London Lights

London Lights

The Minds that Moved the City that Shook the World, 1805–51

JAMES HAMILTON

JOHN MURRAY

First published in Great Britain in 2007 by John Murray (Publishers)
An Hachette Livre UK company

I

© James Hamilton 2007

The right of James Hamilton to be identified as the Author of the
Work has been asserted by him in accordance with the Copyright,
Designs and Patents Act 1988.

I

A CIP catalogue record for this title
is available from the British Library

ISBN 978-0-7195-6639-4

Typeset in Bembo by M Rules

Printed and bound in Great Britain by William Clowes Ltd, Beccles, Suffolk

John Murray policy is to use papers that are natural, renewable and recyclable
products and made from wood grown in sustainable forests. The logging and
manufacturing processes are expected to conform to the environmental
regulations of the country of origin.

John Murray (Publishers)
338 Euston Road
London NW1 3BH

www.johnmurray.co.uk

For Marie

Contents

Illustrations

The author and publisher would like to thank the following for permission to reproduce illustrations: © Bodleian Library, Oxford: 20; © Bridgeman Art Library (Royal Institution, London): 7; © The British Library, London (Willoughby Gordon Papers) 18; © The British Museum, London: 6, 19; © Museum of London: 4, 15, 21, 23, 24; © National Portrait Gallery, London: 1, 2, 9, 10, 11, 12, 13, 14, 25, 26, 27, 28, 29, 30;© Royal Academy of Arts, London / John Hammond: 3, 16; © Royal College of Music, London: 31; © The Royal Society, London: 5; © Sir John Soane's Museum, London: 22; © Tate, London: 17; © Victoria and Albert Museum, London: 8, 32, 33.

Preface

I DO NOT LIVE in London; I do not walk my dog on Hampstead Heath; I am not to be found propping up a bar in Holborn. Living sixty or seventy miles away as I do, I have a detached and sceptical relationship with the city which is, nevertheless, my London. Thus, the perspective of this book may be an unusual one.

My first impression, as I get off the bus at Marble Arch, is the rapidly apparent fact that London is a city of detail, rather than of the grand gesture. Paris, Rome and Bucharest reflect through their street patterns the historical presence of dictators and, layer over layer, of grand plans. London, never having had a dictator, instead has vistas and snatches – a terraced side-street off Park Lane, the views into Regent's Park, a glimpse of Soho from Tottenham Court Road, the steeples and towers of the city from Waterloo Bridge. Even sight of the entire Swiss Re building, the Gherkin, is limited to one or two points near its base – the most we can usually see of it is its tip. London is a living creature; torn down, it grows again; damaged, it heals.

When London has attempted the grand ceremonial in architecture, with the exceptions of Buckingham Palace from the Mall, and perhaps Portland Place, it tends to fail. Take the Royal Institution, a rich golden building flanked by fourteen giant Corinthian columns which would look at home at the end of a wide avenue or parade ground: this is tucked up a side street with no hope of its ever being seen in the way its architecture anticipates. St Martin-in-the-Fields sits at an ungainly angle to the top of Trafalgar Square. Nelson's Column destroys the view of the National Gallery from Whitehall. The British Museum is a breathing dragon in a cage. And St Paul's Cathedral: one of the grandest ecclesiastical edifices in Britain is hemmed in at the end of an upward curving street of shops and offices. Nevertheless it is all, or most of it, unutterably beautiful. As Noël Coward once sang, 'the Italians couldn't bear to; the Spanish wouldn't dare to'. The British, however, take architectural dysfunction as part of normal life. The grand plan and the parish council cannot coexist.

This book grew from the roots of my biographies of Turner and Faraday. Its title, deriving of course from the first two lines of Hubert Gregg's wartime song, came into my head immediately after the initial idea for the book was planted there by Peter Robinson:

> I'm going to get lit up when the lights go up in London;
> I'm going to get lit up as I've never been before.

With this rumbustious but anachronistic song in my head, the book rapidly developed away from a survey of bricks and mortar to an account of some of the bright-eyed men and women who illuminated the circuits of London, who smelt the coal gas and the sewers, who fell out of balloons, who contributed to the hubbub in the lecture theatres and who heard the clatter of Charles Babbage's Difference Engine as the handle turned, the cogs rotated, and out came a long string of numbers.

Among the many archivists, curators, librarians and Londoners who have helped me during the course of researching and writing the three books, I would like to thank Nicola Allen, Bob Arnott, Nick Braunton, Iain G. Brown, Harry Buglass and Louise Buglass (who made the map), David Busby, Emma Butterfield, Alan Carter, Jordi Cat, Hannah Chandler, Stephanie Clarke, Paul Collen, Jessica Collins, Timothy Davies, Sarah Dodgson, Anne Eatwell, Georgina French, Eleanor Gawne, Adrian Gibbs, Hubert Gregg, Colin Harris, Colin Harrison, Trine Hougaard, Neil Iden, Matthew Imms, David Knight, Josie Lister, Anne Locker, David McClay, Sally Matthews, Pieter van der Merwe, Edward Morris, John R. Murray, Virginia Murray, Bernard Nurse, Anselm Nye, Susan Palmer, Justin Pollard, Mark Pomeroy, Jenny Ramkalawon, Vera Ryhajlo, Justine Sambrook, Nicholas Savage, Lucy Scrivener, Jonathan Smith, Anna Stathaki, Lenore Symons, Gary Thorn, Laura Try, Becky Webster, Alex Werner, Stephen Wildman, Sarah Williams, Christine Woollett and Clemency Wright. For permission to quote from written sources, and to reproduce images in their care and ownership I would like to thank in London the Bridgman Art Library, the British Library, the British Museum, the Courtauld Institute of Art, the Institution of Engineering and Technology, the Museum of London, the National Gallery Archive, the National Portrait Gallery, Queen Mary College, University of London, the Royal Academy of Arts, the Royal College of Music, the Royal Institute of British Architects, the Royal Institution, the Royal Society, the Royal Society of Arts, St Bride's Printing Library, the Science Museum, Sir John Soane's Museum, the Society of Antiquaries, Tate Britain, the Victoria and Albert Museum. Outside London, the University Libraries of Birmingham, Bristol, Durham and Reading, the Trinity College Library, Cambridge, the Bodleian and Sackler Libraries, Oxford, the Museum of the History of Science, Oxford, the Oxford University Press, the Ruskin Library, University of Lancaster, the Trustees of the National Library of Scotland for permission to quote from the John Murray Archive, and Chatto and Windus for a quotation from Alexander Herzen.

The Society of Authors has helped in more ways than perhaps they can know, as indeed have my family, friends and colleagues, in particular my wife Kate Eustace, and Marie Hamilton, Patrick Hamilton, Diana Thomas, Thomas and Sarah Hamilton, Elinor and Phil Clift, Chloe Blackburn, Zita Caldecott, James and Mary Miller, Felicity Bryan, Peter Robinson, Roland Philipps, Rowan Yapp, Peter James, Douglas Matthews and Clare Mullett. I thank them all.

James Hamilton
Kidlington
April 2007

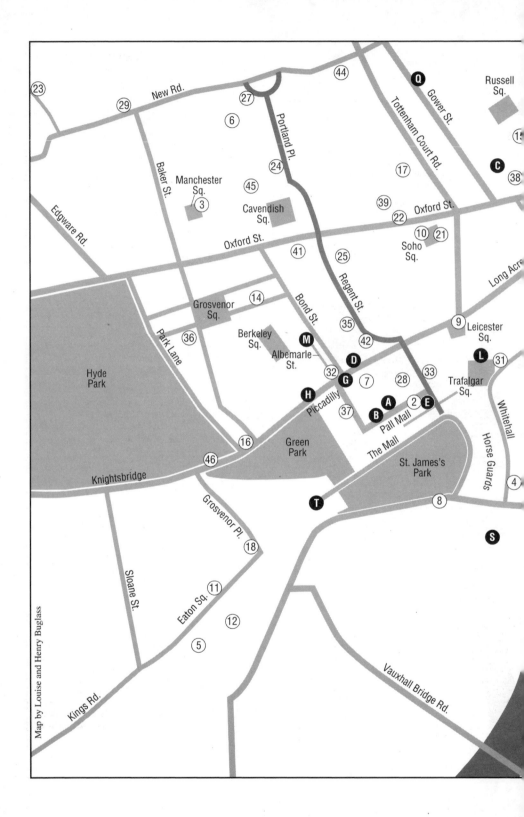

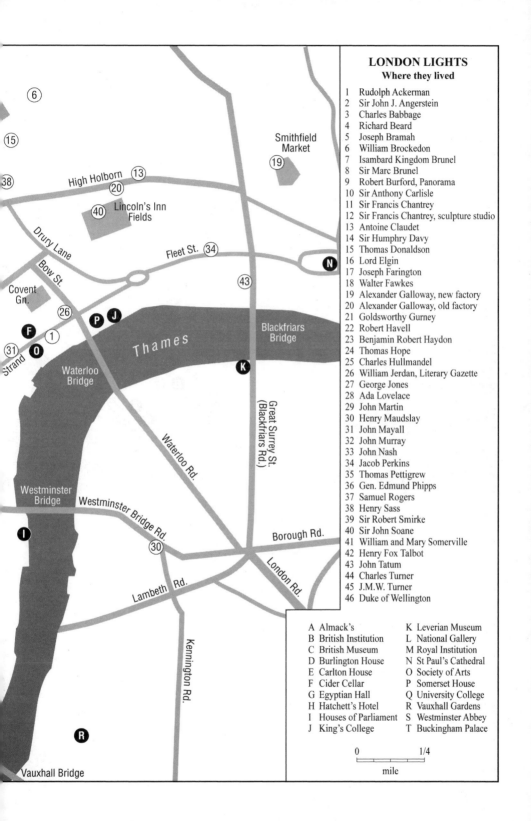

LONDON LIGHTS
Where they lived

1 Rudolph Ackerman
2 Sir John J. Angerstein
3 Charles Babbage
4 Richard Beard
5 Joseph Bramah
6 William Brockedon
7 Isambard Kingdom Brunel
8 Sir Marc Brunel
9 Robert Burford, Panorama
10 Sir Anthony Carlisle
11 Sir Francis Chantrey
12 Sir Francis Chantrey, sculpture studio
13 Antoine Claudet
14 Sir Humphry Davy
15 Thomas Donaldson
16 Lord Elgin
17 Joseph Farington
18 Walter Fawkes
19 Alexander Galloway, new factory
20 Alexander Galloway, old factory
21 Goldsworthy Gurney
22 Robert Havell
23 Benjamin Robert Haydon
24 Thomas Hope
25 Charles Hullmandel
26 William Jerdan, Literary Gazette
27 George Jones
28 Ada Lovelace
29 John Martin
30 Henry Maudslay
31 John Mayall
32 John Murray
33 John Nash
34 Jacob Perkins
35 Thomas Pettigrew
36 Gen. Edmund Phipps
37 Samuel Rogers
38 Henry Sass
39 Sir Robert Smirke
40 Sir John Soane
41 William and Mary Somerville
42 Henry Fox Talbot
43 John Tatum
44 Charles Turner
45 J.M.W. Turner
46 Duke of Wellington

A Almack's
B British Institution
C British Museum
D Burlington House
E Carlton House
F Cider Cellar
G Egyptian Hall
H Hatchett's Hotel
I Houses of Parliament
J King's College
K Leverian Museum
L National Gallery
M Royal Institution
N St Paul's Cathedral
O Society of Arts
P Somerset House
Q University College
R Vauxhall Gardens
S Westminster Abbey
T Buckingham Palace

0   1/4

mile

Quickly, in the Nick of Time, and in Great Quantity

WHEN VICE-ADMIRAL HORATIO Viscount Nelson left London in early September 1805 to join HMS *Victory* at Portsmouth, he departed an eighteenth-century city fearful of invasion. Before two months were over, news from Trafalgar of the shattering of the French and Spanish navies by a British fleet under Nelson's command had burst in the capital with a power that scattered seeds for London's transformation. Fitfully lit by fireworks and flaming torches, crowds cheered the triumph over the monster Napoleon Bonaparte, and wept at Nelson's death in battle. This spontaneous mood of pride and resolution after a naval engagement far away marked the beginning of a tidal flow which carried London through a century of growth and change on a scale unprecedented in human history. With some surprise and misgivings, Londoners began to realise that after more than twenty years of war, first in America, then with France, they just might have reached the threshold of peace. Final allied victory at Waterloo in 1815 recast the map of Europe, and set London on course to becoming the undisputed capital of the world by the time of the Great Exhibition in 1851.

This book is an account of the lives, influences, interrelationships and purpose of men and women whose energy and intellect put in motion the gearing which converted the wartime patriotism of a nation under attack into a new appreciation of the potency and rewards of peace. The 'London Lights' – artists, scientists and writers; architects, manufacturers and engineers – moved mountains, and are the dramatis personae in this biography of the city whose face, direction and ambition they influenced radically. 'The flood of human effort rolls out of it and into it', Thomas Carlyle observed of London in 1824, 'with a violence that almost appals one's every sense.'

Among the London Lights there were partnerships and rivalries, successes and failures, friendships and enmities. Take some of the many relationships that will be observed here: the scientist Michael Faraday with the artist John Martin; Martin with the diarist Joseph Farington; Farington with the surgeon Anthony Carlisle; Carlisle with the steam-car pioneer Goldsworthy Gurney; Gurney with the soldier James Willoughby Gordon; Gordon with the artist J. M. W. Turner; Turner with the banker and poet Samuel Rogers; Rogers with the classicist and drunkard Richard Porson; Porson with the journalist William Jerdan; Jerdan with the artist Benjamin Robert Haydon; Haydon with the sculptor Francis Chantrey; Chantrey with the scientist and writer Mary Somerville; Somerville with Faraday and Turner, and around we go again. Through social contacts, old friendships, affections and *tendresses* do the wheels of change go round, and what may seem at first to be a baldly formal progression of ideas and activity may in fact be driven by more, by intuitive connections, the linking of a circle of people whose fingers meet out of sight. The coincidences of lives weaving in and out over time is not just a phenomenon of the novels of Charles Dickens and Thomas Hardy, Iris Murdoch and Anthony Powell. It is real life, past, present and future; and an exploration of one tiny corner of nineteenth-century real life is the driving force of *London Lights*. Not all of the dozens evoked here are 'great' lives. Indeed, I have missed out many who might together have made this too well trodden a narrative. Dickens, Thackeray, Wedgwood and Darwin barely get a mention, and there is little space for music, the law, politics and religion. My London Lights are, in this volume, men and women, some little known or forgotten, who collectively formed the mould that made the strata that carried the walls that created the place and idea called London.

Securely set nearly forty miles up river from the mouth of the Thames, London began to prove itself as the seedbed of enterprise and human ingenuity when the Romans discovered its potential two thousand years ago. The generous width and reliable tidal flow of the river makes it a highway for friends, while its windings, marked at every turn by forts and batteries, create a perilous course for enemies. As the lobster pot is to the lobster, so to Britain's enemies the Thames was intriguing but deadly. No wonder so few tried it. The American writer Nathaniel Hawthorne observed in 1855 that it was just wide enough: 'as a picturesque object . . . flowing through the midst of a city, [the Thames] would lose by any increase in width'. Within the protective slopes of the Chilterns to the north and the Downs to the south, London had a broad basin to spread into, and plentiful water to refresh it.

In the early nineteenth century London was part of an intricate interdependent system of canals and navigable rivers which enabled goods to travel from town to town, from manufacture to market, crossing the country on a scale that was unique in the world. Britain is a small island, so distances are short: in continental Europe and the United States, such ease of distribution was, then, impossible. While the canals and rivers carried goods, the network of turnpike roads carried people and correspondence. As the Romans found when they built roads that radiated from London, and then criss-crossed the country, natural barriers such as mountains, rivers and marsh were few and surmountable. Using the well-beaten Roman roads as their guide, eighteenth-century engineers built the foundation of the modern road system. And the sea, being no more than 150 miles from any one spot in Britain, was always accessible. Given the sea, so the world.

London had a long historical tradition as a capital; the court was there, as were the institutions. There was plentiful money, a sophisticated society and a vibrant businesslike population of merchants and traders. From whatever direction, coming to England meant coming to London. The momentum gained by the growth of trade, and the ability of the London docks and the river to assimilate and distribute imports and exports, had by the mid-century given London the wealth that created the foundations of the imperial capital of the world. While Europe tore itself apart in revolution, and the United States drove on towards civil war, Britain was for fifty years reaping world harvest. It was not, however, just global imports and exports that kept the capital and the nation buoyant. There was one entirely internal trade without which London would, quite simply, have shrivelled back to the size of a series of riverside fishing villages, if it had ever grown at all. This was the coal trade with the north-east of

England: no coal, no London. Indeed, no coal, no Great Britain. And further, the bends in the river, like the crumples in the human gut, created length and calm water to accommodate the colliers which sailed in and out of the coal wharves, round the clock, day in, day out. Had the Thames been a short straight river to the sea, and its mouth a narrow, rocky or dangerous entrance, the story of London would have been very different. In truth, no story.

An evolving family of institutions in London focused public attention on learning and scientific discovery. Three of them, the Royal Society, the Royal Academy of Arts and the Society of Antiquaries, together occupied meeting rooms which fitted neatly together like fingers in a glove in Somerset House, the complex of government offices off the Strand. One by one these and two other institutions, the Society of Arts, Manufactures and Commerce, and the Royal Institution of Great Britain, had come into being as the eighteenth century closed, and one by one they became the cornerstones upon which the edifice of established learning and artistic and technological development in London was built. Together they formed the fountainhead of the river of knowledge as Humphry Davy described it. In 1805 the poet Samuel Taylor Coleridge expressed succinctly the fecundity that artists and scientists were faced with in the abiding marvel of nature:

> It is her largeness, and her overflow,
> Which being incomplete, disquieteth me so.

These were the decades in which the 'brain drain' flowed from west to east: then, Americans came not just to see this extraordinary place called London, but to investigate closely what was new in science and technology. Steam-engine design, electrical application, refinements in photography were pioneered in London and borrowed to build America. By the time the whole world came to London to see the Great Exhibition in 1851, the river of knowledge had broken up into smaller streams and floods as knowledge expanded and the social landscape through which the river flowed had itself changed radically. Although the roots of the change are social and political, it developed its particular kind of motion through an increasing specialisation in science, the widening professionalisation of scientists, the celebration by

artists of domesticity, and the sheer quantity and wonder of the knowledge and understanding then being obtained through scientific
endeavour. At this golden moment in the history of ideas, when the
beams converged and the light flashed, London was the world's focus
both of intellectual activity and of its practical application.

London, like every great city, changes. The strains of its evolution
across the span of this book can be seen in countless ways: the widening of roads, the demolition of tenements to build factories, new
ways to move around town, the embanking of the river. These
are all big issues. But the small issues also tell, sometimes eloquently.
Here are two: John Goldham, a yeoman of Billingsgate fish market,
told a parliamentary commission inquiring into the supply of water
to London in 1828 that when he was a young man the river was
teeming with fish. He remembered roach, plaice, smelts, flounders,
salmon, shads, eels, gudgeon, dace, dabs; and he recalled that there
were four hundred fishermen, 'each having a boat and a boy', working
between Deptford and Richmond. 'I have known them to take ten
salmon and as many as three hundred smelts in one hawl up towards
Wandsworth,' he told the commission. Across the period of Goldham's
working life, London's population multiplied, as, correspondingly, did
the use of the river as a sewer. The population of fish declined. 'And
now', Goldham said, 'there are not two hundred men engaged in this
fishing, and many of them are selling off their nets and boats.'

In the graveyards and on lesser church monuments erected in
London between about 1815 and 1850 we can see another eloquent
sign of change: if one spouse dies young the name, dates and endear-
ments are cut in the cursive script, appropriately termed 'copperplate',
the facets and angles of the letters being crisply and generously
formed, the flourishes graceful. Space is left on the stone for the
survivor. When the other spouse follows many years later to the
grave, the generation of letter-cutters trained as copperplate engravers
has died out, and the new generation brought up in the age of journals,
newspapers and steam printing has reached maturity. So the spouse
who paid for the copperplate memorial has himself (let's say) to
make do with the harsh, relentless, strident cuts of newspaper letter-
forms. The watchful church visitor can often spot these two opposed
styles coexisting on the same tomb or plaque.

These are local observations; it took a Russian to reflect upon London with detachment. The political theorist and author Alexander Herzen discovered his own technique for surviving the pressures and disappointments of London, and in doing so defined exactly the pace of life and the creative spirit of the capital. Herzen found in 1852 that in London 'nervous and romantic temperaments, fond of living among their fellows, of intellectual sloth and emotional idleness, are bored to death and fall into despair'. Herzen's remedy was this:

> If one is not to be crushed and smothered in London, one must do a great deal of work, and do it smartly, at once, and do what comes first, what is in demand. One must fix the distracted attention of the blasé crowd by intensity, impudence, mass or variety. Ornaments, patterns for embroidery, arabesques, models, photographs, copies, portraits, frames, water-colours, consoles, flowers – anything, so long as it is done quickly, in the nick of time and in great quantity.

I

A Display of Splendour

~

PROFESSOR PORSON WAS lying under the table. He stirred as one
of the party of drinkers in the Cider Cellar, a basement drinking
den in Maiden Lane, tripped and fell over a chair. A dozen or more
men were singing by the fire, their ballad rhythmic still, but increasingly tuneless.

> My cellar's my camp, and my soldiers my flasks,
> All gloriously ranged in review . . .

The cellar, lit by candles guttering in the draught from a street door
high up a stair, smelt of sour wine, mutton fat, smoke and vomit.

> When I cast my eyes round, I consider my casks
> As kingdoms I've yet to subdue,
> My brave boys.

As the singers rolled to their song, their shadows spread and merged
and danced on the ceiling. The professor opened his eyes as his now
senseless companion thudded down beside him. He sat up, hit his
head on the edge of the table, and began to declaim Homer in
Greek. Thus, within shouting distance of the southern edge of
Covent Garden, Richard Porson, Regius Professor of Greek at
Trinity College, Cambridge, and Principal Librarian of the London
Institution, drew his night's entertainment to a close.

Richard Porson was an intellectual literary giant from the same
shelf as Samuel Johnson in the eighteenth century and Samuel Taylor
Coleridge in the early nineteenth. He was one of the greatest classical
scholars of his, or any, era, and his edited editions of Thucydides'
histories and the plays of Euripides became milestones in classical
scholarship. As a young man he had promised a shining future to the

study of Greek in Cambridge, and in his fourteen years at Trinity College he clarified texts which had become inaccurate through copying and reprinting. In doing so he developed a style of penmanship that was of such clarity and elegance that he set new standards in calligraphy. But Porson knew neither charm, tact nor timing. After a series of run-ins at Trinity with colleagues whom he loathed and taunted, and after refusing to sign up to the Thirty-Nine Articles of the Church of England and find a billet-for-life in Cambridge, he plummeted down to London in 1792 and landed with a bump in the Cider Cellar. There he was admired and teased in equal measure, and anecdotes began to accumulate about him like barnacles.

The ever-watchful diarist and topographical artist Joseph Farington knew Richard Porson both as a classical scholar and by reputation as a drinker. After a dinner for Royal Academy members at the Freemason's Tavern in 1797, when the large and fleshy Porson was uncharacteristically silent, Farington remarked that Porson had 'an habitual thoughtful look and sluggish indolence of manner'. Farington may never have been to the Cider Cellar, but this tall, lean man, who drank sparingly, dined carefully, and listened attentively to the conversation around him, reported to his diary with what seems to be perfect recall. Farington, who at six feet was a foxglove among wallflowers, was always the audience, rarely the performer, and was careful, cautious, meticulous. He began to keep his diary in July 1793, at the age of forty-four, and day in, day out for twenty-eight years until the day he died he recorded in a slow, legible hand the doings and sayings of his friends and acquaintances in the interconnecting worlds of art, commerce, fashion, medicine and science. He formed his own and captured others' opinions in the quotidian world of London in a diary that runs to sixteen manuscript volumes.

Farington and Porson were two very different 'London Lights', Farington a thin, persistent, pale flame, Porson flaring richly, then guttering into smoke and ash. They represent two of many shoots from the stock of burgeoning intellectual life in London in the opening years of the nineteenth century: Farington, a highly literate son of a Lancashire parson, a family man whose wife and servants kept neat house for him, a tactician, gregarious and political, and something of a glad-hander. Although he had friends and enemies at the Royal Academy, he had the sense to maintain a wide circle beyond the world of art, and befriended physicians and merchants, churchmen and politicians, connoisseurs and military men. Farington did not gain his place as a luminary of the early nineteenth century through his tidy landscape drawings, but in his dual role as both his profession's fixer and its scribe.

Porson, devastated in 1797 by the death of his wife after less than six months of marriage, soon lost whatever decorum he had developed as a student and later a revered teacher at Trinity. He was the son of Huggin Porson, weaver and parish clerk of East Ruston, Norfolk, who dedicated himself to instilling in his children classical learning and a respect for literature. Porson was a large and awkward boy, but local patronage and his shining intellect paved the way from the Norfolk coast to Eton and Cambridge. Twenty years later, when he ejected himself from Cambridge and arrived in London, he was already a lost soul.

Porson's appetite for food and drink was of gargantuan proportions, as was his ability to starve himself. A near contemporary report tells of how he lived for six weeks on a guinea, dined on milk, or on a pint of porter with some bread and cheese, and could fast for two days. Then, feasting, 'he once nearly ate up a shoulder of mutton at Mr M[altby]'s lodgings, making his apology by speaking of his long previous fast'. Porson went unwashed, wore his clothes to rags, and fixed black patches to swellings on his nose. He looked so disreputable and haggard that when he arrived, invited, for dinner the servants of his hosts would turn him away in disgust. The banker and poet Samuel Rogers claimed to be able to keep Porson 'within bounds' when they dined together, but when they met in other houses Porson would became hopelessly drunk, and after guests had withdrawn would roll back to the dining room to drain the glasses left behind. The radical politician Horne Tooke reflected that Porson would drink ink rather than not drink at all.

Though plagued and degraded by his need for alcohol and the approval of irresponsible company, Porson nonetheless continued his scholarly work in London, editing an early manuscript of *The Odyssey* in the British Museum, and proposing in 1801 a transcription of the

Rosetta Stone for the Society of Antiquaries. He was appointed Principal Librarian of the new London Institution in 1806. With his long recitations in English, Latin and Greek, from Homer, Euripides, Shakespeare and Pope, Porson brought dazzling light and party tricks to his audiences in the Cider Cellar. Drunk as a lord, but with 'dignified deportment, and sonorous utterance', he could 'pour forth a hundred lines of Homer together apparently for no other purpose than to excite the wonder of his audience at what most of them could not understand'. Being shown the chapter 'On Memory' in Thomas Fuller's *The Holy State and the Profane State* (1642), Porson read two pages and repeated them immediately from memory. Urged on by his enthralled audience, he recited them again, backwards, 'and got through, omitting only two words'.

The Cider Cellar had a long history of intellectual and theatrical indulgence for drinkers. It was part of what was once the cellar of the house occupied by Nell Gwyn, the orange-selling actress mistress of Charles II, and by the eighteenth century it had become the gloomy drinking haunt of thinkers and talkers: 'every great Philosopher here had a greater Champion: you are at once surrounded by *Tolanders*, *Tindalists*, *Woolstonists*, *Morganists*, *Mandevellians* and *Chubists*'. Slipping in among the thoughtful swilling crowd in the 1790s was a young man, short in stature, but brightly observant and attentive. This was the son of the local barber, William Turner of Hand Court, 26 Maiden Lane opposite the Cider Cellar. The boy, who would take himself off on long walks into the country to Hampstead or Kent, and was called William after his father, became richly knowledgeable in the classics. This learning, rooted in part in the Cider Cellar 'university' at Porson's feet, emerged as the narrative juice of his paintings when some years later he became better known as J. M. W. Turner RA.

The young journalist William Jerdan aptly described Porson's career as 'accidental and capricious, precarious and erratic'. Jerdan, who first came to London from Kelso in 1801, sat often at Porson's feet in the Cider Cellar, listening to his stories and to his fluid commentary on contemporary events, and marvelled at his 'almost incredible abundance of literary illustrations of antiquity and past times, drawn as it seemed from every channel into which the mind of man could dive'. After an uncertain start, during which he travelled around the south Devon coast reporting on 'indecent sea-bathing', and briefly joined the navy, Jerdan engaged in a bruising, intense and influential career in journalism. He was widely liked, sociable and charming, with, as an early portrait shows, errant tousled hair and a dimple in his chin. He had 'wit, humour, inexhaustible fund of anecdote, and felicitous manner of telling a story', and to this his lilting Scottish accent gave added zest.

Jerdan rose rapidly. By 1808, the year Porson died, he had been editor of the political journals the *Aurora* and the *Pilot*, and wrote for many other papers in London and the provinces before becoming editor of the vociferously Tory *Sun*. He had the knack of being at the right place at the right time, finding himself in the lobby of the House of Commons in the late afternoon of 11 May 1812 when the Prime Minister, Spencer Perceval, was assassinated. Jerdan fell on the murderer, and held him down until he was taken away. Joseph Farington was more than ten years Porson's senior; Jerdan might have considered both of them elderly. Amid the cacophony of London, these three men from afar, from Lancashire, Norfolk and the lowlands of Scotland respectively, maintained and proclaimed the capital's intellectual gold-standard, one from the balcony, one from the gutter, and the third from the newspapers.

Farington had none of Porson's capacity for self-destruction, nor his craving for attention, and by casting brilliant light on the sayings and doings of his contemporaries is lost in his own shadow. He enjoyed dining, and calling on people; he travelled about the country, picking up gossip there and at home in London; he recorded the time he got up in the morning, what the temperature was on the thermometer on his staircase, and how he was feeling that day. One gets the impression that if Joseph Farington was asked how he was, he would respond with a complete run-down of the state of his heart, liver and lungs and of the Royal Academy.

Farington loved intrigue and scandal, and added to and passed on criticism of the work of other artists. He liked to know what other people earned, and what they made or lost in speculation, sifting such information as he dined out with artists, natural philosophers, physicians, peers and the shapers of taste and opinion in London of the day. He reported other people's opinions, their good manners and bad, and their behaviour obscure and bizarre. When he dined in December 1805 at the home in Soho Square of the surgeon Anthony Carlisle conversation turned to surgical operations. The host spoke of an operation he had carried out that morning, and called to his servant to bring a glass bowl containing 'a large excrescence cut from a man's body'. Carlisle lifted it out, turned it over in his hands, and began to give a lecture on this piece of pickle. An expert on muscular action in humans and animals, he enjoyed pugilism, and ranged widely in his conversations over dinner with Farington. Before showing off the 'large excrescence', Carlisle had spoken much about 'training men for bruising and other athletic exertions', and quoted the second-century Greek physician Galen, writing about the training of fighters, as saying 'that men, like game cocks, were bred to *an hour*, which being passed, their mettle fell'.

With Farington's artist and architect friends the conversation was perhaps more circumspect and restrained than it was with medical men. During that December, between Nelson's death at Trafalgar and his burial, Farington ate out with friends on thirteen evenings. This was comparatively reclusive of him – twenty or twenty-five evenings out was his common monthly average – but he was nursing a bad cold and that kept him at home. Topics of conversation that Farington records during this sample of his social life cover religion and books, Royal Academy politics, the weather, the state of the nation, and the British Museum. He urged his friend the lace manufacturer and collector George Butler to bequeath his collection of prints and drawings to the British Museum, and on another evening, as the day of the funeral approached, he heard of Nelson's poor health before the Battle of Trafalgar, and how the Admiral ate macaroni to settle an upset stomach.

After dining with Carlisle, Farington would have walked from Soho Square to his house, 59 Upper Charlotte Street, Fitzroy Square, along Charles Street to the end of Oxford Street, and would then have turned right and sharp left into Tottenham Court Road. With a link-boy walking briskly ahead of him carrying a flaming torch, he would brave the lurking prostitutes and pick-pockets, and five or ten minutes later, keeping to the edge of the road to avoid the mud and filth out in the middle and the splashes from passing carriages, would turn left into Percy Street then walk a hundred yards up Charlotte Street where at number 59, with a rap on the knocker, he would be let in.

Between about eight and ten o'clock on a December night the streets of London were quiet. Shadowy figures moved about. A slamming door. The whinny of a horse, the rattle of wheels and a shout might emerge out of the darkness, before silence descended again. Some windows would show dim lights behind curtains, except where a party or rout was in progress: then there would be a crowd of carriages outside the house, and, as Louis Simond, a French-American traveller put it, 'every curtain, and every shutter of every window wide open showing apartments all in a blaze of light'. Shops were unlit, and after 1809/10, when the first streets in London around Pall Mall were lit by coal gas, the lights were good enough only to reveal the presence of the pole that supported them. Simond, who spent six months in London in 1810, described streets that were 'lit' as being 'edged on either side with two long lines of little brightish dots, indicative of light, but yielding in fact very little'. An opening front door might briefly cast a pale glow on to the pavement before being shut with a rattle of bolts. The carriages that passed Farington as he walked would have been carrying other diners home to bed, or ball-goers off to a late-night rout. At ten o'clock, Simond reveals, 'a *redoublément*' comes on as people return home in their carriages, each with a pair of little staring lights attached. There is 'a universal hubbub; a sort of uniform grinding and shaking, like that experienced in a great mill with fifty pairs of stones . . . it [comes] upon the ear like the fall of Niagara, heard at two miles distance!'

When he travelled around London or to outlying villages by day, however, Farington could use the multitudinous system of competitive coaches which left at all hours of the day, and on summer evenings, from more than 135 different departure points all over the capital. Most of these were inns which, in the crowded narrow streets, attracted travellers and carriage owners to their front doors and to their dining and drinking rooms. The noise, the smell, the mess and danger from bucking and shivering horses, the sheer crush of people milling about with their personalities and pressures, bags and business, coming in and out of the inns was just one contribution to the mêlée. Multiply this by newspaper delivery carts, wagons of meat, furniture drays, an organ-grinder, a woman selling haddock, a midday drunkard, a flock of sheep, a post-chaise, a funeral procession, solo horses carrying single riders, a fire engine and a stray dog, and we can catch a glimpse of what made up the vivacity of London.

Habit or tradition clung around London drinking places in the early nineteenth century, to the extent that some became the exclusive preserves of various occupational groups. Evans's in King Street, Covent Garden, became known at the 'Star Dinner and Coffee Room' because of its exclusivity: 'it was said that it was no uncommon thing for nine dukes to dine here in [the 1830s] in one day'. Stock-jobbers and dealers drank in Jonathan's Coffee House in Lombard Street, watermen at the Old Swan in Upper Thames Street, and city bankers at the Ship and Turtle in Leadenhall Street. William Jerdan knew the inns by their political allegiances: the King's Head was 'ultra Tory'; the Crown 'loyal but more moderate'; the Cockpit 'warlike'; the Olive Tree 'pacific'; the Royal Oak 'patriotic'; the Rummer 'democratic'; the Hole in the Wall 'seditious'.

From the inns – the Goose and Gridiron in St Paul's Churchyard, the New Inn by the Old Bailey, the Spotted Dog in the Strand, the White Bear, Piccadilly, and dozens of others – more than four hundred carriage firms operated, travelling to destinations all over the country. From London in 1805 and 1806 one could climb on to a carriage outside the Angel, the Crown or the Mitre to, say, Manchester or a smaller town like Warwick or Wakefield, and be sure it would leave on time. Seventeen coaches a day went to Manchester, fifteen to Birmingham, three daily to the far west town of Haverfordwest. Even to Aberdeen in northern Scotland the traveller could choose from three coaches leaving daily. Travelling around England, and into Wales and Scotland, from London may have had its problems, but it was not in itself a problem. Coaches would leave promptly: a correspondent reminded the Oxford mathematician Stephen Peter Rigaud that the eleven o'clock stage to Wanstead in Essex left the Royal Exchange every morning 'precisely at Eleven, – that is, the moment the *clock strikes*'. Closer to home, there were forty daily coaches to Barnes, forty-five to Hammersmith and a hundred to Chelsea. It was probably easier to get from Charing Cross to Chelsea in 1805 than it is today on the number 11 bus in the rush hour.

London in 1805 was vast, filthy and growing like a cancer. Most of us cannot even begin to imagine, now, what appalling conditions Londoners took for granted. This remains an obscene secret of history which can only be recreated when civilisation fails. The smell, dirt, smoke, crush, the rubbish not cleared away, the ordure and blood in the streets – horse, cattle, dog, human – the cess piles and pits overflowing behind houses and along streets, huge, wet, evil and rank. The poet Robert Southey, coming from the clear air and water of the Lake District, noticed with disgust how the sewers discharged themselves into the river at Blackfriars 'and blacken the water round about'. He added: 'it is perfectly astonishing that any people should consent to drink it'.

Charles Lamb, the essayist and clerk, was one of the minority of Londoners who lived as comfortably as the age allowed. While he felt joy at the vibrancy of London street-life, he did not have to scrape his living from the mud or the passing crowd, nor did he have to creep home to a filthy, overcrowded room to sleep. The horrors of dilapidated tenement housing, teeming with pallid, sick and ill-fed people, was not fully revealed until Henry Mayhew discovered it for himself in the 1840s and 1850s. For that reason the most telling descriptions of how artisans, tradesmen and manual workers and their families lived come later. Two examples, which throw light on the early lives of a pair of London-born intellectual giants who came to know one another well, the artist J. M. W. Turner and the scientist Michael Faraday, are representative of many. Turner's first biographer, Walter Thornbury, explored Hand Court, behind Maiden Lane, before it was pulled down in 1861: 'It was a gloomy sort of horizontal tunnel, with a low archway and prison-like iron gate of its own, and you had to stand a good minute in the dim light of this archway before you could see the coffin-lid door to the left that in the days of Garrick opened into the small hairdresser's shop.' Michael Faraday, who was brought up a member of the strict Sandemanian Christian sect, worshipped in the Sandemanian chapel in Paul's Alley, to the north of St Paul's Cathedral. Visiting the alley around 1850, the journalist C. C. Walker recalled 'that it was a narrow, dirty court, surrounded by squalid houses of the poorest of the poor'. These were the places of darkness where many thousands suffered miserable lives, but where a significant few first saw light.

The floods and puddles and mud and mess when it rained; the deep shadows, guttering lamps and danger when it was dark; the dust and flies when it was hot; the market rubbish and the rats; and after a snowfall the heaps of blackening snow and ice impeding traffic. Every passer-by knew the irritation of being grimy and smelly; a few deplored the mud on new silk shoes; many noticed silent knots of unwashed, unkempt, ill-clad children with no school to go to; all feared the permanent threat of the pick-pocket. At night the link-boys made a small living by seeing pedestrians and carriages home by torchlight. The streets were so 'dark with light', as the journalist Samuel Carter Hall put it, that in a broad gas-lit highway like the Strand it was impossible to see to the other side.

The air was glum, the water in the rivers of London was dank, black and stinking, and when the sun got through, the light was already tainted. Coffins and corpses within the London graveyards, 'fat with human remains', hid and heaved like rocks in the sea. While the Thames 'glideth at his own sweet will', as Wordsworth put it in 1802, it did its own mead of damage. On opening the burial vault in Westminster Abbey before the Prime Minister William Pitt the younger's funeral in February 1806 his father's coffin was found lying on its side, 'attributed by some to the influx of the Thames, which had covered the vault with slime'. When army records were stored in the riverside cellars of the government offices at Somerset House, irreplaceable material was ruined. The records of the Sick and Hurt Office were kept on a level with the river, which came in and swirled about and flowed away again at its own sweet will. In 1814 the soggy mass was removed and thrown away as rubbish in the foundations of new offices in Cannon Row.

A slime-covered upturned coffin; leather-bound manuscripts water-logged and rotting in heaps: these are images of a Blakean intensity, conditions and happenings that were just repulsive enough in a repulsive age to cause remark. William Blake, the self-contained poet and printer of South Molton Street, saw sights in London which most would tend to take for granted or simply not notice. He went a step further than everybody else, and, as John Bronowski expressed it: 'whatever he imagined he also saw'.

> Minute Particulars in slavery I behold among the brick-kilns
> Disorgani'd; & there is Pharozh in his iron Court
> And the Dragon of the River & the Furnaces of iron.

Wordsworth's eye also fell upon the dark places of London. In *The Prelude* he recalls:

> Private courts,
> Gloomy as coffins, and unsightly lanes
> Thrilled by some female vendor's scream, belike
> The very shrillest of all London cries,
> May then entangle our impatient steps;
> Conducted through those labyrinths, unawares,
> To privileged regions and inviolate,
> Where from their airy lodges studious lawyers
> Look out on waters, walks, and gardens green.

Joseph Farington and the physician Edward Jenner, the discoverer of vaccination, dined together in 1809, and talked of the filth of London. Jenner described how he could tell by the smell of his handkerchief when it was that he came into 'an atmosphere untainted by the *London air*'. Jenner would take his handkerchief out of his pocket at intervals as he travelled away from the capital, and sniff it, and 'while he continued within the *London atmosphere* he could never be sensible of any taint upon it'. But when he approached Blackheath, six miles from the centre, he found his sense had recovered, and he could smell on his handkerchief the traces of the air he had left behind.

More uncomfortable words were written about the noise, filth and smell of London by William Jerdan, who, dreaming of his Scottish homeland, gave himself the pen-name 'Teutha', the Celtic name of the River Tweed. Comparing the capital with the country-side, Jerdan found ballad-singers instead of songbirds, the stink of drains instead of the smell of flowers, the frightened moans of cattle bound for market instead of the soft lowing sound of cows on a hillside, 'the whole forming such a conspiracy of outrageous noise, that one must have a mind similar to the stomach of an ostrich and capable of digesting everything, before an idea of love can enter into the antagonistically crowded precincts'.

Another young journalist Cyrus Redding remembered how the smell of London touched him in his Devon boyhood – he could tell if a letter came from London just by smelling it. The stink of London, as Jenner, Jerdan and Redding variously suggested, had long been its signature, portable by handkerchief to Blackheath and by letter to the far west. There were times when London seemed to be in the grip of its own private depression. One such was the iron-hard winter of 1814 when Redding walked from Blackfriars to London Bridge on the river, frozen with filthy and buckled piles of ice, 'a dreary-looking scene. A rising mist obscured the day almost constantly, so that the season was well characterised as a calamity'. Nevertheless, Londoners took the opportunity to have a party, holding a Frost Fair from 31 January to 5 February. While most pictures of this event, particularly the woodcuts, reveal merry crowds and stalls, and ox-roasting, and fairground games, one rare painting in the Museum of London, by Hablot K. Browne later famous as Dickens's illustrator 'Phiz', captures the same deep melancholy that Redding expresses.

And then there was the traffic: noisy carts, angry drivers, frightened horses, chaotic, dangerous, contrary; carriages trying to make their way up and down narrow streets with never a one-way system (except one – in Albemarle Street, on the days when Humphry Davy was lecturing at the Royal Institution); the crowds, shouting, pushing, hurrying, hawkers clamouring for attention: terrifying. Horses by the thousand moved around London streets and courts, with single riders or pulling vehicles. Occasionally one would break from its traces, and maddened by the noise and tumult would run out of sight scattering pedestrians into side-alleys and turning market stalls and hawkers' trays full-turtle into the mud. Another sudden unheralded eruption might be of a fire engine and helmeted men running after it with pumps and hoses, sending traffic and people haywire. Charles Lamb suggests that fire engines multiplied at the sound of the 'odious cry, quick-reaching from street to street, of the *fired chimney*', drawing 'rattling engines from ten adjacent parishes'.

Such eruptions of volcanic activity, and the slow geological pressure of stratas of people and vehicles, might cause a 'lock', which Thomas De Quincey described as 'a line of carriages . . . inextricably massed and obstructing each other, far as the eye could stretch'. De Quincey went on to evoke the sudden dissolution of the 'lock', when, 'as if under an enchanter's rod . . . motion spread with the fluent race of light or sound through the whole icebound mass'.

Thomas De Quincey, a very bright schoolboy who ran away to London from Manchester at the age of eighteen, reflected with those words on the pressure of the London traffic. He observed, too, how on the approach to London he could feel the city coming. De Quincey, who was to write a classic account of the pleasures and pains of opium, *Confessions of an English Opium Eater* (1822), found like Louis Simond that the exotic and distant Niagara Falls was an apt simile for restlessness at home: 'a *trepidation* increases both audibly and visibly at every half-mile, pretty much as one may suppose the roar of Niagara and the thrilling of the ground to grow upon the sense in the last ten miles of approach, with the wind in its favour, until at length it would absorb and extinguish all other sounds whatsoever'. London's physical extent was, for some, its overwhelming and unsettling novelty. The banker John Julius Angerstein remarked to Farington with some complacency that as a sign of the increase in the size of the capital he could remember how once there was only one fishmonger between Charing Cross and St Paul's, and only one music shop in London: 'nothing was more remarkable', he believed, 'than the increase in the number of Musick shops and Fishmonger stalls'.

De Quincey, however, thinner-skinned, younger and with more nervous sensibility than the sophisticated banker Angerstein, touched on terrors lurking in the never-ending city:

> The great lengths of the streets in many quarters of London; the continual opening of transient glimpses into other vistas equally far-stretching, going off at right angles to the one which you are traversing; and the murky atmosphere which, settling upon the remoter end of every long avenue, wraps its termination in gloom and uncertainty; all these circumstances aiding that sense of vastness and illimitable proportions which for ever brood over the aspect of London in its interior.

A third, less knowing incomer, simply could not take it. A Devon man of property 'who had never been thirty miles from home all his life', travelled to London. All went well until the carriage reached Brentford. The countryman supposed he had nearly come to his journey's end, but expressed impatience and anxiety at seeing the lamps lighting the road, mile after mile after mile. 'Are we not yet in London?' he asked. On reaching Hyde Park Corner he was told that they had now arrived, but so overwhelmed was the countryman by the extent of the city, that he escaped the coach, walked westwards, and was found days later out of his mind in Sherborne, Dorset.

The poet Samuel Taylor Coleridge, another man from the west, was much happier with London. He raised his eyes up from the streets, to watch flocks of starlings circling in the sky,

> in vast flights drove along like smoke, mist . . . now a circular area inclined [in an] arc – now a globe – from ellipse & oblong now a balloon with the car suspended, now a concaved semicircle & [still] it expands & condenses, some [moments] glimmering & shivering dim & shadowy, now thickening, deepening, blackening!

This image of the skies above London pullulating with starlings at dawn and dusk would have been seen daily across hundreds of years from the middle ages to the 1970s. While Coleridge was stuck on the city's pavements, a balloon rising above the River Thames would take the starlings' perspective, and present an unfamiliar view of London as the noise from the streets faded away. Robert Havell, the probable artist of a nine-feet-long panorama drawing of London, took a voyage in a balloon some time around 1806 and saw below him a rough carpet of thousands of buildings set firmly on their erratic acres, tightly compressed like geological strata. This pencil-and-wash drawing on four sheets is the *Rhinebeck Panorama*, now one of the greatest treasures of the Museum of London, and so called after the town in the Hudson Valley, New York State, where in 1941 it was found inexplicably lining a barrel of pistols. The river's edge is sharply defined in the drawing by the warehouses and workshops whose footings are lapped by the water, and roads and streets make tight creases through the city's fabric. The pulse of organic growth makes the press yet tighter, and the city creaks like a boiler at bursting point.

This is no fantasy evocation of a London bursting at the seams, rather a snapshot narrative of activity that dances across the sheets from one side to the other. On the extreme left a fire has broken out among the tightly packed houses; the flames are fierce and the smoke thick and billowing. Some ineffectual efforts to dribble water over it are going on, while fifty or a hundred yards away are lines of black figures in a funeral procession, in which even the open grave and the spade is visible. In the second sheet, where the river curves and fills the fore- and middle ground, smoke issues from chimneys here and there, but the main action is the firing of a salute from one of the ships berthed in the middle of the river. This leads the eye to another ship, on the third sheet, firing back. Painstaking pen and paintwork here delineate the rigging, the sails and, most insistently, the crow's-nest platforms at the top of each ship's mainmast, which give some sense of horizontal security for the artist–balloonist's vertiginous aerial viewpoint. The names of the ships are telling: the lettering on their sterns show that they have come to the Pool of London from Sunderland and Shields in the north-east of England, from Liverpool, from Guernsey in the Channel Islands, and from Viana, the old trading port in northern Portugal, the *Aurora de Vianna*. On the fourth sheet there is another cannon firing, from the turret of the Tower of London, watched by a crowd of people gathered beyond the moat. The reason for this cannonade may be explained by the presence of a ceremonial barge which tries to wend its way through the right-hand group of shipping, past the London Assurance Company's floating fire-tender, to land a dignitary at the Tower of London.

As the panorama carries us high over the city, it is clear that the artist is giving us the four elements here – earth, air, fire and water – the raw ingredients of London. An essential fifth element, which would have obscured Havell's view, and which he reduces to a few small token puffs, is smoke. One of the contributory causes of the filthy state of London was the coal smoke that hung over it constantly like a damp grey blanket of misery. When John Constable first came to London in 1799 he complained that 'I paint by all the daylight we have, but that is little enough . . . I sometimes however see the sky, but imagine to yourself how a pearl must look through a burnt glass.' Unlike Parisians who lived horizontally, in apartments, and burned wood on their fires, Londoners burned coal and lived in families vertically in narrow terraced houses. This came as a surprise to the German traveller Friedrich von Raumer who, delivering letters to addresses in the squares of Bloomsbury, saw that despite the 'pillars and other decorations, the houses are divided into many and comparatively small and narrow houses . . . The English like better to disperse themselves through three storeys, than to inhabit a large suite of apartments, and endure strange occupants above and below.' Von Raumer added that, while houses in Berlin were cheerfully painted in bright colours, if Londoners attempted to paint their houses they would very soon be blackened again. Having multiple floors, each floor had to have one fire at least in the winter, spring and autumn. Though they might avoid having noise from neighbours above and below them, they produced more smoke per household than their French or German counterparts, and turned their city black. The British Museum, in whose basement in Great Russell Street many tons of coal were heaped, had ever-smoking chimneys, producing as a by-product gases perfectly composed to destroy the collections.

Black walls, black grass, black flowers, black snow and a very black Westminster Abbey whose white stone had been obscured for centuries by the time William Henry Fox Talbot took its photograph in 1846. Smoke issued forth from half a million chimneys and hung over London, held cosily a hundred or so feet in the air by the surrounding rim of the Downs and the Chilterns, before dropping to ground level to make the city miserable when the air was damp. This was the 'sea-coal canopy; a huge, dun Cupola' that Byron described in his long poem *Don Juan*, settling above the capital 'like a foolscap crown'. 'By God,' said the painter Henry Fuseli to his friend Benjamin Robert Haydon when in 1806 they looked together across London: 'It's like the smoke of the Israelites making bricks.' 'It is grander,' said Haydon, 'for it is the smoke of a people who would have made the Egyptians make bricks for them.'

Haydon's delight at what he described as the 'sublime canopy' over London was a minority view. The radical author and publisher Sir Richard Phillips saw it otherwise when, looking out over London, he 'obtained a distinct view of a phenomenon which can be seen nowhere in the world but at this distance from London. The smoke of nearly a million of coal fires.' Phillips made a quick though over-estimated calculation, and found that two hundred thousand houses, or half a million chimneys, each produced a bushel (about thirty-six litres) of smoke a second for six hours or more of the day, making a cloud twenty five miles long by two miles high. 'Over this area [twenty or thirty miles' radius from the centre of London] it deposits the volatilized products of three thousand chaldrons, or nine millions of pounds [4,000 tons] of coals per day.'

Phillips went on to assert that the smoke over London 'is found to blight or destroy all vegetation', but Joseph Farington discovered what he thought was its more positive side-effect. He revealed that his friend the architect James Wyatt had found proof of the effect of smoke on the ambient temperature of the metropolis. Smoke made London warmer: 'Wyatt mentioned that as a proof how much the atmosphere of London is affected by the heat of coal fires, on Sunday morning last at ½ *past 7* his thermometer (out of doors) stood at 2 degrees below 0, but at *nine* o'clock it had risen *12 degrees*. NB there was no sun.'

London's smoke was so permanent and consuming a feature of the city's life that the government was forced to take action on one (but only one) of its root causes, the emissions from factories. The House of Commons Select Committee on Steam Engines and Furnaces – the Smoke Committee as it was called – sat in 1819 under the chairmanship of Michael Angelo Taylor, a reforming member of parliament. Taylor was a campaigner for improvements in London's streets, being instrumental in bringing the Metropolitan Paving Act into law in 1817, introducing gas lighting and improving water supply. Taylor's Select Committee was charged with investigating ways of legislating for new standards in the construction of steam engines and furnaces 'in a manner less prejudicial to public health and public comfort', and with finding designs for furnaces that would consume their own smoke. One witness, the physician Edward Roberts, told the committee that he saw Great Russell Street, between Oxford Street and the British Museum, stifled with smoke. 'I have seen the smoke of London in one continuous line for ten miles, like a cloud.' Carried along with it was a foul stink from

23

'steam boilers, brewers' coppers, stills, soap coppers and tallow-melters' coppers . . . a very great nuisance in London'. During the long debate about how best to commemorate Nelson, the idea of erecting a column was widely dismissed. The sculptor Francis Chantrey voiced the mood when he asserted that 'columns have got vulgarised in this country. The steam chimneys in every smoky manufacturing town supply you with columns by the dozen . . . Huddled in such a town as London a column will be lost.' By the 1820s London's smoke had long been a subject for ironic jest. R. C. Kidd, the brother of an Oxford Professor of Physics, suggested that Marc Isambard Brunel, whose tunnel then in construction under the Thames was an abiding marvel, should build another tunnel, 'to convey all the smoke from London to Oxford and there condense it in a Receiver and sell it to the Farmers for manure'.

Robert Southey, the Lakeland poet, saw through the smoke, and felt drawn to London's glitter. He spoke for thousands of incomers about the:

> opulence and splendour of the shops: drapers, stationers, confection-ers, pastry-cooks, seal-cutters, silver-smiths, book-sellers, print-sellers, hosiers, fruiterers, china-sellers, – one close to another, without inter-mission, a shop to every house, street after street, and mile after mile . . . Nothing which I had seen in the country had prepared me for such a display of splendour.

Louis Simond's eye was caught by the print shops, and shops that dis-played mathematical, optical and chemical instruments, 'beautifully arranged; the admirable polish, and learned simplicity of the instru-ments suggests the idea of justness and of perfection'. Native-born Londoners tended to show more circumspection than newcomers, and were more critical and less in awe of the place. They noticed the intermittent water supply and the ineffective drains, the smoke and the bad air, the crowds, the traffic-locks and the crush. 'The passion for crowds', wrote Charles Lamb in 1802, 'is nowhere feasted so full as in London,' and as a result Lamb found his 'natural hypochondria' vanish in the city. He took London's crowds in his stride to the extent that he was horrified when Wordsworth suggested he might leave London to visit Cumberland: 'I don't much care if I never see a mountain in my life,' Lamb replied, adding: 'London itself is a panto-mime and a masquerade, all these things work themselves into my mind and feed me without a power of satiating me. The wonder of these sights impels me into night walks about the crowded streets, and I often shed tears in the motley Strand from fullness of joy at so much *Life*.' Others appreciated the incidental beauties, gifts of the passing moment. Mary Anne Flaxman, sister of the sculptor John Flaxman, took a walk in Portland Place one hot July evening: 'It was like taking an airing in a Dutch oven before a fire. The sun was setting, the New Road very dusty, so that Regents Park appeared through the medium of an atmosphere composed of gold dust.'

The 'display of splendour' that struck Southey so forcibly, the 'vastness and illimitable proportions' that frightened De Quincey, and the horror felt by Cyrus Redding's unnamed Devonian give a consistent picture of the impact of early-nineteenth-century London on three perceptive and susceptible visitors. For Southey it was the variety and wealth of the trades and products to be had; for De Quincey the uncertainty of emptiness; for the Devonian the shock of its tremendous scale. These three, like Porson, Farington and Jerdan, had come to London from afar. London has always been, and con-tinues to be, defined and redefined by outsiders. During the immediate aftermath of the tube and bus bombings of 7 July 2005, the city's mayor, Ken Livingstone, spoke of men and women coming to London from all over the world to fulfil their dreams and to become Londoners.

Joseph Farington was at Rougham, Norfolk, when he heard the news of the victory at the Battle of Trafalgar. During the ten weeks between Nelson's death on 21 October 1805 and his funeral the fol-lowing January, Richard Porson was characteristically mixing scholarship with drinking. William Jerdan, who had not yet taken up his journalistic career, was stuck on the guardship *Gladiator* in Portsmouth dockyard, having joined the navy three weeks before Trafalgar. He was discharged through ill-health after only ten weeks' service, his nautical experience extending only as far as a couple of return journeys to the Isle of Wight. Anthony Carlisle was preparing, and then giving, a lecture to the Fellows of the Royal Society on the muscular action of fish.

Casting the net wider, to catch some of the men and women whose lives will cross and mark these pages, J. M. W. Turner, by now a Royal Academician at the height of his powers, was at thirty years of age already well known in London. He hurried down to Sheerness to see the shattered form of HMS *Victory* and to talk to her sailors, making notes for a dramatic and topical painting of the moment when Nelson was shot. Humphry Davy was preparing and giving his revolutionary series of lectures on the Chemistry of Agriculture at the Royal Institution, and Michael Faraday, then a fifteen-year-old bookbinder's apprentice in Marylebone, was reading, thinking and dreaming about the workings of the natural world, without any particular expectation of a life in science. With the encouragement of his master George Riebau, Faraday constructed ingenious electrical machines in the back of the workshop. One of Reibau's neighbours later recalled Faraday's youthful excitement: 'He amused us in our leisure hours with various chymical experiments. He was very industrious, persevering, and attentive to his master's business, and saved every penny in order to obtain the means of pursuing his favourite studies.'

Further afield, Charles Babbage was then living in his home town of Totnes in Devon teaching himself algebra; William Brockedon was also living in Totnes, making and mending clocks in the shop that he had inherited from his father. This small town two hundred miles from the capital would in due course supply London with two men of uncommon ingenuity, manipulative skill and ill-temper. Charles Babbage would go on to develop a calculating machine, his 'Difference Engine', a forerunner of the computer; while William Brockedon, the creator of dozens of patents, and a portrait artist of great talent, quarrelsome and sycophantic in equal measure, would be rapidly forgotten. Of the other men and women whom we shall read about, Benjamin Robert Haydon had come to London from Devon with no less an ambition than to rise to be a great history painter. His first meeting with Fuseli took place in the autumn of 1805, in the older man's gallery, where he saw: 'Galvanised devils – malicious witches brewing their incantations – Satan bridging Chaos . . . humour, pathos, terror, blood, and murder, met one at every look!'

William Bullock was in his home town of Liverpool, surrounded by the extraordinary museum which he would one day pack up and bring to London. John Tatum, opening his Theatre of Science in Dorset Street off Fleet Street, was beginning his first annual series of lectures to all-comers interested in the study of natural philosophy. Marc Isambard Brunel, some years away yet from designing the Thames Tunnel, was being employed in Portsmouth dockyard to oversee the operation of the block-making machines he had invented for the navy, while Henry Maudslay, an inspired and businesslike mechanical genius, was constructing these same machines to Brunel's designs at his works in Lambeth. Brunel's son Isambard Kingdom was still with his mother, Sophia Brunel, *in utero*, to be born in April 1806. Cyrus Redding made the long carriage journey to London from Devon during these weeks. Reaching the edges of London he was instilled not with excitement, but with the thrill of fear when he saw the guard on his coach cock his pistols and blunderbusses soon after they left Reading, 'a paradoxical mark that we were approaching the more civilized part of the kingdom'.

Robert Smirke had just returned from a continental tour, and was over these same weeks beginning a career as an architect. By invoking his charm as well as his talent, he was already becoming part of dinner-table gossip. Farington reported that one of his first patrons, Lord Lowther, was 'much pleased' that he had commissioned this 'ingenious, modest and gentlemanly' young man to design him a castle in Westmorland. John Martin, to become widely renowned both for his immense apocalyptic paintings and for his unsuccessful plans to revolutionise the water and drainage systems in London, was, as Nelson died on the *Victory*, a young man agitating his parents in Northumberland to allow him to travel to London to become a glass-painter. Mary Somerville, then Mrs Samuel Greig, was living with her first husband, a captain in the Russian navy attached to the Admiralty. Against her husband's will, she surreptitiously studied mathematics while nursing their infant son. The ambitious young army officer James Willoughby Gordon and Julia Bennett, a pupil and friend of J. M. W. Turner, were married on 15 October, nearly a week before the first shots were fired at Trafalgar. All these men and women knew each other, or would come to know of each other, and their paths would cross in London.

Nelson's body had lain in state at Greenwich Naval Hospital since HMS *Victory* had dropped anchor at Sheerness on 22 December. His lead-lined coffin, made from the mast of the French ship *L'Orient*, was itself encased within an ornate mahogany casket, upholstered in black Genoa velvet, and ornamented with ten thousand double-gilt nails. This had been designed by the one of the most influential, and certainly the most expensive, of London silversmiths, Rudolph Ackermann. On 8 January 1806 this weighty, multi-layered casket was taken from Greenwich on the royal barge built for Charles II to Whitehall Stairs, accompanied by a flotilla of sixty or seventy craft of all kinds. A military band played Handel's Dead March, and guns fired every minute: 'the hills in Greenwich Park reverberated the solemn sound between the lofty domes of the Royal Hospital', the *Gentleman's Magazine* reported. The sun shone brightly during Nelson's final river journey, but as the cortège landed at Whitehall a sudden hailstorm and high wind broke out, lashing the water and making the boats pitch and dance. The spectacle, the greatest aquatic procession on the Thames in living memory, caused brave men to weep, and would be matched in grandeur only by the events of the following day.

Overnight the body lay in the Admiralty. When the procession began at half-past ten, it was two hours before the Duke of York could see the cathedral rising up ahead. He rode at the head of the winding column travelling at glacial pace up Whitehall, along the Strand and Fleet Street, and up Ludgate Hill. The military band whispered Handel's Dead March over and over again, breaking its rhythm from time to time with a jauntier Rule Britannia. The black and gold catafalque carrying Nelson's extraordinary coffin rattled as the team of horses pulled it over the cobbles. The tassels masking the wheels danced to the rhythm of the bumps, and the superstructure creaked and lurched like a ship-of-the-line in a gale. Built as a truncated HMS *Victory*, with a glazed and painted poop at the rear displaying a huge white ensign, and on the prow the figure of Fame waving a palm and a laurel wreath, the whole lugubrious machine carried Nelson on his final voyage across a sea of straining faces.

Those at a distance would have seen the canopy, inscribed with Nelson's motto *Palmam qui meruit ferat* rising and dipping; those in the front and in windows above saw a detachment of sailors carrying *Victory*'s ensign, peppered with shot-holes. As the procession passed Somerset House, Royal Academicians, Fellows of the Royal Society, and members of the Society of Antiquaries stood together watching from the upper windows. So long was the procession that, as the leaders took their places in the nave of the cathedral, the tail had not yet left the Admiralty. The Prince of Wales's carriage was near the head of the procession, and the onlookers who cheered the Prince had to wait thirty-five minutes, so Joseph Farington tells us, before Nelson's funeral car passed by. But at least the weather held: 'remarkably fine, the Thermometer on my staircase 48', he cheerfully recorded.

About as many people attended the funeral in the cathedral as there were double-gilt nails in Nelson's coffin. Among them was the painter and engraver Josiah Boydell, present in his capacity of alderman for Cheapside, and as the chairman of a committee formed to raise a monument to Nelson in the City of London. He found the effect in St Paul's, under the gently undulating French and Spanish banners suspended below the dome, to be 'sublime, appearing almost visionary, something like what was described in the Arabian night's entertainments'. Haydon, however, thought that the funeral 'showed the nation's generosity and its utter want of taste'. The coffin was lowered into the deep shadow of a stone-lined vault specially dug for the hero immediately beneath the dome, and with a clamouring shout HMS *Victory*'s tattered flag, paraded so proudly during the procession, was fallen upon and torn into tiny pieces and distributed in shreds and clouds to the crowds inside and out of the cathedral. Haydon got a fragment, but, years later, in his ruin, he lost it.

What soon became clear to all was that after the sea-victory at Trafalgar Britain need no longer be daunted by the spectre of Napoleon; and that when Nelson was buried, uncertainty and the fear of invasion were buried with him. 'All fears of invasion were now over,' Haydon recalled, 'and we looked forward to our pursuits with a degree of confidence which only those can estimate who passed their early days among the excitement of perpetual war.'

Resounding naval victory, and a grand funeral spectacular, brought in their wake a confidence that had not been seen in Britain since the height of the industrial revolution in the 1780s. It led to the continued physical expansion of London, to the redoubling of internal and overseas trade, and, now that the French and Spanish navies had been broken, to a new confidence in the purpose of commerce, the arts and the sciences. Although it took a generation to achieve maturity and direction, London was set on course to become the financial, entrepreneurial and intellectual capital of the world.

2

Chapel, Parliament, Theatre and Pantheon

~

SOON AFTER EIGHT o'clock on a November evening in 1805 Anthony Carlisle stood up in the candlelight in a room full of men in black to talk on one of his favourite subjects, fish. He had 'a fine intellectual face, a brow denoting power, eyes intelligent and impressive, a Phidian nose, a mouth of unquestionable power'. Nevertheless he tended to compromise this fine impression by turning up to his lectures wearing full court dress, a bag-wig and a cockaded hat. Carlisle was about to give the annual Croonian Lecture to the Fellows of the Royal Society and their guests on 'The arrangement and mechanical action of the muscles of fish'. The Croonian Lectures, for which the speaker received £3, were paid for by one-fifth of the annual rent received from the tenant of the King's Head Tavern on Lambeth Hill, a street that ran down towards the river from St Paul's. Thus the sale of beer to lawyers, shopkeepers and watermen contributed directly to the advancement of knowledge. This income had been left to the Royal Society to pay for a series of lectures in perpetuity by the widow of the seventeenth-century physician William Croone. The theme of the lectures, specified under the terms of the bequest, was the nature or laws of muscular motion in humans and animals, to be accompanied by anatomical demonstrations.

The Royal Society of London for the Promotion of Natural Knowledge was a forcing ground and showcase of scientific enterprise, a forum where ideas in science, tested by experiment, were described and discussed, and either made available to be developed into benefits of civilisation, or thrown out and forgotten. Six months after its papers were presented, edited versions were published in the Society's journal, *Philosophical Transactions*. Carlisle's lecture was typical of the learning offered to the Fellows of the Royal Society in the years around Trafalgar. The subject had general appeal – the Fellows ate fish; some caught them in sport; and increased knowledge of muscular action was of benefit to all. On the other hand, unlike the papers presented by, for example, William Herschel, Humphry Davy or William Wollaston, Carlisle's words would never change human perception. For this reason, as an ordinary Fellow, who would be forgotten by the wider world after his death, Carlisle is of particular interest to us here, lingering as he does in the Royal Society's undergrowth. His paper was given in two parts, on the succeeding Thursdays, 7 and 14 November 1805.

Anthony Carlisle was an interesting choice as Croonian lecturer. Charles Lamb called him 'the best story-teller I have ever heard'. Not only was he a practising surgeon and lecturer at Westminster Hospital, but he studied animal as well as human anatomy. Beyond anatomy he had in 1800 published experiments on the electrolysing of water into hydrogen and oxygen, and in 1802 he had tried, with Thomas Wedgwood and Humphry Davy, to capture and hold images by a new chemical method. This came later to be called 'photography'. Carlisle was a keen fisherman, his fishing companions including the President of the Royal Academy, Sir Benjamin West, and Joseph Farington. Through their lobbying and support Carlisle was elected Professor of Anatomy at the Royal Academy in 1808; or, as Haydon put it, 'Carlisle is the man, he knows the effect good dinners have on half starved Academicians.' Carlisle was interested in oddities and the curious. An early contribution he made to the Royal Society in 1801 was an account of a seriously deformed lamb, 'monstrous' as he called it, and he would come in 1814 to publish on the subject of the Colburns of Vermont, USA, a family with a predisposition to polydactyly, that is, the appearance of additional fingers and toes. He wrote on anatomy and the fine arts, and on the oyster. Carlisle was very odd himself: when he suddenly resigned from the Anatomy Professorship at the Royal Academy in 1824, Constable remarked: 'He is considered *insane* by those to whom the Academy is life and death.'

Outlining his approach to the subject of the motion of fish, Carlisle told his audience: 'Their skeleton is simple, and the proportion of muscular flesh is remarkably large, but the muscles have no tendinous chords, their insertions being always fleshy.' Taking the cod as a standard, he described how its bodily motions are performed. In the interests of science he had maimed a tankful of dace, cutting off a variety of combinations of their fins to reveal by comparison the different ways this impeded their motion. One fish had its tail removed, as close to the body as possible, while from another all the fins and the tail were cut off. This latter creature, Carlisle reported, 'remained without motion floating near the surface of the water, with its belly upward.' Hardly surprising, but nevertheless Carlisle repeated his experiments on roach, gudgeon and minnow.

Looking down at Carlisle was the President of the Royal Society, Sir Joseph Banks, who sat above and behind on a red plush throne. Seated at a table beside the speaker, the Society's Secretary, Edward Whitaker Gray, Keeper of the Natural History Collections at the British Museum, took notes with a quill pen which he dipped in and out of one of the three gold inkpots gleaming in the candlelight beside the Society's ceremonial mace. The presence of this regal object, given to the Society by King Charles II in 1663 the year after its foundation, signified that the Royal Society was in session. If the President's concentration drifted, he might look around at the double rows of glum and grimy portraits of his predecessors on either side of the room, at the audience seated before him on brass-studded black leather benches, and feel the warmth from the fire a metre or two behind his throne. The room, directly over the portico of the Strand entrance to Somerset House and looking into the courtyard, was decorated as if it were a grand country-house saloon, and members attending were expected to dress appropriately. The pea-green and pink walls reflected more candlelight, and the stucco ceiling, with intertwining acanthus leaves in grey and pink, asserted the Society's royal allegiances with medallion portraits of its founder King, Charles II, and the reigning King, George III. Carlisle read on:

> The quickness and force of action in the muscles of fishes is coun-
> terpoised by the short duration of their powers. Those accustomed to
> the diversion of angling know how soon the strength of fishes is
> exhausted, for if, when hooked, it be kept in constant action, it soon
> loses even the ability to preserve its balance and turns upon its side,
> fatigued and incapable of motion.

All lecturers read their papers out loud at the weekly evening meetings of the Royal Society, held from early November to early March. Fellows and their guests heard, or tried to hear, these latest reports from the world of natural philosophy, as the candlelight threw fluttering shadows on to the reading desk, and as the audience shifted, itched and coughed. We can only guess at the variety and quality of style of delivery in the unamplified lecture room. Some lecturers mumbled into their scripts, others gabbled. Carlisle was one of the few who knew how to tell a story and hold an audience. While enough information will have been communicated to keep the members listening, and returning for more, much will have been missed by many.

The Royal Society explored the frontiers of knowledge. Science was then known as natural philosophy, a name which connected it directly with over two thousand years of western human thought and experiment since Socrates. As the author Sybille Bedford has eloquently put it, 'physics held no terrors then and the laws of the universe were something a man might deal with pleasantly in a work-shop set up behind the stables'. Occasionally, accounts such as the 'Elephant's tusk with head of spear embedded' had more of a curiosity than a scientific value. Some papers, however, followed fragile threads across rich and exciting scientific territory: Sir William Herschel, the undisputed elder of astronomy, spoke on 'The power of penetrating into space by telescopes' in December 1799. He had discovered the planet Uranus with a forty-foot telescope, the largest in the world, which he had constructed at his home in Slough with the support and enthusiasm of George III. Slough being only a few miles from Windsor Castle, Herschel was frequently bidden to the King's presence to reveal the stars to the royal family. Over the years across the turn of the nineteenth century Herschel spoke to the Royal Society on a number of interlinked astronomical topics, the results of observations that began to transform human understanding of the stars and planets. Thus in June 1797 he lectured on the brightness of the satellites of Jupiter, and gave a paper on the nature of the sun in April 1801. Having looked at the sun through his huge telescope, using a reflector, and filtering the light through a trough of watered ink, he identified for the first time and named the various particular features of the surface of the unseeable sun: openings, shallows, ridges, nodules, corrugations, indentations and pores.

Men who by the early twentieth century would be categorised specifically as mineralogists, physiologists, biologists, botanists or chemists gave papers all of which aimed at expounding and expanding knowledge. There was a rich and teeming variety of subjects: on the impregnation of rabbits, on urinary concretions, on animal electricity, on the growth of plants in pure water, on the stability of ships, on the production of artificial cold, on cretinism. Wherever nature and knowledge rubbed together, there stood the Royal Society analysing the interface, actively and intelligently using its specialised interests to assert collective academic, political and social pressure for change. While the discoveries of Herschel, Davy or Wollaston continue to have resonance into the twenty-first century, the mass of contributors were men whose names have now faded into the dusk, but for whom science was a driving fascination: Charles Hatchett, the pioneering mineral chemist whose geological collection created a foundation for the British Museum, read two papers on 'Sydneia', a mineral lately discovered in New South Wales. The mathematician Sir George Shuckburgh-Evelyn Bt proposed a means of ascertaining a standard of weights and measures. Thomas Andrew Knight, the plant physiologist, spoke on the ascent of sap in trees, and Anthony Carlisle spoke on the 'monstrous lamb', and on muscular motion both in fish and in man.

To survive financially, academically and socially, the Royal Society membership had to strike a balance between the wealthy, the studious and the well connected. Having been founded in 1662, it was the senior of the learned organisations of London, but by the early 1800s it had some active rivals for membership among the amateur elite. The other organisations around which membership ebbed and flowed were the Society of Antiquaries, the Society of Arts, Manufactures and Commerce, the Royal Academy of Arts and the Royal Institution of Great Britain. More than two hundred years after the founding of the Royal Institution, the youngest of the five organisations discussed here, they are all still going strong at the heart of London.

Members of the Royal Society were elected by ballot four times a year, and in attempting to define its balance the Society began to feel a drift during the first two decades of the nineteenth century away from its true scientific mission. By gradually padding the membership with non-scientific men, the Society came to realise in the late 1820s that it was in danger of losing its way. The banker Samuel Rogers, who was also a Fellow of the Society of Antiquaries, a habitué of the Royal Academy and a friend and adviser of artists and writers, was one of many lay members elected not for scientific insight but for their wealth and social and literary connection. Rogers was an amateur poet, writing and publishing at his own expense long reflective works, such as 'The Pleasures of Memory' and 'Italy', and entertaining friends and acquaintances regularly and lavishly. Rogers did not even so much as dabble in science, but nevertheless he was elected a Fellow of the Royal Society in November 1796 under the citation 'Samuel Rogers of the Temple Esqr FSA author of "the Pleasures of memory", a Gentleman well versed in various branches of knowledge . . . desirous of the honor of becoming a Fellow of this Society'.

Of his nine sponsors, only four had any clear connection with science themselves: Sir George Shuckburgh-Evelyn Bt, two physicians Sir Francis Milman Bt and John Grieve, and the astronomer Alexander Aubert. Aubert, who had built observatories in Deptford and Islington, was also a director of the London Assurance Company, and must have been known to Rogers through financial circles. The other Fellows who put Rogers's name forward had literary achievements, and included Thomas Bowdler, Shakespeare's expurgator; Richard Wilson Greatheed, a member of a family of antiquaries from Warwick and a life member of the Royal Institution; Daniel Braithwaite, the Comptroller of the Post Office, a Fellow of the Society of Antiquaries and a member of the Royal Institution; and the Rev. William Tooke, a historian of Russia, and chaplain to the English churches of Kronstadt and St Petersburg. Thus there was already, before the nineteenth century began, a tendency for Fellows to be members of multiple learned organisations, and to elect men in their own image. This had the cumulative effect of pressing the Royal Society away from its founding values, the Promotion of Natural Knowledge.

Twenty men were elected as Fellows in the year of Trafalgar, 1805, and of these, Sir Edward Winnington Bt, MP for Droitwich, died the day before the election, but was elected anyway; nine others seem to have had no particular connection with science, being members of parliament, barristers, earls and landowners; and only six were securely and diligently concerned with scientific advancement. Among these were Thomas Andrew Knight, 'the indefatigable Mr T. A. Knight', as the *Philosophical Magazine* called him, who had earlier supported Samuel Rogers's candidacy; the botanist and antiquary Edward Rudge; the mathematician and astronomer Stephen Peter Rigaud; and the engineer Joseph Whidbey, sailing master to the Royal Navy, who had travelled round the world with George Vancouver and worked with John Rennie on the construction of Plymouth harbour. Of the others there is little or no record. Proceeding in this fashion, the Royal Society was bound in due course to find itself with an identity crisis. This was eventually brought out into the open when Charles Babbage wrote his *Reflections on the Decline of Science in England* (1830), deploring, among much else, the election of non-scientists to the Society.

The second of the older learned societies, the Society of Antiquaries, grew from the meeting of three friends in December 1707 in the Bear Tavern in the Strand. Humphrey Wanley, John Talman and John Bagford came together to discuss their common interest in manuscripts and ancient remains, and proposed to invite others to share their knowledge by forming a society, to meet every Friday. This, they proposed, would be 'limited to the subject of Antiquities; and more particularly, to such things as may Illustrate and Relate to the History of Great Britain'. One early understanding of the Society's fields of interest, published in 1718, asserted that 'the Study of Antiquities has ever been esteem'd a considerable part of good Literature, no less curious than useful'. The Antiquaries appointed themselves keepers of their own registers of manuscripts, monuments and other ancient remains dating from before the reign of James I 'to the end that knowledge of them may become more Universal, be preserved and transmitted to Futurity'.

By the late eighteenth century the Society of Antiquaries had, like the Royal Society, become fully a part of the social and intellectual establishment of London. It had a a president, a director, a secretary, a treasurer, visitors (the Archbishop of Canterbury and the Lord Chancellor), membership, a Royal Charter, a Great Seal, and an address in Chancery Lane. There it had a meeting room, a library and a museum. Nevertheless, the Antiquaries was dogged during the eighteenth and into the nineteenth century by an intermittent lassitude, due to misfortune, ill-timed deaths of officers and patrons, and the shadow of the larger, richer and more glamorous Royal Society. Further, the Antiquaries did not have a leader who matched the public persona, physical and intellectual stamina and sheer bullying capacity of Sir Joseph Banks.

The Royal Society looked forward, driven by discovery and the excitement of the next vista on the course of the twisting river of knowledge; the Society of Antiquaries on the other hand looked back, at the flotsam and jetsam rising up in profusion out of the water. The discoveries announced to the Royal Society came in part as the result of care, method and experiment, and the growing assurance that scientific revelation would come through dogged application. Chance during experiment was for men of science a constant factor, but evidence and raw material was abundant, and even, in practice, infinite. For the Fellows of the Society of Antiquaries, however, material was far-flung, fragmentary, fragile and finite. They sought out and studied man-made remains, ranging from ancient and medieval manuscripts to armour, inscriptions, portraits and evidence of customs and language. They divided their interest into four general areas – the Country, the King, the Church, the People – and set themselves targets, some of which were simply not realistic: 'a Compleat History of Great Britain and Ireland . . . to print Domesday and the Red Book of the Exchequer . . . a Monasticon, enlarged to 30 or 40 volumes'. The 1718 statement of the Antiquaries' area of activity draws wide boundaries. They sought communication from all parts of Great Britain and Ireland on 'old Cities, Stations, Camps, Castles, Theatres, Temples, Roads, Abbeys, Churches, Statues, Tombs, Busts, Inscriptions, Ruins, Altars, Ornaments, Utensils, Habits, Seals, Armour, Portraits, Medals, Urns, Pavements, Maps, Charters, Manuscripts, Genealogies, Histories, Deeds, Letters, Records, Observations, Illustrations, Emendations of Books already publishd and whatever may properly belong to the History of BRITISH ANTIQUITYS'. By the end of the eighteenth century these boundaries had been stretched even wider by the gradual embracing of the study of artefacts discovered in British expeditions and colonies overseas.

Extreme breadth of interest, combined with fragmentation of evidence, demanded a firm guiding hand, and an aggressive and inspirational leadership that was not encumbered by vested interests and indolence. While the more rigorous aspirations of the Royal Society had Sir Joseph Banks in control of them over the forty-two years from 1778 to 1820, the Society of Antiquaries found itself at risk both from poor attendance at meetings and from the perception that for years the Antiquaries had felt that those members who were also Fellows of the Royal Society had 'over grown or over shaded this poor Society'. Indeed, an early president, Martin Folkes, seems to have attempted in 1750 to sell the Society down the river and merge it with the Royal Society – though the fact that he was also President of the Royal Society at the time must have coloured his outlook.

The Antiquaries' only equivalent to Banks in recent times had been Dr Jeremiah Milles, Dean of Exeter, during whose presidency from 1768 until his death in 1784 the Society found a new surge of purpose. Milles, a portly epicurean, brought a new jollity by founding the Antiquaries dining club. He appointed an energetic director for the Society, Richard Gough, who stayed for twenty-six years until 1797. Gough applied his quick mind to the creation and support of publications including the Society's new annual journal *Archaeologia*, his own *Sepulchral Monuments in Great Britain* (1786–96), studies illustrated by engravings of Ely Cathedral (1771), *The Antiquities of England and Wales* (1773–89) by Francis Grose, and volumes on Roman antiquities in Britain (1793), St Stephen's Westminster (1795) and Exeter Cathedral (1797). Never had such a whirlwind of activity emerged from the Antiquaries' offices, and out of the whirlwind came Gough's clear words of guidance for members: 'The arrangement and proper use of facts is HISTORY; – not a mere narrative taken up at random and embellished with poetic diction, but a regular and elaborate enquiry into every ancient record and proof that can elucidate or establish them.' Under

Milles and Gough the Antiquaries established foreign contacts with equivalents in Paris, St Petersburg, Hesse and elsewhere, and found a new seam of topicality to excite their membership in papers on subjects including recently discovered druidical remains in Yorkshire, on the opening of the tomb of Edward I in Westminster Abbey, and on discoveries in Pompeii.

During this period the Antiquaries took the evolutionary step, with the Royal Society, of moving into new premises behind the Strand façade of Somerset House. The buildings were now in construction on the site of a previous Somerset House, which was being nibbled away bit by bit by demolition as the sharp, shiny white new edifice, designed by Sir William Chambers, building went up in its place. Known briefly as Somerset Place, this was the first part of the complex to be completed. For the first time, these two established bodies, who had shared members but had never shared a staircase and lobby, were to be obliged to live cheek by jowl. The Royal Society moved in November, and the Society of Antiquaries in December 1780. The Royal Academy was already in residence. So close were they that applause in one of the meeting rooms could be heard through the wall in another: a paper on astronomy in the Royal Society might be punctuated by the sound of a row between artists in the Royal Academy, and this might also disturb proceedings in the Antiquaries.

Over their front door their names were incised in stone, suggesting that a marriage had been arranged: ROYAL & ANTIQ^N SOCIETIES. To make the stern point that it was the Royal Society that was the senior of the two, a bust of Sir Isaac Newton was placed over the door. As the historian of science Sophie Forgan has written, 'to put up a bust of such symbolic significance was rather like planting the regimental standard'. To the particular displeasure of both, the Antiquaries' rooms and those of the Royal Society interlocked. At the outset, the Royal Society was deeply offended that it had to share the main staircase with the Antiquaries, and they unilaterally colonised the porter's lodge, complaining to the architect about the lack of space. The Royal Society also complained that they had no room for their museum, and very soon after they moved to Somerset Place, from Crane Court off Fleet Street, they gave the greater part of their collection of natural and artificial curiosities to the British Museum. Even the basement, with its cellar, kitchen and privy, was a bone of contention for the two learned groups.

Somerset House was being built in Portland stone between Somerset Place and the bank of the river as the home of government bureaucracy. It would gather offices of state, conveniently close together and under the eye of Whitehall. The deal that George III struck with the government on relinquishing the site was that the societies whose work and ambitions he cherished should be housed within the new structure. Thus it was that the societies, accommodated on the Strand side of the courtyard, acted as a screen of science, art and history before the winding of the endless corridors of the Tax Office, the Salt Office, the Office of the Comptroller of the Pipe, the Navy Pay Office, the Treasurers' Remembrancers' Office, the Sick and Wounded Office, the Hawkers and Pedlars Office, and the Lost-Monkey-and-Mislaid-Poodle Department. This last was an invention of the journalist G. A. Sala; the rest are real. Sala was one of many writers who came to satirise the purpose of the government offices in Somerset House. Another, John Williams, under the pseudonym 'Anthony Pasquin', wrote:

> In these damp, black and comfortless recesses, the clerks of the nation grope about like moles immersed in Tartarean gloom, and stamp, sign, examine, indict, doze and swear as unconscious of the revolving sun as so many miserable demons of romance condemned to toil for ages in the centre. Methinks I hear the Isle of Portland mourn for this misapplication and prostitution of its entrails.

In the years around 1805 the Society of Antiquaries went to sleep. The gap between the publication of the volumes of *Archaeologia* widened from an average of two or three years to six. This should be compared with the publication of the Royal Society's *Philosophical Transactions*, which appeared like clockwork, a large volume every year. Richard Gough's successor as Director, Samuel Lysons, was criticised for having turned the Society into a 'temple of Morpheus'. The Secretary at this time, elected in 1807, was Nicholas Carlisle, Anthony Carlisle's half-brother, described as 'one of the Society of

Antiquaries' most gifted exponents of the art of inactivity'. He was objected to by Lysons on account of his 'strong provincial accent of the West Riding of Yorkshire. It is also uncertain', added Farington, 'if he read Greek.' As a measure of the inattention now given to the quality of papers, Nicholas Carlisle published in *Archaeologia* a letter from his half-brother Anthony describing, but not discussing or illuminating in any way, a group of five ceremonial maces discovered by the British army at Agra in India.

To make matters worse, the Society was caught in the backwash of scandal when its senior Vice-President, Sir Henry Englefield Bt, was taken to court by a former soldier, Major-General Richard Crewe, for allegedly having had 'criminal conversation', that is, adultery, with Crewe's wife in Brighton. Crewe divorced his wife, and Englefield was ordered to pay £3,000 in damages. The affair led to rows in the Society, one Fellow noting that, although Englefield was a good antiquary, 'his reputation was much injured by the crim. con. trial in which he was proved to have committed adultery'. Englefield had a high opinion of himself which may have been one of the reasons he got himself into such trouble. He believed he naturally smelt of violets. 'Bless me, what a smell of violets!' an acquaintance standing beside him once said. 'Yes, it comes from me,' replied Sir Henry.

Dull and unproductive of scholarship though it might have been at this time, scandal and lethargy among the old men of the Antiquaries created an opportunity for the emergence of youth and energy. Having just returned from the continent, Robert Smirke the younger submitted an account of Gothic architecture in Italy and Sicily which blew some welcome life back into the 'temple of Morpheus', and prompted a rapid response from Sir Henry Englefield, followed by a robust defence from Smirke. William Jerdan tried his best to be a diligent member, contributing two papers to the Society for discussion, but even his unbounded energy came up against the Antiquaries' slough, and he found he could not get the volumes of *Archaeologia* that he asked for from the 'fat, contented, and rosy official', and he discontinued his membership.

Discussion from objects was central to the Antiquaries' process, and, to reflect this, their meeting room was of a different configuration to the Royal Society's across the hall. Where the Royal Society's meeting room was arranged like a chapel, with the dais at the far end of the two rows of benches, the Antiquaries sat in two triple banks of seats facing each other, as in the British Houses of Parliament, across a long central table with the President at the head. This arrangement reflected the fundamental difference between the Antiquaries' and the Royal Society's approach to study. Royal Society members were a non-participatory audience, listening to prepared papers; the Antiquaries, on the other hand, encircled the objects that members brought for discussion, and spoke about them together on an equal basis, expecting free discussion, object handling and instruction.

A third learned body which promoted research and teaching was the Royal Institution of Great Britain, founded in 1799. At the head of its first minute book is written its founding intention in bold lettering: 'INSTITUTION for diffusing the Knowledge, and facilitating the general Introduction of Useful Mechanical Inventions and Improvements; and for teaching, by Courses of Philosophical Lectures and Experiments, the application of Science to the common Purposes of Life.' Sir Joseph Banks PRS chaired the founding meeting, and played a central role in the Royal Institution's first two decades. One of its co-founders, Benjamin Thompson, Count Rumford, made it quite clear that this was not just a London organisation, but one which would deliver benefits to the nation as a whole. It did not call itself the Royal Institution of Great Britain for nothing. Writing to the printers of its prospectus, Rumford instructed:

> We wish it might be sent to all the booksellers of note in London with a particular request that it might be exposed to view in their windows, or in some very conspicuous part of their shops. We likewise wish that it might be sent to Bath, Birmingham, Manchester, Liverpool, and all the other great towns. In short we wish to make it as public as possible.

The mission of the Royal Institution was to spread experimental discoveries of science as far into everyday usage as the farmyard and the family hearth. Indeed, following these very threads of intention, Humphry Davy discussed the chemistry of manure, and Count

Rumford invented, and lectured upon, an improved domestic fire-place. Only a few months after the Institution's foundation it announced an account of its labours in *The Times*. First in a long list was the Institution's ambition to investigate improvements in making bread and 'cheap and nutritious soups for feeding the poor', while at the bottom was improving iron and steel refining. In the years around the victory at Trafalgar, the Royal Institution was the youngest and by far the most enterprising and trend-setting of the London learned societies. It was, as its name indicates, not a 'society', but a teaching and research organisation, open to subscribers who became members. Unlike the Royal Society and the Antiquaries, anybody could join who could afford the annual four-guinea fee, had a member as sponsor, and came respectably dressed. Flushed with the early success of its aims, and the rapid growth of its membership, the Royal Institution's managers proudly announced that it was estab-lished on a basis 'so prim and respectable that no doubt can be entertained of its success and of its permanent utility'.

The Royal Institution's horseshoe-shaped lecture hall, at the heart of its town house at 21 Albemarle Street, off Piccadilly, was a theatre for the mind. Its audiences watched scientific performances from rows of seats which raked down steeply to a large mahogany demon-stration bench. The configuration of the Royal Institution meeting room, designed in 1800 by John Soane and Henry Holland, was dif-ferent yet again from those of both the Royal Society and the Society of Antiquaries. It reflected the priority of the Royal Institution to teach large numbers of people at the same time, with everybody get-ting as good a view of the proceedings as possible. The form of the room mirrored the design of medical theatres, but for enlightenment and pleasure rather than pain and horror. With a central bench for the lecturer, the surrounding ring of tiered seats rose twenty feet towards the ceiling. The lectures, particularly when given by the first professor, Thomas Garnett, and subsequently by Humphry Davy from 1801 to 1812, were at their best dramatic and sensational per-formances attracting one thousand or more each time to watch the forces of nature being encouraged to perform at the lecturers' com-mand. The Royal Institution was for the people, as much as for specialists, and on another night audience members might entertain themselves at the Drury Lane theatres, or watch the acrobats and trick horsemen, and the 'Patagonian Samson', the seven-feet tall Giovanni Belzoni, performing at Astley's Royal Amphitheatre in Lambeth.

On the resignation of Thomas Garnett, the Royal Institution Proprietors searched the nation for a new guiding light, preferably one who was young like the Institution, practical like its purpose, and eloquent like its ambition. Humphry Davy was the obvious choice. He was brought to London from Bristol in 1801 trailing clouds of glory after a successful period of two years as a lecturer on scientific matters at Bristol's Pneumatic Institute. Before that he had come from even further west, practically off the map both socially and geographically, being the son of a wood carver from Penzance. Davy was charming, charismatic, handsome, ambitious and a mere twenty-two years old, a breath of fresh air among the crusty metropolitans of London. His easy way with an audience soon captivated the subscribers to the Royal Institution, and led to a rapid increase in membership and attendance.

Davy filled the Royal Institution's auditorium with people and filled its laboratory with the smells and noise of scientific experiment, and as a result its coffers began to fill with money. Casting its net more widely, and drawing audiences from a general, eager and impressionable public, the Royal Institution found its income beginning to emerge from different pockets. Small monies from the many began to challenge the privilege of the larger sums from the few. Tickets to Royal Institution lectures were distributed by members who themselves paid an annual subscription. As an example of the drift into wider and richer social fields, three-quarters of the Royal Institution membership of over four hundred in 1816 was composed of 'Esquires'; titled members were by now heavily in the minority. Nevertheless, in a capricious aside Samuel Taylor Coleridge, who attended Davy's lectures, wrote in his notebook: 'If all aristocrats here, how easily Davy might *poison* them all – 15 parts Ox[ygen]. 85 Muriatic acid gas [hydrochloric acid].'

Davy's first series of lectures at the Royal Institution in 1802 incorporated aspects of chemistry that were both fascinating in themselves and of a topicality and an economic importance to the nation that cannot be over-estimated: in tune with the Royal Institution's principles, the application of science to the common purposes of life, Davy lectured on the chemistry of tanning, dyeing and colour printing of fabric. Over the next few years he carried out research and lectured on the chemistry of agriculture, to find scientific ways of improving the quality and use of land, perfecting fertilisers, and by soil analysis strengthening crop yield.

But the Royal Institution had a broader outlook. It ran courses on Moral Philosophy by Sydney Smith, on the principles of poetry by Samuel Taylor Coleridge, and then there was music, architecture, mechanics, Persian literature and watercolour painting among the subjects on offer. The artist William Marshall Craig, drawing master to Princess Charlotte and miniature painter to the Queen, gave a series of lectures in 1806 on watercolour painting, 'The Complete Instructor in Drawing', to an audience that included artists, antiquarians and scientists. Craig's ideas found little favour with some members of the audience, and Joseph Farington made a note of gossip that he heard afterwards:

> [Robert] Smirke [the elder] called in the evening. Mary Smirke [his daughter] heard one of Craig's Lectures at the [Royal] Institute [Institution]. The principal object of it seemed to be to shew the superiority of *Water* over *Coloured* [that is, oil] painting. He encouraged Amateurs to practise in Water Colour and by the example of Mr [John White] Abbott of Exeter who had produced in the Exhibitions pictures universally admired, invited them to acquire fame which might easily be obtained.

Craig had gone on to suggest a formula for the balance of light and shade that amateurs should follow, four-fifths of shade to one of light. This easy way to apparent success drew delighted applause from the audience, but Mary Smirke, herself an exhibiting artist at the Academy, was 'disgusted' by Craig's 'presumption and folly'. Her brother, the architectural draughtsman Richard Smirke, who made drawings of buildings for the Society of Antiquaries, found the lectures 'absurd and presumptuous'.

Watercolour painting was not at that time taught at the Royal Academy, and this intervention at the Royal Institution challenged the programme and practice of the Academy. To get formal tuition in watercolour, a young artist hired his or her own tutor, as Julia Bennett and Clarissa Wells hired J. M. W. Turner, or went to one of the few private art schools such as that run in Bloomsbury by Henry Sass. The difficulty that the various members of the Smirke family had with the lectures was that Craig, who consorted with water-colour painters and royalty but remained aloof from the Royal Academy, should pronounce on painting over the heads of the 'pro-fessionals' whose main market was the very men and women who supported the Royal Institution lectures. By speaking on the Royal Institution's independent platform, which was managed by a group of men whose principle interest was science, Craig was a loose cannon, out of the Academy's control.

But the same lecture was discussed among those members of the Royal Society who were in the Royal Institution audience. Here Craig found support for his teaching of the use of watercolour, as Farington again reported:

> Mr Simmonds mentioned Craig's Lecture at the Royal Institute and Mr Parsons expressed his approbation of it, being, with Craig, of opinion that *Water Colour* painting is superior to *oil painting*. He formed the opinion on seeing Ducros drawings in Italy, and the Exhibition in Brook Street last year. Seeing Lysons smile he said, 'You think I talk very foolishly.' Lysons replied 'Not very wisely'. Sir Harry Englefield told Lysons that Craig seemed capable of teaching people to make bad drawings – that is, to attempt something without knowledge.

This argumentative conversation about the art of watercolour paint-ing between a physician (Samuel Simmonds FRS), a natural philosopher (William Parsons FRS), the Director of the Society of Antiquaries (Samuel Lysons FRS, FSA), and the Vice-President of the Antiquaries (Sir Henry Englefield FRS, FSA), all recorded by an artist (Joseph Farington RA FSA), is a living example of an intellec-tual argument in which the participants came from a variety of disciplines, each professing a determined view of the practice of watercolour painting. The interesting point about it is that an anti-quarian (Lysons) tells a man of science (Parsons) in the presence of an Academician (Farington, who was noting all this down) that he is not being very sensible in expressing a view counter to practice and opinion in the Royal Academy. There, oil painting was seen as the highest medium of pictorial art.

At the other end of the Strand from Somerset House, in John Adam Street, the Society of Arts encouraged progress in invention, manufacture, commerce, engineering, architecture and social development. Founded in 1754, this was both an influential catalyst for the improvement of the infrastructure of the nation and a social club with a membership in 1805 of around 1,400. The Society's committees devised challenges for men and women from all walks of life, and from all parts of Britain and the colonies. It sought ideas and solutions for invention, for technical and mechanical advance, for new ways of encouraging trade and industry, for geographical exploration, for improvements in husbandry. One hundred and seventy or eighty specific improvements or advances might be advertised annually through the Society's published *Transactions*, with the offer of a medal and sometimes a generous cash 'Premium' to the entry considered to be the most successful in each category. A premium was not a prize, but, as Dr Johnson had defined it in his Dictionary, 'something given to invite a loan or bargain'. Thus the Society expected more than just gratitude from the recipient; it trusted that a premium might be the beginnings of the development of the idea into a fact of modern living, and, ultimately, that the invention or practice would be seen in the fields, in the shops, or running about on the roads.

In the distributions of 1805, for example, George Smart of Ordnance Wharf, Westminster Bridge, won a gold medal for a mechanical chimney cleaner; Gilbert Gilpin of Old Park Iron Works, Shifnal, Shropshire, a silver medal and thirty guineas for a crane of a new design; Robert Salmon of Woburn a silver medal and ten guineas for improvements to canal locks; and John Farey of Westminster a silver medal for tree-planting in Buckinghamshire. Every sort and kind of technical advance or enhancement was sought out and rewarded among the dozens of categories competed for. While the twentieth-century desire for convenience was not yet the Society's target, it did seek utility. Entrants brought or sent models, plans and descriptions of their entries to John Adam Street, where they were displayed in the ground-floor repository. This was a museum of a kind, or a long-running trade fair. Inevitably the repository became overfilled: too much stuff came in, not enough was taken away, to the extent that by 1808 the Society was at crisis point, and made an attempt at self-improvement by declaring the intention that deposited models 'may receive a more methodical arrangement, be better preserved, and more distinctly viewed, than they can be in the present promiscuous state of their disposition'.

The Society of Arts was not, like the Royal Society, the Society of Antiquaries and the Royal Institution, a place principally for lecturing and teaching. It did not compete with those three other organisations in that way, but instead its members met at regular gatherings, in particular the annual reward distributions in May, and saw their two-guinea membership fee contributing to the costs of the reward system. The largest category in which premiums were offered was, however, not mechanics or manufacturing, but what was termed the Polite Arts. In 1808 the twenty-three rewards given for these Polite Arts – outline drawing, drawing after plaster casts, landscape painting in oil, and engraving – were balanced by only thirteen for Agriculture, ten for Mechanics, and two each for Chemistry, Manufactures, and Colonies and Trade. The prizes for the Polite Arts were medals, designed appropriately as gold and silver palettes, handed out to both men and women. The inclusion of painting and drawing in the reward system prompted rivalry among amateur artists and helped to increase membership to fuel and fund the technical improvements. It was also, as with William Craig's watercolour lectures in the Royal Institution, a means to broaden the audience and to sweeten the pill of science.

The manner in which an institution presented knowledge to its members and beyond defined its interface with the world, and its meeting room was its symbol. The Royal Society had its chapel, the Society of Antiquaries its parliament, the Royal Institution its theatre. The Great Room of the Society of Arts was different yet again: meetings were held in what presented itself as a national pantheon, a nearly square, high room surrounded by the mural cycle, *The Progress of Human Culture* painted by James Barry RA in 1784. In the language of classical iconography, the work presented London as the apogee of civilisation, where the world's thought, trade, arts and technologies came together. Father Thames is there, sitting in state on a water-borne chariot, drawn by four great English seafarers, Drake, Raleigh, Cabot and Cook. To the right, in a vision of British patronage at the peak of its power and prestige, is a group portrait of members of the Society of Arts giving and receiving premiums for invention, ingenuity and foresight. On another wall is a procession of victors of the first Olympic games, seen in a frieze below the Parthenon; and opposite are the Elysian Fields, populated by dozens of men of genius from all ages. In these canvases, Barry depicted 'one great maxim of moral truth, viz. that the obtaining of happiness, individual as well as public, depends upon cultivating the human faculties'.

The Royal Academy of Arts, founded in 1768, moved into rooms in Somerset Place in May 1780, six months before its new neighbours, the Royal Society and the Society of Antiquaries. Its front door was to the right of the entrance colonnade on the Strand, just forty feet from the door of the Royal Society and the Society of Antiquaries. The primary aim of the Royal Academy was to foster national genius in painting, sculpture and architecture, to organise annual exhibitions of work by living artists in which the works of its associates and academicians would feature largely, and to run and maintain a free art school for talented young men and women. The 'meeting room' of the Royal Academy was neither chapel, parliament, theatre nor pantheon, but an art gallery where for a modest entry fee anybody could submit their works for display, and all could come to see the annual exhibition. Teaching was the lifeblood of the Academy: that indeed was why it called itself an 'Academy'. In the closing words of his final address to students, the founding President, Sir Joshua Reynolds, invoked in 1790 the name of that 'truly divine man' Michelangelo, whom Reynolds urged all students to study. Underlining his centrality to its work, there above the doorway of the Academy was placed (and remains) a bust of Michelangelo looking across to the bust of Sir Isaac Newton at the Royal Society and Antiquaries opposite.

Like both of its neighbours, the Academy was going through difficult years. In the first decade of the nineteenth century artists were split between a court faction, Sir Francis Bourgeois, Sir William Beechey and James Wyatt among them, which supported their comparatively brief but nonetheless traditional links with the Crown, while the 'Academicals', including Robert Smirke and his father, Robert Smirke the elder, Henry Fuseli, James Barry and Thomas Banks, had sympathy for Napoleon's France, and entertained democracy and radicalism. These 'Academicals' left an indelible stamp on London, in neo-classical architecture, public monuments and impetus for cultural change, while the members of the royalist faction are now practically forgotten. Thus stand-up rows and altercations about the explosive topics of democracy took place across the entrance to the offices of a repressive Tory government.

In the same year that Humphry Davy exploded into the presence of the Royal Institution, Joseph Mallord William Turner, an arrogant, unpredictable but brilliant twenty-five-year-old artist, stood for election as one of the forty Academicians at the Royal Academy. When a few months later, in February 1802, he was elected, Turner became a focus of the divisions between the two camps in the Academy. Not only did he cause a good deal of trouble through aggressive behaviour in committee meetings, and upsetting the traditional master–servant relationship between patrons and artists, but he also probably helped to save the organisation by fomenting rows that had been too long simmering, and by blowing air into the stuffy and complacent membership.

It was a rough ride at first: within a year, Turner was on the Academy Council, taking part volubly. At the first meeting he attended things began to liven up. In an echo of the practice at the Society of Arts, premiums with gold and silver medals were proposed for specific subjects: for a historical painting, 'Achilles frantic for the loss of Patroclus'; for a sculpture, 'The Death of Meleager'; for an architectural design of an Exchange; for a drawing of the Park front of Horse Guards. Such details had not been recorded in the minutes for years. At the next meeting Turner seconded a divisive motion proposed by John Soane, another difficult and irascible man, that the Council admit and listen to a deputation of members demanding higher salaries for Academy officers. Turner was proposed as a member of the hanging committee for the 1803 exhibition, but was struck out at the next. Then at that meeting he was voted into the chair, and he struck himself back in again. Turner did not last long on the Council, for in May the following year he stormed out following a slanging match with Sir Francis Bourgeois, who had called him 'a little reptile', and accused him of setting a bad example to the young. A year or two later Turner was back: in 1811 he voted to prevent members from removing from Somerset House works of art belonging to the Academy (a long-running and casual practice), and he voted to sack his friend John Soane from the post of Professor of Architecture, because Soane had openly criticised Robert Smirke the younger in one of his lectures. Turner was also conscious of how the Academy looked – before a visit by the Prince Regent to the 1811 exhibition he moved in Council that the shabby chairs in the Council Room be replaced. Turner was difficult and ambitious, not at all the charming and eager-to-please young man that was Humphry Davy.

By the end of 1805, these two comparatively young men had risen to positions of great influence in the cultural politics of the day. Neither had been born with any useful social, family or monied connections, but, having bundles of energy and ambition, and being critical of current tradition, both rapidly turned their institutions upside down in their attempts to reform and update them. In the process these two charismatic men became celebrated for their personalities and character, and set a course of art and science practice and management that continued into the twentieth century.

3

The Circuits that Illuminated London

~

THE YOUTH, ENERGY and genius of Humphry Davy and J. M. W. Turner caught the focused attention of the world of culture in London. Each in his own way, both instinctively and deliberately, worked to reveal the truths of art and science, and the nature of their interdependency: Davy through his writings, his experiments and his acknowledgement of the union of truth and beauty in intellectual life, Turner through his consistent and growing excitement at the visual manifestations of scientific understanding – modern geology, meteorology and images of contemporary technology all exercised his pencil and paintbrush. The presence of Davy and Turner together in the culture of London marked the beginning of the break-up of the river of knowledge into its smaller streams. It is a paradox that as much as they severally indicated and advocated the unified roots of art and science, so their huge public followings lent particular attention to Turner's art and to Davy's science. By applying such pressures upon the two young men to respond, the weight of public demand for education and enlightenment fractured the threads uniting the subjects that the public craved to understand.

Davy wrote eloquently in these years about the interweaving of art and natural science, and saw knowledge as being 'like a river, which, unless its springs are constantly supplied, soon becomes exhausted, and ceases to flow on, and to fertilize'. He placed science, with literature, music and art, as part of an integrated system of knowledge built up, repaired and rebuilt from Antiquity:

> The perception of truth is almost as simple a feeling as the perception of beauty: and the genius of Newton, of Shakespeare, of Michelangelo, and of Handel, are not very remote in character from each other. Imagination, as well as reason, is necessary to perfection in the

philosophical mind. A rapidity of combination, a power of perceiving, and of comparing them by facts is the creative source of discovery. Discrimination and delicacy of sensation, so important in physical research, are other words for *taste*; and the love of the magnificent, the sublime, and the beautiful.

In Humphry Davy we have a man who shimmered with sensibility. He spent his childhood in and near the Cornish moors behind Penzance, told his friends 'stories of romance and tales of chivalry, with all the fluency of an Italian improvisatore', and wrote and declaimed poetry. He numbered poets among his closest friends. For him, 'everything seemed alive, and myself part of the series of visible impressions; I should have felt pain in tearing a leaf from one of the trees'. In the laboratory he would break and remake equipment as he needed it, moving at the speed of a rising gas bubble; in the lecture theatre he raised his arms and his voice to embrace and uplift his audience, spoke directly and clearly with barely a glance at his notes, and moved with grace and speed to set his demonstrations in motion. In the evening he put on a clean shirt (over his dirty one) and rushed out for dinner, being greatly in demand. To fellow guests, 'he must have appeared a votary of fashion rather than of science'. Nevertheless, he was considered to be a bit too smart for his own good: what was described as his 'uncouth address' meant his rough Cornish accent; and he carried 'a smirk on his countenance and a pertness in his manner, which . . . were considered as indicating an unbecoming confidence'.

Generally speaking, Humphry Davy was a happy man. Going to bed, so his younger brother John recalled, he might be heard reciting verse, or 'humming some angler's song'. Lady members of his Royal Institution audience sent him declaratory poems to read in his room, he was sent love-tokens to wear, and shining from his smiling face were a pair of eyes that it was said 'were made for something besides poring over crucibles'. As the poet Laetitia Barbauld expressed it,

> where mute crowds on Davy's lips reposed,
> And Nature's coyest secrets were disclosed.

Davy carried his learning and his creative energies lightly, to the extent that when a thespian friend rushed into the laboratory in panic at not having a prologue for a play that was to open at Drury Lane the next evening, Davy put down his crucibles, wiped his hands, went upstairs and in two hours produced some workmanlike verse:

> Hence Genius draws his novel copious store;
> And hence the new creations we adore:
> And hence the scenic art's undying skill
> Submits our feeling to its potent will.

On his election as an Academician, J. M. W. Turner, the barber's son from the streets below Covent Garden market, began to appreciate the silky prestige of the Royal Academy, the most exclusive of London clubs. He stopped referring to himself, or signing his work, as 'William Turner', and formally added his grand triad of initials to his surname. He was known as J. M. W. Turner for the rest of his life, and thereafter. His father continued to call him Billy, but nobody else did. Where Humphry Davy was charming, and had winning ways, Turner managed quite successfully to get on the wrong side of his colleagues in the Academy and, worse, with many of his patrons. There were other oppositions between these two men: Davy courted and married a rich and well-connected widow, Jane Apreece, and they held regular soirées for the social and cultural elite of London. Living in Upper Grosvenor Street, Mayfair, they became the talk of the town. Turner found a widow too, Sarah Danby, whose musician husband had died in 1798 leaving her a meagre pension and three daughters to bring up. Turner and Sarah never married; he kept her well out of sight, in a terraced house some way north of Oxford Street, and had two daughters by her. It is possible that in the early 1810s he packed Sarah and the five girls off to a cottage on the Chilterns near Great Missenden in Buckinghamshire. It was not differences in achievement or their areas of activity but the behavioural gap between Davy and Turner that kept them in separate social boxes in early-nineteenth-century London.

In his professional life, Humphry Davy was a natural teacher whom audiences flocked to hear; for Turner, however, teaching was a heavy burden, and, in front of an audience he was uneasy and frequently tongue-tied. But he diligently prepared his lectures at the Royal Academy schools where he taught as Professor of Perspective from 1811. Speaking on the perception of nature and the uses of colour, he declared: 'Nature and her effects are the materials offered to our pattern of imitation with the combinations of the science of art which we received . . . Nature and her effects are every day offered to our choice of imitation, to be collated with the science of art, and united by theory to practical inference.' Such lumpy and unpretending language is at odds with Davy's smooth and flickering presentation of thoughts and ideas. After he had retired from teaching, Davy wrote, in Rome in 1819, words which are so rich in imagery that they might come to describe Turner's use of colour in the latter years of his life:

> From what appeared to me to be analogous to masses of bright blue ice, streams of the richest tints of rose-colour or purple burst forth and flowed into basins, forming lakes or seas of the same colour. Looking through the atmosphere towards the heavens I saw brilliant opaque clouds of an azure colour that reflected the light of the sun.

Newly emerging scientific discovery, elbowing its way into the world of arts and letters, generated a refreshed explanatory vocabulary. Coleridge remarked that he attended Davy's lectures 'to renew my stock of metaphors', and at the Royal Institution he could have seen once again Davy's demonstration of nitrous oxide, the 'laughing gas' that Coleridge had himself breathed in Davy's company in Bristol. Davy described the 'highly pleasurable thrilling' that the gas produced in him, and the hallucinations where 'objects around me became dazzling and my hearing more acute'. During the three-and-a-half-minute 'trip' that Davy experienced under the gas, he declared: 'Nothing exists but thoughts! – the universe is composed of impressions, ideas, pleasures and pains!' Scientific experiment lifted Davy out of the quotidian, and transported him on to another plane, one in which he was quite at home.

Through the pens of Humphry Davy, Samuel Taylor Coleridge and later Thomas De Quincey and Michael Faraday, subjects which may have begun their lives in the laboratory and lecture theatre overflowed into the illuminating and visual orbit of literary metaphor. Davy and Faraday spoke and wrote in the 1810s, 1820s and 1830s of magnetic poles, attraction, lines of force; and Thomas De Quincey, recalling in 1834 his first arrival in London as a fifteen-year-old in 1800, lifted this language and bound it with the vocabulary of mathematics to create an alarming image of the power of the presence of London on the surrounding nation. De Quincey expressed the nature of the invisible and irresistible force that London exerted on Britain and the globe. He felt 'the sublime expression' of London's scale in the:

> vast droves of cattle . . . all with their heads directed to London, and expounding the size of the attracting body, together with the force of its attractive power, by the never-ending succession of these droves, and the remoteness from the capital of the lines upon which they were moving. A suction so powerful, felt along radii so vast, and . . . other radii still more vast, both by land and sea, the same suction is operating, night and day, summer and winter, and hurrying for ever into one centre the infinite means needed for her infinite purposes . . .

Substitute 'droves of cattle' with 'iron filings', and we are in the laboratory discussing magnetism; accept the metaphor as De Quincey has proposed it, and we inhabit, with him, the globe's terrible beating heart. Scientists needed language and imagery to express new ideas, just as a lamp needs oil and a wick to spread light. Thus, to reach the new public that controlled political support and the money-supply, scientists, artists and writers required a trace of an understanding of the particular magic of each other's specialities.

They also needed the presence of an audience, and in the circuits that illuminated London at the Royal Institution and the Society of Arts they could find it. Of the thousands who filled the Royal Institution lecture theatre weekly, a few have left echoes of their presence. Jane Marcet (née Haldimand) was a banker's daughter, a child of a family rich in books, friends and conversation who soaked up what she heard of contemporary thought. When she married the physician Alexander Marcet, her intellectual aspirations were yet more encouraged, and she attended Davy's lectures in Albemarle Street. This, and her connections with the literary world, led her to write *Conversations on Chemistry, Intended more Especially for the Female*

Sex (1805), which became one of the most popular and reprinted chemistry text books of the early nineteenth century. Jane Marcet had attended experimental lectures elsewhere, but 'found it almost impossible to derive any clear or satisfactory information from the rapid demonstrations which are . . . crowded into popular courses of this kind.' Until, that is, she discovered Humphry Davy, and she was caught for life: 'Every fact or experiment attracted her attention . . . the numerous and elegant illustrations [that is, experiments] for which that school is so much distinguished, seldom failed to produce on her mind the effect for which they were intended'.

Roderick Murchison, a fox-hunting spendthrift from Easter Ross in the Scottish Western Isles, and latterly from Barnard Castle and land-locked Leicestershire, was propelled by his wife into Royal Institution lectures when by the early 1820s he had run through his fortune. There, and through meeting Humphry Davy, he was struck by the potency of science, and in particular by geology. From such beginnings, Murchison went on to become one of the greatest geologists of his age. He learned and discovered so much so quickly that, within twelve years of his first walking through the door of the Royal Institution, he had devised and named the Silurian system of strata, and revolutionised understanding of the age and composition of the earth. A third impressionable member of the Royal Institution audience was Elizabeth Porden, the daughter of the London architect William Porden. She was taken to Royal Institution lectures in 1804 or 1805, at the age of nine, and so must have been one of the youngest people to have seen Humphry Davy in performance. Elizabeth Porden, who came to marry the polar explorer Sir John Franklin, wrote long atmospheric poems, containing much vague scientific imagery. Her work *The Veils, or the Triumph of Constancy* was published by John Murray in 1815.

A fourth curious onlooker at the Royal Institution was Cyrus Redding, who heard Davy give his lectures on agriculture, and a fifth was a pompous young connoisseur Robert Finch. Graduating from Balliol College, Oxford in 1805, Finch tried half-heartedly to become a parson. In 1810, however, he inherited money and no longer had to work. He spent the next four years, as his extensive diaries and correspondence in the Bodleian Library, Oxford tell us, living as a cultivated but studious man-about-town before leaving for Italy where his expenses were lighter and his opportunities for enjoyment and study boundless. There he decided he would become 'Colonel Finch' for ease of passage on the continent, with an invented history of military service in Portugal. This elaborate self-deception, which contributed to his being described as a 'pretentious ass', may throw some doubt on the reliability of his London diaries. Nevertheless, within their context, and before Finch's lie about the Colonel, they have the ring of truth, and shed much light on our period and milieu.

Finch does not seem to have been a man who chattered; his conversations, as he briefly records them, were wide ranging, and may be typical of men and women of his period, intelligence and class. In December 1813, for example, he 'drank tea' with his friend Dr Henry Fly, the Sub-Dean of St Paul's, and a Fellow of the Royal Society. Finch lists their topics of conversation: 'Mr West. Styles of writing. Sagacity of dogs. The deluge. Science. Astronomy. The Elliotts. The Wells's. Music. Mr Hoare. The Leeds family.' He gives incidental detail about his attendance at lectures, having been, a few days before his tea with Fly, 'to Dr Evans's Astronomical Lecture at Christ's hospital which was scientific & good. I wish him to enliven it more, before he lectures at the Royal Institution. He must read too slower.' Finch's experience as a member of audiences led him to offer Evans advice on content and delivery. They dined together, and 'Evans's introductory lecture for the Royal Institution was corrected by me. Talked of instances of caprice and ingratitude. Mathematics. Chemistry. Chances of life. Evans's eldest boy understands seven languages.'

One of Finch's close friends was Clarissa Wells, the beautiful, mettlesome daughter of the watercolour painter William Wells. Finch, indeed, was besotted with her, describing her as 'good, amiable Clarissa', and revealing 'how happy it renders me to see her so serene and blest!' He was thoroughly put out when it became clear that she was very fond of their mutual friend J. M. W. Turner, to the extent that Finch and others became convinced in gossip that she and Turner would marry. While Finch, like so many others, admired Turner's paintings, the artist's gracelessness was becoming famous beyond the Royal Academy. Finch met him from time to time at the Wellses' and elsewhere, describing him as 'no gentleman, in appearance or in manners'.

The rumour of marriage to Clarissa, or anyone, would have been news to Turner, even though by this time he had loosened his ties with Sarah Danby. But what Turner, and others in their circle, will have known was that Clarissa was an enthusiastic member of the audience at Royal Institution lectures. Finch notes in his diary:

> Called at the Royal Institution for Clarissa, and afterwards proceeded to York Buildings [on New Road, where Clarissa lived with her parents] . . . I quiz Clarissa for attending Chemical Lectures, as she never can understand it, I am very sure. Indeed I deem it a sad waste of time for her to throw away. She had much better attend to more solid and really useful pursuits.

This may not have been the benign questioning that the word 'quiz' tends to mean today, but an interrogative and even unkind mockery. But Clarissa dismissed Finch's criticism, retorting: 'You shall not quiz poor chemistry. It is a fine science tho' I am a very humble dabbler in the art – I shall be happy to read any chemical work you may please to put into my hands.'

A seventh attentive member of the Royal Institution audiences was John Tatum, a silversmith who became one of the most exuberant teachers, in the demonstrative mould of Humphry Davy, of what he boldly proclaimed in the name of his establishment as 'Science'. Tatum opened his 'Theatre of Science', where he gave a series of lectures to all-comers, at 53 Dorset Street, off Fleet Street, in October 1805. Students could learn about Electricity, Galvanism, Mechanics, Hydrostatics, Optics, indeed practically every division of natural philosophy. As one of his students put it in a long poem, 'Quarterly Night, Oct 2nd 1816', Tatum would:

> Explain why smoke ascends why water flows
> Why lightning kills and wind tempestuous blows
> Who tell the wand'ring world whence earthquakes rise
> And dread volcanoes thund'ring towards the skies.

By the time he came to advertise his tenth annual series, in September

1815, Tatum had developed a busy organisation which emphasised the theatrical nature of his performances by using the terminology of theatres: seats in the pit could be had for one and a half guineas a session, and those in the gallery for one guinea. The surroundings were, or came to be, equally theatrical. The Theatre, next door to the City Gas-Light Company's works, was gas-lit, as one potential student discovered:

> And turning up her meek enquiring eyes
> Astonished view'd the flaming gas arise
> On each door post (with shame my heart is smitten)
> Was 'Theatre of Science' badly written
> Concluding straight without deliberation
> This was the place where wisdom held her station.
> She knock'd and asked admission but was told
> To enter there she first must be enrolled.

The theatre's ceiling was painted with bulging clouds, a large eagle and a balloon carrying a pair of aeronauts, a man and a woman. Tatum rigged up electrical circuits which sparkled and fizzed when he connected the batteries, and in one case lit up the word SCIENCE in burning letters. He would get members of his audience to stand in a ring holding hands, and pass an electrical current though them, to great consternation and sudden shock. In Optical lectures he threw images on to the wall with a candle-lit magic lantern. His audiences loved it, and one at least, Michael Faraday, wrote detailed notes of what he had learned, evoking the atmosphere and camaraderie of the place.

Tatum taught amateurs and aspiring professionals alike, the former attending on Monday evenings, the latter on Wednesdays. The aspirants, with Tatum's encouragement, formed themselves into the City Philosophical Society, listening to and discussing Tatum's teaching, and preparing and giving their own lectures in turn. The City Philosophical Society, a cohesive and amiable group of young men, included Michael Faraday, the artist Cornelius Varley, the reformer and satirist William Hone, and Robert Cocking who was to find some brief fame as the inventor of a parachute which, in 1837, failed to carry him safely to earth. Cocking died as a result. Between 1808 and the Society's disbanding in the mid-1820s, these and others helped each other in their learning, many becoming lifelong friends. Guided by the quality of Tatum's teaching some rose to influential positions in science, administration and commerce. Tatum himself got involved in the cut-and-thrust of scientific debate, publishing controversial plant-respiratory and electrical experiments in the *Philosophical Magazine* in 1817 and 1818. Cornelius Varley, later a distinguished landscape and portrait artist, invented his Patent Graphic Telescope, a device designed to throw a brightly lit image on to a sheet of paper. This would then be drawn round, precisely and carefully, to create a neat but characteristically rather flat landscape or portrait. Among Varley's subjects was John Tatum himself, revealed in an elegant drawing as a well-dressed middle-aged man with a double chin.

There was a high public craving for the kind of lectures that Tatum offered. To take a slice at random through those advertised to the public in the autumn and winter of 1808/9, we find, in addition to Davy at the Royal Institution, George Singer speaking at the Scientific Institution off Cavendish Square on the nature, use and properties of the atmosphere; Friedrich Accum at the Chemical Laboratory, Soho on experimental chemistry and analytical mineralogy; James Sowerby on Chromatometry at his house in Mead Place; the Rev. William Crowe on ancient Greek history and historians at the Royal Institution; and many others in addition.

Michael Faraday first attended Humphry Davy's Royal Institution lectures in February 1812, having been with Tatum for two years. Sixteen months later, when he had been taken on as Davy's laboratory assistant, Faraday had garnered enough experience as a member of an audience both with Tatum and with Davy to give his views on the design of lecture theatres. He and his friend Benjamin Abbott, a city clerk whom he had met at Tatum's, corresponded at great length from 1812 to the early 1820s, discussing everything in science that struck them as exciting, novel and puzzling. 'The best form for a lecture room in general,' Faraday told Abbott in 1813,

> is without dispute a circular one tho in particular circumstances deviations may with propriety be adopted. The seats should be so arranged that no obstruction intervene between the spectator & the lecture table. If there is a gallery each person in it should be situated in a manner the most convenient for observation and hearing.

Faraday went on to say that those which pleased him most included the Theatre Royal, Haymarket, and the Royal Institution's own theatre, whose construction had been overseen both by its architects Soane and Holland, and by George Saunders, the Institution's buildings surveyor, and the architect of the British Museum's Townley Gallery. Drawing instruction from entertainment and pleasure as well as from learning, Faraday went on to discuss lighting, and reflected that theatre lighting 'fatigue[s] the eyes of those who are situated low in the house'. He thought highly of the way the popular lecturer William Walker demonstrated his twenty-feet-diameter orrery, which was dramatically lit by strong artificial light to cast shadows of the turning planets. For the teaching of science, however, Faraday found that 'day light is the most eligible and convenient', particularly from a skylight. Ventilation was also most important: these were the days when candles and later gaslight consumed ambient oxygen, and without proper ventilation replaced it with carbon monoxide and carbon dioxide:

> How have I wished the Lecture finished, the lights extinguished, and myself away merely to obtain a fresh supply of [air]. The want of it caused the want of attention, of pleasure, and even of comfort . . . Attention to this is more particularly necessary in a lecture room intended for night delivery, as the lights burning add considerably to the oppression produced on the body.

Faraday's other concern was the quality of the lecturer's diction, and the way he presented himself to the audience. The advice given to Benjamin Abbott by the young man who was to become the greatest teacher of science of his generation, but who had not, as far as we know, yet given any lectures himself, was clear, sensible and direct. So appropriate and timeless were Faraday's words that extracts were published by the Royal Institution in 1974 in the booklet *Advice to Lecturers*. In short, Faraday advised that the lecturer should not speak too quickly, 'but slow and deliberate conveying ideas with ease from the Lecturer and infusing them with clearness and readiness into the minds of the audience'. He should obtain a 'facility of utterance and the power of clothing his thoughts and ideas in language smooth and harmonious', and make gentle and deliberate movements so that it would not look as if he were screwed to the floor. A most important skill for the lecturer, he said, is the ability to engage the audience from the outset, and 'irresistibly to make them join in his ideas to the end of the subject . . . and by a series of imperceptible gradations unnoticed by the company keep [their interest] alive as long as the subject demands it'.

Michael Faraday, Robert Finch, Jane Marcet, Roderick Murchison, Elizabeth Porden, Cyrus Redding, Clarissa Wells and John Tatum were men and women of very different kinds, representing the breadth of audience that the Royal Institution aimed to engage in the study of science. Clarissa Wells became an accomplished botanical artist, having been taught by her father. She was also taught by Turner, their proximity over the paint-box no doubt encouraging a mutual fondness. Nothing propinks like propinquity, as Dorothy Parker later put it. Wells's botanical illustrations, which were bequeathed to the University of Oxford in the 1870s, were cherished by the unctuous Finch: 'Clara has begun to draw for me, and I hope to possess, if it pleases God to prolong my life, a charming treasure in her works.' In Marcet, Faraday and Murchison the Royal Institution struck gold: Marcet, Porden and Redding wrote for publication, Tatum taught the next generation, and Faraday and Murchison altered human perceptions of the world.

The fluidity between the learned organisations in London was such that membership was effectively interchangeable. Given the ease with which a man of wealth and standing could gain membership of the Royal Society, he could also get himself elected to membership of the Society of Antiquaries, the Royal Institution and the Society of Arts. Across the eighteenth century, many men had been members of both the Royal Society and the Antiquaries, and when attendance at Antiquaries' meetings slumped, the latter postponed their meeting time by one and a half hours so that joint Fellows could attend both. The Society of Arts had many members who were also Fellows of the Royal Society, the Antiquaries, or both, as had the Royal Institution. Only the Royal Academy was exclusive. An Associate or a Royal Academician had to be a practising artist or architect of contemporary distinction, elected by his peers. In theory, therefore, to complete the grand slam and be a fellow or a member of all five organisations, one first had to be a distinguished and successful artist or architect. One man actually did accomplish such a technical feat: John Soane was a Fellow of the Royal Society, a Fellow of the Society of Antiquaries, a member of the Royal Institution, a member of the Society of Arts, and a Royal Academician, all at the same time.

Women were not able to join the Royal Society or the Antiquaries until the twentieth century, but from the beginning they were welcome at the Royal Institution, and as contributors to the Society of Arts. Only months after the Royal Institution was founded, women were invited to become subscribing members, on the advocacy of Thomas Garnett who told the managers 'that the fair Sex constituted a large proportion . . . of his numerous auditory, which sometimes bordered on 1000 persons'. In the first decade of the century the societies were driven by the expectation that alongside the knowledge to be gained there were also friendships and business contacts to be made. Thus the Society of Antiquaries shared artists, architects and scientists as members – Academicians Richard Westmacott, Francis Chantrey, Thomas Phillips, Thomas Lawrence and C. R. Cockerell all became active in the Antiquaries, as did Royal Society fellows Humphry Davy, Everard Home, John Children, William Whewell and Davies Gilbert. Early members of the Royal Institution included Alexander Aubert, Anthony Carlisle, John Children and Sir Henry Englefield, all of whom were also Fellows of both the Royal Society and the Society of Antiquaries. Among the members of the Society of Arts who were active in some of the other organisations were Francis Chantrey, John Children, Davies Gilbert, Sir Henry Englefield and Thomas Hope. At the end of a tiring day at Somerset Place, as they left to go home, the following exchange might have been heard between the gentlemen of art, science and history bidding each other farewell in the Strand lamplight:

'Good night, Babbage!'
'Good night, Chantrey!'
'Good night, Hope!'

4

A Pelican in a Chicken Run

~

B Y 1808, WHEN its first guidebook, or *Synopsis*, was published, the British Museum had become the greatest public collection of antiquities, natural history, manuscripts and printed books in the world. From its opening in 1759 the Museum's responsibility was to encourage and enable study, learning and enlightenment 'in all studious and curious persons'. It was one of the few places in London where both men and women of common interest and curiosity for the world, who were not necessarily members of any group or society, could go for pleasure and instruction. Its nineteenth Director, Neil Macgregor, with a perspective of 250 years, told the *Guardian* newspaper in 2005 that the British Museum's founding principle was an expression of the ideas of the seventeenth-century philosopher John Locke that all knowledge should have a civic outcome; that is, knowledge gained should be spread and shared. Whether they took advantage of it or not, and many did, the British Museum was also the place where the paths of our 'London Lights' could cross, where they were free to come and go as they pleased, and where their knowledge could be gained and shared.

The British Museum occupied Montagu House in Great Russell Street, 'the largest, the completest and the most magnificent' house in London. This had been built in the 1660s for the Duke of Montagu in the manner of a French château, with a courtyard in front and a large formal knot garden of box and herbs at the back. From its upper rooms, looking north, the green hills of Hampstead and Highgate could be clearly seen. Capacious, exotic and odd, it was, beside the dense and hurried streets of London, as if a pelican had flapped down and landed in a chicken run. Less a mansion, more 'a palace for the abode of a prince than that of a subject',

Montagu House, deserted by its Duke, had by the 1750s become dismal and shabby, and its drains backed up from Great Russell Street. With money raised through a public lottery, it was bought in 1754 to house the multitudinous collections of natural history, antiquities, manuscripts and curiosities acquired for the nation from Sir Hans Sloane, Sir Robert Cotton and Robert Harley. The British Museum's trustees were charged with creating some semblance of rational order in the storage and display of a deep fluorescing pool of patient inanimate objects. Cartloads rattled into the Museum month after month, stacked here, shelved there, until all its cupboards creaked. 'The collections . . . are in the greatest confusion,' the Swedish naturalist Carl Linnaeus was told in 1755, 'and many articles have been lost, either through neglect, or from being placed in a bad situation; but they receive acquisitions daily from every part of the globe.'

Having in its first few decades levied an entrance charge, and admitted people only in groups to be guided through the rooms, the Museum became in 1805 free to the public, and a weekly average of about three hundred people made their way through its doors. It was open from ten until four o'clock from Monday to Thursday, and closed in August and September, and at Easter, Whitsun and Christmas. Artists were admitted to draw from the collections on Fridays and every day in August and September. No children 'apparently under 10 years of age' were allowed in. In 1810 obligatory guided tours were abolished, and the opening days changed to Monday, Wednesday and Friday. Thus the Museum was more likely to be shut than open, and because visitors will have come in groups and surges, there will have been long periods when the building was practically empty. On a cold, wet Wednesday afternoon in February the best place to be alone in London would have been the British Museum.

There were other places in London to see amassed curiosities in the years around 1805. At the Rotunda in Albion Street, at the southern end of Blackfriars Bridge, the Leverian Museum displayed in fifteen rooms more than thirty thousand objects, mainly stuffed animals and fish, 'brought together from almost all the known parts of the world'. Among its collections of man-made objects was the traveller Edward Wortley Montague's Turkish costume, Oliver Cromwell's helmet and body armour, and a sixteen-inch-high stilt used by Venetian women to make them appear taller than the men, and to help keep their feet dry in the flooded piazzas. The collection had been formed by a Manchester landowner, Ashton Lever, who displayed it as the 'Holophusikon' (holo = entire; phusikon = physical world) in Leicester Square. Running out of money, however, Lever did the converse of the British Museum trustees and disposed of his museum by lottery in 1786. The winning ticket was held, extraordinarily, by a man who had a serious and practical plan for the collection. James Parkinson, a successful land agent, moved the Museum in 1790 to the mansion which he built for the purpose, the Rotunda, in Albion Street. There, the Leverian Museum was run as a commercial operation, and was the British Museum's only serious rival in London. As its guidebook reveals, the Leverian Museum was well organised, a model of reasonable clarity and order. 'An inexhaustible fund of entertainment to the naturalist,' said one satisfied visitor from afar, the Rev. William MacRitchie of Clunie, Perthshire, who came briefly to London during a tour of Britain in 1795. The Leverian Museum had a Fish Room, a Monkey Room, a Reptile Room, even a Sandwich Room – though this was not a café, but the room in which objects from the Sandwich Islands, collected on Captain Cook's final voyage, were displayed. A prized exhibit was the lottery ticket with which James Parkinson won the Museum. With weaker political and curatorial pressures upon it, the Leverian Museum in its prime made a better job of creating rational order than did the British Museum. The American naturalist Charles Willson Peale found the Leverian Museum easier to get into than the British Museum: 'The trouble to obtain a sight of the British Museum renders it of less value to the public than a private collection belonging to Parkinson called the Leverian Museum.'

But the Leverian had failed to survive in Leicester Square, and neither could it survive so far off the beaten track on the south bank of the Thames. In 1804–6 Parkinson tried, and repeatedly failed, to sell the collection to the British Museum. The proposal was blocked by the Museum's most dominant trustee, Sir Joseph Banks. As Farington remarked, 'Parkinson says Sir Joseph hated Sir Ashton

Lever, therefore hates the Collection.' In the end it had to be auctioned, in a sale which lasted sixty-five days between May and July 1806, and became scattered around the curiosity shops and raree shows of London. Years later William Jerdan described it as 'a most heterogeneous medley of stuffed animals, without order or classification', though he saw it at the end of its days, only when it was being sold.

Looking back more than fifty years later, Jerdan also remembered that up to about 1812 the British Museum was 'not yet a place of popular resort, and visitors were still received with reluctance'. From the street, Montagu House gave no air of welcome whatsoever. Visitors would pass under a ten-feet-high brick wall to a dark-arched entrance gate with a wooden pepper-pot cupola on top. The entrance was guarded by a pair of armed sentries in red coats. Admitted, visitors found themselves under an Ionic colonnade looking across a wide courtyard, over 150 feet square, with three-storey wings to right and left, and the imposing face of the four-storeyed, multi-fenestrated, multi-chimneyed, brick-fronted, grey-slate-roofed building towering ahead of them. Beside the visitors, under the colonnade and in the courtyard, were pieces of Egyptian and Roman antiquity, and a mummy case or two, left there because they were too big to get in through the front door, or too heavy for the floors.

Having climbed the wide steps to the front door of the Museum, and fallen under the eyes of two more armed sentries, the visitors would find themselves in the airy entrance hall where statuary, Latin, Greek and runic inscriptions, Chinese figures, seven huge lumps of stone from the Giant's Causeway in County Antrim, a piece of the Appian Way south of Rome, and miscellaneous other curiosities would beguile them. Ahead, the door to the Department of Printed Books, Maps, Globes and Drawings was 'rich in panels, wherein are Roman shields and trophies, a cross torus of oak leaves also', and here the visitors would first notice the green flock wallpaper which was 'general in all the rooms'. After a while, they would also be very well aware of the spread of damp stains across the walls, rainwater lines running down the frescoes, ceilings propped up by bookcases, and marks of puddles on the floors. Montagu House was plagued by dry rot and damp, and, despite half-hearted efforts to keep it in repair, it was by 1808 beginning gradually and gracefully to fall to bits.

Access to so grand a building remained a novelty to most visitors. While the collections were breathtaking in their quantity and scope, the building, despite its deterioration, provoked a wonder of its own. Montagu House was truly a splendid old wreck, as extraordinary and imposing in London in the eighteenth century as Somerset House was to become in the nineteenth. In the entrance hall and all the way up the stairs, on the landings and on the attic ceiling, were wide landscape frescoes and bas-reliefs by fashionable seventeenth-century French artists, celebrating such stories as Diana and Actaeon, Phaeton and the chariot of the sun, and various Roman battles and orgies.

The figures painted on the walls would have greatly outnumbered visitors on most days. The floors across which the visitors tramped were laid in oak marquetry decorated with diamond and other geometrical forms, so that, full of objects though the house was, there was also plenty to discover on the walls and floors. Entering the British Museum, the visitor saw many wonders; one of these was the building around them.

If the visitors turned left and left again at the top of the stairs they would pass through the Department of Natural and Artificial Production, rooms of minerals, shells and fossils, stuffed animals and birds, many falling apart in the sun, plumage fading, butterflies crumbling away. They might pause to look at the roomful of exotic objects brought back by Captain Cook, and be stopped in their tracks by a twenty-one-feet-long stuffed crocodile from the River Indus, which guarded the top of the back stairs. Eventually, passing cases holding precious stones and diamonds, brittle wasps' nests, hats from around the world, gallstones from cows' bladders, they would come to the rooms displaying some of the Museum's peerless collection of smaller Egyptian and antique sculpture where young artists studying at the Royal Academy Schools might be seen drawing. Against its ubiquitous green flock wallpaper, this west side of the building held everything that was not books and manuscripts, coins, maps and medals: object representatives of the whole world of artifice and nature were crammed chaotically, though with an ambition for order, into these five rooms of the British Museum.

If on the other hand they turned left and immediately right at the top of the stairs into the Department of Manuscripts, Medals and Coins they would find the collections of Greek and Latin texts to be rather more ordered. There in high cases and bookshelves which propped up the sagging ceilings were some of the world's finest and most fragile manuscripts, from papyri rescued from the Egyptian deserts, to Carolingian, Ottonian and Anglo-Saxon manuscripts of the European Christian world. Here the Utrecht Psalter could be seen, there the Lindisfarne Gospels, and near by yet more antiquities, and coins and medals of all ages and nations. On the south side of the building the sun streamed in through the windows, but while the coins and medals just reflected it, the fading of the manuscripts and their bindings was only arrested by the rough curatorship of the Museum's scanty staff, and by London's poor weather and the filthy smoke-filled atmosphere absorbing the rays of the sun.

A visitor with a special pass could go through the door to the Museum's Reading Room. Only men were admitted as readers, on the recommendation of a member of staff or a respected and known outsider. Thus in the Reading Room Register for the years 1795–1810 phrases such as 'known to Mr Planta', 'known to Mr Ayscough', and 'at the recommendation of Sir Joseph Banks' crop up in the margins. Richard Porson is first listed as a reader in 1796, perhaps when starting work on the *Odyssey*, his pass being renewed in 1798. Robert Smirke the younger was given a six-month pass in March 1805 indicating that the man who would become the Museum's architect was busy at work in the building very soon after he returned from his two-year tour of the continent. Charles Lamb first registered in May 1804, and Benjamin Robert Haydon in April 1806. Other readers include the topographical print engraver and publisher John Britton, Henry Sass 'to make drawings', and 'Willm M. Turner Esq of 64 Harley St' (that is, J. M. W. Turner) for three months in June 1809: this was at the time when Turner was preparing his lectures as Professor of Perspective at the Royal Academy, and perhaps consulting some early texts on perspective that he could not find in the Academy library. There was a way for a woman to gain formal admittance: by going in under the wing of a man. Thus, in January 1809, 'Mr Paytherus, 108 Great Russell Street, for his two daughters to make drawings', was given a six-month pass.

One foreign visitor to the museum in or around 1800 was the German traveller Johanna Schopenhauer. She was impressed by the attention of the curators, 'very kind and helpful in showing items of special interest', and was shown the letters of Elizabeth I to the Earl of Essex, Pope's first draft of his *Essay on Man*, and 'framed under glass on a desk . . . the most sacred document of the English, the Magna Carta . . . Even though a little faded and ravaged by time, it is kept safely here for posterity and looked at reverently, by every true Briton.' Another, Louis Simond, was shown round with a party of fifteen people at high speed, '*au pas de charge*', as he put it:

> We had no time allowed to examine anything: our conductor pushed on without minding questions, or unable to answer them, but treating the company with *double entendres* and witticisms on various subjects of natural history, in a style of vulgarity and impudence which I should not have expected to have met in this place, and in this country.

What Johanna Schopenhauer, Louis Simond and other visitors may not have fully realised was that the British Museum was at bursting point. The rate of influx of objects and collections was such that space and the limited and compromised staff time just could not manage the flow. It took the Keeper of the Natural History Collections, Edward Gray, more than three years to begin to list and organise 'the large and well-chosen collection of minerals of every class' bought for £700 in 1799 from Charles Hatchett. By 1803, when the trustees engaged the refugee French aristocrat scientist Count Jacques de Bournon to help this process, Gray was still casting about for parts of the collection 'scattered and lost in the dust of the basement'. The keepers in charge of antiquities were also with difficulty assimilating Sir William Hamilton's large collections of ancient Greek and Roman pottery, and massive pieces of Egyptian granite carving. In 1806 they had to face the impending arrival of the heaving crowd of classical figures bought from the heirs of the collector Charles Townley.

But while things came in, things also went out. The mass of minerals which came with the founding Hans Sloane collection were by the turn of the nineteenth century being sold, given or thrown away. Of more than ten thousand minerals that Sloane collected, only about three hundred remain in the British Museum. Natural history material was dumped, as stuffed creatures fell apart, and bones and skeletons were sent to the Royal College of Surgeons. The painter and teacher Richard Reinagle, who studied in the British Museum in the first decade of the century,

> amused himself with a general examination of the numerous objects of natural history, unstuffed birds, animals and reptiles, which were heaped together in the then lumber room. After turning over a vast pile he discovered the head and beak with the short thick legs of a dodo . . . Mr Reinagle has not been able to learn what became of the fragments, but they ought still to be somewhere in the British Museum.

Manuscripts and prints were also lost, stolen or strayed. Soon after the collection arrived, many prints from the bequest of Clayton Mordaunt Cracherode were stolen. One habitual Reading Room thief was the Charing Cross engraver and print-seller Robert Dighton who was allowed to come and go when he pleased with a portfolio, and be left on his own. With such freedom of action, Dighton, who was also well known as a popular singer at Vauxhall Gardens and Sadler's Wells, quietly slipped prints into his portfolio, and took them away to sell. The librarian in charge, William Beloe, was too trusting, and had allowed Dighton to distract him with presents of geese, chickens, fish and peas. As a result, Beloe was sacked from his £200 a year job, 'with very good apartments and fire and Candle'. While there were concerted attempts to keep the displays in the public rooms of the Museum ordered, clearly laid out and secure, the keepers were fighting a losing battle. Internal rivalries and conflicts over space between the officers responsible for the libraries, the man-made artefacts and the natural specimens caused the use of the rooms to ebb and flow from one discipline to another, so that the room arrangement of 1806 bore little resemblance to that of 1790; nor that of 1806 to, say, 1820.

The British Museum trustee whose imposing character, scientific knowledge and breadth of vision led the transformation of the philosophy of the museum from a warehouse of curiosities to a place of learning and enlightenment was the President of the Royal Society, Sir Joseph Banks. As a young man, Banks had accompanied Captain Cook to the South Seas, and had brought back the many thousands of plant species that gave a new set of perspectives to the understanding of botany. Under the King's patronage Banks guided the development of the royal gardens at Kew, sowing the seeds that transformed this series of picturesque riverside walks into a living museum of plants. But it was in his role as Royal Society President that Banks became an ex-officio member of the board of trustees of the British Museum, whose collections he continuously enhanced, and whose root problem he faced with determination.

Banks was the gatekeeper of scientific learning in early-nineteenth-century London, and as chairman of the British Museum's building committee he tackled the matter of space, reporting that the solution lay not in piecemeal additions, but in a grand scheme that filled the gardens of Montagu House with a simple quadrangle of long galleries, east, west and north. A petition to parliament, a £4,000 grant, and the impending arrival of the Townley Collection led not, however, to the generous spaces that Banks had dreamed of, but to the relatively modest, 220-feet-long Townley Wing. This had also to accommodate Egyptian antiquities and Sir William Hamilton's collection of classical vases, bronzes and gems, the whole display being arranged by Royal Academicians Richard Westmacott and Henry Tresham. This modest building was the first in the western world to have been designed and constructed specifically for the display of works of art, for free, to the general public. Queen Charlotte, the wife of King George III, was invited to open the Townley Wing, but before her arrival the Museum and garden staff set about tidying up. The flower beds were weeded, rubbish thrown into the back of the Museum was removed, and the gravel was rolled. Shortly afterwards, the gardener made representations for his garden roller to be repaired. When the Queen, accompanied by her eldest son the Prince of Wales and a line of the Prince's brothers and sisters, opened the

Townley Wing on 3 June 1808 *The Times* reported: 'it is twenty years since Her Majesty was [at the Museum]'.

In embarking on the building of the Townley Wing, the trustees drew from their architect, George Saunders, a progressive design which introduced the relatively new idea of top-lit galleries. This created the best possible lighting conditions for the showing of sculpture, allowing light to filter down and reflect from the pale surrounding walls. Saunders was a learned and accomplished architect. He was an expert on the design of theatres, having written a treatise on the subject that tackled the problems of sight-lines and acoustics, and on the strength of that had designed the Theatre Royal and Assembly Rooms in Birmingham (1793). Under the eyes of Soane and Holland, Saunders had supervised the building of the lecture theatre at the Royal Institution in 1800. In commissioning the Townley Wing from Saunders, the trustees got one of the most experienced architects that could be found.

But even as the Queen cut the ribbon to open the new extension, an 'ingenious' young man had begun to weave himself inextricably into the fabric of London's architectural development. Robert Smirke had been apprenticed as a boy to two leading London architects, George Dance and John Soane, and attended the Royal Academy Schools. He braved the fire of John Soane's bad temper and moodiness, and learned the rudiments of architecture and its practice both from Soane and from the more mellow George Dance the younger. In September 1802, with his elder brother Richard, Robert Smirke had set off on a long tour of Europe, beginning at Calais and travelling as far as Greece. The Smirkes' route followed the well-trodden paths taken by the English and Scottish Grand Tourists of the eighteenth century, and at Athens Robert witnessed the beginnings of the long journey to London of the Elgin Marbles. Watching parts of the frieze being prised off the Parthenon and crashing to the ground, Smirke wrote, 'each stone as it fell shook the ground with its ponderous weight with a deep hollow noise. It seemed like a convulsive groan of the injured spirit of the Temple.'

After his training with the architects, and his studentship at the Academy, Robert Smirke's finishing school had been Europe. His was the perfect balanced education for a young man destined to become a fashionable and successful architect – he had observed how architectural practices are run, how clients are managed, and how to handle a tempestuous master. On his travels he had made copious drawings from French, Italian and Greek architecture, some of which he used to impress the Society of Antiquaries whose members were a potential source of lucrative employment, and he later published a brief account of the most striking buildings. When he returned to London in January 1805, Smirke was made a fuss of in society, and it appeared very rapidly that he was the golden future of English architecture.

Robert Smirke's father, another Robert Smirke, was an influential Royal Academician, and with recommendations from his father and from colleagues including Joseph Farington, Thomas Lawrence and George Dance, Robert Smirke the younger began to build up a group of moneyed and influential clients in London and the country. One of his first clients was the immensely rich Lord Lowther, later Earl of Lonsdale, who commissioned a new country house within months of Smirke's return from the continent. This came to please Lowther so much that he engaged J. M. W. Turner to make a pair of paintings of the house under construction, when the artist was on a northern tour of Britain in 1809. Smirke's good nature and courtesy also pleased Lowther, who made sure the word got round. By the time it reached Farington, it was public knowledge: 'Lord Lowther had written to Sir George [Beaumont] expressing his pleasure at finding Robert Smirke so ingenious – modest and gentlemanly in his manners; and desiring Sir George to thank Mr Dance for recommending him.'

Lowther Castle is in Westmorland, hundreds of miles from London, and although this brought Smirke prestige among landowners, it could not in itself bring his architecture down to street-level in London. The commission that put his name on the town map came as a result of the burning down in September 1808 of the Theatre Royal, Covent Garden. Smirke was quickly named as the architect by the theatre's actor–manager Philip Kemble, and at rapid pace produced plans for what was one of the largest theatres in the world. George Saunders had already expressed the political and cultural importance of a theatre for a great city in his *Treatise on the Design of Theatres* (1790): 'When a foreigner first arrives at a town his curiosity naturally leads him in the first place to visit the theatre. Here he receives his first impressions of the state of the arts, of the genius and the manners of the people.'

Smirke's Theatre Royal, whose foundation stone was laid by the Prince of Wales within three months of the fire, gave London an extraordinary new architectural experience. Following on from Saunders's top-lit sculpture gallery for the British Museum, London now had England's first giant Doric portico modelled directly on the Parthenon. Smirke took account of the sight-line and acoustic advice that Saunders had advocated in his *Treatise on Theatres*, and delivered the building so rapidly that it was opened two days short of a year after its predecessor was destroyed. The attack with which Smirke approached this commission meant that money flowed into his practice to the extent that Farington was able to point out that Smirke 'now pays *clerks* who assist him to the amount of about £700 per annum'.

Good reputation and appreciation followed, and it soon became clear that Robert Smirke was the man to be entrusted with complex and prestigious public works, which would be completed on time. While the British Museum trustees were accepting that they would have to make do with the Townley Wing, and that their 'simple quadrangle' might never be built, Smirke was embarking on commissions that took him to the Royal Mint on Tower Hill, the county court in Carlisle, the bridge and cathedral in Gloucester, and country-house commissions in Kent, Sussex, Middlesex, Radnor, Dumfriesshire, Yorkshire and Gloucestershire. He had earned £10,000 for his work on the Theatre Royal, Covent Garden, a fee that became, so it was rumoured, his minimum. Although it may not have been clear at the time, the British Museum's purpose and Smirke's genius were already naturally aligned, and within ten years the trustees and Robert Smirke would together begin to construct the British Museum that we know today.

Until he broke his neck when his speeding coach overturned in September 1813 outside Marlborough, James Wyatt was Surveyor-General and Comptroller of the government's Office of Works. He had held the post since 1796, and as a manager, administrator and financial controller had been a disaster. The then Prime Minister, Lord Liverpool, remembered Wyatt as being 'certainly one of the worst public servants I recollect in any office'. The rapid consequence of Wyatt's death, largely unmourned within his profession, was an energetic jockeying for position as his successor in his prestigious and lucrative post. Three architects, John Nash, John Soane and Robert Smirke, were immediately the leaders in the race, and in the event Wyatt's job was reorganised and divided between them. Nash took on the enlargements to Buckingham Palace for the Prince of Wales, by now the Prince Regent, Soane took responsibility for the Law Courts, and Smirke the Royal Mint, the Custom House and the General Post Office. Each man seemed content with his lot, as Nash put it to Soane: 'Our appointments are perfectly Constitutional, I the King, you the Lords, and *your* friend Smirke the Commons.'

Taking on 'the Commons' brought Smirke what would become his greatest challenge, occupying and dogging him all his working life, the rebuilding of the British Museum. Although the portico and the wings surrounding the Great Court may now appear to be one grand conception in which all consideration of Montagu House has been dismissed, what we see in the twenty-first century is the product of a gradual evolution whose course depended wholly on the physical presence and involvement of Montagu House at its centre. It could hardly be otherwise. The Museum grew as all museums grow, in bursts, as the tidal pressures of the collection aided by patronage overcome the opposing pressures of the availability of money and political will. In 1818 the trustees brought the Museum kicking and screaming into the nineteenth century when they installed gas lighting in the courtyard. This was probably generally welcomed, but the Museum was soundly criticised a year later in some lines of doggerel published in *The Times* for killing a husky dog for its skin:

> Is this the place where taste and science reign?
> This charnel-house of cruelty and pain!
> Where sages to preserve the coat and skin,
> Murder the harmless animal within!

'One of the poor dogs brought to England from Baffin's Bay, was killed at the MUSEUM, that its skin might be stuffed *while the coat was in fine order!!!*'

By the first decade of the nineteenth century, the tide had become a torrent as an onrushing flood of books, manuscripts and productions of art and nature entered the building from all corners of the globe. In 1809 the Reading Room had to move upstairs, one of many stops on its peregrination around the building. Everything that was anything sat in cupboards, in display cases, in boxes and on shelves, hung on the walls or lay on the floor, within the buildings, courtyards, colonnades and curtilage of Montagu House. This influx included portraits of distinguished men and women, which became the roots of the collections of the National Portrait Gallery, founded in 1856. Until 1824 when they began to find a home in the embryonic National Gallery in Pall Mall, the British Museum also collected old master paintings.

In 1815 the Temple of Apollo, an entire Greek temple, with columns, pediment, roof, walls, friezes and associated sculpture, was brought to the museum from Bassae in Greece. The collection, known as the Phigaelian Marbles, completely overwhelmed the abilities of Montagu House to cope, and became the catalyst of a very slow chain-reaction of development. In August the following year the Parthenon marbles, bought at last by the government from Lord Elgin, and trundled down to the gates of Montagu House, arrived like overweight and grubby orphans. The 'Elgin Marbles', all 120 tons of them, had spent nearly ten years stranded on quaysides, sunk in the Aegean Sea, detained by officialdom and parked in sheds and gardens in Park Lane and Burlington House. Only now were committees of government ministers, groups of artists and influential fixers and politicians beginning to reach agreement, and to find the right moment to raise government money to buy them for the nation.

Benjamin Robert Haydon and his friend the painter David Wilkie saw the Marbles while they were at Park Lane one summer's day in 1808. Many other artists badgered Lord Elgin to be allowed to draw from them: the young Royal Academy student William Brockedon applied to his tutor Thomas Daniell RA, who asked Elgin's secretary

William Richard Hamilton, who promised to ask Lord Elgin. The Marbles immediately justified artists' diligent study of anatomy. Haydon was one of the first – certainly the most persistently elo-quent – of English artists to express wonder at the subtlety of the anatomical and muscular detail that the ancient Greek sculptor could command:

> The first thing I fixed my eyes on was the wrist of a figure in one of the female groups, in which were visible . . . the radius and ulna . . . I darted my eye to the elbow, and saw the outer condyle visibly affecting the shape as in nature. I saw the arm was in repose and the soft parts in relaxation . . . My heart beat! If I had seen nothing else I had beheld sufficient to keep me to nature for the rest of my life.

Sensing victory in advance of the Marbles' arrival, the British Museum trustees brought in Robert Smirke to design not what they really wanted, a second wing for Montagu House, but instead another temporary shed built in Baltic fir, brick and iron, attached to the west of the Townley Gallery, to be a home for the Phigaelian and the Elgin Marbles.

Looking with renewed urgency for a solution to their problems, the trustees seriously considered abandoning Montagu House, and moving lock, stock and marble to another large unwanted building, Carlton House, the vacated home of the Prince Regent at the end of Pall Mall. But in 1820, they engaged Smirke to look again at the Museum and its needs, and to propose a new radical solution for Montagu House, which demanded the demolition of the short-lived Townley Wing. This led to the confirmation and expansion of their original plan for two new side wings, a further wing at the far north-ern end of the garden to complete a quadrangle, and the replacement of Montagu House itself by a giant classical portico to proclaim that this was not just the *British* Museum, but the World's Museum, known and yet unknowable, the repository of knowledge.

Knowledge in the British Museum emerged in many forms and guises. The curators diligently arranged and displayed the objects as best they could be so that the Museum would not be an endless jumble of curiosities. Curiosity was encouraged in the public, but it was the curators' job to break the curiosity of objects. Order and explication was the aim, despite the pressure of the unending stream of objects, the complexity of the stories that they had to tell, and the modest capacity and poor physical condition of the building. The scientist John Children told the 1835 Select Committee on the Condition, Management and Affairs of the British Museum that a 'great many' natural history specimens kept in spirit bottles had been lost, having been 'stowed away in the damp rooms of the basement storey'. In 1823 King George IV gave the library that his father George III had collected to the British Museum. This galvanised government and trustees, and parliament voted £40,000 to begin the reconstruction of the British Museum with a new library worthy of the royal gift. The King's Library, designed by Robert Smirke, was built with the innovative use of iron beams, the only material that could span the library's forty-one-foot width.

One of the Museum's attendants, Thomas Conrath, kept a diary and noted the beginning of the construction of Smirke's grand library: 'Monday Septr 8th 1823. The first bricks were laid for the foundation of the new building at the British Museum near the east end of the old house, the ground being springy I saw the bricks and mortar laid in water. The foundation is about twelve feet deep.' The purpose of the new wing was not only to have the book collection of George III shelved on the ground floor, but also to house, on its upper floor, a large picture gallery showing the growing nucleus of the nation's collection of old master paintings. The connoisseur Sir George Beaumont had been encouraged by the Paymaster-General Sir Charles Long to bequeath his art collection, which included paintings by Claude, Poussin, Rembrandt and Canaletto, to the British Museum. Events, however, overtook this proposal, and when Sir John Angerstein's collection, and his house 100 Pall Mall, were acquired as the National Gallery in 1824, the need for a picture gallery in the British Museum withered. Instead, the Museum's natural history collections were shown upstairs.

Attendances grew steadily at the Museum, exceeding 112,000 in 1824, and after a drop to about 68,000 in 1829, climbed rapidly to over 383,000 in 1836 when it fell again steadily until a new rise to over half a million in 1842. This was despite the evident difficulties for the public in finding the doors open. The Common Place Book, kept throughout his life by Michael Faraday, gives a note of the Museum's tortuous opening arrangements:

> Mondays, Wednesdays and Fridays in every week (except in the Christmas, Easter and Whitsun weeks; also on the 30th January, Ash Wednesday, Good Friday and any Fast or Thanksgiving days ordered by proclamation, and during the month of August and September.) The hours of admission are from 10 till 2 [sic] o'clock.

The King's Library was, nevertheless, a public success. The Museum's committee reported forty-thousand visits to the yet again relocated Reading Room in 1831, a figure which no doubt helped to persuade the committee to grant £250 for the installation of two water closets for readers the following year. Books could be at a reader's desk within minutes, those shelved on the upper gallery of the King's Library being hauled up and down in rope-bound parcels by assistants straining with a foot against the lower bar of the railings. One reader who asked for fifty-five books to be delivered to him in one morning got the lot, without question. The Treasury gave £8,000 in 1831 to the Museum to complete the west wing housing the Elgin, Phigaelian and Townley marbles, and although Smirke agreed that this would be enough to complete the building, he would need more to resite and display the sculpture. The British Museum was now being used by its public with determination, to the extent that the crush created its own dangers: two fingers were knocked off the Townley Venus in 1832 when a young artist carelessly moved his easel.

Before the King's Library was completed in 1827, construction began on the western wing of the Museum, the work moving from north to south, and slowly encroaching upon the Townley Wing. It was a permanent building site. George Scharf's drawing of the progress of the work shows where things had got to in July 1828. The viewpoint is to the east of the courtyard looking towards the Townley Wing, and the northern half of the west wing is by now built as far as the central portico. Montagu House is visible beyond a heap of sand on the left. In the foreground are piles of logs, a winch and other equipment, and men are cutting, polishing, dressing and transporting stone. Most of the new building is covered in scaffolding and ladders, and the arches of the cellars can be seen under construction.

There were long pauses in the progress of the work when money ran out, or was delayed. A new room for the Elgin Marbles, to replace the temporary shed, was opened in 1832. Richard Westmacott described the Elgin Gallery as 'one of the finest rooms in the world; and, I think, as an artist, that it is as finely lighted as any room I know'. Montagu House, with its 'guarded gateways, its square turrets, its front of dirty red brick, its old crazy cupola', finally vanished in 1843, its parts being divided into lots and sold by public auction. It was demolished before it could fall down, as Robert Smirke told the Select Committee which continued to discuss the complex affairs of the British Museum into 1836. 'The building is in a very insecure state,' Smirke reported. 'Most of the floors are supported by props concealed by the bookcases.' Smirke and the Museum trustees scuffled inconclusively over details of the building and its decoration, the historian and politician Thomas Macaulay finding himself apologising to Smirke for what might have seemed an intrusion: 'I must have expressed myself ill if I led you to think I disapproved of the manner in which you propose to decorate the museum. I am entirely with you as to that matter, and have expressed my opinion repeatedly and strongly at the Board.' Macaulay went on to give his views on the bright colours that Smirke proposed for the Greek galleries:

> I might perhaps say that I didn't recollect any similar decoration in the Vatican Museum. For in truth I did not recollect the red and green marble which you mention, and, when I think of the Laocoön, the Apollo and the Demosthenes, the background always presents itself to me as grey or very pale blue. It is very possible that the excellencies of those masterpieces of sculpture may have drawn away my attention from the architectural accessories.

For the Egyptian sculpture galleries Smirke proposed a light tone: 'What I should much prefer myself would be no other colour than that of stone – for we have no other superfluous quantity of light in the Centre Gallery and any other colour like that given to the Greek Rooms would be ruinously dark.' Nevertheless, the trustees would not take Smirke's expert advice until they could consult each other, and determined to ask Sir Charles Long (by then Lord Farnborough) and Sir Martin Archer Shee, President of the Royal Academy, to 'examine the effect of two or three patterns and give directions as they think best'. In the event, the light tone that Smirke recommended for the Egyptian rooms was a failure. The architect's brother Sydney Smirke, who took on the mantle of Museum architect, pointed out to the trustees twenty-six years later that 'formerly the walls of the Egyptian Gallery were *very light*. The effect was constantly complained of, as being cold, unfinished, & dirty; for the soot & dust that unavoidably settles on the walls became of course very apparent on so light a ground'. As a result the Egyptian Gallery was repainted in a strong red.

Progress on the building continued painfully, and it looked as if it would never be finished. In September 1837 seven painters where killed when the scaffolding carrying them collapsed, throwing them twenty feet to the ground. While the architectural design had its own predictability and rigour, Smirke admitted that the new wings' pattern of use could never be predicted, and nor could their suitability for the task in hand. The reason for this, as outlined by Smirke, was that the extent of public interest in any one area of the Museum was an unknown quantity, as were both the direction and the speed of the growth of the collection. None of these could be clearly foreseen. In 1838 yet another Select Committee, this one on the Plans and Estimates for the Completion of the Building of the British Museum, was appointed to see why everything was taking so long. It was told by Joshua Forshall, the Museum's Secretary, that the collections were increasing so rapidly, and visitor numbers were now so large, that it was imperative that the building be completed 'within the next five or six years'. But even by 1851 it was unfinished, and as the Keeper of Antiquities, Edward Hawkins, reported: 'scarcely a room remains as it was originally constructed . . . it may be asserted with truth that Europe cannot show any building so ill adapted for its intended purpose, as the British Museum.'

Nevertheless, active use was being made of the collections, casts of the Elgin Marbles and the Townley Collection, for example, being in great demand. This provided a small income for the Museum from the mould shop in the cellars of the new west wing. The making of plaster casts was a lucrative and fashionable trade serving domestic, artistic and academic markets in Europe and America, and the British Museum attempted to dominate a corner of it. Cast making in the Museum had since the 1820s been overseen by Richard Westmacott, who also advised on the cleaning of the marbles. The Select Committee was told that a complete set of the Elgin Marbles had been made for the King of the French, a gift from the British government, and further sets had gone to the University of Edinburgh and the Royal Hibernian Academy in Dublin. The committee learned that a complete set of Elgin Marble plaster casts cost 350 guineas to make, and weighed sixty-eight tons at the dockside.

Thomas Conrath, who sat patiently with the Elgin Marbles for so many years, was not the only museum attendant to keep a diary. Charles Rice, a twenty-three-year-old who had been appointed as an attendant in 1837, worked all day at the Museum, and then went off to the taverns of Soho and St Pancras where he was a popular and energetic singer. One of the songs he performed made fun of Humphry Davy's reputation as a chemist, still shining more than ten years after his death, and thirty after his fame had reached its height:

> What are mortals made of?
> By analyzation, I've tried all the nation;
> defined each gradation, and proved every station;
> with Sir Humphry's best, new chemical test; –
> And I've found out what mortals are made of!

Rice must have been one of the more ruminative and interesting of museum attendants, as he sat all day long keeping watch over cases of insects or Egyptian mummies. If challenged for what he had written in his small pocket book, he would have been obliged to declare that the previous night 'I sang "Age of India Rubber," "St. Anthony," encore "Jackdaw!" "King of Otaheite!" encore "On the Spur!" "Ballooning", encore "Safely follow him", "The Wolf", encore "Dramatic Lexicon." Closed at ¼ to 12.'

5

The Traffic of Mind

~

WHEN THE CELEBRATED Italian sculptor Antonio Canova came to London on 3 November 1815, he experienced every kind of entertainment and hospitality that the intelligentsia of the capital could decently supply. He and his half-brother, Giovanni Battista Sartori Canova, were taking a few weeks' rest and recreation in the company of friends, after two months in Paris where they had tensely but successfully negotiated the return of the art treasures that Napoleon's armies had removed from conquered nations and displayed in the Louvre. The restitution of the works of art, to the Vatican, Venice, the Netherlands, Austria, was not universally popular in Paris. Canova had feared for his life, while the Duke of Wellington, one of the masterminds behind the clearing of the Louvre, was hissed at the theatre. Canova's host in London was William Richard Hamilton, Lord Elgin's former secretary, and now Under-Secretary of State for Foreign Affairs, who had prepared and smoothed diplomatic routes for the sculptor in Paris.

Canova had many friends in London, all delighted to see him. For thirty years he had offered open house in Rome to English artists and collectors, including John Flaxman, by now the Professor of Sculpture at the Royal Academy, Richard Westmacott, a former pupil, and Charles Rossi, who had been in Rome for three years in the 1780s on a Royal Academy travelling scholarship. These three Englishmen, along with Francis Chantrey, the fashionable sculptor who had not yet been to Italy, were part of the present and future of sculpture in England, each of them in his own way aspiring to be a worthy successor to the Italian master.

London's artists wanted to thank Canova, and show him what London's entertainment was like. So through his many friends he met painters, sculptors, scientists, entrepreneurs, peers of the realm, politicians and royalty. Treated like royalty himself, he was taken to Westminster Abbey and St Paul's to see the monuments, to the British Museum to inspect the Egyptian and Greek sculpture, to Burlington House where the Elgin Marbles were still resting. At the Royal Society he listened to lectures by Sir Humphry Davy and Anthony Carlisle, and there he met Sir Joseph Banks who took him to see Richard Payne Knight's fabulous collection of drawings and sculpture at 3 Soho Square. He lunched with William Richard Hamilton in Stanley Grove, Chelsea, he dined with Lord and Lady Holland at Holland House, and among the many parties he attended was one crowded with welcoming artists at the workshop and show-room in Tenterden Street, off Hanover Square, of the cabinet-maker George Bullock. Accompanied by Benjamin Robert Haydon, Canova called on the Duke of Devonshire in Piccadilly to see his art collection, and on Turner in Harley Street where he exclaimed 'grand génie' – great genius – in front of his pictures: among them would have been *Dido Building Carthage* (London, National Gallery), lately shown for the first time at the Royal Academy.

In the two months he was in England Canova's feet barely touched the ground. Sir Charles Long, the Paymaster-General, took him up to the heights of Sydenham to look down upon the prospect of London, shining and smoking in the autumn light. The Duke of Bedford whisked him off to Woburn Abbey, Bedfordshire, where he saw the Sculpture Gallery and Temple of Liberty, and discussed the siting of *The Three Graces* that the Duke had ordered from Canova. The days that were perhaps the most memorable for Canova were those on which he saw the Elgin Marbles, commenting, as Farington reported, that 'he never before saw sculpture at such a height of per-fection'. He later confided that 'to see the Elgin Marbles was alone worth the journey from Rome,' and made the same remark in response to John Rennie's Waterloo Bridge, then in construction. This, he said, was also 'alone worth the journey from Rome,' so his remark may just have been a characteristic courtesy to please his hosts.

Canova's charm and gentleness had made him many friends throughout Europe. This led Haydon to remark that 'when he smiles the feeling sent forth is so exquisite that one fancied that music would follow the motion of his lips'. London's farewell to Canova befitted the Italian both as an artist and as an eminent diplomatic guest. Royal Academicians feasted him on 1 December in Somerset House, a dinner which, as the *Courier* put it, 'presented a most pleasing example of the harmony and cordiality which should subsist in the community of the Fine Arts'. Just before he and his half-brother left London he was presented by the Foreign Secretary Lord Castlereagh to the Prince Regent at a Carlton House levée. The Prince gave him a gold snuffbox with a cheque for £500 tucked inside it.

Canova's London holiday was unique in its context and circumstances, and is a litmus test of the capital's powers of sophisticated welcome and entertainment. But as an example of London being used as a crucible of hospitality for a distinguished visitor by a welcoming social and political circle it was one of a countless number repeated in varying degrees again and again. To thank his host, and those in England chiefly responsible for aiding the return of the looted works of art, Canova made a grand personal gesture with his gift the following year of four marble *Ideal Heads* to the chief protagonists in what had been, as W. R. Hamilton described it, 'the happy year of 1815, which has established the peace of Europe, and returned to Italy her greatest works of art'.

The motive force behind gatherings of the kind that Canova attended was the social, commercial and intellectual benefit that would accrue from the meeting of men and women from all parts of the spectrum of achievement. Liaisons were affected, business transacted, marriages made: friends around a dining table fired the engine of the turning world. So intricate and multi-layered were the circuits of London, and so rich the private entertainment available, that accomplished hosts and hostesses could make choices with ease and without offence. While this was impossible in the country, where every house had eyes, in London, as the author Edward Nares put it, 'neighbourhood is of no account at all'. Writing under the portmanteau pseudonym 'Thinks-I-to-Myself', Nares analysed the machinery of society in the capital: 'The people we hate most in the world, are welcome to live next door to us, and there is nobody too far off, if any pleasure or profit, amusement or delight, but above all any credit or *éclat* are to be derived from visiting them.' Nares, who was both a professor of history at Oxford, and the vicar of Biddenden in Kent, 'a country living, out of sight', remarked:

> In London, wherever you are *not*, nobody, probably, of all the company, knows where you *are*, so that you may . . . decline any troublesome or unpleasant invitation . . . houses enough are open generally every night to enable you in the way of visiting, to kill *twenty* or *thirty* head of *game* (as Mrs Fidget would say) in one evening . . . in London preferences at least are possible, not being very easy to detect.

Samuel Rogers gave parties at breakfast, which usually meant about noon, as did the engraver and publisher John Britton, and the publisher John Murray. Francis Chantrey, and Sir Humphry and Lady Davy entertained on a Sunday, John Martin on a Monday, the painter William Etty on a Tuesday, the Somervilles on a Wednesday (this was also Humphry Davy's open evening for Royal Society Fellows), John Murray on a Thursday, Faraday's Royal Institution discourses were held on a Friday, and Charles Babbage entertained on a Saturday evening. Etty's Tuesday breakfasts were open house, largely for artists, 'none being invited, many coming': Etty, characteristically shy, looked on silently. John Martin's parties, at his home in Allsop Terrace, comprised singing, discussion, playful badinage and chess. Artists, writers and scientists mixed there freely and companionably: Michael Faraday asked if he could come without his wife. Among the many other guests, Martin invited Charles Landseer the engraver, John Britton, William Jerdan and William Etty, 'a short, thick-set, slip-shod, slovenly person, strongly marked with smallpox', according to Martin's son, Leopold. Ellen Jacobson, the daughter of the botanist, antiquarian and banker Dawson Turner, was one of the guests at a Murray Thursday party at 50 Albemarle Street in 1828. Her letter to her father gives a vivid idea of the crush and bustle:

> I speak more by report than experience; for Mrs Murray expressed her fears of being crowded, and I remained out of the room with her second daughter. But even to see such people as Crabbe, Callcott etc

is a great pleasure, and it was quite delightful to see the animation and vivacity with which that very old man Crabbe conversed with Mrs Callcott.

Before she married the painter Augustus Wall Callcott in 1827, Maria Callcott was Mrs Thomas Graham, a noted travel author and widow of the naval officer Captain Thomas Graham. Together the Grahams had travelled to India, Italy and South America, where, in the Pacific in 1822 en route to Valparaiso, Thomas Graham fell ill and died at sea. Maria Graham, later as Maria Callcott, had a long correspondence with John Murray, stretching over thirty years. She described herself to Murray as a 'plain matter of fact person. I like plain question & answer & that given I am always tractable & satisfied.' John Murray, who in 1820 had published both her journal *Three Months in the Mountains East of Rome* and her pioneering life of the painter Nicolas Poussin, was in Maria Graham's affectionate words 'an arch bookseller . . . Every body on the Continent is so convinced that you can do what you please, that they don't think a thing is worth reading unless your name appears on the title page.' Maria, gregarious and ebullient, liked to share hospitality and friendship, and proposed to introduce to Murray's circle a young painter, Charles Eastlake, whom she and Thomas Graham had met in Rome: 'I want [Mr Eastlake] to see the sort of thing that one only sees at your house at your many levées, the traffic of mind and literature if I may call it so.'

William Jerdan was another frequent guest of John Murray. Jerdan found Murray, quizzical in expression with his one good eye, to be 'joyous and festive; and, as far as his constitution allowed . . . an exceedingly pleasant boon companion, full of information, cheerful in converse, humorous in remark and repartee, and gentlemanly in manners'. Around the walls of the upper rooms in 50 Albemarle Street were – still are – portraits of poets, travellers and writers, including Byron, Coleridge and Southey, some of whom, as Jerdan noticed, 'generally formed a portion of the convivial group below', joining in with the party. One regular gathering might spawn yet more. Jerdan, with John Britton and others, founded the Pot-Luck Club which was to meet weekly at members' houses in turn for a simple meal and conversation. This rapidly got out of hand. Jerdan, being a bon viveur, laid on a rich and expensive supper. At the second meeting, the Bond Street bookseller Andrews offered fare that was richer still: 'then Martin and the others took fright and further meetings were indefinitely postponed'. Another convivial grouping was the Graphic Society, founded in 1833 by William Brockedon to bring artists and scientists together. Among its early members were scientists Michael Faraday and Charles Wheatstone, and artists and architects including John Pye, J. T. Willmore, Peter Robinson and Thomas L. Donaldson – all of whom we will hear of in later chapters.

In London society, breakfast gatherings could last a long time, and elided with lunch. Breakfast was often an entertainment, stretching way out into the afternoon, an apparently endless path of fun. One Monday morning in June 1808 a crowd of men admired a naked boxer posing in a London drawing room. Anthony Carlisle had invited Joseph Farington and twenty or more other painters, sculptors and medical men to his house in Langham Place to consider 'Gregson, the Pugilist, stripped naked . . . exhibited to us on acct. of the fineness of His form. He is 6 feet 2 inches high, all admired the beauty of His proportions.' This was not a sporting event, but an opportunity for physicians and artists to observe supreme human form in motion and repose. The pleasure at the sight of Gregson was mixed with criticism, for the President of the Royal Academy, Sir Benjamin West, found that the bones of the boxer's legs were too short, his toes were not long enough, and there was some heaviness about the thighs and knees. That apart, the company generally agreed that in front of them stood 'the finest figure the persons present had seen'. They told him to take up a variety of 'attitudes', which would mean that he might have swung his arms out and twisted at the waist to pose in the classical form of the Discus Thrower, have sat on a stool with his left leg pulled over his right knee as the Spinario, a boy pulling a thorn out of the sole of his foot, then a Dying Gladiator, or perhaps an Apollo, posed standing bravely with his head turned to one side, his right arm reaching out both defiantly and in welcome.

The entertainment and instruction that these erudite men were seeking was to compare a living being with the finest productions of classical sculpture then known. This was now practically possible, for the Elgin Marbles, on their slow, interrupted journey to the British Museum, were in 1808 displayed in Lord Elgin's house and garden at the southern end of Park Lane. They had not yet reached Burlington House where Canova saw them. Having seen Gregson's beauty, Carlisle's guests arranged to meet the boxer again at Lord Elgin's 'to compare his form with some of the antique figures'. Gregson posed for two hours among the carvings: once again, 'he was placed in many attitudes', Farington remarked. The following month the entertainment reached a climax when at least five boxers fought each other before an audience of Academicians and others in front of the battered Marbles. 'Lord Elgin's I went to at one o'clock,' Farington recorded, 'to a Pugilistic Sparring match. Gulley sparred with Belcher, Dutch Sam with Belcher Junior, Jackson with Gulley.' As the boxers pummelled each other, thoughts of art and sport mingled in the minds of some of the onlookers. Charles Rossi particularly admired 'Dutch Sam' (Samuel Elias), 'on account of the *Symmetry* and the *parts being expressed*'. The artists would see Gregson again: in January 1809 Carlisle used this 'well made man' in his anatomy lectures at the Academy as his model 'to demonstrate the general divisions of the human body on the living figure'.

With the sight of boxers sparring in front of the Elgin Marbles we have an extreme example of the interlocking of intellectual and social circles for mutual enlightenment through entertainment in art, sport and anatomy. The Colburn family, with the twelve-year-old Zerah as their star turn, was another special social attraction with some light intellectual content. The Colburns came from Vermont, USA, to London in 1812 to demonstrate Zerah's extraordinary mathematical powers. The family took rooms in Spring Gardens, where Zerah could be visited, for a fee, by the curious, and from whence he paid calls on London drawing rooms and on royalty to answer whatever mathematical memory questions might be thrown at him.

'How many seconds since the commencement of the Christian era, 1813 years, 7 months, 27 days,' he was asked at one of the soirées.

Zerah thought for a moment, and replied: 'Fifty-seven thousand two hundred and thirty-four million three hundred and eighty-four thousand [57,234,384,000].'

'What is eight to the power of sixteen?'

'Two hundred and eighty-one million four hundred and seventy-four thousand nine hundred and seventy-six million seven hundred and ten thousand six hundred and fifty-six [281,474,976,710,656].'

Zerah was examined by physicians and Fellows of the Royal Society, Humphry Davy sending his amanuensis Michael Faraday off to quiz him about his tricks of memory. Faraday was highly impressed: 'He can retain three or four lines each containing six or seven figures in his mind at once and he can blend those figures together without confusion, adding, subtracting, noting the sum or remainder and substituting these numbers for those he commenced with.'

The Colburns had additional curiosities about them: they were the polydactylic family that Anthony Carlisle examined in 1813, and wrote up for the Royal Society. Both Zerah and his father had five fingers and a thumb on each hand, and six toes on each foot; some of Zerah's brothers and sisters were similarly endowed, like a biblical giant, as Carlisle reminded his readers. Haydon met Zerah in May 1813 and drew his portrait. He was enraptured by the boy and his powers: 'it is a probable, natural, common power, which everyone has in some degree, carried to the highest perfection, so that there is no saying where it may end'.

The most significant social event, however, was dinner, 'everyday social and set dinners', as defined by Thomas Walker, a barrister who wrote both on the Poor Law and on 'aristology', the art of dining – 'ariston' being Greek for dinner. Walker had a third category, 'solitary dinners', but these, he advised, 'ought to be avoided as much as possible, because solitude tends to produce thought, and thought tends to the suspension of the digestive powers'. Everyday social dinners were organised spontaneously, while set dinners were planned with great care. The time of dinner changed gradually as the early nineteenth century progressed. It had been two or three o'clock in the afternoon in the mid-eighteenth century, and by the 1790s it had crept forward to five o'clock, 'hitherto unheard of' as a time to dine, according to John Hogg. By the 1830s, 'The hour at which this meal is taken by the upper classes in the metropolis is 8 or 9 o'clock . . . it is the chief meal still.' The cause of the change of time, according to Hogg, was 'pressure of business and increased duties'. A further refinement on the types of meal available was supper, taken at about half-past nine or ten o'clock. 'In all times', as Walker put it, supper was 'consecrated to mental enjoyment . . . Dinner may be considered the meal of the body, and supper that of the mind . . . Dinner is a business, supper an amusement.'

Joseph Farington was a regular and active diner, variously as a host, a guest and alone. In his case reflective thought produced not as far as we know indigestion, but a reliable diary. Farington gave an 'everyday social dinner' when three men joined him in Upper Charlotte Street in April 1817 to discuss a small crisis in London journalism. John Taylor, the journalist co-proprietor of the Tory newspaper the *Sun*, had invited himself over to lick his wounds with Farington, who brought in the painters Henry Thomson RA and Thomas Lawrence for support. Taylor wanted to gather sympathy for the rough treatment he was receiving from the young editor of the paper, half his age, William Jerdan. Behind Taylor's back, Jerdan had secured the editorship with a nine-hundred-year contract, and despite the fact that Taylor had subsequently bought nine of the ten shares in the paper (Jerdan held the tenth), the new editor was as despotic as anybody might be who had the security of a nine-hundred-year lease on a job. He refused Taylor's contributions, egregious articles supporting the government, gossip paragraphs and puffs about parties, 'so objectionable', as Jerdan remarked, 'to my notions of . . . public propriety, that I would not publish them'. 'He thought of nothing,' Jerdan added, 'he talked of nothing, he wrote of nothing, he dreamed of nothing but my villainy and oppression; he worried ministers with them, he distressed friends, he bored the town, he disturbed the office, he ruined the paper.'

Taylor, by now in his sixties, was desperately trying to re-establish his credibility with influential men like Farington and his friends. But he failed to convince, having presided over the *Sun*'s decline, 'going down, in a very hazy set'. Jerdan saw Taylor as a figure of fun, who threw tantrums in the *Sun* offices: 'frenzies . . . at once ludicrous and afflicting . . . he would cast himself down upon his knees, clasp his hands, gnash his teeth, and imprecate curses on my head for five minutes together, till someone humanely lifted him up and led him away to privacy'.

The feud between Taylor and Jerdan came to an end when the latter sold out of the *Sun* in 1817, and went off to be editor of the *Literary Gazette* – full title: *The Literary Gazette; and Journal of Belles Lettres, Arts, Sciences, &c.* There Jerdan came to revolutionise the reporting and record of the world of letters, science and art, while Taylor got what he wanted, the editorship of the *Sun* once more. Taylor also wrote and published jaunty and sycophantic verses which illuminate the character of some of the parties and other gatherings that he attended, and praised his hosts and their hospitality. Running through the poems is the clear indication that the key to the success of a good party was the extent of the collective brainpower of the guests; the keyword which crops up in Taylor's verses, indeed, is 'mental'. The 'Lines on Mr Ackermann's Evenings' Conversazione' reveal that the intention of the publisher and bookseller Rudolph Ackermann was to spread a 'rich . . . mental banquet' in his shop and rooms in the Strand. In Taylor's lines 'On the Evening Parties at Henry Sass's, Esq., Bloomsbury', we read that:

> No worthless guests are summon'd there,
> But men of sense and lib'ral hearts,
> Props of the fine and useful arts,

and that the 'mental banquet' at Sass's gatherings was 'cheerful, instructive, and refin'd'.

Henry Sass, who came to his parties wearing one of his characteristically 'extravagant waistcoats of cut velvet', ran his own art school, Sass's School for Drawing and Painting, opposite the British Museum at 50 Great Russell Street. There he aspired to bring young men and women to a high enough standard in drawing from the antique and the human figure to pass into the Royal Academy Schools. The proximity of the Museum and its collections was central to the school's success, and finding a lucrative market among the new social and artistic aspirants of west London, it flourished. Remaining in the Museum's neighbourhood, Sass moved in 1820 to 6 Charlotte Street, Bedford Square, a house with a bust of Minerva, the Greek goddess of wisdom, over the door. When the students had gone home, Sass displayed his own works to his evening guests, 'proofs of a fruitful, cultur'd mind', for discussion and admiration.

The surgeon and antiquary Thomas Pettigrew entertained 'men of science, artists, wits, and bards' at 8 Savile Row, behind Burlington House, and there laid on a 'varied mental treat'. Feeding the minds and the conversation in these and many other evening parties, and keeping conversation in focus, were the libraries and collections of art, antiquities and *objets de vertù* which impressed the guests, and defined the host's own credibility. Bent though he was on flattery, Taylor did nevertheless evoke an atmosphere of enjoyable scholarship, made even more impressive by glittering candlelight on a winter evening. At these evening parties, the books and collections surrounding the guests were to be contemplated, discussed and used. At Sass's,

> The dome with various treasures stor'd,
> Rare books and prints enrich the board.

And at Pettigrew's,

> Works of rare value o'er the rooms abound,
> That gratify and elevate the mind.

While at Ackermann's,

> Sculpture and Painting well adorn the place,
> And classic stores the spacious tables grace.
> Study and converse with alternate pow'r,
> Engage, amuse, instruct, the passing hour.

At private parties guests ate, drank and talked, but there would have been no music for dancing. This was provided at another level of social activity, the balls and routs that took place constantly in the season. When in 1806 he first arrived in London from Devon, Cyrus Redding put up at Hatchett's Hotel in Piccadilly, and was kept awake all night by a rout in Arlington Street, and by the noise and clatter of the carriages. The acme of these gatherings was Almack's, in Pall Mall, a fashionable and exclusive ballroom run in the 1820s by a committee of seven inquisitive ladies, the Countess of Jersey, the Marchioness of Londonderry, Lady Cowper, the Countess of Brownlow, Lady Willoughby D'Eresby, the Countess of Euston and the Countess of Litchfield. Together, these women, dripping with jewels and top-heavy with titles, wielded absolute power, 'often exercised in the most capricious manner'. If they refused to admit an applicant to a dance, that was that; there was no appeal. Almack's ballroom, one of the most beautiful in London, opened for business on ball evenings (Wednesdays) at ten o'clock at night, and for the following hour at least the street was packed with carriages coming and going and dropping off their stiff-cravatted, silk- and ostrich-feather-encumbered passengers. The average attendance, according to one source, was five hundred. There was strictly no admission after midnight, unless (this was a late amendment to the otherwise inflexible rules) the applicant was a member of parliament or of the House of Lords, and had been held up by a vote. Dancing began at eleven, and went on non-stop until four o'clock in the morning.

> Mark how the married and the single,
> In yon gay groupes delighted mingle:
> Midst diamonds blazing, tapers beaming,
> Midst Georges, Stars, and Crosses gleaming.
> We gaze on beauty, catch the sound
> Of music, and of mirth around,
> And discord feels her empire ended
> At ALMACK's – or at least suspended.

In the hands of the playwright and author Pierce Egan, fashionable meeting places themselves became the settings of theatrical entertainment. Egan, who evoked the spirit of Regency London in books and plays featuring his pair of lads-about-town Tom and Jerry and their friends, carried his audience around the capital in his play *Life in London*, first staged at the Adelphi Theatre in November 1821. He introduced the largely knowing audience to Burlington Arcade, 'a sort of hurly-burly market, where everything is to be had good in its kind for money, except one thing – "And what's that one thing, Mr Impudence?" said a pert little miss in her teens: – "Modesty, Miss, and I think you missed your share when it was serving out to Dame Virtue's customers."'

Tom and Jerry, the Hon. Tom Dashall and Jerry Hawthorne, were a gregarious pair of sophisticates. They took themselves around the shops and exhibitions, markets, parks and public gardens. In Soho they went to George and William Cooke's gallery to see an exhibition of engravings, and at the British Museum joined a party being taken round by a 'Conductor'. In the courtyard, still vainly waiting for a home within the building, were Egyptian monuments and a porphyry sarcophagus housed in 'two large sheds'. Under the grand staircase they noticed the fragments from the Giant's Causeway, still sitting there gathering dust after twenty or thirty years.

Over the few days of their perambulation, the friends attended a fancy-dress ball at Almack's, passed through Covent Garden market, 'an emporium unquestionably . . . not excelled by any other of a similar description in the universe', and in Leicester Square visited Miss Linwood's Gallery of Needlework, 'the very extraordinary production of female genius'. In Spring Gardens they discovered at Wigley's Promenade Rooms 'Mr Theodon's grand *Mechanical and Picturesque Theatre* displaying dramatic views of the Island of St Helena, and the St Bernard's Pass', and were shown a model of a pedal carriage which could travel at six miles per hour. At nightfall they wondered at the newly installed gas lighting which ran along the Mall and around St James's Park, shedding 'a noon-tide splendour on the solitude of midnight'.

Candles were gradually being banished in wealthy houses, as hosts invested in the new gas lighting. Rudolph Ackermann's premises at 101 Strand, The Repository of Arts, was, by 1814, fully illuminated with coal gas, 'from the kitchen to the drawing room, his extensive warehouses, shop, printing-office, and manufactory'. One of the wealthiest collectors in London, and one who was particularly generous with invitations to his house, was the connoisseur, author and designer Thomas Hope. His collection defined neo-classical taste in London, being strict in its parameters and vast and varied in extent. In his mansion, designed by Robert Adam on the corner of Duchess Street and Mansfield Street, Hope entertained lavishly showing off his antique pottery, classical sculpture, and paintings, furnishings and objets d'art. One particular rout, reported in *The Times* in 1802, was attended by nearly a thousand people, who spread themselves around sixteen rooms each at that time still illuminated by 250 wax lamps. Hope distributed tickets for entry, and published a catalogue of the collections and a guide to the house so that visitors might recognise the objects. Royal Academicians were offered free tickets in 1804, an inducement which did not amuse them.

Hope's visitors saw the three vase rooms, the Egyptian and Indian rooms, a room given over entirely to the sculpture of John Flaxman, his dining room, drawing room and grand staircase, all the epitome of a taste at the sharp end of fashion. Hope even had that rare thing a Lararium, a Roman shrine to the guardian spirits of the house, used here for the display of Hope's Egyptian, Chinese and Hindu idols on an elaborate stepped mantelpiece. So free was Hope with his invitations that Maria Edgeworth, asking her host in 1813 the name of one of the guests in a party of about nine hundred, had the reply, 'I really don't know. I don't know half the people here nor do they know me or Mrs Hope even by sight. Just now I was behind a lady who was making *her speech*, as she thought, to Mrs Hope but she was addressing her compliments to some stranger.' But even Hope's crisp house was subject to the depredations of London. A few months after the collector's death, a German artist Johann Passavant visited Duchess Street and found 'a heavy gloomy building, almost entirely devoid of windows, blackened with accumulations of soot, and to all outward appearance conveying the idea of a large brewery, than of an opulent banker's residence'. Every building in London, however grand, very soon became filthy.

Perfection in a party of diners was, as Thomas Walker maintained, eight people, 'the golden number, never to be exceeded without weakening the efficacy of concentration'. Walker described one near-perfect occasion, when he had entertained some friends in chambers in the Temple, probably in the early 1830s. They were six (not the golden eight): the soldier Sir James Scarlett (later Lord Abinger), the MP for Scarborough Sir John Johnstone, Thomas Young the private secretary to Lord Melbourne, Robert Bell of the lawyers Bell and Brothers, the Hon. George Lamb, the politician brother of Lord Melbourne, and Thomas Walker the host. When inviting these men, in writing, to dine, Walker made sure to state plainly 'what I meant to attempt, and the names of the party'. He advocated absolute clarity in the invitations, making sure that the guests even knew what they were going to eat, as well as who they were to share a table with. Walker added that a large formal card was not appropriate for a simple dinner: 'it leads to disappointment'.

Walker's dinner in the Temple was of the 'set' kind, and its menu reflects the rich abundance of supplies in London, and the intricacy of the contemporary catering industry: take-away food is not just a late-twentieth-century phenomenon. They ate 'quite delicious' Spring soup from Birch's on Cornhill, a moderate-sized turbot, 'bought in the city, beautifully boiled, with first-rate lobster sauce, cucumber and new potatoes', ribs of beef from Leadenhall market, 'roasted to a turn, and smoking from the spit', with French beans and salad. This was followed by a 'very fine dressed crab' and jelly, with orange and biscuits and anchovy toast for dessert. 'The fish and beef were dressed by a Temple laundress . . . the proximity of the kitchen was not the least annoyance to us in any way, or indeed perceptible, except in the excellence of the serving up.' They drank champagne, port and claret. Although lawyers have always enjoyed the best cuts, dinners like this would have been going on every evening all over the City of London, in the fashionable western districts, and in the large houses in London's fringe villages.

Before a large party, beds, cupboards and chairs were moved out of sight, and the house practically stripped to make room for the crowds. At the London house of a notable host or hostess the guests who arrived on foot would rap the knocker or ring the bell. Those who came by carriage, however, would make an infinitely more dramatic arrival. The coachman would jump off his seat, leap up to the front door and give the knocker one enormous rap enough to rattle the windows, then a series of rap-rap-rap-raps, then, after a theatrical pause, a high-speed flourish 'as on a drum, with an art, and an air, and a delicacy of touch, which denotes the quality, the rank, and the fortune of his master'. W. M. Thackeray enjoyed watching dinner guests making their way through the streets:

> Every evening between seven and eight o'clock, I like to look at the men dressed for dinner, perambulating the western districts of our city. I like to see the smile on their countenances lighted up with an indescribable self-importance and good-humour . . . the coaxing twiddle which they give to the ties of their white chokers – the caress of a fond parent to an innocent child.

In the entrance hall the guests would hand over hats, umbrellas and coats to the footman, and go upstairs to the drawing room where their names would be announced. Walker felt he had to state the obvious, and warn the host not to look bored at this point: 'It is usually seen that the host receives his guests almost as if they were strangers to him, and, after a word or two, leaves them to manage for themselves.' Evidently some hosts did not feel it necessary to introduce their guests to each other, and, as in Thomas Hope's case, many guests were strangers even to the host. Walker also advised the host to know how to command the situation, 'and not let his guests run riot'. An inconvenience of autumn or winter gatherings was that the drawing-room assembly took place in the dark. Inadequate candles would flutter on sconces or chandeliers, and in the dim light guests would fumble around in descending gloom: 'such obscurity, that it is impossible to see. Then there is often a tedious and stupefying interval of waiting, caused perhaps by some affected fashionable.'

The decorative painter David Hay, who wrote an influential and popular guide to interior decoration, *Laws of Harmonious Colouring Adapted to House Painting* (1828), recommended for the drawing room 'vivacity, gaiety and light cheerfulness' in the colouring, with the brightest colours and strongest contrasts being on the furniture. The decoration of a dining room, on the other hand, played its part in encouraging harmony. With a bright, blazing fire which 'has a very inspiring effect on entering', the dining room should, Hay advised, be 'warm, rich and substantial, and where contrasts are introduced they should not be vivid'.

An evening in a London town house was a strenuous walking activity which began with a journey up to the drawing room to assemble, down to the dining room to eat, and then up again to the drawing room for coffee. Staircases, where guests tended to spend quite some time as they traversed up and down, were ideally 'of a rather cool tone and the style of colour should be simple and free of contrast. The effect to be produced is that of architectural grandeur.' The first descent to the dining room when the days were short ended when a 'blaze of light produces by degrees sundry recognitions; but many a slight acquaintance is prevented from being renewed by the chilling mode of assembling'. The importance of good lighting in the dining room was recognised by Samuel Rogers, who installed 'Ellesmere' gas lamps to show off his pictures. Where Rudolph Ackermann had led, his clients followed. Many of Rogers's paintings were masterpieces: he owned Titian's *Noli Me Tangere*, Rubens's *Roman Triumph* and a Raphael *Madonna and Child*, all now in the National Gallery in London. He asked Sydney Smith one evening how he liked the dining-room lighting. 'Not at all,' Smith replied. 'Above, there is a blaze of light, and below, nothing but darkness and gnashing of teeth.' The lighting in Rogers's dining room was the latest and brightest picture lighting available. A young visitor to his house, Mary Potter, who years later as Mary Lloyd was to write what she called her 'sunny memories' of celebrated characters she had met in her youth, noticed how Rogers's Ellesmere lamps were fixed on the walls at intervals between the pictures, each having a metal shade to direct their light: 'This mode of lighting I there saw for the first time and then greatly admired. There is no doubt that it is the best light for pictures, and it is better than daylight in most London houses.' After coffee in the drawing room upstairs, guests would begin to take their leave, passing the door to the dining room, with its flickering or by now extinguished lamps, collecting hats, coats and umbrellas from the servant in the hall, and out into the dark, and home.

6

A Mutton Chop at 5 O'Clock

~

BENJAMIN ROBERT HAYDON held what he came to call 'the Immortal Dinner' in his painting room at 22 Lisson Grove on 28 December 1817. His enormous canvas *Christ's Entry into Jerusalem* 'tower[ed] up behind us as background', he wrote afterwards. It was an all-male affair, an opportunity for Haydon to bring together for an evening his friend the twenty-two-year-old John Keats and the older and now celebrated poet William Wordsworth, with Charles Lamb and Wordsworth's wife's cousin Tom Monkhouse, a friend of Keats. Haydon also wanted to show his guests the nearly completed painting that he was convinced would prove to the world the depth of his genius, and to reveal the high and well-lit painting room that he had recently begun to rent from Charles Rossi. Penelope Hughes-Hallett suggests that Haydon would have given his guests two somewhat complex courses, the first of soup with a roast joint, fish, meat pie and vegetables, and the second, the 'remove' – game, savoury dishes, meat patties, and it being so near Christmas perhaps also roast turkey. This would be followed by dessert, and all accompanied by expansive conversation, loosened up as they were by port. The dinner began soon after three o'clock, in the last light of the day, candles being lit and flickering in advance of the guests' arrivals.

'We had a glorious set-to,' Haydon recalled, 'on Homer, Shakespeare, Milton and Virgil. Lamb got exceedingly merry and exquisitely witty; and his fun in the midst of Wordsworth's solemn intonations of oratory was like the sarcasm and wit of the fool in the intervals of Lear's passion.' They all got drunk, and Lamb called a vote to send Haydon out of the room, when they drank his health. Then they began to talk about the painting behind them, and argued about Voltaire and Newton whose portraits Haydon had worked into the composition as an unbeliever and a believer respectively. Wordsworth and Keats recognised portraits of themselves among the crowd welcoming Christ's arrival on a donkey into Jerusalem. The climax of the dinner conversation as recorded by Haydon defines the distance that was gradually appearing between art and the understanding of science:

> [Lamb] then, in a strain of humour beyond description, abused me for putting Newton's head into my picture; 'a fellow', said he, 'who believed nothing unless it was as clear as the three sides of a triangle.' And then he and Keats agreed he had destroyed all the poetry of the rainbow by reducing it to the prismatic colours. It was impossible to resist him, and we all drank 'Newton's health, and confusion to mathematics.'

This classic gathering might have been what Thomas Walker would describe as a 'set dinner' – written invitations, the list of guests known to all in advance, table laid with the best family silver and napery, menu planned down to the last blancmange. Other guests, expected and unexpected, came later, including the surgeon and future African explorer Joseph Ritchie, the engraver John Landseer, and, clattering up in a cab from Somerset House, uninvited, John Kingston, a Comptroller of the Stamp Office, 'frilled, dressed, and official', who particularly wanted to meet Wordsworth, the official distributor of stamps in Westmorland.

But rather than end with handshakes, bows and farewells at the front door, as was accepted social practice, Haydon's evening descended into farce. The Comptroller of Stamps tried to engage Wordsworth in a discussion about Milton, while Lamb, drunk as a lord, told Kingston in his froggings and fancy that he was a 'silly fellow'. Watching it all was deaf-as-a-post Landseer, with his hand to his ear saying 'What? What? What's that he said?', and Keats, Ritchie and Haydon falling about with laughter. Lamb went on and on about the shape of Kingston's head, his 'phrenology', and appeared to taunt him:

> Diddle iddle don, my son John
> Went to bed with his breeches on.

They all bundled Lamb out of the room, as he shouted 'do let me have another look at that gentleman's organs!' Monkhouse took Lamb home.

The sculptor Francis Chantrey was five years older than Haydon, and by 1817 already finding the worldly success that was to elude Haydon all his life. He was widely praised during his first Royal Academy exhibition in 1811, when he exhibited his bust of John Horne Tooke, and claimed over the period of the exhibition to have received £5,000 worth of orders for busts: ''tis the most money-making part of my business', he once remarked. Haydon regarded Chantrey with irritable admiration, meeting him, after an eight-year gap, in Brighton in 1827: 'His nose at the tip was bottled, large and brown, his cheeks full, his person corpulent, his air indolent, his tone a little pompous. Such were the effects of eight years' success. He sat and talked, easily, lazily – gazing at the sun with his legs crossed.' They talked of the colossal sculpture of Satan that Chantrey was making for Lord Egremont, and Chantrey said he had stopped work on it, 'till I am perfectly independent, and then you shall see what I will do in poetical subjects'. This drew from Haydon one of his most reflective remarks about creativity, characteristically using himself as a measure:

> To see a man of Chantrey's genius so impose on himself was affecting. Here he was, for that day at least, quite independent; gazing at the sun, sure of his dinner, his fire, his wine, his bed. Why was he not at that moment inventing? Good God! If I had waited till I had been perfectly independent, what should I have done? Invention presses upon a man like a nightmare. I composed the Crucifixion, in part, while going in a hackney coach to sign a warrant of attorney. I began Solomon without a candle for the evening. I finished it without food – at least meat – for the last fortnight. And here is Chantrey putting off poetical inventions till he is perfectly independent!

Chantrey, a good-hearted, popular and energetic host, was direct and engaging in his approach, with a cheerfulness that would have impressed Thomas Walker. He had deeply sunk, reflective eyes, and described himself as 'an honest, dull-headed, perhaps stupid, Englishman, but I am not a fool for all that'. Chantrey's cheerfulness also impressed Jerdan, who remarked on his 'lively and entertaining' conversation, and on his 'comical and mirth-provoking expressions'. So characteristic was this jollity that the painter C. R. Leslie used Chantrey as the model for Sancho Panza in his paintings of scenes from *Don Quixote*. Chantrey attracted friends and patrons to his house in Belgrave Place for Sunday dinner, and to his studio and foundry in nearby Eccleston Street, Pimlico: patrons became friends, friends became patrons. When working on busts he would encourage the sitters to move about the studio and converse freely in a relaxed manner so that he could draw out their personal characteristics. Mary Somerville told her son of Chantrey's informal manner. 'He never asks me to *sit*,' she said. 'He works a little, then sits down and quietly takes his pinch of snuff without even looking at the clay, and after talking and laughing for ten minutes begins again.'

Finding one of his usual Sunday gatherings to be perhaps a bit thin, he dashed off a letter to his old friend and future biographer Captain George Jones RA. As Walker had advised, Chantrey leaped straight in to tell Jones the menu, and who was also to be present:

> Mackerel, roast beef, Yorkshire pudding, and an excellent hen pheasant roasted sweet as a nut! This 14th day of March, and tender as a chicken, at *six o'clock*! Only Stokes! Pray come if nothing better [on] offer. I could not reach you yesterday. Turner dines with Boddington. I tried a new horse yesterday; won't do.

On another occasion, inviting Jones to Sunday dinner, Chantrey urged him to dress up a bit, to 'put on silk stockings', because fellow guests were to include Mary Somerville and the antiquary Edward Utterson. Chantrey's generosity was such that, as Jones remarked, 'no hospitality short of Lord Essex's, Lord Spencer's and Lord Holland's could compare'. His parties were held in his dining room, and for small meetings and discussions he and his guests retired to his library. 'In this room, sitting by the fire in his easy chair, commodious for writing and reading, close to his desk, Chantrey received the dignified and scientific of the land, ready to listen to the requests and inquiries of all . . . his attention was always ready, his observations reasonable, and often mixed with facetiousness.'

Chantrey was fascinated as much by the science of the marble he carved and the bronze he cast as by the art and undertaking of sculpture. His profound understanding of the character and requirements of his material was one of the keys to his success. When he was in Italy in October 1819 he visited the marble quarries at Carrara, where 'he secured marble of the finest quality, and his sagacious liberality was rewarded by having the choicest blocks reserved for his use'. In Rome he went to the Quirinal Palace with Lady Davy, who was in the city with her husband, and it must have been Chantrey who was behind the request given to Sir Humphry Davy 'to determine if the spots in Carrara marble are *iron oxide* and if they can be eliminated'. His sometime fishing companion William Wollaston thought that Chantrey's mind was capable of 'maturing any subject to which it might be steadily directed', and Jones paid a further high tribute, although it is one that should be taken with caution, for Jones's admiration for Chantrey was overwhelming: 'Chantrey did well all he undertook, and some things pre-eminently . . . in geology, chemistry, and optics, as well as in the exact sciences, he had considerable knowledge, and enough to give him a lively interest in all.' Ada Byron, the argumentative daughter of Lord Byron, who was already causing consternation in social circles by the acuteness of her mathematical mind, would not be taken in, and managed adroitly to resist Chantrey's professional friendship. She told her friend Mary Somerville: 'I'm afraid I shall never like Mr Chantrey, and declare I won't admire his bust of you, out of spite.'

Enjoyment of scientific and literary matters led Chantrey to continue to fire off invitations to men and women outside his own professional sphere, and to mix artists, scientists and writers together in a rich cultural soup. Charles Babbage was a regular target of Chantrey's amiable barrage, and remained so despite the fact that he never sat to the sculptor. There is a scattering of letters which reflect their friendship's ease. One invitation of May 1826 to dine goes on to say 'and I will instruct you in the Art and Mystery of Sculpture'. Another, of November 1829, summons Babbage and Banks's successor as President of the Royal Society, Davies Gilbert, to meet another Royal Society Fellow, Captain Henry Kater, 'on Wednesday next at ¼ past 3 o'clock for the purpose of looking over my foundry and eating a mutton chop at 5 o'clock – come in boots. Rejoice in your success with the Prime Minister.' Then another in April 1832: 'On Sunday I shall be most glad to see you, & if you can enjoy a dinner of Roast Beef in the company of Stokes – Turner – Jones – Calcott – Landseer & Hilton all artists except Stokes, I shall be most happy.'

A few years later, in December 1839, he asked Babbage again:

> The life of James Watt is in print.
> Mr Boulton and Mr Watt will dine with me on Sunday next at six o'clock (in Boots). Will you do me and them the kindness to dine here also?

'Mr Boulton and Mr Watt' were Matthew Boulton's and James Watt's sons, who were confusingly, and dynastically, also called Matthew and James. The younger James Watt was a rich source of patronage for Chantrey, being instrumental in commissioning the sculptor to make six marble busts of his father, at least fifty plaster casts and five full-size seated statues in marble and bronze. The net income that James Watt junior directly or indirectly drew down towards Francis Chantrey through these commissions between 1814 and 1835 was £15,306 4s 0d. No wonder Chantrey's square-jawed indomitable image of James Watt is so well known; no wonder Chantrey gave Watt's son dinner. Matthew Boulton junior was by comparison a less forthcoming patron, commissioning Chantrey to make one work only, a marble memorial to his wife Mary Anne in St Michael's Church, Great Tew, Oxfordshire, completed in 1834. For this the younger Boulton paid £1,500. References to boots in Chantrey's letter suggests that the sculptor is telling Babbage that there is no need to dress up, and to remember that they would be going into the foundry where the floors were treacherous with debris, and hot. 'Wear boots' was an alternative dress code to 'put on silk stockings' in Chantrey's social lexicon.

Chantrey was inordinately proud of his studio, with its furnaces and cranes, its industrial appearance, and work-in-progress standing nonchalantly about like an enchanted theatrical cast of characters – there were probably three or four James Watts in there at any one time. The industrial equipment (one of the furnaces was fourteen feet by twelve feet by twelve feet high) was installed in 1827 by the engineer Henry Maudslay, another of Chantrey's professional friends, who welcomed Chantrey as 'the most attractive visitor' at his workshop in Lambeth. Chantrey's studio in Eccleston Place was very conveniently close to Pimlico Wharf, where his sculptures could be floated off on barges for distribution. He was close also to other useful engineering works, including the factory of the inventor of the security lock, Joseph Bramah, in Eaton Street, where he could have any piece of necessary metalwork, such as a sculpture armature, run up for him with ease.

The gathering at Chantrey's studio 'for the purpose of looking over my foundry' in early December 1829 may be the same one that Babbage recalls in his autobiography when he met Chantrey, Kater and Thomas Lawrence, President of the Royal Academy. At Chantrey's invitation, Babbage and Kater went into the oven, which was then at a high temperature for drying moulds for 'a large bronze sculpture', possibly the equestrian figure of the former Governor of Madras, Sir Thomas Munro, in early progress by 1829. Lawrence did not follow them into the furnace as he was unwell; he died two or three days later. That was some hot party, as Babbage explained, after he and Kater entered the oven and had the doors closed upon them:

> The further *corner* of the room, which was paved with squared stones, was visibly of a dull-red heat. The thermometer marked, if I recollect rightly, 265°. The pulse was quickened, and I ought to have counted . . . the number of inspirations per minute. Perspiration commenced immediately and was very copious. We remained, I believe, about five or six minutes without very great discomfort, and I experienced no subsequent inconvenience from the result of the experiment.

Chantrey made a habit of taking visitors into his furnace. Another friend, who braved the oven with Chantrey and 'five or six others', was the Edinburgh mathematician David Brewster. They all went in for two minutes when the thermometer read 320°F, and variously suffered, according to Brewster, sharp pains in their ears and in the septum of the nose.

Chantrey is an exemplar of the successful businessman–artist, the antithesis of Haydon, and one for whom hospitality was part of the game, and easy friendship a business asset. He was always on the ball, always on the look-out. Likewise, Charles Babbage saw entertainment as an applied science, and science part of entertainment. When David Brewster came to town in June 1831, Babbage swept him up and entertained him by taking him to hear the Italian violinist Nicolò Paganini, who was giving a series of terrifyingly brilliant performances in London that summer. They may have gone together to Chantrey's foundry and experienced the oven, and together they examined the Thames Tunnel, which had been languishing and incomplete since being flooded out in January 1828:

> I have seen much of [Brewster] and hope to see more. We *Paganinied* it last night; tomorrow the tunnel, and on Sunday I have asked Lord Oxmantown and H[enry] F[ox] Talbot and [. . .] Musgrave to meet him here at breakfast and then visit the machine which progresses well. He has been making some queer discoveries on the spectrum.

Babbage's parties were large affairs, designed to entertain friends and influence reluctant politicians in his efforts to raise capital to develop his Difference Engine, the most complex piece of mechanical equipment yet made. The Difference Engine was a calculating machine intended ultimately to be the size of a large garden shed. Made of many thousands of individually crafted or die-stamped parts, the machine carried out through the crank of a handle complex mathematical and logarithmic calculations. The Difference Engine was not just a big toy: what it could do was to make tables of longitude, lunar phases, the movements of the stars, the planets and the tides that reached a level of accuracy and reliability that had never before been matched by clerks and mathematicians scratching their quill pens and doing their sums by hand. It was an essential piece of equipment for successful social and technical development, particularly as Zerah Colburn's feats of memory could not yet be bottled and carried in the pocket. Accurate tables were of critical importance because on them depended, for example, the safety of ships at sea. Tables of longitude told the captain where he and his ship were in relation to a shoal of rocks on the map, and on safety at sea depended the nation's security, self-esteem, social cohesion and wealth. By April

1829 Babbage had spent nearly £4,000 of his own money on developing the Engine, with an additional £3,000 being granted by the Treasury. This was soon spent and, after successfully lobbying the Duke of Wellington in 1829, he received a further £7,500 of government money.

Babbage's triumph in capturing this support was the event that led Chantrey to urge him to 'rejoice in your success with the Prime Minister'. He gave parties not only at his home in Dorset Street, near Manchester Square, but on an occasion in 1832 around 180 people came at his invitation to hired rooms at Sir Hugh Myddleton's Inn at New River Head. There he displayed his Difference Engine. He told John Herschel: 'I propose that the Calculating Engine shall hold a Drawing Room but of this you shall have more notice . . . A part of the engine, 15 figures, is quite completed and stands in a glass case in my library. It will make cubes, eat a bit of its tail, and tabulate queer functions.'

There were dozens of people at each of Babbage's events. Charles Lyell confided to Charles Darwin, 'Babbage's parties are the best in the way of literary people in London – and . . . there is a good mixture of pretty women.' The rooms in his house in Dorset Street 'were ordinary rooms, with folding doors, not large or handsomely furnished', with a working section of the Difference Engine gleaming in polished brass in one of the rooms, and, after 1834 when he bought her at auction from Weekes's mechanical exhibition in Cockspur Street, a shining silver clockwork woman in the other. 'This figure moved her arms and head most gracefully, and even moved her eyes, and almost smiled, as if she was amused with your astonishment.' Most guests preferred the dancing woman to the Difference Engine: on one evening only two foreign visitors admired the Engine, while everybody else crowded to watch the dancer. 'In that room – England,' Babbage remarked. 'Look again at this – two foreigners.'

One of Babbage's youngest guests was Mary Potter, already a good friend of Samuel Rogers, and a regular habituée of London drawing rooms: 'a shy young girl expecting to meet a "Lion"'. She was the daughter of the Rev. John Phillips Potter of Kensington Square, a subscriber to the Royal Institution, and an attender of lectures there. In *Sunny Memories* she recalled some of the many distinguished people she met at Babbage's, evoking an Elysian Field full of the great and the good. Her large cast of men and women who impressed her includes Ada Lovelace, David Livingstone, Edwin Landseer, Charles Dickens, Archbishop Richard Whately, Sir Charles Eastlake, J. M. W. Turner, Samuel Rogers, the historian Henry Hallam, Sir Charles and Lady Lyell, the educationist Leonard Horner and his family, the physician James Carrick Moore and his artist daughter Harriet Moore, the poet Barry Cornwall, Lady Davy, Lady Chantrey, Caroline Norton and 'many others well known in London society'.

Mary Potter discovered that Babbage had come to organise his soirées to entertain his aged mother, and to give his mother some idea of the extraordinary range of people he was mixing with. He sat her in a chair in a corner of the drawing room, 'and then she could see the guests I had invited without the fatigue of conversing with them'. Babbage took Mary under his wing, and advised her to attend carefully to what went on around her, and to have a notebook handy. 'If a thing occurs once,' he told her, 'it is an *incident*; if twice it is a *coincident*; and if it occurs three times, note it, examine it well, for on it may possibly hang a discovery useful to mankind.' Mary could have found Babbage something of a pedant, but does not admit to have done so. He assured her that his Difference Engine would 'analyse everything, and reduce everything to its first principles and so include future inventions, and in short almost supersede the human mind . . . It will even analyse wit.' 'How would it do that?' Mary asked him. 'It will divide wit into two kinds,' Babbage persevered boldly. '"Exaggeration" is Sydney Smith's favourite kind of wit, "Sympathy with the wrong object" is another,' he said, and proceeded to give examples. One might think he was teasing her; but actually he was being perfectly serious, if not seriously misguided. Babbage believed that everything in life and nature was susceptible to clear mathematical analysis.

A more considered account of the Difference Engine, the 'Leviathan', as Babbage called it, came from the American historian and professor of literature, George Ticknor, on a visit to London in 1835. He was given an introduction to the invention,

by [Babbage's] special invitation . . . I must say, that during an explanation which lasted between two and three hours, given by himself
with great spirit, the wonder at its incomprehensible powers grew
upon us every moment. The first thing that struck me was its small
size, being only about two feet wide, two feet deep, and two and a
half high. The second very striking circumstance was the fact that the
inventor himself does not profess to know all the powers of the
machine; that he has sometimes been quite surprised at some of its
capabilities; and that without previous calculation he cannot always
tell whether it will, or will not work out a given table. The third was
that he can set it to do a certain regular operation, as, for instance,
counting 1, 2, 3, 4; and then determine that, at any given number, say
the 10,000th, it shall *change* and take a different ratio, like triangular
numbers, 1, 3, 6, 9, 12, etc; and afterwards at any other given point,
say, 10,550, change again to another ratio. The whole, of course,
seems incomprehensible, without the exercise of volition and
thought.

Babbage was relentless in advocating the intricacies and the purpose of his invention, and never missed an opportunity to talk about
it. The German traveller Friedrich von Raumer was sceptical: 'Mr
Babbage would have been burned for a conjuror a few centuries
ago,' he wrote in 1835. When Babbage explained it to the Duke of
Wellington, he found himself to be at a loss for the right kind of
analogy for the 'almost innumerable combinations' that the machine
could handle, 'a number so vast, that no human mind could examine them all'. Then inspiration struck him: 'a similar difficulty must
present itself to a general commanding a vast army, when about to
engage in a conflict'. 'I know that difficulty well,' responded the
Duke. Visiting Paris, Babbage met the Empress Eugénie. 'Oh Mr
Babbage,' she chided, 'I cannot think how you can devote so much
time to figures, they are so *dull*.' 'Precisely, your Majesty, because
they *are* so dull, I thought I would invent a machine to do the
work.'

Guests came alone and in groups to Babbage's. William and Mary
Somerville accompanied Ada Byron, later Lady Lovelace, who one
evening found herself stranded: 'If you are going to Mr Babbage's
tonight, will you do me so great a favour as to call for me at 10

Wimpole Street, and take me there. I am at a loss for a chaperone, or should not have taken such a liberty. I particularly want to talk to you about something else.' Ada must have first attended a Babbage soirée in March 1834, when the mathematician invited her through the 'rare and priceless' Charlotte Murchison, who saved her husband, the geologist Roderick Murchison, from a life of profligacy, indolence and debt. Ada and Babbage became close friends, and by November Babbage, having recognised Ada's mathematical dexterity, lent his printed and illustrated account of the Difference Engine for her to study. The following season, Babbage invited Ada again. 'I hope you intend to patronise the "Silver Lady". She is to appear in new dresses and decorations.' Charlotte Murchison could find no words to describe the Difference Engine when she confided to Mary Somerville: 'I saw [Mrs Charles Lyell] at a soirée Babbage gave to his *fair* admirers (great & little), to introduce them to the Machine. It looked bright in a glass case, & this is all *I* can say for it. *You* would have been more worthy of its performances.'

Babbage's friends worried about his becoming exhausted by the strain of developing and displaying his Difference Engine. Mary Somerville tried to tell him to take care, writing in 1836 to tell Ada how ill Babbage was looking: 'I do fear the Machine will be the death of him, for certain I am that the human machine cannot stand that restless energy of mind which all but persecutes him.' Ada Byron began to make a habit of going to Babbage's with the Somervilles. She asked them in November 1834 to pick her up at Wimpole Street on their way to Dorset Street from Chelsea, so that their carriages could go in convoy; and the following season, having spotted the Somervilles in Albemarle Street on their way to a Thursday morning 'Drawing Room', probably one of John Murray's parties, she asked if they would take her to Babbage's the following Sunday. Ada Byron was intense by nature. A highly articulate, overwrought mathematical genius from a high social background, she attended lectures at the Royal Institution, routs in glittering ballrooms, soirées at Babbage's, and, aged seventeen in 1833, was presented to the King and Queen at court. Her natural brilliance in the abstract language of mathematics that few understood, her disturbed upbringing as

Byron's daughter and the elevated position in society that it was her lot to display and maintain created a confused and uncertain young woman. 'You know I am a d—d odd animal!' she wrote to Mary Somerville's son Woronzow Greig. 'But if you knew one half of the *harum-scarum* extraordinary things I do, you would certainly incline to the idea that I have a spell of *some* sorts about me. I am positive that no other *she* creature of *my years* <u>could</u> possibly attempt many of my everyday performances with any impunity.' It was a rare piece of real good fortune for Ada, however, that she had the sensible and structured example of Mary and William Somerville's family life to balance her self-absorption, the insistence of her many suitors, and Charles Babbage's frantic self-certainty. 'I hope you still find pleasure and improvement in the lectures,' Mary Somerville asked her with concern.

Mary Greig, the elegant and eligible Scottish widow, and William Somerville had married in Edinburgh in 1812. When William was appointed principal inspector to the Army Medical Board four years later they moved to London with Mary's two sons and their own two daughters to a house in Hanover Square. Mary was lionised among her scientist contemporaries when in February 1826 she became the first woman to present a paper to the Royal Society outlining her controversial findings on the apparent magnetism of the colour violet in the spectrum. As a woman however she was not permitted by the rules of the Royal Society to present the paper herself, so it was read on her behalf by her husband, who was a Fellow. Mary Somerville's book *The Mechanism of the Heavens*, published in 1831, confirmed her brilliance, which matched her charm, her beauty and the delight of her company. Everybody loved Mary. The writer Maria Edgeworth described her as being 'naturally modest with a degree of self-possession through it which . . . adds a prepossessing charm to her manner and takes off all the dread of her superior scientific learning'.

So concerned was Maria Edgeworth that Mary should always appear at her best when attending parties, she knitted her a pair of 'little bootikins . . . to be drawn over dress shoes to keep them from wet or dirt in getting in and out of a carriage'. The naval captain and author Basil Hall was overcome with the elegance of *Mechanism of the Heavens* when Mary Somerville sent him a draft copy:

The style is easy, clear and vigorous; it flows along . . . like one of your own Planets . . . Knowledge is power, they say – but that power is not always the power of expression: and you are therefore most happy in possessing both in a degree which enables you to give others so much information in such an agreeable shape.

This was one of many such notes that Mary Somerville received from baffled men, a river of congratulation that became a torrent when her *On the Connexions of the Physical Sciences* was published in 1834. It became an immediate bestseller. The President of the Royal Academy, Martin Archer Shee, thanked her for a copy of *Mechanism of the Heavens* in a convoluted and anxious manner: 'Humble a man of art as I am, I absolutely begin to suppose myself a man of Science on the strength of the distinction which you have conferred on me.'

It was a serious loss to the brightness of London's social and intellectual sparkle when in 1837, having found they had been swindled by a cousin, the Somervilles could no longer afford to live in Hanover Square. Mary was forced the following year to mortgage her copyright in *On the Connexions of the Physical Sciences* to John Murray to raise money, and pay off a loan that the publisher had made to her husband. William Somerville, physician to the Royal Hospital in Chelsea, took his family to live in this unregarded and insanitary village far from the centre of fashion. When the Somervilles' financial crisis turned into a disaster, and William became ill in 1838, the family left England for a peripatetic life in Italy. During their few years in Hanover Square, the Somervilles were loved and attended, and Mary's affection treasured. When in 1834 the physician Henry Holland became engaged to Sydney Smith's daughter Saba he told Mary that he hoped that 'if [Saba] is not already your friend . . . she will become it'. Charles Lyell the geologist, while revealing the pressure that the social roundabout placed upon those in demand, reflected on the wider feelings for Mary Somerville: 'I shall be happy to come on Wednesday. I will also continue to get to Lady Davy's Sunday Evening though I unfortunately dine at Clapham. I am glad she keeps you in countenance in spending Sunday Evening and part of Monday Morning in so rational a way.' The Somervilles were not, however, at the pinnacle of the invitation tree – if a better, or higher, invitation came along they could be sidelined rapidly, as Edward Nares had implied. William Wollaston performed this social sidestep, as he told Chantrey:

> Having found no difficulty in extricating myself from my engagement to the Somervilles so that I could make my movements accord better with the plans of Lord Essex, I have determined upon going to Cassiobury on Sunday. I must therefore endeavour to find you at home at some earlier hour than we agreed upon, & shall hope to be with you about 1 o'clock, unless by return of post I receive a forbidding line.

Running alongside the parties given by artists and scientists were those which added writers to the cultural mix. One particular focus for these was the Royal Society of Literature, founded in 1823, which held monthly meetings first in Lincoln's Inn Fields and latterly St Martin's Place. Its charter directed it to advance the study of literature, to publish obscure and uncommercial texts, 'and to preserve the purity of the English language'. London needed an equivalent of the French Academy of Belles Lettres, it was argued, and this reached the ears of George IV. With an upsurge of enthusiasm, the King propelled the Society into being with the promise of 1,000 guineas a year to be paid as pensions for authors. William Jerdan was one of the co-founders of the Society, and early members included John Britton, Francis Chantrey, Samuel Taylor Coleridge and John Murray, who published the Society's *Transactions*. Jerdan was also closely connected to the management of the Royal Literary Fund, a body established in 1790 to assist writers suffering financial hardship. 'The literary man', Jerdan wrote, 'is the Saint Sebastian of his days, stript and bound for every cruel hand to shoot an arrow into him.' Jerdan instanced Thomas Moore, 'courted and flattered by the high and fair for many a bright year', who lived his final years in a 'lowly Wiltshire cottage'; Thomas Campbell who could 'scarcely have kept a decent house over his head' but for income from the periodical press; and John Britton who, aged eighty in the 1850s, was 'much consoled by the grant of even a paltry pension'. Cyrus Redding wrote about the gatherings of literary men and women, some of whom would come to be grateful to the Royal Literary Fund's work:

Mr Soane used to receive parties at his home in Lincoln's Inn Fields, and Mr Britton, who was then labouring at his Cathedral Antiquities, gave breakfast parties. The great bookselling houses, too, kept up their old customs of dinners on stated days where there was much agreeable intercourse . . . I remember Godwin at some of these parties, Archdeacon [Robert] Nares, [Henry] Bone the enamel painter, and some distinguished men. There was then much society and little jealousy among literary persons.

Redding noticed Samuel Taylor Coleridge at some of these gatherings. He 'sacrificed his eminent abilities to his love of conversation . . . rich with ideas – soap-bubbles, brilliant with colour, and sparkling with light, which flashed upon the vision a moment and vanished'. That corroborates a view of Coleridge which the historian and essayist Thomas Carlyle put even more tartly than did Redding: 'Never did I see such apparatus got ready for thinking, and so little thought. He mounts scaffolding, pulleys, and tackle, gathers all the tools in the neighbourhood with labour, with noise, demonstration, precept, abuse, and sets – three bricks.' Redding recorded that Walter Scott spoke with an English northern dialect, rather than 'Scotch', and, quoting Byron, remarked on Samuel Rogers's 'epigrammatic mouth – a mouth characterised by a contractile quality, the power of a sort of pincer's squeeze lurks about it'. Rogers had moved into 22 St James's Place in 1803, and lived there until he died, giving breakfast parties to eager and flattered guests. A speciality of his was Americans – he entertained literary figures who sailed into London from the United States, including Washington Irving and one much younger American, the author Herman Melville, who noted with a cruel accuracy in 1849, 'for all the pomp and splendour of his social life, he was a shy man and a frightened man, one who knew all too well the extreme thinness of his own talent'.

People like Cyrus Redding – and there were other people like Redding, observant, catty, probably reasonably reliable, such as Thomas Carlyle, William Jerdan and Joseph Farington – hand down the life-blood of early-nineteenth-century London gatherings, and give us insights that have survived only because they were set down hot. Of Madame de Staël, Redding remarked that her drawing room was a daily levée. 'All the world went to see her, and she to see all the world.' Walking home late at night, Redding evoked London in the small hours, and described the silence of the streets in contrast to the noisy tumult of a party he had just left,

> when, in a moonlight morning, at two or three o'clock, I traversed the streets of London. There was no murmuring of the waves, no brilliant scenery of nature to be observed, it is true, but I imagined myself in a city of the dead, in streets of catacombs, where all before had been noisy and animated . . . Under the old *régime* of watchmen, who were generally in comfort asleep in their boxes, as the pedestrian paced homewards, the silence and the similitude were more perfect. There are few things more impressive, except it be the same city at sun-rise, from the top of St Paul's; but that is more of real vision than deceptive reality, for we seem beyond all connection with things below.

Thomas Carlyle took a more jaundiced view as he walked home at the same sort of hour:

> The world looks often quite spectral to me; sometimes, as in Regent Street the other night (my nerves being all shattered), quite hideous, discordant, almost infernal. I had been at Mrs Austin's, heard Sydney Smith for the first time guffawing, other persons prating, jargoning. To me through these thin cobwebs Death and Eternity sate glaring. Coming homewards along Regent Street, through street-walkers, through – *Ach Gott!* unspeakable pity swallowed up unspeakable abhorrence of it and of myself. The moon and the serene nightly sky in Sloane Street consoled me a little. Smith, a mass of fat and muscularity, with massive Roman nose, piercing hazel eyes, huge cheeks, shrewdness and fun, not humour or even wit, seemingly without soul altogether. Mrs Marcet ill-looking, honest, rigorous, commonplace. The rest babble, babble. Woe's me that I in Meshech am! To work.

Carlyle claimed to hate dinner parties, his dissident, dyspeptic, calcu-latedly disagreeable manner generating a sourness which energised him. The American writer Ralph Waldo Emerson described him as 'the voice of London – a true Londoner with no sweet country breath in him'. After dining 'greatly against wont' with Samuel Rogers, the Rev. Henry Milman, Rector of St Margaret's, Westminster, Charles Dickens, Charles Lyell, Charles

Babbage and 'sundry indifferent-favoured women. A dull evening', Carlyle wrote to his brother: 'Babbage continues eminently unpleasant to me, with his frog mouth and viper eyes, with his hidebound wooden irony, and the acridest egoism looking thro' it.' But Carlyle would pick and choose where he went, and whom he called upon. Having had a 'small quiet party, and . . . blithe serious talk' one evening, he called on Harriet Martineau who was also giving a soirée. 'There were fat people, and fair people, lords and others, fidgeting, elbowing; all very *braw*, and hot: "*What's ta use on't?*" I said to myself, and came off *early*, while they were still arriving, at eleven at night!' Then he went home to Chelsea, and to his wife Jane, dreaming of how he preferred to end the day, 'a book at home . . . with a quiet pipe twice in the evening; innocent "spoonful of porridge" at ten, and bed at eleven in such composure as one can'.

The most popular and best-attended gatherings were those in which the host, like Ackermann, Pettigrew, Hope and Sass, had a collection to show off. An idiosyncratic private collection of antique sculpture fragments and architectural offcuts of great quantity had been assembled by Sir John Soane in the incomparable setting of his house in Lincoln's Inn Fields. Once a private house, this is now a singular public museum. Sir John Soane's house is a warren of rooms and passages on the ground floor, the entrance hall only very gradually widening from the front door to the curving stair. Then a turn to the right takes the visitor to the dining room and library, with its glazed book and display cases, busts on corbels and trio of arches suspended in the air. A door from the dining room leads to the breakfast room where mirrors lurk in spandrels, a Roman lamp hangs from the cupola, and there is a plethora of neo-classical decoration. The ceiling, resting neatly on discreet and practically invisible mirrored columns, hangs above the visitor like the inside of his or her own skull. Beyond the breakfast room runs what is perhaps the busiest corridor in the western world, busy not from people going to and fro, but from the fragments of architectural carving – triglyph, anthemion, dentil and swag, urns, bits of leg and foot, a head or two, some nymphs and an acanthus-rich Corinthian column supporting nothing. And so the little house goes on, with a tantalising glimpse beyond of a painting by Canaletto, a Hogarth or two and perhaps the lingering shade of a hermit. Johann Passavant wrote in 1831:

> These various objects of virtù, for which enormous sums have been paid by their owner, are disposed with the greatest attention to the picturesque, in the small space allotted to them. The assortment of such heterogeneous articles, with the striking effect produced by the architectural fragments, heightened by a most skilful arrangement of light, form a coup d'oeil which can ill be described.

Soane was as learned and passionate a collector as he was an architect, and, while bad-tempered and vain, he had a steely determination to acquire what he wanted and to reject what he disliked. He generously supported the Royal Literary Fund, but threatened in 1836 to withdraw in fury when he took grave exception to a portrait painted of him by Daniel Maclise, and hung by the Fund in its boardroom. 'Sir John will not live or die in peace with the Society,' Britton told Jerdan, 'unless it be exchanged – he is *violent* on the subject.' Jerdan resolved the issue by cutting the portrait into shreds, an act which caused ribald comment in the press and this poetic squib in *The Ingoldsby Legends*:

> Ochone! Ochone!
> For the portrait of Soane,
> J[erdan]! you ought to have let it alone;
> Don't you see that instead or removing the bone
> Of contention, the apple of discord you've thrown?
> One general moan,
> Like a tragedy groan,
> Burst forth when the picturecide deed became known.

Soane was an impressive party-giver. He gave one particularly memorable entertainment on three successive evenings in late March 1825 to his wide circle of friends, acquaintances and influential power-brokers. The main reason for the party was for Soane to show off the sarcophagus of the Egyptian pharaoh Seti I, which had been discovered in 1817 by the circus-performer and 'Patagonian Sampson', who had latterly turned archaeological obsessive, Giovanni Battista Belzoni. The sarcophagus had been offered to the

British Museum in 1821 for £2,000, but the trustees declined it. Soane, who had second refusal, stepped in and paid up. Though his life and achievements would have been much discussed during the evenings, Belzoni had been dead two years. Soane's event was planned both to show the sarcophagus and to benefit Belzoni's widow. It was a rare event. Few parties bringing together the intelligentsia of London matched its combination of the exotic, the glamorous, the dramatic, the mysterious. If Haydon's was the 'Immortal Dinner', this must have been the 'Immortal Three-Day Event'.

The guests mainly assembled upstairs, in the yellow drawing room, for where else apart from the library could they comfortably have stood in such numbers – four or five hundred people seem to have been present on at least one of the evenings. Today, the maximum allowed in the building at any one time is eighty. The star attraction of the party, Seti's sarcophagus, lay brooding in the basement. All or most braved the narrow steps to find it, for, with the house as a whole, it had been dramatically lit by lamplight under Soane's direction. Benjamin Robert Haydon was among the guests, and he left a vivid account of the evening he was there:

> The first person I met . . . was . . . Coleridge . . . [then] I was pushed up against Turner, the landscape painter with his red face and white waistcoat, and . . . was carried off my legs, and irretrievably bustled to where the sarcophagus lay . . . It was the finest fun imaginable to see the people come into the Library after wandering about below, amidst tombs and capitals, and shafts, and noseless heads, with a sort of delighted relief at finding themselves among the living, and with coffee and cake. Fancy delicate ladies of fashion dipping their pretty heads into an old mouldy, fusty, hierogliphicked coffin, blessing their stars at its age, wondering whom it contained . . . Just as I was beginning to meditate, the Duke of Sussex, with a star on his breast, and an asthma inside it, came squeezing and wheezing along the narrow passage, driving all the women before him like a Blue-Beard, and, putting his royal head into the coffin, added his wonder to the wonder of the rest.

More modest and very much shyer than the rumbustious Haydon was another guest, Mary Anne Turner. She told her father Dawson

Turner all about the hubbub and the crush, and described the crowds of carriages, and the policemen, and the 'living throng' which was itself 'as interesting and as diversified as the decoration which covered the walls'. Mary Anne spotted the painters C. R. Leslie, Thomas and William Daniell, Richard Reinagle, William Newton; the architect C. R. Cockerell, the engravers John Landseer, John Britton and Henry Le Keux. There was Samuel Rogers, who made a profession of party-going, and ministers and statesmen including the current Prime Minister, Lord Liverpool, and a future Prime Minister, Robert Peel. 'They formed a distinct group by themselves, and moved about in a compact body, and Mr Soane attended upon them and was their cicerone.' Then there were:

> *fine ladies & gentlemen*, [who] only gazed slightly about, and supplied the air of fashion in dress and in appearance – but there was a great preponderance of *character* and great variety of expression in the motley crowd of inferior authors, and translators and magazine compilers . . . The action and expression and dress of these less brilliant stars was not chastised into the uniformity and decorum observable in those of greater magnitude, and therefore it was the more piquant . . . There were several foreigners made evident by their air and dress, and in the buzz of voices I frequently caught words of French and Italian. But the finest living sight was an Egyptian Moslem who stood looking with sulky pleasure upon his fellow countryman, the sarcophagus. This very interesting monument was placed in a ground floor apartment, which is surrounded & overlooked by the upper rooms. We staid about two hours but so short a view of this immense collection was only tantalizing. I could have great pleasure spending a month there.

Haydon and Coleridge, Turner and the Duke of Sussex, Samuel Rogers, John Landseer, the Prime Minister Lord Liverpool, Robert Peel, C. R. Cockerell and John Britton: all these men and hundreds of other 'fine ladies & gentlemen' gathered together under the London lamplights in John Soane's house. With in addition a 'motley crowd of inferior authors, and translators and magazine compilers' Soane's three-day party for Mrs Belzoni was a classic of early-nineteenth-century metropolitan entertainment, at once a prototype, an exemplar and a measure.

7

Every Tool Had a Purpose

~

ALEXANDER GALLOWAY, MACHINIST and engineer, 69 High Holborn, fired off a strongly worded letter in November 1814 to Stephen Peter Rigaud, Professor of Geometry at Oxford: 'It was to oblige you that I took [this trifling order] in hand. I have written first last very near 20 letters on this business and it is this great trouble that deters one to undertake such a job of its . . . magnitude because they are always attend[ed] with loss.' What had appeared to be a straightforward order for an accurate steam-driven saw became complex and time-consuming. This was a small job for Galloway, an active and ambitious engineer–businessman who employed dozens of men in his factory. He catered for a growing demand for the supply of technical equipment, a result of the compound interest in learning and understanding in science, translated into technical and mechanical activity. As his advertisements revealed, Galloway made 'Machinery constructed and manufactured for experimental and scientific elucidation to any scale of magnitude. Steam engines made on any principle to order . . . Variety of tool chests for Gentlemen, Portable Forges of Iron . . . Cranes and Jibs, Jacks, Blocks and Pullies for lifting heavy weights.' Everything, from the screws needed to bolt the saw mill together to the mahogany frame and the blades of the saw, was made in the factory: raw material and men went in; working machine tools came out. By the mid-1820s, Galloway had become one of the largest employers in London, with about eighty men on his payroll.

Running a successful factory was second nature to Galloway, and when his dealing with Rigaud went sour he hit back to protect his good reputation. He did eventually supply Rigaud with the new equipment which included, as the invoice reads, 'an Iron Bench with parallel and angle cutting apparatus, spindle, pulley, Iron poppet Heads, two saws, a mahogany bolted frame, and 4 screws and nuts to fix the Mill to a stone floor, and two Keys for the different screws of Mill: £26.10.0'. With a wrought-iron frame, clutch apparatus, repairs, cleaning and lacquering to parts of the existing steam engine, miscellaneous bits and pieces and transport to Oxford, the whole order came to £51 0s 6d. The elegantly set-out invoice and the increasingly terse letters Galloway sent to his irritable customer in Oxford reveal an effective businessman unafraid of confrontation. Fed up with Rigaud's pernickety attitude, he fired off a final broadside:

> The flywheel of your engine is preposterously too large namely 2 feet 10 inches diam. Pray Sir by what principle of fatality was I to know this . . . You surely ought to have known all these particulars, before you ordered attachments to your Engine . . . I have had a great deal of trouble and devoted a great deal of time one way and another about this trifling order.

Galloway was far more than an efficient, skilled and impatient employing engineer. As a leading member of the London Corresponding Society he was influential, radical, brave and eloquent. This group was formed in 1792 to campaign for improved conditions for working people, to extend the franchise and to rid parliament of corruption and misrepresentation. Ultimately its work would lead to the passing of the Reform Bill in 1832. Galloway was described by one of the Corresponding Society's leading figures, Francis Place, as 'one of the cleverest men' in the Society. He was among those who in 1795 attempted to present a petition for parliamentary reform to the Home Secretary, Henry Dundas, thirty-seven years before the Reform Act came into effect. Galloway became President of the London Corresponding Society in 1797, aged only twenty-one, and when the principle of habeas corpus (no imprisonment without trial) was suspended the following year, he spent nearly two years in Newgate Prison. He had a broad and ruminative definition of radicalism, which he expressed to Francis Place, as the motive power required 'to assist the grand work of national regeneration', and to promote 'the cause of truth'. Galloway remained active

as a radical, having in 1815 successfully led a campaign to end restrict-
ive and outmoded apprenticeship clauses in the 250-year-old Statute
of Artificers. He was described in 1826 as 'a man entirely devoted to
the cause of freedom, and possessing great influence in the election
of the members of Parliament, in London and its environs.'

Being an active campaigning voice for engineering in London,
Galloway was invited to give evidence to the 1824 Parliamentary
Select Committee on Artizans and Machinery. This had been set up
to meet the growing disquiet at the continuous draining away from
Britain to the continent and America of engineering expertise, and
the flagrant pirating abroad of designs for machine tools. British
machine manufacture was hampered by this and yet more outmoded
practices, such as the export ban, dating from the eighteenth-century
wars with France, on some classes of machinery. Galloway explained
to the committee that he had many times presented himself at the
Custom House by London Bridge to try to convince customs officers that the export of such-and-such a piece of machinery would
not harm British interests abroad. It was becoming increasingly the
case that the difficulties of export were actively injuring the national
economy, and that the law was more honoured in the breach than
the observance. Galloway cited how he was currently manufacturing
'one of the largest presses ever made in England', for packing cotton,
for an Egyptian customer whom he did not name, but who was
none other than Mehmet Ali Pasha, the Ottoman Turkish Viceroy of
Egypt. He applied for special permission to export the press, which
was granted: 'that is, in plain English, permission to offend the law'.

It was part of Galloway's contract with the customer that his own
employees, the men who had made the machinery, had themselves
to travel abroad to erect it in the customers' works and to set it
going. This was one of his problems with Rigaud: Galloway had sent
a man to Oxford, but because the new parts would not work with
the old, the machinery could not be assembled. Given the state of
the law which banned Britons from travelling abroad to erect
machinery, Galloway and other engineers had to pretend that their
employees were travelling for reasons other than their proper business. Some employees just did not come back. Galloway had visited
Paris in 1823 and was astonished at the progress France had made in

manufacture since the end of the Napoleonic Wars. 'There were specimens of excellence as I have never seen surpassed in this country,' he told the committee, adding that 'a great many of the most considerable manufactories in the neighbourhood of Paris are conducted by Englishmen; at Chaillot, at Charenton, and several on the banks of the Seine, where from 1000 to 1200 engineers are employed; and I have no doubt that in Paris alone there is from 3000 to 4000 working engineers'. The engineering now being produced in Paris was being largely managed by Britons, and, according to Galloway, was of a standard comparable to English-made machinery.

One of the causes of this dangerous state of affairs for British technology was the very success and the international respect of scientific societies and, in particular, the Society of Arts. The Society's annual *Transactions* published measured plans of prize-winning machinery in such detail that anybody with any basic mechanical skill could build the machines anywhere in the world, with no credit needing to be given to the inventors. Galloway's colleague the engineer Bryan Donkin, then the chairman of the Committee of Mechanics of the Society of Arts, gave a further clear answer to questioning by the parliamentary committee when asked about the distribution of Society of Arts *Transactions*:

'Do not these volumes circulate all over the world?'

'Yes,' Donkin replied.

'Cannot an able workman, from those plans and specifications, produce or make the machinery there described?'

'Most undoubtedly.'

'Is it not the policy of our laws prohibiting machinery therefore at variance with the whole proceedings of that society and other scientific societies existing in this country?'

'Entirely so.'

The assembly and wide distribution of information, the driving purpose of the Society of Arts, acted against the law of the land, and created a situation that was ludicrous and damaging, and could not be maintained.

In the 1760s and 1770s British mechanical engineers had created the market for steam power-production, and, without any significant foreign competition, had taken it to the world. Engineering companies had ridden this surging wave ever since. Matthew Boulton, whose partnership with James Watt created the mechanical engineering company which dominated the late-eighteenth-cen tury market in steam engines, welcomed visitors to his Soho works in Birmingham from Europe and further afield: 'I had lords and ladies to wait on yesterday. I have Spaniards today; and tomorrow I shall have Germans, Russians and Norwegians.' Boulton's charm and enthusiasm as a guide around his works, and his energy as a sales-man, found customers for his steam engines in Coalbrookdale, Cornwall, Derbyshire, Lancashire, Leicestershire, Staffordshire, Tyneside, Yorkshire and London. Wherever water needed to be pumped, there were Boulton and Watt engines hammering away at the job. Rapidly, Boulton's salesmanship opened up foreign markets all around the world's trade routes – Paris, where they pumped the city's water supply, Naples, St Petersburg, Madras. The results of Boulton's entrepreneurship were clearly visible in London – there were Boulton and Watt engines in Whitbread's brewery, the Straw Paper Mill at Millbank, the Albion Mill at Lambeth and in dozens of other places. But Boulton's vision went further. In harnessing his machines for commercial production, he sold the manufactured goods, from pressed buttons to fine plated candlesticks, in the nation's shops. And yet further, from the mints in London and Birmingham, his engines produced the coins which rattled in the pockets of all, to be spent in shops and markets and to create the medium for a fluid economy. By 1821, the London Mint expected to produce 200,000 guinea coins every week.

London had been the site of the most ambitious experiment in steam-powered mass-production: by the southern end of Blackfriars Bridge, Boulton and a group of City moneymen built in the mid-1780s Albion Mill, a four-storey flour mill designed with arches and columns to resemble a grand country house. So high was it that the artist–entrepreneur Robert Barker used its roof as the viewpoint for the first painted panorama of London, exhibited in 1792. Behind the façade of Albion Mill, however, were two Boulton and Watt fifty-horsepower steam engines, which lifted to the top of the building sacks of corn delivered by barges on the river below. They fanned, sifted and dressed the corn for production, drove twenty pairs of millstones to grind it to flour, and finally lowered the flour into barges and carts for distribution. When the stones were running at speed the building and the ground around it shivered. Albion Mill was the very pinnacle of late-eighteenth-century industrial production, which, on the pretext of feeding the people, sucked up arable production, forced down the price of wheat, and threatened to put farmers, merchants and windmillers out of work. On 2 March 1791 the mill caught fire; grindstones crashed through the burning floors and smashed to bits; the flames lit the sky for hours; farmers, merchants, millers and the mob danced with glee, and in the Leverian Museum near by exhibits were wreathed in an intermediate tincture of smoke. The building was left a blackened festering ruin to seep gradually into the mind of London, and to become one of the inspirations for William Blake's phrase 'dark, Satanic mills'.

A commercial disaster though this was, what also went up in smoke with Boulton's ambition as an industrial miller was the pair of James Watt's double-acting steam engines. Mechanical engineers remembered these machines with admiration, because they were the perfected engines from which all others sprang. Writing more than fifty years later in his *Treatise on the Steam Engine*, the engineer John Bourne recalled that the Albion Mill engines 'contained all the improvements . . .[and] are the type from which land engines, up to the present time, have been constructed . . . [They] have been very little exceeded in their performance by the best modern engines, which work with the same measure of expansion.'

While Boulton and Watt led the market in engines and their products at the turn of the century, by the 1820s the company was displaying, to their competitors at least, 'an uncommon degree of mystery', as Alexander Galloway put it in his evidence to the 1824 Select Committee. Matthew Boulton had died in 1809; the world had changed. Boulton and Watt's period of dominance of the market was over. The ebullient delight with which Matthew Boulton had shown all sorts and conditions of people over his works from the 1760s had been replaced by the stern pragmatism of his successors in the business: 'the Public are requested to observe that this manufactory cannot be shewn in consequence of any Application or recommendation whatever', ran the advertisement placed in the press by the company in 1802. So complete did this exclusion become that Galloway, who perhaps never knew the extent of Matthew Boulton's generosity of spirit, recalled that Boulton and Watt had 'always *shut* their works against any competent judge in England', adding, 'therefore foreigners have been no worse treated than anybody else; but my opinion is decidedly that [Boulton and Watt] have nothing to show beyond what is well known in other places; they continue from pride that exclusion which before was dictated by interest'.

Entrepreneurs and engineers alike saw the steam engine as the greatest invention of humanity, outshining all others in the extent of its transformation of civilisation. John Farey, a mechanical draughts-man, inventor and writer, and one of the most widely travelled engineers of his generation, published a treatise on steam engines, twenty years before John Bourne's, in which he saw the steam engine as surpassing the ship in significance in the scale of human invention: 'when we consider the steam-engine as a production of genius, it must be allowed to take the lead of all other inventions'. Driven by its endless possibilities, the steam engine spawned a chain-reaction of further combinations of cogs, cranks and axles, creating inventions with no known beginning and no apparent end. It released not only motive power, but also the imagination, ingenuity and ambition of craftsmen–engineers from the village forge to the factory drawing board. The intricacy of steam-driven machinery was overwhelming. A natural drive for greater efficiency and econ-omy prompted the evolution of complex mechanical parts each of which had one task only in the transfer of power: the easing of mechanical restriction, the richer employment of the last drop of steam, the staunching of escape, the storing of energy, the conversion of heat to work. And these early engines were efficient and prodi-giously powerful: a report on steam engines in Cornwall found in 1818 that one bushel of coal (that is, one-third of a sack) could power an engine to raise 23,005,446 pounds, more than 10,000 tons, of water one foot high.

When steam engines began to be applied to ships, however, the engineers had the new task of adapting a nervous, flailing machine to fit within the smooth form of a ship's hull, like a hermit crab into its shell. This was a problem that was not faced by land engines, which could sprawl as wide as they reasonably wished. Marine engines were steam engines with additional responsibility thrust upon them, machines which had come of age. All these small evolutionary steps within a multitude of extraordinary machines took place over let's say eighty to one hundred years, rather than the multi-million years of biological evolution. If in John Farey's view 'the steam-engine follows next to the ship in the scale of invention', the development of the marine engine was the greatest mechanical achievement of mankind before the aeroplane.

John Farey was fully aware of the steam engine's transforming power. Only the coming of the computer and the internet is comparable as a radical and bloodless intervention in the course of human history. Farey wrote in his *Treatise on the Steam Engine*, published in 1827, but written over the course of the preceding seven years,

> The productiveness of labour has been so greatly increased by this gigantic auxiliary, and by the improved system of manufactures and commerce to which it has given birth, that those conveniences of life, and attributes of wealth, which were formerly considered to be one of the distinctions of the first classes of the community, are now acknowledged to belong equally to that middle class which may be said to consist of labourers, who apply their minds to useful industry, instead of their hands.

Farey did not, however, seem quite able to engage the entire population, without exception, in the benefits of the steam engine. There is always a caveat: 'Unless the industry of the working class is systematically applied, and aided by the use of machines, there can be but little surplus wealth to maintain an educated class in society, and produce that state of general affluence which is conducive to the progress of civilisation, and the development of intellect.'

Farey was the exemplar of the early-nineteenth-century pluralist born of the cornucopia of opportunities that the steam engine presented. Nevertheless, he failed to imagine what social damage it might do. As well as being a distinguished and successful engineer who worked in Britain, France and Russia, he had interests in geology, surveying, astronomy and mathematics, wrote and drew with accuracy and invention for journals and encyclopaedias, and patented a number of his own inventions while also acting as a patent agent. He started early, initially working with his father, John Farey the elder, a musician, mathematician, geologist and surveyor, who won the medal for tree-planting at the Society of Arts in 1805. The younger John Farey filed his first patent at the age of fourteen, and was elected a member of the Society of Arts at fifteen, one of the youngest members ever. Having worked in Tiverton soon after he married, he spent two years in the mid-1820s managing the steam engines (Boulton and Watt, of course) in John Marshall's Flax Mill at Holbeck, Leeds. This was one of the most advanced of its kind, comparable in the 1820s Yorkshire clothing industry to the Albion Mill in 1780s London. Back in London, where he worked for the rest of his life, Farey became a sought-after engineering consultant, and appeared at many trials and public inquiries as an expert witness.

John Farey was a product of the first generation to benefit from the systematic broadening of access to artistic and scientific knowledge in London. With the added benefit of being the son of a sympathetic polymath, Farey took every advantage offered to him to broaden and express his education. He contributed articles to the *Transactions* of the Society of Arts and to the *Philosophical Magazine*, and wrote the entry on 'Steam Engines' in *Rees's Cyclopaedia* of 1816. He made drawings using the recently invented *camera lucida*, and designed a longer slide-rule for mathematical calculations, and a machine for drawing accurate ellipses. He is described in the *Oxford Dictionary of National Biography* (2004) as having interests ranging across 'engineering, chemistry, astronomy, mathematics, geography, geology and theology; and as a young man he was proficient in music, singing, painting and engraving. He was also a prolific writer . . .' With such a rich spread of talents to be nourished, London was the only place in Britain where Farey could truly shine.

By the 1820s Boulton and Watt's contemporaries and competitors in London alone included Alexander Galloway, who moved in 1821 from High Holborn to an enlarged works in Smithfield; Henry Maudslay, who was in partnership with Josiah Field at Westminster Bridge Road, Lambeth; Bryan Donkin, who developed paper-making machinery, food-canning processes and astronomical equipment from his works in Spa Lane, Bermondsey; Joseph Bramah, who developed complex locks, machine tools and a hydraulic press in his works at Eaton Street, Pimlico; Joseph Clement, a tool-maker of unbounded ingenuity who solved the manufacturing problems of Babbage's Difference Engine; John Braithwaite, whose steam engine the *Novelty* came a close second to Stephenson's *Rocket* in the Rainhill Trials in 1829; and Jacob Perkins, who emigrated to London from Philadelphia in 1819 to develop his techniques for printing engraved banknotes. Later Perkins diversified into the possibilities of steam power, notably a steam gun and refrigeration, and exhibited them at the privately owned museum of scientific endeavour, the National Gallery of Science, in Adelaide Street, off the Strand.

Engineering went down in families. Marc and Isambard Brunel were father and son. James Watt's father, also James, was a shipwright in Greenock; his son, James again, carried on as a director of Boulton and Watt. Bryan Donkin went into partnership with his son, as did Alexander Galloway and Henry Maudslay with theirs. John Farey's brothers and a nephew were engineers, and his second wife Elizabeth Pugsley worked beside them, with what was described as 'almost masculine scientific abilities'. The high capital investment, the long development time and the profession's overwhelming personal and physical demands on its members drove successful engineers to hand their achievements down to their sons, to keep fortune in the family and a name alive: thus Maudslay, Son and Field; Donkyn and Sons; Bramah and Sons; and countless others.

Alexander Galloway went from strength to strength after his move to Smithfield. To build his new factory, in which he claimed he had invested £30,000, he demolished an acre of property, including a large soap factory, some stables, warehouses, four houses in West Street, all the houses in the adjacent Thatch Alley, and Wright's and Hosier's buildings where there were 'crowded together about *400* inhabitants, chiefly composed of the lower Irish and their distressed families'. Galloway used, at his own estimate to the 1824 Select Committee, between 100 and 150 tons of bar iron a year to manufacture his products, and in the 'six or eight different branches' of his business, employed 'workers in wood . . . pattern makers . . . good cabinet makers, joiners, millwrights, and others employed in wood; iron and brass founders; smiths, firemen and hammermen . . . vice-men and filers; and brass, iron and wood turners in all their variety'. Despite his activities as a campaigner for reform and improved working conditions, Galloway was not universally liked by his employees. Joseph Clement, who had worked for him briefly in 1814, described him as 'only a mouthing common-council man, the height of whose ambition was to be an alderman'. Hardly fair, or indeed accurate. Clement walked out of Galloway's works, carrying his genius away with his toolbag, and rose rapidly first through Joseph Bramah's works, and then through Henry Maudslay's, before setting up on his own in Southwark where he came to revolutionise machine-tool design and manufacture.

Henry Maudslay, who also gave evidence to the 1824 Select Committee, had as a young man been Joseph Bramah's works manager until they fell out over pay. He had self-assurance, a good-natured temperament and, at six feet two inches tall, the physical presence to give him the confidence to set up on his own. This he did in 1797, initially making lathes and screw-thread cutters. In 1800 he began to work with Marc Isambard Brunel on the manufacture of ships' block-making machines, designed by Brunel to speed the production of wooden pulley-blocks for naval ships' rigging. Maudslay's ingenuity drew him to design precision instruments such as micrometer gauges which reached their apogee in the micrometer known as 'The Lord Chancellor'. This was called on as the final legal arbiter in engineering measurement disputes, having an accuracy of one-thousandth of an inch. Maudslay's smallest yet most influential innovation was the standardisation of screw and bolt threads so that every quarter-inch nut would attach to any quarter-inch bolt, non-negotiably, reliably and regularly. Charles Holtzapffel, the father and son of lathe-makers, and the author of a five-volume treatise on lathes and what they could do, held Maudslay in the highest esteem. He gave him the credit for effecting 'nearly the entire change from the old, imperfect and accidental practice of screw-making . . . to the modern, exact and systematic mode now generally followed by engineers; and he pursued the subject of the screw with more or less ardour, and at enormous expense, until his death in 1831'.

Maudslay diversified into marine engineering, making engines and paddle-wheels for many dozens of steamships of all sizes. Big engines could be manufactured in quantity only in wide, tall factories; and the fewer columns that were needed to support the roof, and interfere with the working space, the better. Thus wood gave way to iron for roofing in both Galloway's and Maudslay's works. When part of Galloway's new building collapsed during construction in 1824 the inquest on two dead men heard that the girders supporting the roof weighed about twenty-eight hundredweight each. Two years later, when Maudslay expanded, and his new factory extension fell down with about six or eight men dead and many more injured, the cause of the accident was in the weakness of the walls which 'appeared [to have] given way under the pressure of its ponderous roof'. These were very large buildings: Galloway's collapsed walls were about thirty feet high, and Maudslay's twenty feet, surrounding a factory one hundred by thirty to forty feet. To meet the demand of the market, to create engines of all sizes for pumping, draining, cutting, sawing, driving and paddling, and for anything else that moved or wanted to be moved, engineering works devoured the London streetscape, displacing families, demolishing acres of run-down property, and, in their hasty and untidy construction, sometimes demolishing themselves.

For the rapidly growing market for small-scale engines designed to perform modest quasi-domestic tasks, Maudslay developed a machine that sat on a small iron framework, or even a kitchen or workshop table. It was this compact little 'table engine', whose piston was set vertically above a low-slung central flywheel, that particularly impressed the German architect Karl Friedrich Schinkel when he visited London in June 1826. Calling at Maudslay's works, Schinkel remarked as he picked his way around the partly collapsed factory:

> [Maudslay] a stout, friendly man, his iron roof had collapsed, much damage. He took us round. A steam-engine, his own invention, with one cylinder takes up little room. Magnificent lathes, iron roofs. Iron vaulting. Iron staircases. The slender iron columns supporting the roof of one of the rooms also function as outlets for waste water. The

foundry is installed on an iron-and-brick vault; a roller which makes holes, slits and incisions, for nail holes in the steam boiler. A hammer simultaneously punching profiles, with a clamped head. A cut-off worm acts as a brake on the fall of the hammer.

Schinkel was one of a growing flood of continentals who came to London in the first decades of the nineteenth century to see and report what was going on in the acknowledged 'World City': others whom we have met in these pages include the Germans Johanna Schopenhauer, Friedrich von Raumer and Johann Passavant, the Italian Antonio Canova, and the French-American Louis Simond. Seeking trade as well as social and religious liberties, thousands followed in the wake of the peaceful Huguenot 'invasion' of a hundred years earlier and stayed on to set up their own businesses. Among the many that flourished were John Jacob Holtzapffel, Charles Holtzapffel's father, from Strasbourg, and George Deyerlein who had come to London in the 1790s. They worked together as lathe- and tool-makers in Long Acre, and subsequently Cockspur Street. Holtzapffel and Deyerlein made some of the most precise and reliable lathes for both amateur and tradesmen's use, the finest of them being built with mahogany or rosewood cases to resemble furniture of the highest quality. Before a Holtzapffel lathe's lid was raised it would be hard to tell if the object was a machine tool or a piano: only context would be a guide here, because few people would install a lathe in a drawing room. Schinkel and his travelling companion P. C. W. Beuth had visited Holtzapffel and Deyerlein on the same morning that they toured Maudslay's works, and watched a workman spinning a fluted oak hemisphere on a lathe to varnish it: 'the instruments for this can be bought', Schinkel reported. Beuth, head of the Prussian Department of Trade and Industry, and Director of the Design and Technical School in Berlin, promptly bought one to send home.

The detail and quality of the work and activity that Schinkel and Beuth saw in London were adequately matched by their reports of their delight at seeing it. Beuth had preceded Schinkel to England, and had indeed urged him to visit the country. Writing from Manchester in 1823, he urged Schinkel: 'It is only here my friend that the machinery and buildings can be found commensurate with the miracles of modern times – they are called factories. Such a barn of a place is eight or nine storeys high, up to forty windows long and usually four windows deep.'

Schinkel and Beuth's 1826 tour of England was an official visit. Already the architect of important public buildings in Berlin, Schinkel was a leading member of the Prussian Public Works Committee. The delegation was of high status, being sent by King Frederick William III 'to travel to Paris and London, there to take precise cognizance of the construction of the Museums with a view to the future erection of a Museum here in Berlin'. Within hours of arriving in London the pair were delighting in the new architecture of the capital and at the physical evidence of Britain's burgeoning industrial power. Their itinerary was comparable in extent to Canova's of eleven years earlier, but this was an industrial fact-finding mission, rather than the weeks of fun and friendship that Canova had enjoyed. Schinkel and Beuth spent their first full day visiting Regent's Park and the Panorama and Diorama there, and admiring the construction of Westminster, Blackfriars and Southwark bridges. The following day they made their first visit to the British Museum where Schinkel noted that antiquities were still being stored in the Museum's forecourt in the open air. Smirke's first architectural schemes were being realised in the King's Library, and Schinkel saw how the iron beams were encased in wooden coffering: 'none of the construction very praiseworthy', he felt.

After visiting Hampton Court and Richmond, Schinkel and Beuth attended an annual prize-giving ceremony at the Society of Arts, '(Boring)', visited the Royal Academy exhibition in Somerset House, and saw performances of *Robinson Crusoe* at the Covent Garden theatre and 'grotesque dancers' at Sadler's Wells. They visited Edmund Turrell, who had engraved architectural plates for C. R. Cockerell, saw die- and medal-making at the Mint on Tower Hill and iron smelting and casting at Joseph Bramah's factory, before calling on Maudslay at the end of their first week in London. This was a highly compressed seventeen-day tour, which gave the two Germans a near-complete picture of the life and work of social, artistic and engineering London.

Schinkel and Beuth were two continental sophisticates in London on official business, and Maudslay's works were high on their list of places they must see. Three years later, a younger man, eager, impressionable and ambitious, arrived from Edinburgh with his father specifically to visit Maudslay's and perhaps to meet the master engineer himself. James Nasmyth, then a few months short of his twenty-first birthday, had grown up as the youngest of a large family of artists. Immersed as he was in an understanding of both landscape and engineering through his father, the artist and amateur engineer Alexander Nasmyth, James Nasmyth turned for his early career to professional engineering and amateur art. His father and friends provided James with early opportunities which he richly justified – his youth and training in engineering in Edinburgh had reached a climax with the construction and public trial on the Queensferry Road of a steam carriage capable of carrying eight passengers for five miles. But he had always nursed a desire, which developed into a passion, to see Maudslay's works:

> I was told that his works were the very centre and climax of all that was excellent in mechanical workmanship . . . The chief object of my ambition was now to be taken on at Henry Maudslay's works in London. I had heard so much of his engineering work, of his assortment of machine-making tools, and of the admirable organisation of his manufactory, that I longed to obtain employment there.

James Nasmyth left a vivid, but thoroughly unreal, description of Maudslay's factory, which suggests he was recalling some kind of well-orchestrated mime or ballet. He was deceiving himself about the silence: the punishing noise and activity of the factory is self-evident, not least in Schinkel's description of the iron roller and profile-punching hammer. Nasmyth, however, recalled:

> The beautiful machine tools, the silent smooth whirl of the machinery, the active movements of the men, the excellent quality of the work in progress, and the admirable order and management that pervaded the whole establishment, rendered me more tremblingly anxious than ever to obtain some employment *there*, in however humble a capacity.

Nasmyth's detachment, an infection from Maudslay's own personality, is the successful mechanical engineer's natural state of mind in a world of whirring, incurious machinery. Schinkel had noticed

Maudslay's coolness when he showed off his plant to the high-level German visitors only a week after his new iron roof had collapsed, with fatalities. Nasmyth's description of Maudslay's private workshop reflects further on the self-control and desire for order of both men:

> The workshop was surrounded with cabinets and drawers, filled with evidence of the master's skill and industry. Every tool had a purpose. It was invented for some special reason. Sometimes it struck the keynote, as it were, to many of the important contrivances which enable man to obtain a complete mastery over materials.

Maudslay showed the young Nasmyth a chest of drawers near his workbench. Inside, each tool nestling in its own perfect place, was Maudslay's neat collection of taps, dies and screw-tackle, which he had himself made. 'There was a look of tidiness about the collection that was very characteristic of the man,' Nasmyth remarked.

Nasmyth immediately impressed Maudslay, who took him on as his assistant. He was one of a number of young men who attached themselves to Maudslay, and who went on to form the generation of ingenious engineers who brought a teeming population of lively progeny from the simple steam engine: Joseph Clement not only made Babbage's Difference Engine an infinitely complex reality, but he became one of the finest teachers of practical mechanics of his generation; William Muir developed the railway ticket-counting machine, and machinery for manufacturing interchangeable rifle sights; Richard Roberts developed cotton-spinning machines and power looms for the northern textile industries; Samuel Seaward improved marine engines for steam ships and patented such inventions as the detachable crank for paddle-wheels, and the telescopic ship's funnel; and Joseph Whitworth devised with Maudslay's and Clement's assistance the means to make a perfect plane surface on iron plates, among very many other innovations for shipbuilding, civil-engineering construction and manufacturing. The paths of almost every successful and innovative mid- and late-Victorian engineer who set up in business in London, Manchester, Leeds, Birmingham and Glasgow can be traced back to Henry Maudslay's works in Lambeth, and to the tall, commanding and good-natured figure whom his workmen respectfully called 'the guv'nor'.

Maudslay and Nasmyth were drawn together by something other than machinery: they both had wider interests. James Nasmyth's father who, as an amateur engineer, had invented the 'bow-and-string', an early form of suspension principle for roofs and bridges, had taken his son on drawing expeditions around Scotland, and had helped him to develop his natural artistic talent and judgement. This gave James a further 'bow-and-string' for life, leading him to paint landscape and industrial subjects, among them an illuminating oil painting, now in the Science Museum, London, of his own most influential invention, the steam hammer, at work in his Manchester factory. When giving evidence to the 1836 Select Committee on Arts and their Connexion with Manufactures, Nasmyth referred to his father as 'an artist of some celebrity', and, asked if he had himself studied drawing, replied, 'Yes, very intimately.'

Maudslay was impressed by Nasmyth's skill as an artist, and set him to work to make a drawing of a pair of 200-horsepower marine engines, 'a noble object in the great erecting shop', which were ultimately used to drive a new Post Office mail packet, the Paddle-Steamer *Dee*. 'Indeed, such a class of drawing was rarely to be had from an engineering draughtsman,' Nasmyth wrote. 'Mere geometrical drawing could not give a proper idea, as a whole, of so grand a piece of mechanism. It required something of the artistic spirit to fairly represent it. At all events my performance won the entire approval of my master.' Another of Nasmyth's interests was astronomy, and this too he shared with Maudslay, who had become enraptured with the subject while on a visit to Berlin to erect new machinery at the Prussian mint in 1830. Among the additional entertainments laid on in Berlin for Maudslay were meetings with the explorer Humboldt, and with his old acquaintance Friedrich Schinkel who gave him a set of engravings of his architectural designs, and impressed Maudslay (if he had not already done so in 1826) with 'his minute attention to detail, and his fine artistic feeling'. But Maudslay was also shown the Prussian Royal Observatory, where he saw Jupiter, Saturn and the moon through some of the most advanced pieces of astronomical equipment, and this fired him on his return to acquire an advanced telescope of his own. Nasmyth took it upon himself to grind an eight-inch mirror for Maudslay's use in a reflecting telescope, but the older man wanted nothing less than a twenty-four-inch model, and engaged his abundant energy to find a house in Norwood where he could set up an observatory away from the smoke of London. Alas Maudslay's observatory was never built; he died in 1831 a few months after his return from Berlin.

Nasmyth came late to Maudslay's life, working with him only for two brief years. Theirs, however, was one of the lucky associations of the enthusiasm of youth and the experience of age with which Maudslay and his apprentices were blessed. Young men with ideas and nimble fingers were gold dust for engineers in London, and the young men knew it. Nasmyth was to return to Edinburgh, and ultimately to set up his own engineering factory in Manchester; but he learned the rudiments of factory management from Maudslay, as did Muir, Seaward, Whitworth and many others. They all grasped some of the ground-rules of mechanical engineering that were undoubtedly obvious to them all, but which Nasmyth had the generosity to ascribe to Maudslay's own pithy, ruminative nature:

> First, *get a clear notion* of what you desire to accomplish, and then in all probability you will succeed in doing it . . . Keep a sharp look-out upon your materials; get rid of every pound of material you can *do without*; put to yourself the question, 'What business has it to be there?' Avoid complexities, and make everything as simple as possible.

Within those maxims there are three universal truths of successful machine-making, which all came out of a noisy early-nineteenth-century Lambeth factory. They can be applied to practically any creative activity, from making jam to building a moon rocket: Understanding; Economy; Simplicity.

8

The Very Pulse of the Machine

~

HENRY MAUDSLAY'S APPROVAL of James Nasmyth's draughts-manship was indicative of his consideration of the intertwining of art and mechanics, and of how much this should be acknowledged and even encouraged. The machinery that came out of Maudslay's works, and indeed from Galloway, Perkins, Donkin, Braithwaite and Bramah, and the dozens of other engineers of their generation, was self-evidently beautiful. The movement of the parts, the parabolas and ellipses that their pistons and cranks drew as they went through their motions, the shimmer on the brass and steel, the suck of oil and hiss of air, all generated an intrinsic and indefinable satisfaction. To this is added the natural delight that, against all the odds, these heavy pieces of assembled metal would actually do what they were designed to accomplish, to perform a specific mechanical task, and effect one link in a chain of ordered events. No wonder that Maudslay, like his fellow engineers, honoured their mechanical creations with fine settings and physical presentations of their own. As an accomplished painting is honoured by an appropriate frame, so Maudslay's machines were deliv-ered to customers mounted on supporting framework designed in the language of fashionable architecture or furniture. His early products, the machines for making ships' blocks, were supported on Doric columns, with, in some cases, additional framework echoing the shape of Hepplewhite or Hope furniture – the sort of fine, expensive and fashionable goods that the furniture dealer Rudolph Ackermann might have sold in his Strand emporium – but here made in iron. A later product, the pair of 200-horsepower marine engines for the *Dee*, were set within a framework of elegant Gothic arches.

Such infrastructure was second nature to the thoughtful engineer; the idea that an intricate and beautiful machine should be bolted on to any old plank was anathema. One of the causes of Galloway's anger with Rigaud had been that the latter had compromised Galloway's ability to deliver a good-looking job well done. At the 1836 Arts and Manufactures Select Committee, an understanding of the philosophy of beauty in machinery, which underpinned the natural instincts of mechanical engineers, was revealed for the first time in a formal public arena. Discussing the way a machine should be presented, and how the framework on which it stands should be designed, James Nasmyth asserted that:

> The most economical disposition of the materials coincides with such a form as presents the most elegant appearance to the eye; this is especially the case where the elliptic or parabolic curves are employed in the form of the parts which connect one part of the machine with another, so that when viewed as one design it shall present a perfectly graceful form, and at the same time completely attain the object in view.

Nasmyth went on to say that an understanding of the relationship between economy and appearance can be understood only if the mechanic is instructed in the arts of design. Education, he stressed, was the root of the 'intimate connexion . . . between the arts of design and practical mechanics'.

Means to attain the ideal of education in art and design for the mechanic were outlined to the 1836 committee by Charles Toplis, Vice-President of the London Mechanics' Institution. Toplis listed some of the many organisations in London where training could be found: at his own institution in Chancery Lane, in Leicester Square, Marylebone, Finsbury, Spitalfields, Islington, the City, Borough, Deptford, Stepney, Stratford, Wandsworth. Far from being difficult to find, scientific, literary and art training for the 'engineer, builder, carpenter, mechanist' was widespread and more or less well organised. In the reality of early-nineteenth-century London, despite the difficulties of communication and financial uncertainty for many, a reasonable liberal education, with a generous range of subjects including English grammar, arithmetic, mechanical drawing and French, was theoretically available in evening classes for those tradesmen who were able to take it up.

A theme that emerged repeatedly in the evidence to the 1836 Select Committee was the crucial importance of the role of museums in the education of tradesmen. 'The formations of museums,' Charles Toplis said, 'for the collection of models of construction, of specimens of skilful workmanship, and of examples of tasteful design and graceful form, cannot fail to advance, in a conspicuous degree, both the fine and useful arts of the country. Our national greatness rests on the skilled industry of our people.' James Nasmyth took things one step further in his evidence, and advocated the exhibition of works of art and design, ancient and modern, within the factory itself. Nasmyth wanted to see a museum in every workplace. In that way, the mechanic could spend his brief leisure time looking at the exhibits, and considering 'in company with each other . . . the merits of such objects as would materially tend to increase their taste . . . which object is so completely attainable without the slightest interruption to their daily occupation'. Despite Nasmyth's utilitarian assurance that contemplation of art objects would not effect factory output, this is a Ruskinian principle uttered twenty years before John Ruskin gave his *Political Economy of Art* lectures in Manchester, and forty years before he opened the Museum of the Guild of St George at Walkley, Sheffield, specifically for the education and enlightenment of the Sheffield metalworkers.

The artist Henry Sass, the host of soirées at 6 Charlotte Street, Bloomsbury, was another witness before the Select Committee. He advocated free and constant public entry to museums and galleries: 'the advance of intellectual improvement would be great, and France and Italy give a very good example of that'. Sass himself took advantage of the British Museum on his doorstep; he was, as we have seen, the holder of a ticket allowing him to draw in the Reading Room. Sass urged the setting up of museums in every town in Britain to develop a system of 'teaching persons how to see with their own eyes'. Quoting Ovid, lines which recall John Taylor's jaunty verses in praise of Sass himself and other savants, he assured the committee:

> These polish'd arts which humanize mankind,
> Soften the manners and refine the mind.

Richard Porson (1759–1808) by Giovanni Domenico Gianelli; classical scholar. An intellectual literary giant, with a capacity for self-destruction and a craving for attention

William Jerdan (1782–1869) by Daniel Maclise; journalist. The ambitious and vociferous editor of the *Literary Gazette*, a man with a 900-year lease on his job

Joseph Farington RA (1747–1821) by Henry Singleton RA; artist, diarist. In profile, fourth from left. A careful and attentive diarist who, six feet tall, dominated his contemporaries while he privately recorded their lives and opinions

Left: Joseph Mallord William Turner RA (1775–1851) by John Thomas Smith; artist. Turner, an artist both studious and revolutionary, is shown looking at drawings in the Print Room of the British Museum

Below: Sir Humphry Davy, Bt (1778–1829); chemist, teacher. Davy's profile on the Davy Medal, instituted by the Royal Society in 1869 for an outstandingly important recent discovery in chemistry

Above: The Rhinebeck Panorama of London, c.1806 by Robert Havell. Discovered in 1941 lining a barrel of pistols, in Rhinebeck, New York State, this is the most evocative and painstaking panorama of London of its period

Right: Michael Faraday (1791–1857); scientist, teacher. This daguerreotype, showing a relatively youthful Faraday, may have been taken in 1839 in the Royal Institution laboratory. Alternatively it may have been taken c.1841 by the coal-merchant turned entrepreneur of photography, Richard Beard. Among his wide scientific interests, Faraday was also a pioneer of photographic technique

Left: John Tatum (c.1776–?) by Cornelius Varley; chemist, teacher. An enthusiastic and influential teacher of science, the proprietor of the Theatre of Science off Fleet Street. This was drawn with Varley's Patent Graphic Telescope

Below left: John Murray (1778–1843) by William Brockedon; publisher. The one-eyed entrepreneur–publisher who orchestrated the 'traffic of mind and literature' from his Albemarle Street house. Murray was also a pioneer of enormous advances to authors

Below right: Maria Graham, later Mrs Callcott (1785–1842), by Thomas Lawrence; traveller and writer. Gregarious, ebullient and brave, her travels took her from bandit-country in Italy to the Pacific coast of South America

William Brockedon (1787–1854) by Clarkson Stanfield; artist, writer, traveller, inventor. 'London is intolerably dull. Nobody left except myself. There is one advantage in this. I work without interruption'

John Pye (1782–1874) by Henry Behnes Burlowe; engraver. 'He truly was a gigantic man . . . His was indeed a stupendous life of rigid work and self-denial'

John Martin (1789–1854) by William Brockedon; artist. A natty dresser, smart and trim, whose personal dynamism connected with an understanding of how to work the system. Ultimately, this failed him

Benjamin Robert Haydon (1786–1846), plaster cast of a life mask by an unknown artist; artist, diarist. Bulky, bullet-headed and uncompromising, he was a scourge of the Royal Academy and the despair of his friends

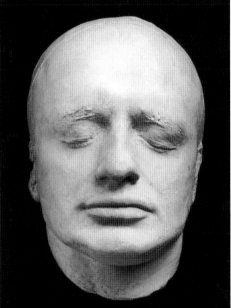

'One of the Lions' – or, the Living Statues at the London Museum by
George Cruikshank: A guard at the door of Bullock's Museum in the
Egyptian Hall, Piccadilly, in 1817

Right: John Constable RA (1776–1837) by Charles Robert Leslie RA; artist. A gentle artist, given to conceit, whose paintings have shaped modern perception of the English landscape. He described Turner as 'watchful and savage'

Below: James Willoughby Gordon (mid-1770s–1851) by David Wilkie; soldier, administrator. An amiable old soldier who indulged his wife's affection for Turner, and had a thing about cheese. He is shown here with his daughter at home at Niton, Isle of Wight

Goldsworthy Gurney's pioneering steam carriage and its entourage making their journey from Middlesex to Bath, by Sir Charles Dance. Accomplished in July 1829, this was the longest return journey (220 miles) yet made by a steam carriage. 'At our quickest pace the post horses were kept at a gallop'

The west wing of the British Museum under construction, by George Scharf. Left: the old Montagu House; centre: the Townley Wing. Both would be demolished. Scharf has inscribed the drawing 'There will be 44 Columns to the Facade, and 10,000 Tons of Stones used as Mr Baker the Builder told me'

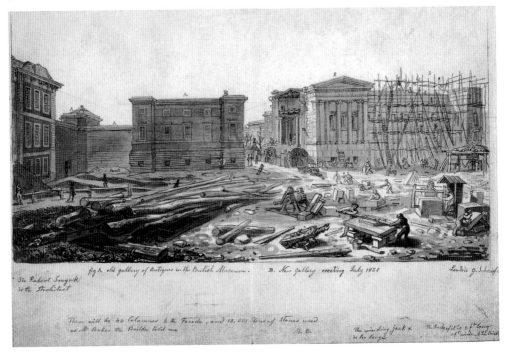

The uses of museums, especially the British Museum, also exercised John Martin in his evidence to the Select Committee. Martin had himself sent his sons off to the British Museum to make drawings of costume from books in the Reading Room. His proposal, which was characteristically revolutionary, was to institute what would now be called education departments in museums, appointing professors to teach anatomy, perspective and proportion. This would not become accepted practice until the late twentieth century. 'Would a young man learn all these merely by a museum?' he mused aloud in front of the committee.

> I think so, by proper masters . . . Indeed professors might be appointed to teach every branch of art, science and literature, as in the British Museum everything requisite is on the spot, and few alterations of the establishment would be needed. The National Gallery and the National Gallery of Practical Science might become branches of the British Museum . . . I firmly believe that the arts are useful to every branch of manufacture in the land.

Martin added wryly that 'even to our legislators drawing is useful, for they are not capable of judging a plan without a knowledge of it'.

Dry though they may sound by their titles, the House of Commons Select Committee reports are deep and fertile sources of information and opinion. The committees were part of the machinery of government then as now, and the steam that they produced each year came in the form of many tons of paper. In 1833, for example, forty-four volumes of official papers were produced by the Houses of Parliament, from Select Committee reports to Estimates and Accounts, and State Papers. The average length of the volumes is seven hundred pages; at about sixty lines per page, that is about 63,000 words per volume, or twenty-eight million words a year just to report to government. The leading dramatis personae of the committees (that is not too strong an epithet, for there were theatrical moments), the expert witnesses, the chairmen and members, were chosen carefully, and the recorded evidence justifies this. Whether they be the bluff and reflective Henry Maudslay, the belligerent and watchful Alexander Galloway or the practised committeeman John Martin, the information that comes across is direct and spontaneous, and may be reasonably read as an authentic voice of the period. James Nasmyth the engineer–artist and John Martin the artist–engineer appeared by their evidence to be in general agreement with each other, although there was one point of emphasis that they differed on. Nasmyth illustrated the importance of improved design to the exterior of factories, their chimneys and outbuildings, to render 'elegance of form . . . familiar to the eyes of mechanics'. This would lead further to the increased elegance of manufacturing towns. Martin, on the other hand, took porcelain (or 'china' as he called it) as his indicator of taste, revealing the great distance he had travelled, both socially and geographically, from being the son of a Newcastle-on-Tyne fencing master, to the acclaimed metropolitan artist whose soirées were noted events in the London social calendar. He asserted that:

> china painting . . . has fallen so low that what is done is not worthy of being called invention; the French are beating us hollow . . . China is perpetually before us; every day we see china; at all our meals the elegant and beautiful china is always before us; we are delighted with a piece of beautiful workmanship, and it might be rendered very cheap if there were a great number of clever draughtsmen as china painters, but we cannot find them now.

John Martin is a unique example of an artist of high significance with a passionate and highly constructive interest in a particular branch of the sciences. A surviving sketchbook shows architectural details and engineering ideas jostling for position on the page. Like Galloway, one of Martin's passions was that British manufacturers should not be outdone by the French. If we were to propose a scale of genius effective in both the arts and the sciences where Leonardo da Vinci scored ten points, Martin might perhaps reach five or six, while Nasmyth, marked up by his painting, would be two or three. Faraday, practical and effective as he was in the development of steel-engraving, lithography and photography, might settle around Martin's level. The little-known figure of William Brockedon, however, would reach a higher score than both Martin and Faraday, say seven or eight. A portrait and history painter of great accomplishment, and incidentally an energetic and purposeful continental traveller and alpinist, Brockedon crammed a variety of successful careers into his sixty-seven years. Born in Totnes, and trained there by his father as a watchmaker, he came to London in 1809 to study painting at the Royal Academy Schools. His painting career was enthusiastic and energetic. Beginning as it did during the period in which Fuseli was Professor of Painting at the Royal Academy, Turner a powerful and aggressive force and Benjamin Robert Haydon a controversial presence, Brockedon became captivated by large-scale historical painting and by portraiture. Over a period of twenty-five years he exhibited extensively at the Academy and the British Institution, and embarked on a self-imposed project to draw the portraits of what came eventually to be 104 accomplished and in-ventive men and women, whom he called his 'Prominent People'. These, which he drew for his son as 'little Philip's book of his father's friends', are now in the National Portrait Gallery, London. Brockedon became obsessed with discovering the route of Hannibal's army, and in the 1820s crossed the Alps nearly sixty times by thirty different routes to gather evidence. He eventually came to the now generally accepted conclusion that Hannibal's route had been across the Petit St Bernard Pass, above Aosta. Brockedon drew in the Alps, in Egypt and the Holy Land, and published volumes of engravings from his work, and travel books. A period in Rome (1821–2), where his *Vision of Zechariah* was exhibited in the Pantheon, led to his being elected a member of the Academies of Rome and Florence.

Most of his paintings were presented as gifts by the artist, evidence that, like Haydon, he found large-scale religious subjects to be unsaleable. Brockedon settled in Devonshire Street, Bloomsbury, not far from John Martin in the New Road and Charles Babbage (another son of Totnes) in Dorset Street. He was a good friend of Michael Faraday, who fostered the natural mechanical ingenuity that had led to his becoming a watchmaker. Faraday also spotted the breadth of Brockedon's interests, inviting him to the Royal Institution to speak on wire-drawing machinery (1827), on firearm wadding (1828), colour perception (1830), Hannibal's Alpine cross-ing (1831), an improved ship's anchor (1832), the uses of India rubber (1833), the Alpine storms of 1834 (1835), and medal and cameo engraving (1837). Brockedon's mechanical turn of mind led him also to develop and take out patents for a machine for drawing wire, for an oblique pen nib (1831), a rubberised felt substitute for corks and bungs (1838), firearm wadding (1843), an artificial plumbago for lead pencils (1843), a pill-making machine (1843), and a domestic gas fire (1847). He coined the term 'vulcanisation' for the chemical means of strengthening rubber.

His activity as a traveller led him to become a founder member of the Royal Geographical Society (1830). He was an active member of the Society of Arts and the Athenaeum Club, the founder of the Graphic Society in 1833, a Fellow of the Royal Society, and an expert witness at parliamentary select committees. As an author he contributed articles to Charles Dickens's *Household Words*, and wrote passages on Egypt, the Holy Land, Italy and Switzerland for illustrated publications by David Roberts, Clarkson Stanfield, Samuel Prout and others.

Brockedon was an extraordinary figure, even in a period which produced so many men and women whose achievements covered a wide intellectual span. His single-mindedness, a paradox in a man who had such a multitude of interests, induced an irritable, argumentative side which brought conflict upon him. In correspondence with John Murray, one of his travelling companions on the continent, Brockedon heaped scorn on the historian and sometime trustee of the British Museum Henry Hallam, who failed to turn up as expected at the inaugural meeting of the Graphic Society. Listing those who did attend, Brockedon adds:

> goodly company even for Mr Hallam. Mr Hallam's autograph [that is, on the society's membership roll] therefore would give me no pleasure since whatever respect I may have for his talents I have none for his courtesy. If he be a collector of autographs, you may send him *this* as *mine*. Yours sincerely, William Brockedon.

Self-centred, driven and not to be disturbed when he was working, Brockedon observed in his staccato manner in September 1837: 'London is intolerably dull. Nobody left except myself. There is one advantage in this. I work without interruption.' When his own portrait, engraved by Charles Turner, was published in 1835, the *Literary Gazette* described it as 'a striking and animated resemblance full of original expression of the highly gifted original'.

Active as Brockedon was across a broad spectrum of practical and intellectual life, his work was both ephemeral and anachronistic, and this has been a direct cause of his obscurity. The inventions and patents lasted only as long in the public mind as their commercial need; and his huge paintings, unsaleable from conception, were given away to the damp anonymity of country churches. While his continental and Middle Eastern landscapes are period pieces, it may be that Brockedon's lasting contribution to cultural history is the group of portraits of 'Prominent People'.

A select committee to which John Farey was called was the 1831 inquiry into Steam Carriages which was ordered to investigate the level of road tolls that steam carriages should pay, and to look at steam transport's 'Probable Utility to the Public'. Steam carriages were by 1830 puffing along the roads and the gentler slopes of industrial England and Scotland, blowing up, breaking down, and frightening the horses. The vehicles had been mobbed by cattle, stoned by Luddites, driven into walls and ditches and abandoned by infuriated drivers and passengers. The young James Nasmyth was one pioneer of the steam carriage, having given his four-wheeled monster a test drive outside Edinburgh in the mid-1820s. Walter Hancock, working from his factory in Stratford, east London, introduced steam carriages to compete with horse-drawn passenger transport on routes between Stratford and the City of London in 1831, then on other busy routes within London, and between London and Brighton. Encouraged by Henry Maudslay, William Muir built a steam carriage at the Maudslay works in Lambeth. The steam carriage represented, briefly, a new means of approach to the expanding frontier of swift travel to distant places, and many engineers turned their minds to its mechanical problems. To flourish at a reasonable cost, steam carriages depended on reliable road surfaces and an economic level of toll charge, and had to take on the vested interests of horse-drawn carriage companies, canal owners, the government and, fatally for them, the railways. The differential, it emerged at the Select Committee, between tolls for horse-drawn and steam-driven carriages was as much as 1,300 per cent – for example, the toll for horse-drawn carriage on the Ashburnham-to-Totnes toll road in Devon was three shillings, while for a steam-carriage it was

£2, that is, forty shillings, more than thirteen times the cost of a horse-drawn carriage.

The most determined and voluble motor engineer of the period was the surgeon and inventor Goldsworthy Gurney, a friend and near neighbour of Sir Anthony Carlisle in Soho. Gurney lectured in chemistry at the Surrey Institute, and there discovered ways of making intense light from a jet of burning oxygen and hydrogen played on to lime. Gurney's principle obsession in the late 1820s, however, was the development of steam carriages, which he constructed in a series of sheds in Albany Street, Regent's Park, and tested on the roads to Edgware, Stanmore and other villages north of London. Over seven days in July 1829 he drove his most highly developed prototype from Cranford, Middlesex, to Bath and back, 110 miles each way at an average speed of 10 m.p.h. It was a cavalcade that puttered along the turnpikes in a westerly direction, a phaeton in front with four passengers, pulled by two horses; the steam car itself controlled by Goldsworthy Gurney, pulling a barouche with four more passengers; and a carriage drawn by two horses carrying a team of engineers, and the coke to make the steam. Among the passengers were two senior soldiers, Colonel Sir Charles Dance and General Sir James Willoughby Gordon: the former wrote a rapid and full report on the journey. The latter, who travelled with his wife, was the Quarter-Master General for the army, and a Fellow of the Royal Society.

The trip was peppered with incident, but nonetheless it was the first long-distance journey for a steam carriage, and a giant leap for mankind. Dance's report on the event claimed that although they were crashed into by a mail coach on a bridge soon after leaving Cranford, there were mitigating circumstances, and the accident was the fault neither of the mail coach nor of the steam car. Thereafter, Dance writes that 'at our quickest pace the post horses were kept at a gallop, and when we stopped were in a *White Lather*. The Light Phaeton could keep up very well, but the Post Carriage [in the rear] was so heavy that the Post Boys said no pair of horses could keep up, and we were obliged to take Four all the rest of the Journey.'

No horses were startled by the steam carriage for the whole length of the journey (save for the early incident on the bridge), Dance claimed, and the coke produced no sparks or smoke. They were able to climb Devizes Hill 'without stopping at the rate of 5 to 6 miles an hour'. They did, however, get into difficulties in Melksham:

> On our arrival . . . there was a Fair in the Town and the streets full of People. Mr Gurney . . . fearing to injure any person, moved slowly as possible . . . unfortunately the people here had taken a dislike to the Steam Carriage, and after abusing us shamefully, attacked us with stones and flints, and after having wounded the stoker and another engineer severely in their Heads . . . a violent scuffle took place between us.

Despite the fracas in Melksham, aggravated by the fear of steam engines taking away the livelihood of Wiltshire weavers, the successful outcome of Gurney's pioneering journey led to his setting up a public steam-transport service between Cheltenham and Gloucester, using a carriage which weighed three tons and carried eighteen passengers. Gurney was one of a number of motor engineers who gave robust evidence to the 1831 Select Committee on Steam Carriages. He showed off his carriages proudly, assuring the committee, worried about the effect of steam carriages on horses, that he had been very frequently in a steam carriage in and around London and the country: 'I have certainly seen horses shy often, but never saw a horse make a dead stop.'

Gurney's was the most persistent voice on behalf of steam carriages, against a rising determination of the owners of horse-drawn carriages to put him out of business before he ruined them. The Select Committee was set up to investigate all aspects of this new transport method, and to report on levels of annoyance, pollution, the wear and tear on roads, the level of road toll and the safety of the machines. Gurney proposed that 'an iron horse of the same weight as one of flesh and bones' should pay the same toll, and he believed that four wheels did less damage to the road surface than four hooves. The committee agreed with him. He also claimed that the cost of running a steam carriage, 'depending on the cost of coke and labour', was about half the cost of keeping a coach-and-four.

John Farey was called to speak after Gurney. His evidence was succinct and detached, and he made it clear that steam carriages were the transport of the future: he had 'no doubt whatever but that a steady perseverance in such trials will lead to the general adoption of Steam Carriages', and added that 'the danger of explosion is less than the danger attendant on the use of horses in draught'. Steam carriages, the committee believed after hearing the evidence, were cheaper, safer and cleaner than horse-drawn transport, and would not run away in fear, or bolt down hills, or fall over when travelling fast round corners as horses might. 'Every witness examined has given the fullest and most satisfactory evidence of the perfect control which the conductor has over the movement of the Carriage. With the slightest exertion it can be stopped or turned, under circumstances when horses would be totally unmanageable.'

Gurney's view was that the steam carriage would replace the one thousand horses employed 'in Hounslow alone . . . in stage coaches and posting'. He gave the same figure for the post-horses on Paddington Road, and multiplied these to assert that throughout Great Britain there were 'millions [of horses] in posting and stage coaches'. By this time Gurney was well into his stride before the Select Committee, and continued with his amateur statistics. 'The consumption of a horse is equal to that for the maintenance of eight individuals. So for every horse that is removed we make way for the maintenance of eight individuals.' Gurney hazarded a guess that in five years steam carriages would be generally employed throughout England. There he was dead wrong. The railway lobby intervened and introduced protective legislation which effectively did for the motor car in Britain, and resulted in its development passing to France, Germany and the United States. Despite bravely championing his advanced mode of transport, Gurney was the loser in all this. The Toll Relief Bill (1834), aimed at modifying tolls for steam carriages, failed to become law, and Gurney went bankrupt. He went back to his country home at Bude in Cornwall, where he turned his attention to the development of artificial light.

The steam engine was during the 1820s and 1830s getting everywhere – on the roads, on the sea and the fields. Somewhere by the river near Kew, William Jerdan claimed in 1829 to have spotted:

the patent Philosophical Hay-tosser, a stupendous machine, invented expressly to prevent the degradation and slavery to which thousands of our fellow men are subjected during hay-harvest. It must gratify every friend to the amelioration of his species to learn, that the humane intention of the inventor is likely to be realised, as there are already three thousand Irishmen out of employ.

This was probably meant to be funny, but as poets, painters and authors were beginning to reveal, nowhere was immune from 'the very pulse of the machine'. Wordsworth, in love in his youth with a Scots girl, used in 1807 the machine as a bizarre metaphor of hope and beauty:

> She was a phantom of delight
> When first she gleamed upon my sight . . .
> And now I see with eye serene
> The very pulse of the machine;
> A Being breathing thoughtful breath,
> A Traveller between life and death . . .

Twenty-six years later in 1833 his attitude had hardened:

> What change shall happen next to Nunnery Dell?
> Canal, and Viaduct, and Railway, tell!

By 1844, it had hardened still more. He wrote to the *Morning Post* about the invasion by the railway of the Lake District, and opened his poem 'On the Projected Kendal and Windermere Railway', with the words 'Is then no nook of English ground secure / From rash assault?'

The triumph of horse-drawn transport businesses over the steam carriage was brief. The railway, after the opening of the Stockton and Darlington railway in 1825 and the Rainhill trials on the line between Manchester and Liverpool in October 1829, was already signalling the end of the stage coach, and smothering the steam car at birth. The Rainhill steam-engine trials, won ultimately by Robert Stephenson's *Rocket*, was, but for a broken pipe, nearly a triumph for the London engineer John Braithwaite and his partner John Ericsson. Taking their turn to run along the three miles of straight line near Rainhill Bridge, Manchester, the steam engines assembled for the seven-day trial in bright party colours before a huge holiday crowd: John Braithwaite and John Ericsson, of Paddington, paraded the *Novelty* in the jaunty colours of copper and blue. Mr Ackworth, of Darlington, entered the *Sans Pareil* in green, yellow and black. Robert Stephenson, from Newcastle-on-Tyne, showed off the *Rocket* with its shining white chimney and yellow and black livery. After undergoing tests of speed, pulling power, endurance and fuel economy, Stephenson's *Rocket* eventually won the trials. But the London entry, the *Novelty*, which at two tons fifteen hundredweight was about half the size of the *Rocket*, challenged it and won 'the grand prize of public opinion'. The *Novelty* impressed the crowds particularly through its 'compactness, and its beautiful workmanship'. It ran at a steady 28 m.p.h., and in one burst of speed covered a mile in seven seconds short of two minutes: 'Had the railway been completed, the engine would, at this rate, have gone nearly the whole way from Liverpool to Manchester within the hour; and Mr. Braithwaite has, indeed, publicly offered to stake a thousand pounds, that as soon as the road is opened, he will perform the entire distance in that time.' The *Mechanics Magazine* believed that the principle and arrangement of the Braithwaite and Ericsson engine would be followed in the construction of all future locomotives:

> The powerful introduction of a blast bellows, the position of the water tank below the body of the carriage, by which means the centre of gravity is brought below the line of central motion, the beautiful mechanism of the connecting movement of the wheels, the absolute absence of all smell, smoke, noise, vibration, or unpleasant feeling of any kind, the elegance of the machinery, in short the *tout ensemble* proclaims the perfection of the principle.

The engineering world of London was a rich mixture of eccentric technical obsessives like Gurney, clever businessmen and managers like Maudslay and Galloway, and analysts and chroniclers like Farey. There were men who came to machinery from other professions — medicine seems to have produced a number, such as Gurney, who told the 1831 Select Committee that he had 'left an honorable and lucrative profession' to develop steam carriages, and Charles Fox, who worked with Braithwaite and Ericsson on the

Novelty and went on to manufacture iron-frame buildings. Others, such as Joseph Perkins, came to London from the United States, while Bramah, Clement, Nasmyth and Muir saw London as the place of engineering opportunity, and came to the city from Yorkshire, Westmorland and Scotland.

Towards the end of the 1820s, an employee of the London and Edinburgh Shipping Company, which carried passengers between the two capitals along Britain's North Sea coast, pasted a printed leaflet into a pile of copies of *Reid's Leith & London Smack Directory*. This little pamphlet, published in 1819, detailed the times and procedure for passengers proposing to travel in the small and versatile single-masted sailing boats which for decades had been taking passengers between London and Edinburgh. The leaflet, gummed into the back cover, was a harbinger of profound change:

> These smacks are now replaced by the splendid steamers of the London and Edinburgh Shipping Company, sailing three times a week between Hermitage Wharf, London, and Victoria Dock, Leith. First class fare 22s 1d in place of 73s 6d by smack!
>
> Average time of journey: 5 days.
>
> Cost of ticket: £3 13s 6d, compared to £8 9s by coach to Edinburgh, with coachmen, guards and subsistence brings it to £12–£13.

The paddle-steamer quartered the cost of both the sailing smack and the coach, reduced the travelling time and was able to keep to a timetable which the weather barely affected. The smack could carry only about eight or ten passengers in reasonable comfort, and, of those, half would have to spend the voyage on deck as there were not enough cabins for all. Michael Faraday found this to be the case in 1813 when he sailed from Plymouth to France with Sir Humphry and Lady Davy. The Davys bedded down in the rough comfort of the cabin, while Faraday spent the night on deck, variously pacing up and down or wrapped in a blanket. When Turner travelled to Scotland in 1822 to witness the royal visit to Edinburgh by King George IV he will probably have gone by smack. During the journey he made a long series of pencilled horizons of the East Anglian and Lincolnshire coastline, an unhurried diary of the distant landscape, the sunsets and the busy shipping traffic. For the creak of the rigging and the heave of the vessel as it responded to the changing wind, passengers on the new steam boats exchanged the incessant chugging of the engine, the curling smoke and steam, and the suck of sea water around the paddle wheels. They reached their destination faster, but the passengers also had to endure each other's company in greater numbers than before, as the steam boats were larger than their sail predecessors, and, being more expensive to commission and run, their owners had an urgent economic incentive to pack people on board, hurry the timetables, break speed records, and make money.

Directly after the Select Committee on Steam Carriages had finished its deliberations in the Houses of Parliament in September 1831, another select committee looked into the matter of 'Frequent Calamities by Steam Navigation' in and around the Pool of London. This is the two-and-a-quarter-mile stretch of river from below London Bridge to the bend of the river at Limehouse Reach. The overcrowding in this stretch, the churning up of the water by wash from paddle-steamers and indeed continual instances of dangerous seamanship had led to the entire issue of the management of the river as a transport route being discussed in the House of Commons and in select committee. One MP, John Maberly, protested that it was ridiculous to bring in a law regulating the speed of steam vessels. Speed was their 'chief excellence', he claimed. 'If it were successful [the Commons] would next be called upon to regulate the speed of coaches, and probably the rate at which men were to walk.'

The Select Committee was charged with investigating the types of causes of accidents to steam vessels by bursting boilers, the 'undulation occasioned by the motion of vessels', the methods of construction of vessels, and what speed limits should be imposed. The practice of paddle-steamers owned by rival companies racing each other to get into mid-channel in the river was one concern:

> A Margate and a Gravesend boat start at 9 a.m. from the wharf near London Bridge; by the time they are abreast of St Katherine's [half a mile downstream] [another] Margate and a Gravesend boat are steering out from that place of embarkation also, and thus four powerful vessels are passing down the Pool at the same instant . . . There are

deep-loaded craft in many of the reaches of the river, and two vessels racing for mastery necessarily create a greater swell by the meeting of the waters thrown off by the wheels.

Another regular complaint was that steamboat captains allowed their vessels to be overloaded with passengers. A witness to the committee said that he had repeatedly seen around seven hundred people on board a modest 250-ton paddle-steamer, and had seen the *Albion* (250 tons) en route to Margate with a thousand passengers. Most of the passengers would be on the top deck when the steamer was leaving her berth, and they would run to one side when something interesting appeared in the riverscape, making the ship unstable.

The problem with paddle-steamer racing and deliberate ramming was not so much that it was dangerous in itself, but that it damaged the river's banks and interfered with the smooth flow of London's supplies. The Thames was still principally a waterway for sailing ships; the paddle-steamers were a modern nuisance. In 1818 there were nine running on the Thames, and even as late as 1860 there were only 350 steamers compared with three thousand sailing vessels registered at the Port of London. All along the length of the Pool of London, in the middle of the river, a complex of moorings created rows of eight berths abreast for the continual stream of colliers that sailed into London with coal from the north-east, the raw material which ultimately created London's 'dun cupola crown' of smoke. On either side of the moorings traffic passed along a channel three hundred feet wide, and it was this that had to be kept clear at all costs. As well as coal, there was a constant flow of imports and exports into the Pool of London, and into the rapidly developing London docks.

The coal kept London on the move, its steam engines running and its fires burning. There was nothing else to burn: coal was for the nineteenth-century economy what oil has been, and is, for the twentieth and twenty-first centuries. The coal merchant Richard Beard, a voluble and ambitious businessman, asserted in a series of letters to *The Times* that 2,006,633 tons were sold on the London coal market in 1833 – a weight which approximated to twenty to twenty-five thousand shiploads, or about seventy to a hundred ship movements in and out of the Thames every day of the year. John Herschel accepted the figure of 1,500,000 chaldrons of coal burned in London in 1830, that is about two million tons – so his and Beard's figures more or less concur. Then as now the fuel was a rich source of government tax, the City of London taking one guinea for every ton of coal delivered. At any one time there might have been around 1,500 colliers in the middle of the river, a long, winding, ever-evolving sea-porcupine tracing its way downstream. From London Bridge the ships looked like 'the avenues of a forest in the leafless winter'.

In the first two decades of the nineteenth century, before Brighton and London were connected by rail, Margate was the only coastal town that rivalled Brighton as a holiday spot for Londoners. As Cyrus Redding put it, 'The cockney talked of a jaunt to Margate as of an important event in his life, and the time consumed was of real importance, amounting to three or four days going backwards and forwards.' Margate had burgeoned from the sheer pressure of numbers of Londoners who wanted to taste its salty and saucy delights. Until the new steamer service opened in 1815, the town was served from London by a kind of fat smack, the Margate hoy, which could take two days and nights to make the journey. Charles Lamb, in his most archaic voice, evoked the pleasures of the old hoy,

> when the o'er-washing billows drove us below deck (for it was far gone in October, and we had stiff and blowing weather) how did thy officious ministerings, still catering for our comfort, with cards, and cordials, and thy more cordial conversation, alleviate the closeness and the confinement of thy else (truth to say) not very savoury, nor very inviting, cabin.

To cope with the traffic generated by the steamers, the town's harbour company commissioned a new stone pier designed by John Rennie. This gave a haven to 'the foppery and fresh-water niceness of the modern steam-packet', as Lamb put it, with its 'magic fumes, and spells, and boiling cauldrons . . . poisoning the breath of ocean with sulphureous smoke . . . chimneying and furnacing the deep'. Rennie's harbour wall curved round like a claw, and had, mounted on top of it, the Droit House for the handling of customs and other revenue payments, and a lighthouse. The pier could not however cope for long with the numbers of visitors from London, which between 1815 and 1827 tripled from about 25,000 to 78,000 a year. Nor was it really suitable for landing steamer passengers, because the foreshore at Margate shelves slowly and has dangerous shoals. The solution was to build a structure 1,100 feet long pointing out to sea with a platform at the end, Jarvis's Landing Place, opened in 1824.

Negotiating her way past the colliers in the Pool of London, the *Albion* carried passengers in their thousands to Margate in the 1820s. Her predecessor on the route, the *London Engineer* (launched 1818), one of the first paddle-steamers to ply the river, had been built at Samuel and Daniel Brent's shipyard at Greenland Dock, Rotherhithe, with engines supplied by Maudslay's, specifically to take advantage of the Margate trade. She was sumptuously fitted out for passenger comfort, with lofty well-ventilated saloons and elegant painted and carved decoration. The *London Engineer* had her paddle wheels installed in a central well amidships, in a novel design patented by Richard Trevithick in 1808. This was supposed to make the vessel relatively safe from cannon fire and other damage, and it also created a mystery about how precisely she moved through the water without sails, and with no visibly splashing paddles.

The Brent shipyard had built naval ships since the yard was established in the 1750s, but when naval orders reduced drastically after the Napoleonic Wars the company turned to other ways of building ships and making money. Brent's first steam-driven warship was the *Rising Star* (launched 1821), built for Thomas, Lord Cochrane, the buccaneering naval officer who sought glory in the years after Trafalgar. With Britain now firmly ruling the waves Cochrane had to travel thousands of miles for action, specifically in 1818 to the Pacific coast of Chile where he commanded the Chilean navy in the war of independence from Spain. The *Rising Star*, with Maudslay engines adapted by Galloway, was to be Cochrane's secret weapon against the Spanish. But she arrived too late; the war was already won by the time she entered Valparaiso harbour in April 1822, having been delayed by malfunctions during her crossing of the Atlantic. She was the first steamboat to make the Atlantic crossing, though she did most of the journey under auxiliary sail, and the first to round Cape Horn and enter the Pacific Ocean.

Although she missed the war, the *Rising Star* did catch one of the most formidable of British women travellers of the age. Who should appear on the other side of the globe as the *Rising Star*, with its polar-bear figurehead, nosed into the Pacific dawn but Maria Graham, who had just buried her husband in Valparaiso. Nursing her grief, Maria Graham nevertheless found the words to express a seminal moment in the history of man's spread around the world:

> The first thing I did was to visit the machinery, which consists of two steam-engines each of forty-five horse power, and the wheels covered so as not to show in the water from without . . . It was with no small delight that I set my foot on the deck of the first steam-vessel that ever navigated the Pacific, and I thought, with exultation, of the triumphs of man over the obstacles nature seems to have placed between him and the accomplishment of his imaginations.

With Samuel and Daniel Brent as the main contractor, Alexander Galloway, whose engines had drawn Maria Graham and the *Rising Star* together, entered a deal in March 1825 with a mysterious pair of Graecophile bankers, Jacob and Samson Ricardo. They eventually produced £160,000 on behalf of Greece to purchase first one, then five more steam-driven warships for the embryonic (that is, practically non-existent) Greek navy to fight for independence from Ottoman Turkish domination. The navy was to be under the command of Cochrane, now looking for fresh fields of action after turning up late in Chile. Maria Graham found Cochrane to be 'a most extraordinary man – as gentle as he is determined, as kind-hearted as he is courageous, and as generous as either. I grudge him to these foreign services & hope before I die to see him where he should be.'

The boats were needed rapidly, by Christmas 1825, and to speed things up the understanding was that they were to be purchased as ready-made vessels, converted for war. But misunderstanding crept in, and the order was placed for the boats to be built from scratch. They were substantial vessels, designed to impress and to frighten: three were to be 150 feet long, the others 100 feet. The Greek war of independence had become an emotional issue in England. The Elgin Marbles, though removed from Athens when Greek power and self-esteem were at their lowest ebb, were a perpetual reminder for Britons of the heights that Greek culture had reached. The slaughter in 1822 by the Turks of 25,000 Greek inhabitants of Chios, an island just off the Turkish coast, had shaken public opinion in Britain. Chios, a rich and cosmopolitan island with a population of merchants, bankers, lawyers and farmers who had dominated trade in the eastern Mediterranean for centuries, was devastated and forcibly depopulated. The international offence that this gave was expressed by Delacroix in his painting *Massacre at Chios* (1824), presented to the Louvre by King Charles X of France. The massacre led to the formation of the London Greek Committee in 1823, its membership including Lord Byron, Sir Francis Burdett and John Cam Hobhouse. Byron, who supported the suggestion that steam warships should be used against Turkey, died fighting for Greek freedom at Missolonghi in April 1824. This timely, dramatic and unnecessary death galvanised the cause.

Alexander Galloway had been given the task of making the engines for the warships because he was 'considered a man entirely devoted to the cause of freedom . . . and consequently a man enjoying the reputation of a Philhellene'. He and Cochrane had done business together before, having been jointly granted a patent in 1818 for a means of removing gases from stoves and transferring them to useful purposes. Nonetheless Galloway did not win Cochrane's complete confidence in the matter of the building of the ships. Despite the short time available, Galloway appears to have become 'fertile in promises', but continually letting Cochrane down: 'it was always "three weeks hence"', Cochrane was told. The first boat, the *Perseverance*, later renamed *Karteria*, did not sail for Greece until May 1826, leading the bankers to the expedition to complain: 'Galloway is the evil genius that pursues us everywhere: his presumption is only equalled by his incompetency. Whatever he has to do with is miserably deficient. We do not think his misconduct has been intentional; but it has proved most fatal to the interests of Greece, and of those engaged on her behalf.'

Galloway dismissed the odium heaped on him as 'calumnious misrepresentations'. His enemies had misjudged not only his skill as an engineer, but also his clarity and determination in rebutting their claims. The man who had challenged the Home Secretary in 1795, and had taken on the Professor of Geometry at Oxford in 1814, could equally take on his critics in 1826 and 1827. The boats as supplied by Brent turned out to settle twice as low in the water as expected, so that the engines had to overcome additional heavy resistance from the sea.

> If upon this discovery I had acted the part of a *prudent man* instead of that of an *ardent and generous friend to liberty*, I should have refused to place the engines into such vessels, but my zeal for the cause of the Greeks . . . induced me to propose to alter the engines . . . to overcome these difficulties. This created not only unavoidable delays, but opened the door to a chain of events, by which I have lost many thousand pounds, besides having my reputation unjustly assailed, and my integrity as a man undeservedly suspected.

The Greek boats, with internal paddle wheels like the *Rising Star*, were using:

> novel and experimental machinery [which] (especially for navigation) is what every engineer dreads, *because it invariably gives him vast additional trouble and anxiety, and is never a source of profit to him* . . . The novel construction of the vessels was found to deprive them of all *steering-capability*, and this caused numerous alterations to be made in the construction of the vessels themselves.

Another problem that beset Galloway was that his business interests were so wide and complex that they extended, as we have seen, deep into the Ottoman Empire itself. Having built the world's largest cotton press for Mehmet Ali Pasha in Alexandria, he had to write a letter to *The Times* to counter press criticism that he was in the pay of the Ottoman Turks. His son John was also implicated in converting the *London Engineer*, lately taken off the London-to-Margate run, into a warship for the Turks to use against the Greeks. Intrigue built on intrigue, and Galloway was further accused of 'having private connections with the Pasha of Egypt', and that he 'never intended to do the work [for the Greek cause] he was employed to do'.

The radical politician and journalist William Cobbett tore into Galloway and the bankers in *Cobbett's Weekly Register*. It was Cobbett's political campaigning that would come to fire up the

Wiltshire weavers to attack Gurney's steam carriage in Melksham in 1829. Referring to the bankers allegedly pocketing £64,000 in the Greek gunboat deal, Cobbett wrote: 'Oh brave Greeks! to have such *patriots* to aid you with their financial skill; such *patriots* as Mr Galloway to make engines of war for you when his son is making them for the Turks.' In the next issue, Cobbett attacked again. The £160,000 was meant to purchase vessels, not to have them built:

> and strange to say ONE ENGINEER ALONE WAS EMPLOYED TO PREPARE ALL THE STEAM ENGINES AND MACHIN-ERY! . . . We have been . . . *told that the matter rested entirely with Mr Galloway* the Engineer; whilst [Galloway] . . . *more than once hesitated to answer our enquiries.* Will it be credited that it was left to *one Engineer to prepare the engines and machinery for six vessels,* which were to be got ready for sea within two months and a half, and *that the Engineer charged with this service on behalf of Greece should be one who is employed by, and has, for a long time past had a son at Alexandria, in the pay of the Pasha of Egypt?*

Things did not look good for Galloway, but nevertheless he robustly defended himself against Cobbett's attacks. John Galloway's employment in Egypt had been widely known long before the Greek gunboat affair, and when Galloway first met the bankers in his factory, 'I not only then stated to them the employment of my son in Egypt, but pointed out several engines I was then finishing for the Pasha of that country. There was therefore neither mystery nor concealment in my conduct.'

This controversy coloured the latter part of Galloway's career as an engineer, but despite being severely damaged financially by it, he came to take a sanguine attitude to Cobbett. 'If Cobbett was not so bad a fellow,' he wrote to Francis Place three years later, 'I should like to see him in the House [of Commons], as I think he would break down *that courtesy amongst its members, which has so often destroyed good men and so long and successfully humbugged the people.'* The second ship, the *Enterprize,* renamed *Epicheiresis,* eventually sailed in April 1827, and the third, the *Irresistible,* later *Hermes,* did not get to Greece until September 1828. The fourth, the *Mercury,* arrived three months later, and the fifth and sixth never left the shipyard, and rotted away on the river. As did the *Rising Star* in Chile, Galloway's steamboats missed the action off Greece: the Turks were annihilated at the Battle of Navarino in October 1827 with the old technology, a force of sailing ships. With this crisis, the public got an early taste of the financial, political and technological problems which are endemic in advanced engineering enterprises conducted under political pressure. Successful technological research cannot simply be bought. Such crises were common in the twentieth century – the nuclear bomb, the Apollo programme, Concorde – but the Greek gunboat affair of 1825–7, with the radical politician–engineer Alexander Galloway at its heart, was perhaps the earliest nineteenth-century precursor.

9

Haydon, Géricault and Bullock at the
Egyptian Hall

~

THREE VERY LARGE soldiers from the King's Life Guard came heaving, puffing and cursing out of a side gate on Alpha Road, a dozen or more paces from its corner with Lisson Grove. One stumbled as his foot slipped on a cold paving stone wet from February rain. A long roll of canvas, like a steamboat's chimney stack, was a dead weight on their shoulders. For six years, since 1814, the thirteen-by-fifteen feet canvas had been stretched across the back wall of Benjamin Robert Haydon's painting room, causing 'struggle, ill-health and pecuniary distress', as upon it the artist created what he considered to be his masterpiece, *Christ's Entry into Jerusalem*. By turns, Haydon had been deep in despair, and then like a rising bubble buoyed by 'aspiration and glowing elasticity of imagination', and yet more by enthusiasm for the painting and encouragement from 'fashion, beauty and rank, by genius and by royalty'.

The progress of Haydon's painting was a source of some interest to artists and patrons in London, but perhaps not as much as the artist hoped. 'Charmante, charmante,' Canova said doubtfully, adding, 'Vous êtes un brave homme . . . La composition est très belle.' Haydon opened his painting room every Sunday from two until five o'clock and it was 'generally crowded with visitors – from the citizen up to the prince', or so Haydon claimed. The French natural scientist Georges Cuvier came to see it, as had the Grand Duke Michael of Russia, the brother of the future Czar Nicholas I, who found amusement in sitting down on top of his attendant physician, as if by mistake, and did this regularly. When Haydon gave his 'Immortal Dinner' in December 1817, the unfinished painting dominated the proceedings, and gleamed in the firelight behind

Wordsworth, Keats and Lamb. 'Wear thy own green palm, Haydon, triumphantly', Lamb wrote in a poem praising the painting. The expectation for *Christ's Entry into Jerusalem* was, as Haydon put it, 'very high indeed'.

There were three very different, but in their own way equally distinguished exhibition places in London, where Haydon could have chosen to display *Christ's Entry into Jerusalem*. One was the Royal Academy, where in April he could have submitted the painting to the mercy of the hanging committee, among whom this year was Joseph Farington. But in the Academy's Great Rooms Haydon would have been obliged to give up all control of how his painting should be treated, and risk its being displayed obscurely or with disrespect. He had experienced rough treatment by an Academy hanging committee before: his *Dentatus*, depicting the frugal Roman tribune who refused to be bribed, was poorly hung in 1809. 'God forgive him, I can't,' Haydon wrote of the mild-mannered Thomas Phillips who with Martin Archer Shee was a member of that year's hanging committee. 'The bitterest enemy from the beginning I ever had, except Shee.' This was one of the first steps in Haydon's alienation from the Royal Academy. To Haydon, 'all the world were fools; he was the little bit of leaven that was to bring the stolid lump to fermentation; the one wise man whose presence rescued the mass of mankind from unqualified insignificance and fatuity.' He would not toe the line; he spoke his mind and annoyed people; he swore. Bulky, bullet-headed, self-opinionated and uncompromising, Haydon effectively cast himself out of the care and ken of the Academy. 'I was opposed, calumniated and run down by the Academy for what they called my impertinence in thinking of such a picture [*The Judgement of Solomon*] without being commissioned.'

The second possibility for Haydon was the British Institution at 52 Pall Mall, on the north side of the street near St James's Palace. The British Institution, which is not to be confused with the Royal Institution in Albemarle Street, was probably the finest and most sympathetic space for showing large paintings. It had been built as an art gallery in 1789 for Alderman John Boydell's commercial venture of commissioning, for engraving and publication, paintings of scenes and characters from Shakespeare. When the business failed in 1805, the building and its entire contents were sold up, like the Leverian Museum in 1786, by lottery. The gallery, which was bought by a consortium of connoisseurs and members of the aristocracy, had generous interlocking exhibition rooms, high walls and top lighting, and presented all the best conditions for displaying grand art. Despite an initial indulgence towards having artists among its management, the aristocratic and moneyed empire of the British Institution struck back to give connoisseurs control over what the public saw in the art world of London.

The British Institution and the Academy began as friendly rivals with complementary aims – the one as an academy for students run by artists, the other a showcase for mature artists, dead and alive, run by connoisseurs and collectors. Nevertheless, the two organisations circled around each other in their search for influence. The British Institution cleverly came to an agreement with the Academy to open its exhibitions in February, thus taking priority from the Academy whose annual exhibition opened in late April when the British Institution closed. To underline the point that the two would not interfere with each other in the market place, the British Institution rules specified that, 'being intended to extend and increase the beneficial effects of the Royal Academy . . . the British Institution will be shut up during their annual exhibition'.

The market that both sought was limited. There was a finite number of wealthy men, and many organisations and causes seeking their support. The attraction that art held for the general public also had its natural limits. Private collectors, such as Thomas Hope, Sir John Soane, the Marquis of Stafford and the Marquis of Westminster, threw their houses and collections open to the public from time to time, Soane on Sundays, Stafford and Westminster in May and June. The cumulative effect of this added to the amenities of London, even if it began to be taken for granted, as the critic and pioneer art historian Anna Jameson recalled:

> We can all remember the loiterers and loungers . . . people who instead of moving amid these wonders and beauties 'all silent and divine' . . . strutting about as if they had the right to be there, talking, flirting, peeping and prying, lifting up covers of chairs to examine the furniture, touching the ornaments – even the pictures.

Some collectors on opening their houses to the public got more than they bargained for. Walter Fawkes, the friend and patron of Turner, who opened his collection at his house, 45 Grosvenor Place, in 1819, witnessed a crush as one group of visitors met another on the stairs:

> [We] remained jammed in on the landing-place for at least half an hour, during which we saw rouge melted, teeth dropped, feathers broken, bonnets crushed, flounces torn, humps pulled off, heard Dandy laces give, and in the end saw emerge from the doorway the truly suffocated Easterns we had so long before left struggling there.

Another, William Beckford in his country palace Fonthill Abbey, Wiltshire, employed an enthusiastic housekeeper who grandly pointed out the old masters, saying, this is by Og of Bassan; this is a Watersouchy of Amsterdam; and this a genuine Blunderbussiana of Venice.

The new dimension that the British Institution brought to cultural life in London was its series of exhibitions of old master and recent British artists drawn from aristocratic art collections in London and the country. Thus in 1813 the British Institution showed the paintings of Sir Joshua Reynolds, the deceased first President of the Royal Academy; in 1815 paintings by Rubens, Rembrandt and Van Dyck; and in 1818 Italian and Spanish masters. This was something the Royal Academy, then, could not and did not do, and it was a conscious attempt not only to show off private riches, but also to create an approximation of a national gallery in London, in the years before the National Gallery was established in its first home at 100 Pall Mall, on the south side of the road, close to Carlton House, in 1824. The British Institution's exhibitions gave the public an opportunity to see 'the most perfect specimens of every school of painting', and to save those who were capable of such travel 'the fatigue and expense of a long, and perhaps a *fruitless* journey, to a palace, in one of the most distant of the English counties, in which [works of art] may have been deposited'.

High in prestige though the British Institution was in 1820, Haydon did not choose to show *Christ's Entry into Jerusalem* there. Falling out with the Royal Academy was not enough for him: he had crossed swords with the British Institution management also. In 1816 he had suggested to its directors that the Institution organise a system of annual prizes ('premiums') for various categories of art, including Historical Painting, Poetical Landscape, and genre – 'Subjects of peasant life and humour', as Haydon described it. The directors considered Haydon's proposal, and announced a diluted variation of it. Whether or not he understood the reasons for the variation, Haydon later uttered some withering remarks on the subject:

> This was nothing but that usual want of confidence in their own judgment which has ever fettered, and will ever fetter, the directors of the Gallery and all committees or commissioners composed of the same class. High bred, and feeling that the patronage of Art is a part of their duty as an aristocracy, they are very much to be pitied for their want of knowledge of Art as a class.

During an earlier skirmish with the British Institution directors, Haydon believed himself to have been cheated out of the chance of a three-hundred-guinea prize for his *Macbeth* (1812). He blamed Academicians on the jury for leaving him without any prize, and thirty guineas short of the price of the picture's frame. 'What should I do? I owed my landlord £200. How was I to go on? Would he allow it? How was I to dine – to live, in fact?' Thus he intricately mixed in his imagination members of the Royal Academy and British Institution officials as fools at best and villains at worst, creating in his own mind conditions that made it impossible for him to show *Christ's Entry into Jerusalem* at either institution.

There was one more place left for him, however. This was the most fashionable exhibition hall available for hire in London, the Egyptian Hall, which sat between prim Georgian terraces on the south side of Piccadilly, almost directly opposite the junction with Bond Street. The Egyptian Hall had the façade of a pharaonic temple and the internal volume of a Nile hippopotamus. It had been designed in 1812 by Peter Frederick Robinson to house the huge collection of natural history specimens, arms and armour, curiosities from the South Seas and much else – 32,000 or more objects – brought together by the showman William Bullock. This self-confident entrepreneur from the north-west of England had bought many hundreds of items, including South Seas ethnography, from the former Leverian Museum by Blackfriars Bridge, which had closed for the last time in 1806. Some of the material in the Leverian Museum had itself been bought from a defunct museum in Leicester Square. So it was that curiosities circulated among the glass cabinets of London: what may be sold off as no longer interesting to the public in one part of the capital might surface again in a different context, tidied up and re-presented under the ebullient authority of a new proprietor.

William Bullock, whose brother the cabinet maker George Bullock ran a successful business off Hanover Square, had brought the bulk of his 'museum' to London from Liverpool in 1809. He showed it first at 22 Piccadilly, on the north side of the street, where in a central rotunda, well lit under a glazed dome, visitors saw stuffed wild animals – elephant, rhinoceros, ostrich and other creatures cor-ralled together with palm trees and exotic ferns. There were cases of yet more stuffed animals and birds around the room, and further rooms of antiquity and oddity. Jane Austen saw Bullock's museum and the British Institution, and, as she told her sister, had some amusement at each, 'tho' my preference for Men & Women, always inclines me to attend more to the company than the sight'. Having generated great public interest at number 22, Bullock moved the col-lection across to his new Egyptian building on the sunny side of the street in 1812.

Bullock first named his collection the Liverpool Museum, but then strategically retitled it the London Museum, even though its only connection with the capital was that it happened to be there. Visitors passed under figures of Isis and Osiris when they entered the building, and paid their shilling for admission. In one of the main display rooms Bullock installed his 'Pantherion', an exhibition dis-playing what he claimed was 'the whole of the known Quadrupeds, in a manner that will convey a more perfect idea of their haunts and mode of life'. This was a direct challenge to the authority of the British Museum, which, with public funds, was attempting much the same thing, with education attached. Being a showman, Bullock opted for the total experience when preparing his displays. He arranged his animals in an 'Indian Hut, situated in a Tropical Forest', to which visitors gained access by passing through a basaltic cave modelled on the Giant's Causeway in County Antrim, and Fingal's Cave on Staffa. Supplying his visitors with a true sense of geographical continuity was not what Bullock was aiming for. Nonetheless, as William Jerdan noted, Bullock realised that London provided ample opportunity for him, and that 'the town was absolutely astonished by . . . so vast and marvellous a treasure'. 'The Tower, and a wild beast show at Exeter Change in the Strand, comprehended their [that is, Londoners'] zoology, and Covent Garden and the unadorned Parks their botany – all else was desert . . . Bullock dispelled this crass condition of mind in everything beyond the daily routine of trade.' Jerdan held Bullock in high admiration.

> Such a man does infinite good. He does not set up as a teacher . . . but he conveys more intelligence to the public mind, than a multitude of pseudo-dogmatists, and even able lecturers and writers . . . I held with Mr Bullock in all his undertakings, admired his indefatigable energy, and wondered at the tact by which he perceived attraction after attraction, and never failed to gratify the 'world'.

Like all good businessmen, Bullock looked for ways to keep the money flowing. In 1813 he was offered for sale the head of Oliver Cromwell, 'still intire with the flesh on having been embalmed and fixed on part of the pike on which it was exposed by order of Charles the Second'. This had been displayed off Old Bond Street in the recent past, John Constable having described it as 'an old, rusty, fusty head with a spike in it'. Sensing perhaps an opportunity for self-publicity, Bullock consulted the Prime Minister, Lord Liverpool, for advice 'on the propriety of exhibiting such an article', but got a dampening response. Over the winter of 1815–16 he began a series of special exhibitions of whatever he felt would attract visitors in large numbers. He acquired Napoleon's dark blue and gold bullet-proof carriage used at Waterloo, in which the Emperor ate, slept, wrote and planned his campaign. This attracted tens of thousands of visitors who, despite the presence of a small army of severe museum guards, practically broke the carriage to bits in their desire to see it. Also in 1816, perhaps across the same period as Napoleon's carriage, Bullock showed the twenty-six-feet-long canvas

Brutus Condemning his Sons by the French painter Guillaume Lethière: 'a very fine work of art', Joseph Farington pronounced, seen by 'many connoisseurs'. This monster was hung on the ground floor in what Bullock now called the Roman Gallery, which may have replaced the Pantherion, and in which he displayed antiquities.

Following this success, Bullock moved even more ambitiously into big art by purchasing and displaying in 1817 the thirty-feet-long canvas *The Son of the Widow of Nain* by Jean-Baptiste Joseph Wicar. This was 'much inferior', to the Lethière, according to Farington. These enormous French paintings were a challenge to the dominance of the Royal Academy and the British Institution, neither of which could hope to display works of such size and dramatic impact, and their presence suggests that Bullock was trying to raise the tone of the Egyptian Hall by displaying art. If this was the case, it failed in the eyes of Academicians, many of whom returned the free entry tickets Bullock sent to them. They appreciated the gesture even less than their colleagues had in 1804 when Thomas Hope handed out tickets to Academicians to see his collection.

Realising that newsworthy objects could make him more money, and that stuffed animals and curiosities had only a finite attraction for the public, Bullock sold his collection in 1819. He was feeling the pressure from the decision of the British Museum trustees to make Montagu House more accessible, as we might put it in the twenty-first century, or, as Bullock put it, 'finding that the throwing open the British Museum to the public which in itself is a measure most praiseworthy . . . has so far diminished the profits of his private Museum . . . he can no longer support it to his own advantage'. Thus he offered his collection to the nation for £9,000. The Prime Minister turned him down, and at an auction the ethnographical material went to the Berlin Museum, and other objects to the University of Edinburgh.

The sale gave Bullock the opportunity to remodel the Egyptian Hall. In the Great Room he went conclusively overboard by creating a gaudy pastiche of an Egyptian interior, and used it for crowd-pulling shows. In 1821 its architecture suited to perfection the items from the tomb of Seti I which Giovanni Belzoni had discovered, with its centrepiece the sarcophagus that soon found its home in Sir John Soane's Museum. In that same year the Society of Painters in Watercolour held their exhibition in the Great Room. A family of Laplanders, with their reindeers, sledges and clothing, was Bullock's sensation of 1822: the Egyptian Great Room would not have been appropriate for them, and Rowlandson's aquatint suggests they were camped in a top-lit panelled room elsewhere in the building. In the Egyptian Room that year casts of a group of highly coloured reliefs from Luxor were shown, 'which, being coloured from the originals', one young visitor enthused, 'it is absolutely the same thing as going to Egypt to see the originals'. Then in 1822–3 Bullock went wandering in the New World and Central America, and brought back Mexican artefacts which he displayed in 1824.

Haydon saw the point of Bullock's entrepreneurship. They were kindred spirits, sharing enthusiasm for extravagant and daring productions, a delight in the exotic and a cavalier way with money. Bullock, however, was able to judge public mood and had the sense to try to keep ahead of fashion, and to get out before the wind changed. He was sure of himself; he made a fortune. Haydon on the other hand persisted obstinately with historical and religious subjects of a kind that had run out of fashion, and which sucked up his time and energies. In a typical moment of piteous self-examination he wrote: 'Passed an acute and miserable morning in comparing myself with Raphael. At my age he had completed a Vatican Room.' Haydon's work had many admirers, but no real market, and he found it impossible to accumulate money. He borrowed with extravagant purpose, against the remote possibility of a purchase from an influential patron, or of a large cash prize. 'Thus reasoning,' he had written in 1810 of a miscalculation, 'I borrowed . . . *And here began debt and obligation, out of which I never have been, and never shall be, extricated, as long as I live.*'

One contributory cause of Haydon's financial difficulties was that each painting took him so long to complete, and he insisted and worked towards an impossible perfection. 'Bitter anxieties!' he would exclaim; 'Cast down!' he would say, as he described his tribulations with patrons, paintings and prizes. In 1828 he beseeched John Murray for employment in designing, sketching or painting. 'I have a large family, and between the sale of one Picture and another, I am sure to get with debt, unless I can establish some practice that will obtain ready money.' This went on for a lifetime. In 1823, 1827, 1830 and 1836 he was thrown into the King's Bench Prison, 'that blessed refuge for the miserable', for debt. Nevertheless, when he entertained Haydon insisted on the best linen, the best wine and cuts, and a table laid to perfection with the best silver. This he usually borrowed. For one party he demanded from his landlord William Newton '4 more large knives and forks, two small decanters – and 8 wine glasses all which shall be safely returned'. The attention to detail and standards that drove his entertaining also drove Haydon as an artist. Difficulty empowered him, as did his profound religious faith and the strength that it brought him. 'I look upon all difficulties as stimulants to action. I have £200 to pay the twenty-first of next month. As yet I have not a sixpence towards it; but in God I trust who has always relieved me. Let me be successful in realising my conceptions in my day's labour, and what shall subdue me but extinction?'

The six years it took Haydon to paint *Christ's Entry into Jerusalem* were filled with the painstaking preparation of the canvas, and the careful making of dozens of studies of his friends and models for figures in the painting – William Hazlitt, John Keats and Wordsworth appear as themselves; Newton and Voltaire are there also. He drew extensively from the Elgin Marbles and from the Raphael Cartoons, two of which had been lent by the Prince Regent for display in the British Institution in 1816. Across this time also, Haydon had involved himself in the whirlwind controversy over the government's purchase of the Elgin Marbles. The pressure had made him ill. 'Shaking like an aspen leaf I was obliged to stop, to the regret of everybody. My room was so small, the air so confined, the effluvium of paint so overpowering, that many people of fashion advised me to move if I wished to save my life.' Haydon had long been the butt of humour and malice within the fraternity of Academicians. 'The Academicians now say I am an artful designing politic fellow; first I was a rash, thoughtless fool . . . They always attribute the actions of those they envy to any cause but principle, and the excellence of their works to any cause but talent.' When at last *Christ's Entry* was finished, and Haydon had approached Bullock to show the work at the Egyptian Hall, an Academician advised Bullock: 'Take care of your rent!'

With immense physical effort, grunting and heaving, the rolled canvas found its way into the Great Room on the first floor of the Egyptian Hall. Then in four long golden lengths, to be assembled *in situ*, came the frame. *Christ's Entry into Jerusalem* was not alone: with it Haydon exhibited his *Joseph and Mary, Dentatus, Macbeth* and *The Judgement of Solomon*. The paintings will have looked completely out of place in Bullock's Egyptian fantasy, but so determined and driven was Haydon that he probably took no notice. The first time his hired Life Guards heaved *Christ's Entry* up in its frame to the wall its weight snapped an iron ring with a supposed six-hundred-pound breaking strain. 'The strongest soldiers were as nervous as infants, but at last we lifted it by machinery and pitched it without accident right on its proper support.' An army of women sewed deep purple fabric to hang in folds around the painting, and a troop of boys cleared and tidied the room as Haydon dashed off to borrow £50 to pay for everything. Bullock came in and shook his head: 'Goodbye, rent.'

Across the three days of preparation, Haydon sent out eight hundred tickets for the private viewing days, and, on Saturday 25 March 1820 sat in a coffee house near by to have a long lunch and to watch as his guests rolled up. Though they came slowly at first, they gradually began to come by dozens in their carriages. All closely inspected *Christ's Entry into Jerusalem*; they looked at the head of Christ; they observed the crowds thronging the background of the painting; they discussed the contemplative head of Wordsworth and the sneering head of the atheist Voltaire. Few were brave enough to tender an opinion, until in walked the celebrated actress Mrs Siddons, 'with all the dignity of her majestic presence . . . like a Ceres or a Juno'. The crowds parted; the room fell silent. Somebody asked Mrs Siddons carefully what she thought of the head of Christ. She paused, then spoke deeply, loudly and with a tragic timbre: 'It is completely successful.' Cheers and chatter and hurrahs for Haydon: 'It is completely successful!' 'It is completely successful!' 'It is completely successful!'

Until Bullock energetically began to change the tradition, artists exhibited their work either in their own studios and private galleries, with picture dealers, or in mixed exhibitions such as those at the British Institution and the Royal Academy. Gainsborough and Reynolds were successful enough to have had their own private galleries at the end of the eighteenth century, as Turner had in the first half of the nineteenth. The Egyptian Hall became the first 'venue' to enable artists to mount their own individual shows of current work, and Haydon and, two years later, John Martin were the first to take advantage of this opportunity. An allied opportunity for artists was the Panorama, but in these the artist was generally anonymous, with credit and profit returning to the entrepreneur. Haydon's Egyptian Hall venture had, in embryo, all the panoply of the exhibition private view that has come to characterise gallery openings in the early-twenty-first century: the frantic set-up, the owner worrying about the rent, the invitation cards and mailing list, the catalogue, the cultural and social elite on parade, the anxious artist, the guests waiting for a prominent critic to take a view, the critical verdict. In this, as in little else, Haydon scored a world 'first'.

The *London Magazine* supported Mrs Siddons's opinion of Haydon's exhibition. 'This is certainly the finest historical picture which England has ever produced,' it wrote, 'and she might fairly challenge all Europe at present to produce anything like it.' The magazine sympathised with the artist's plight by regretting that he, like other historical painters in England before him, had been obliged 'to advertise himself like a quack doctor, to squeeze that support from the shillings of the people which he has vainly hoped to obtain from public patronage'.

In the meantime, across the English Channel, a painting at twenty-four feet by eighteen larger yet than Haydon's had been a *succès de scandale* at the 1819 Paris Salon. *The Raft of the Medusa* by Théodore Géricault was a painting representing not Christian celebration, nor a moment of French naval glory, but an event which brought severe embarrassment to the government of post-Napoleonic France. The subject was the last few hours of the ordeal of survivors of the wrecked French naval flagship *Medusa*, sent in 1816 to re-establish a colony in Senegal in West Africa. They had been on the raft for thirteen days and their numbers had shrunk through mutiny, starvation and drowning from 150 people to (according to the painting) fourteen, until they were rescued by the British ship *Argus*. Reports circulated that the survivors had resorted to cannibalism.

Sensing perhaps that Haydon's *Christ's Entry into Jerusalem* was not going to pay its way, Bullock welcomed Géricault to the Egyptian Hall in April 1820. The pair agreed that *The Raft of the Medusa* should be shown without delay in the Hall's Roman Gallery. There was something slightly dubious about Haydon that Bullock, wary old showman that he was, would have been able to detect if not to analyse. Haydon could be charming one minute and wheedling the next; bombastic, full of bluster and self-pity, and not reliable. He was not a man to do business with lightly; he was a trial and a worry to his friends. Bullock was more comfortable with a real, dark, Saturnine, silent, Gallic artist like Géricault, a man with an inner mystery that he had no need (or inclination) to fathom.

Géricault's *Raft of the Medusa* was shipped from Paris, and installed in the Egyptian Hall where the exhibition opened on 12 June. Unlike the arrangement with Haydon, who rented his space, with Géricault Bullock took the commercial risk and offered the artist a share of the receipts. Bullock also placed the advertisements, twenty-two on the front pages of *The Times* during the showing of the painting, and many more in other London papers. On some days, Géricault's *Times* advertisement (paid for by Bullock) and Haydon's (paid for by Haydon) jockeyed for attention next to each other. 'MR HAYDON'S PICTURE of CHRIST'S TRIUMPHANT ENTRY into JERUSALEM, which has been nearly 6 years on the easel, is now exhibiting at Bullock's Museum, Piccadilly, with all his other Pictures and Drawings, from 10 to 6,' said one; 'MONSIEUR JERRICAULT'S GREAT PICTURE . . . is now OPEN for public inspection in the Roman Gallery at the Egyptian Hall, Piccadilly . . . this chef-d'oeuvre of foreign art,' said the other. As had Haydon, Géricault wrote out his own invitations. Two of these survive, one addressed to 'Mr Philips', and another to the art dealer Colnaghi. Géricault, however, went one better than Haydon: he wrote his invitations on the back of a small lithograph of the painting, and gave these out to all visitors so that everybody went home with an image.

With Haydon upstairs and Géricault downstairs, Bullock's

Egyptian Hall contained, in the summer of 1820, two paintings which are the twin poles of early-nineteenth-century European painting. Both attracted people in large numbers: Haydon characteristically complained that during the summer 'people had left town and forgotten me and my picture'. Nevertheless, though takings fluctuated, by June he had made £1,000 according to David Wilkie, and ended the exhibition on 4 November with £1,760 7s 6d in his pocket. Haydon tells us he took £1,547 8s in shilling tickets, which reveals that he must have admitted at least 30,948 people. Many of these, from early June until early November, would have stumped up two shillings to see both paintings.

The Raft of the Medusa and *Christ's Entry into Jerusalem* had a great deal in common: both were the product of years of obsessive mental and physical labour by two men working largely alone. Haydon spent six years on his work (the time interspersed with other things); Géricault took perhaps two. Haydon (or rather his servant, on his behalf) turned down an offer of £1,000 for the painting, the equivalent of perhaps £50,000 in the early twenty-first century. The British Institution declined to buy it, and Sir George Beaumont tried to organise a subscription to buy the painting for the new St Luke's Church, Chelsea. To Haydon's chagrin, Beaumont limited each subscriber to ten guineas, and the venture failed. 'It was my destiny always to suffer by the mismanagement of friends,' Haydon complained afterwards. Three years later, after exhibitions in Edinburgh and Glasgow, the work was sold to creditors for £240. It was bought in 1831 by Cephas Childs, a Philadelphia engraver, who took it to the United States where it was shown at the Pennsylvania Academy of Fine Arts in Philadelphia. Having been rescued from a fire in 1846, it was presented to Cincinnati cathedral. From there it found its way to the atrium of the Athenaeum of Mount St Mary's Seminary, 6616 Beechmont Avenue, Cincinnati, where it is one of the seminary treasures. Géricault's *Raft of the Medusa* was offered, on its return to Paris, for purchase for the French royal collections for 6,000 francs. The offer was ignored three times, and it was secured for the Louvre only when it was auctioned after the artist's death in 1824. Subsequently, it became one of the world's treasures.

The Raft of the Medusa was overwhelmingly praised by the London press. Connoisseurs and collectors including the Marquis of Stafford, Sir Thomas Baring and several Royal Academicians attended the private view, and at the close on 30 December Bullock claimed it had been seen by fifty-thousand visitors. The *Literary Gazette*, in a passage probably written by William Jerdan who claimed he never missed a show at the Egyptian Hall, declared: 'In this tremendous picture of human sufferings, the bold hand of the artist has laid bare the details of the horrid facts, with the severity of Michel Angelo and the gloom of Caravaggio . . . Taken all together, his work is . . . one of the finest specimens of the French school ever brought to this country.' Farington admitted that it was 'a fine performance which does honour to the French school'. Significantly, Haydon does not mention it in his surviving writings. Its theme was taken up by a rapidly composed melodrama at the Coburg Theatre, *The Shipwreck of the Medusa, or the Fatal Raft*, which played to 'overflowing audiences'. Nobody considered making a theatrical performance of Christ's entry into Jerusalem to cash in on Haydon.

In reflecting on an event which had neither religious nor patriotic sentiments – except for the fact that the survivors were rescued by a British ship – *The Raft of the Medusa* caught the public mood of post-war humanity, being a tragic account of survival in the face of a civilian rather than a military disaster. Whether Bullock's claim for visitor figures is accurate or not, both he and Géricault made handsome profits, the artist taking home between 17,000 and 20,000 francs, the equivalent of perhaps around £50,000 or £60,000 today.

Géricault remained in London until the end of December 1821. While the Royal Academy took him under its wing – he was a guest at the May 1821 banquet – it was not with the same enthusiasm that they had welcomed the charming Canova five years earlier. Once at least in London Géricault had reportedly tried to kill himself, his instability and fragile mental state making it difficult for other artists to warm to him: this was one quality he shared with Haydon. Géricault mixed with expatriate Frenchmen, and also with English artists and architects such as Wilkie and C. R. Cockerell, who had:

great admiration for his talent. His modesty so unusual and remarkable in a Frenchman his deep feeling of pity, the pathetique at the same time vigour fire and animation of his works . . . lying torpid days and weeks then rising to violent exertions. Riding tearing driving exposing himself to heat cold violence of all sorts.

William Bullock continued to strive for effect in his public displays. In 1822 he mounted in the Egyptian Hall's Great Room an exhibition of paintings and engravings by John Martin. The central exhibit, *Destruction of Pompeii and Herculaneum*, was, at five by eight feet, a mere bagatelle compared to Haydon's and Géricault's offerings; and a scrap compared to Lethière's and Wicar's monsters. Nevertheless, interspersed among the bulbous Egyptian pillars, looking very much at home there, were twenty-six of Martin's cataclysmic paintings, large and small, including *Sadak in Search of the Waters of Oblivion* (1812), *Joshua Commanding the Sun to Stand Still* (1816) and *The Fall of Babylon* (1819).

By exhibiting at the Egyptian Hall, Martin was making a decisive statement. He had in the past shown at both the Royal Academy and the British Institution, his first exhibit at the Academy being *Sadak in Search of the Waters of Oblivion* in 1812. This had been hung in the gloomy light of the ante-room to the Great Rooms at Somerset House, but to Martin's 'inexpressible delight' it was reviewed in the press, and found a buyer. Two years later when he showed his landscape *Clytie* at the Academy, he was devastated when a careless Academician allowed a pot of dark varnish to spill down the middle and ruin it. This accident was one of the factors that fuelled Martin's antipathy towards the Academy, giving him a resentment against it which lasted all his life.

Being an autonomous and rule-bound organisation, run by artists for artists, the Academy was an easy target for voluble and disaffected members and non-members. James Barry had ended his career there in 1799 by vilifying the Academy and by being the first Academician to be stripped of his rank. Haydon found rich targets among Academicians for his antagonisms. When he committed suicide in 1846, Turner was less than sympathetic, muttering in a characteristically lateral reference to the Academy, 'he stabbed his mother; he stabbed his mother'. The damage to Martin's *Clytie* was a catalyst to his fury against the Royal Academy. He felt his work did not get the best positions in the annual exhibitions: *Sadak* had been tucked away in the ante-room, as was *Joshua Commanding the Sun to Stand Still* in 1816. *The Bard* made it to the Great Room in 1817, but there it was hung too high for Martin's complete satisfaction.

One gets the impression that Martin was over-sensitive, not to say petulant. His paintings were, despite their positions on the Academy walls, receiving high public praise, and demand for engravings of them developed rapidly. *Joshua* 'acquired immense applause' for Martin, and when in 1819 he chose to show his *Fall of Babylon* at the British Institution rather than the Academy the visitors to the exhibition were entranced by the painting's detail, colour and drama: 'The spectators crowd around it, some with silence, some with exclamatory admiration; sometimes very near to look at the numerous small objects . . . sometimes further off to feast upon the grandeur of the whole.'

Martin had now turned his back on the Academy. Like Barry and Haydon, who called the Academy 'an inquisition without a Pope', Martin objected to what he called the Academy's 'unjust and illiberal laws.' Having chosen to show his *Macbeth* at the Institution rather than the Academy in 1820, he can hardly have been surprised to receive no votes when standing as one of forty-eight candidates for election as a Royal Academy Associate that same year. Among the electors who could have voted for him but did not were Callcott, Chantrey, Flaxman, Fuseli, Lawrence, Rossi, Smirke and Turner. The following year Martin showed the dynamic *Belshazzar's Feast* at the Institution to such acclaim that, as his biographer Thomas Balston put it, 'the day before Martin had been a painter of promise; that day he became famous'. So great was the crush that an iron rail had to be put in front of the picture.

Choosing to exhibit a new work at the British Institution, Martin had taken an aggressive step against the Royal Academy in response to 'their ill usage, or what I considered ill usage'. Had his paintings been mild landscapes, few would have noticed or cared. But Martin's paintings were, by everyday exhibition standards, huge – five by eight or nine feet, and not of cows and rivers in gentle greens and browns, but of flaming red and orange, with buildings on fire, lightning strikes, people going to their deaths, civilisations being destroyed, and the whole panoply of biblical apocalypse being visited upon the uncomprehending. And all this hanging on the Institution's scarlet-papered walls, 'so vivid . . . that it is said to have fatigued and distressed the eye and to have overpowered the brightest reds in the pictures'.

In taking his considered decision in 1822 to exhibit at the Egyptian Hall, the place where, once, stuffed animal displays had shared a building with vast neo-classical canvases, Martin, like Haydon, was moving even further from the Royal Academy. He was encouraging Bullock's attempt to drag the Egyptian Hall upmarket, to raise its tone away from a place of raree shows where a display of the rotting head of Oliver Cromwell could even be considered, to a gallery where thematic, controversial and challenging exhibitions were held.

10

As the Art Advances

~

JOHN MARTIN WAS an artist with the natural ability to connect a talent for pictorial invention, personal dynamism, social savoir-faire, natural physical strength, an aptitude for friendship and an understanding of the way the system worked. He was also a natty dresser, smart and trim, favouring a light primrose-coloured waistcoat with bright metal buttons, a blue coat with shiny buttons, and curled hair glowing with macassar oil. According to the young artist William Powell Frith, John Martin was 'one of the most beautiful beings I ever beheld'. Martin was quite unlike Haydon, who did indeed have all those same qualities, except the physical beauty, but whose character had the inconvenient addition of a volcanic temper, a mischievous talent for the disruption of systems, a disregard for money and a delight in the calculated insult. Martin knew how to work with the market and to spot opportunities; Haydon appeared to believe that the market, and fashion, would conform to his fantasies.

By the time he exhibited at the Egyptian Hall, Martin was doing well enough to live in a substantial house, 30 Allsop's Buildings on the north side of the New Road, now Marylebone Road. He was on the northern edge of the eighteenth-century expansion of London, within the Portman estate, and a short walk from the Grosvenor and Portland estates. This is where the smart money was, and where potential patrons shimmered in the urban undergrowth like large fat multicoloured beetles. To the north and east were fields and the Regent's Park, to the south and east was Portland Place, where Mary Anne Flaxman had seen the Park in the distance 'through the medium of an atmosphere composed of gold dust'. Martin now had a painting room big enough to take his large and yet larger canvases with ease, space for an engraving and printing room below, and the breadth of comfort required for him and his family to entertain friends and associates at his Monday soirées on a generous scale. After the Egyptian Hall experience, and the popularity that his paintings aroused, Martin took the publication of his images into his own hands, avoiding as far as he could the interference of engravers. He had made his own etchings in the past, but to translate his dramatically lit compositions into black and white he now took up mezzotint engraving, a medium which produces rich velvety blacks from which the image emerges as if light were coming out of darkness. The traditional engraving material was copper, but copper is soft, unable to produce prints in the quantity that Martin's public demanded. So instead he turned to the new process of engraving on steel, a technique which used all of the current expertise on the manufacture and use of steel as an alloyed and chemically amended variant of iron.

Among Martin's artist contemporaries, the engravers William Say and Thomas Lupton had experimented with varying degrees of success in engraving on steel around 1819 and 1820. In these same years Michael Faraday and the cutler James Stodart, who had a business making and selling surgical instruments, experimented with varieties of steel including the ancient Indian recipe for steel, 'wootz'. Together they published an account of their work in the *Quarterly Journal of Science* of 1820. Perhaps the man most determined to get the right kind of steel for engraving was not an artist engraver, but the American-born engineer and entrepreneur Jacob Perkins. At stake for him was a contract from the Bank of England to make secure and durable plates for printing banknotes in infinitely greater quantity than any artist would require for a print. Faraday visited Perkins's premises in Fleet Street in February 1820:

> He takes blocks of steel, softens them by some process of de-carbonization so that a knife cuts them almost in the manner of lead. Exquisite engravings are then made on them by hand and by lathes. The blocks are re-carbonized and converted into hard steel and this is in such an admirable way that the engraving suffers not the slightest injury. A roller of softened steel is then passed over this hard engraved plate under pressure and the engraving is reversed on to it,

i.e. reversed from the first plate. The roller is then carbonized and hardened and is the piece from which steel or copper plates are made for use. Thus the roller by being passed over a soft steel or a copper plate makes an impression on it exactly like the original plate and to appearance as sharp and fine. If of steel it is carbonized and hardened and will then give numberless impressions on paper without being injured. If of copper it works in the usual way, but on being worn out a second is made in a few moments.

Perkins's technique, so admired by Faraday, enabled him to create engraving plates on an industrial scale. Thomas Lupton, who won the Isis Medal at the Society of Arts in 1822, successfully alloyed steel with nickel and copper to make an engravable plate that produced more than 1,500 impressions. John Martin, who by the mid-1820s at least was in contact with Faraday at the Royal Institution, was fully abreast of the latest developments in engraving technology, either through Lupton who worked with Martin in the later 1820s, through Faraday, or perhaps through Perkins himself. Martin's popularity as an artist drew the publisher Septimus Prowett to invest £2,000 in him by commissioning in 1823 a set of twenty-four mezzotints of scenes from Milton's *Paradise Lost*. Prowett made another commission for £1,500 for a further set at smaller dimensions. Drawings from these, or perhaps the engravings themselves, were displayed at Faraday's invitation at a Friday-evening discourse at the Royal Institution in March 1827, and the following year Faraday helped Martin broadcast his engravings by sending a set to France through diplomatic channels.

Martin's mezzotints from *Paradise Lost* were unique in that they were designed straight on to the plate. Although there will have been preliminary drawings, the mezzotints were not reproductions of paintings, and for their successful sale relied solely on Martin's name and skill as an artist, and his reputation in the art market. As the prospectus put it: 'the Engravings . . . possess as originals the charm of being the first conceptions of the Artist, and have all the spirit and finish of the Painter's touch'. From now on Martin's business as an engraver went into overdrive. He announced an engraving of *Belshazzar's Feast* in 1826, 'the first large steel plate ever engraved in mezzotint', and promptly sacked Charles Turner from the task of engraving *Joshua Commanding the Sun to Stand Still*, an image Turner had been working on for years. Martin started the image afresh in mezzotint, and went on to engrave his *Deluge* (painting, 1826; mezzotint, 1828) and *Fall of Nineveh* (painting, 1828; mezzotint, 1830).

Martin did not do this all on his own, of course. Realising that large-scale demand required large-scale production he fitted out his basement printing room with the latest equipment, and employed a team of printers. Martin's son Leopold, recalling the printing venture, described the workshop as:

> nearly as perfect as art could make it. He had fly-wheel and screw-presses of the latest construction; ink-grinders, glass and iron; closets for paper French, India and English; drawers for canvas, blankets, inks, whiting, leather-shavings, etc; outdoor cupboards for charcoal and ashes; in fact every appliance necessary for what my father was converting into a fine art.

When Martin took something on, he entered into it with ambition and determination. He was rewarded not only with satisfactory sales – 482 first-run proofs of *The Deluge* were sold – but also with plaudits and a demand for a return to the large canvases with which he had made his name. He was praised in verse, by the Quaker poet Bernard Barton who wrote at least four poems inspired by his paintings. Martin's *Joshua* elicited from Barton lines that caught the blood and violence of the Battle of Gibeon in bucketsful:

> Look on the horrid conflict; mark the stream
> Of lurid and unnatural light that falls,
> Like some wild meteor'd bright terrific gleam,
> On Gibeon's steep and battlemented walls.

Martin was tapping into a rich market for imagery, spawned by the fertile supply of art exhibitions in London and beyond. Dozens of artists and publishers supplied prints, some working together in more or less rigid contractual agreement, others independently, and yet others trying to do the whole process themselves. Martin was, once he saw the profits to be made, one of the latter. Other artists made multiple arrangements: J. M. W. Turner worked with up to about eighty different engravers including George and

William Cooke, Charles Heath, Thomas Lupton, John Pye, Charles Turner and J. T. Willmore. Turner played his engravers like fish on a line, falling out with some and, like a father-figure, taking others such as the young Birmingham-born engraver J. T. Willmore under his wing. Willmore had already worked on engravings after Turner for a decade or more when the artist gave him an hour's lecture 'with many most cordial grunts . . . difficult to understand, on the art of engraving', and advised him 'to sacrifice everything to your art'. Turner could be encouraging one day and difficult and dismissive the next, and always stubborn and determined in his business relations with his engravers and publishers. His business methods were exasperating, as Francis Chantrey and George Jones found when in 1832 they tried to reason with him over a matter of pricing engravings. Chantrey told Murray:

> I have had a long conversation with Turner, supported by my friend Jones R.A. *We both agreed in your view* and so we told him, *again* and *again*. He argued stoutly that we have no right to injure speculations previously entered into (meaning Heath of course). On this we could come to no very clear understanding. You must now make the best you can of him. You will find him stiff to move.

Other individuals in the printmaking trade, such as John Britton, harnessed the publishing side of the business. While being a considerable artist in his own right, Britton made his greatest contribution as an entrepreneur publisher of other men's engravings. The search by an author or a publisher for an engraver could be a long job, as William Hyett, the author of a study of Northamptonshire's monuments, found:

> George Baker has recommended one very strongly of the name of 'Radclyffe' . . . Nichols has also recommended *'Woolnoth'* – whose Cathedrals you have probably seen . . . *Stothard* I have . . . Do you know anything of *Cooke* the engraver who executed a plate of Ld Bacon's monument for Mr Clutterbuck? I want also to find one *'Thompson'* a wood-engraver whom Mr Britton has employed.

The engraving market was further fuelled by the technological improvements in printing, by now steam-driven, which allowed much larger runs of books and journals to be produced to satisfy the burgeoning middle classes. One innovation was the publication of small-format annuals, such as the *Amulet* and the *Keepsake*, handy for the pocket or reticule, ideal for reading in the carriage or steam boat.

John Pye, one of the most distinguished and long-lived engravers of the period, was a regular contributor of engravings to the *Amulet* and other pocket journals. He devised improvements to his art, winning a Society of Arts silver medal for a new method of preparing charcoal and chalk for drawing. What raised Pye above the mass of engravers of his generation, however, was his physical energy and drive, and his bloody-minded campaigning to raise and maintain the status of engravers in Britain. He fought for the Artists' General Benevolent Fund, the charitable body that raised money to assist impoverished artists and their families, and organised engravers to join together and to publish their own prints in an effort to reduce the share of the profits taken by picture dealers. Like Haydon and Martin, Pye was a vehement critic of the Royal Academy, actively organising fellow engravers to campaign against the exclusion of engravers from full membership of the Academy. One tactic he used was to exhort his colleagues to make a declaration that they would pledge not to stand for election for Associateship of the Royal Academy 'until it shall render to the Art of Engraving that degree of importance which is attached to it in other countries of Europe'. Like Haydon and Martin also, Pye was called as a witness to parliamentary select committees, on Arts and Manufactures in 1835 and Art Unions in 1844. His clearest expression, however, of his zeal for fluid and fair support for artists comes in his book *Patronage of British Art* (1845), a polemic which enthusiastically recounts the battles fought by engravers for recognition by the Royal Academy, and for protection from the art trade.

Pye did not expect engravers to be exceptionally treated, just fairly treated. Engraving, like all trades, was subject to the market. Britain's power, he pointed out, was dependent on manufacture and commerce, and, as a result of this, had 'perhaps, more occasion than any other country for the aid of the fine arts'. He objected strongly to government money being used to foster art that would be 'looked upon as jewels of the state', to confer 'rank on the members of the

Royal Academy in their pursuit of portrait painting and of the other branches of art applicable to the decoration of the mansions of wealth and fashion'. He railed against the practice of the Academy of charging admission for its exhibitions 'intimating to the public . . . that the pleasure and instruction derivable from the contemplation of works of art were, in Britain, due only to affluence and ease'. And rounding on to his central complaint:

> British engraving has . . . enabled native genius in painting to live . . . it has turned the eyes of Europe full on British art; and . . . in so doing, it has brought a considerable revenue to the British treasury. And . . . been spreading throughout the civilized world the moral influence and other merits of the original works of rising British painters.

Pye was an obsessive keeper of his own records and of family correspondence, and made a unique collection of proof prints which he sold to the British Museum in 1869. He was in constant contact with professional associates and friends, writing, visiting, encouraging, to the extent that when his descendent E. R. J. Radcliffe presented his papers to the Victoria and Albert Museum in 1920 he could say that Pye:

> kept . . . everything – I have destroyed already heaps of [letters] . . . The letters he poured into his daughter – even when a child of 12 – would have suited the occasion of the enthronement of a Bishop – frequently four square pages of solid homily. He never spared himself, and he never spared them . . . He truly was a gigantic man . . . His was indeed a stupendous life of rigid work and self-denial.

In 1827, three years after the National Gallery opened in Pall Mall, Pye led the administration of the project to engrave some of the major paintings in the nation's collection. This was a bold enterprise, which required financial and moral support of a high order, as well as the commitment of a large number of competent engravers. Ventures of this kind were financed by subscribers, who paid in advance with the promise of, eventually, receiving the engravings by instalment. The subscribers had to be approached gently and with due deference, a slow and frustrating process which Pye described all too clearly in his notebooks:

30 April 1828: Sent to the Earl of Egremont for the book [of sub-
scribers] which was returned, His Lordship declining to subscribe.

The last five applications [Earl Cowper, Marquis of Aylesbury,
Earl Grosvenor, Earl of Dartmouth, Earl of Egremont] were made by
sending a messenger and the whole of them have failed, not one of
the Noblemen having subscribed – I feel afraid from the known
character of the individuals applied to that, had I applied personally
for interview, some if not every one of them would have subscribed . . . This experiment proves that the end is not to be obtained
without great personal diligence. J.P.

Sent to the Duke of Buccleuch. This is the fifth application to his
Grace.

To secure the Duke of Buccleuch's subscription, Pye called on him
four more times. He left notes at his house in Grosvenor Square,
dashed across London in a cabriolet in anticipation of an audience,
cooled his heels in Hyde Park while finding the Duke was 'from
home', and, after another fruitless attempt, 'it being now almost 9
o'clock I returned home accompanied by some feelings of dissatis-
faction and I may say fatigued mentally and bodily'. Ultimately Pye
secured the subscription, but thus did the National Gallery engravings initiative progress.

The project was especially long drawn out and financially risky
because the engravings had to be taken from neat and careful drawings of the paintings. The usual practice was for the engraver to
borrow the original canvas from the artist and have it on an easel
beside his bench. The original might be away from the artist or
owner for one or two years, although exceptionally, when Pye was
engraving Turner's *Ehrenbreitstein*, he had the painting in his workshop for ten years. During this time (c.1835–45) the picture found
a buyer, but nevertheless it remained with Pye, who kept it for so
long because he could not live solely on engraving *Ehrenbreitstein*: 'It
meant starvation . . . owing to the enormous labour required and
the time occupied . . . every stroke of the graver having to be deeply
considered'. Such arrangements were out of the question for
National Gallery pictures, and so Pye had to engage not only a
group of engravers, but a cohort of draughtsmen also. John Linnell
estimated that it would take him two years to make a drawing of *The*

Raising of Lazarus by Sebastiano del Piombo, and quoted sixty guineas to make a twelve-inch drawing of Poussin's *Bacchanalian Revel*, 'the least possible price that I think I can afford'. When the project was brought to an early close in 1840, thirty-one engravings had been commissioned, and twenty-nine finally published in a gold-tooled, red-leather-bound volume entitled *Engravings from the Pictures of the National Gallery*. Of them, Pye's own plate of *The Annunciation* by Claude had taken nearly five years to complete, and Finden's *Village Festival* by Wilkie over ten years.

The engraving market in London in the 1820s was buoyant and fiercely competitive. Charles Heath, writing to Dawson Turner in 1825, observed that 'the Art of Engraving never flourished as it now does – there is so much doing that every Engraver is full'. Ten years later the situation was just as buoyant: the engraver John Burnet giving evidence to the 1836 committee said that too many students were coming forward to be trained in this booming trade. 'As the art advances, and so many prints are sold, everyone wishes to send his son to learn engraving.' Though the number of engravers in employment rose, what none of them could do was increase the speed of production without compromising quality, and market forces prompted a decline:

> Eight or ten years ago [that is, in the late 1820s] there was an immense demand for Annuals . . . Formerly a sale of 10,000 copies was not deemed extraordinary . . . now I doubt if half that number be disposed of any of them. Nothing short of a sale of 4500 copies will pay the expenses of getting up an Annual, provided the engravings are executed in a respectable manner.

This opened the way for a new, faster, slicker technique of reproducing images, which had been hovering in the margins of the market and respectability for a decade or more, lithography.

When Géricault was in London in 1820–1 he spent much of his time working on an extensive body of lithographs of street scenes and people, horses and landscapes. Writing to his friend Pierre-Joseph Dedreux-Dorcy, he said: 'I work a lot in my room, and then roam the streets for relaxation. They are so full of constant movement and variety . . . [I] turn out lithographs with all my might. I have for some time been devoting myself to this art which is a novelty in London and is having an incredible vogue here.' The 'incredible vogue' that Géricault discovered in London was the direct side-effect of the volcanic energy of the artist and entrepreneur Charles Hullmandel. He was the son of the French composer Nicolas-Joseph Hullmandel and his wife Camille-Aurore Ducazan, the niece of a former Receiver-General of France. The family had fled Paris as the French revolution was brewing, and came to London where Charles was born on 15 June 1789, four weeks before the fall of the Bastille. The Hullmandels had been a notable family in *ancien régime* France. Not only would Camille-Aurore's slight connection with the royalist system of taxation have put her life at risk, but Nicolas-Joseph, as a musician and teacher, a piano virtuoso and a composer of sonatas for piano, drew his living and audiences from the French court and its edges. Nicholas-Joseph brought his family to Queen Street, Mayfair, from where he continued to perform and write. He contributed the article on the clavichord to the 1791 edition of Diderot's *Encyclopédie*, and published a piano manual, *Principles of Music*, in 1796. Charles Hullmandel grew up in London, but as a young man during the latter years of the Napoleonic Wars studied art in Paris, and travelled in France, Italy and Germany. There, in Munich in 1817, he met Aloys Senefelder, who taught him the principles of lithography, and launched his life's work. When he came home from Germany Hullmandel immediately set about translating his drawings of Italian views into his first group of lithographs, published as *Twenty-Four Views of Italy* (1818).

Lithography was not quite the novelty in London that Géricault had suggested. It had for some years been known by the portmanteau term 'polyautography', and was practised by artists including Philip André and Henry Bankes. Both published treatises on the subject in 1803 and 1813 respectively. Rudolph Ackermann, the high-flying salesman of objets d'art to the rich, used and discussed lithography in his illustrated volumes *Repository of Arts* from 1817. When Lieutenant-Colonel James Willoughby Gordon, one of Goldsworthy Gurney's courageous steam-carriage passengers, was appointed Quarter-Master General in 1812, he saw the point of lithography as a cheap and reliable way of making maps and drawing

terrain, and introduced it as the standard, portable medium of reproduction: 'The first application of [lithography] to purposes of
usefulness unconnected with the fine arts, was made by the Duke of
Wellington in the Peninsular War, for the purposes of accompanying
the general orders, instructions &c with sketches of positions.' James
Willoughby Gordon was an amiable old soldier who indulged his
wife's affection for Turner, and had a thing about cheese. Julia
Willoughby Gordon (née Bennet), a fellow traveller with her husband in the steam-carriage journey to Bath, had for many years
been a pupil and close friend of Turner, and during the 1820s and
1830s she and her daughter, also Julia, practised lithography themselves. Turner, who kept in touch with the Gordons and visited
them on the Isle of Wight, maintained his affection for the couple
and painted pictures for them.

Hullmandel saw a further potential to lithography, not just as a
cheap mimic-engraving technique, but as a new and incomparable
graphic medium which could equally be described as 'reproductive'
and as 'original'. The *Philosophical Magazine* saw the difference
clearly, describing it as 'the art of multiplying originals; engraving, as
that of multiplying copies'. Looking both ways, lithography was the
Janus-art, the medium that stood at the gateway between laborious
reproductive engraving and fine-art mass-production.

Géricault and Hullmandel first worked in partnership in 1820
when Hullmandel printed the lithograph of *The Raft of the Medusa*,
to be distributed as advertising material. In the same year he won
the Society of Arts silver medal for the advances he had made in
lithography. Hullmandel had set up a lithographic press at 51 Great
Marlborough Street, where he lived with his father, a street that
ran at right angles to Swallow Street. This was soon to be consumed
by the John Nash developments which created Regent Street.
Géricault's Gallic impetuosity and melancholy would have struck a
homely chord in Hullmandel, while Hullmandel's determination
to explore new ways of conjuring light and darkness out of the greasy
surface of the lithographic stone chimed with the energy with
which Géricault went about drawing his characteristically sullen
London street scenes. These, of the poor and indigent, of tradesmen,
of crumbling buildings and large overpowering architectural forms,

created a sequence of images of London matched only by the sad-eyed wood engravings of all levels of London life by Gustav Doré a generation later.

Working together as they must have done over the same set of lithographic stones in Great Marlborough Street, Hullmandel and Géricault had more than the French language in common: they shared a brusque and abrasively direct manner. Hullmandel refused to be characterised as a jobbing printer, seeing himself as an artistic innovator and collaborator. He was furious with the geologist James Bowerbank who sneered at him and his work, despite the high cost he was incurring in developing lithography: 'now I am looked upon as a fool, a dreamer and a quack and by Mr Bowerbank as anything but an *honest* man'. Some artists found Hullmandel hard to take. James Ward RA described him as 'this high and lofty one', writing to Sir John Leicester, 'he being as he says in possession of some things in that art of printing peculiar to himself – and being as it would appear more proud than any of his fellow mortals, thinks proper to make it appear that the artists are under an obligation in his printing for them'.

By the time Géricault and Hullmandel had come together, the latter was approaching variety and perfection in his lithographic process, and could offer his own tried and tested technique to the public. As his father had taught piano through the written word, so Charles Hullmandel published his English translation of Brégeaut's *A Manual of Lithography* (1820), and four years later brought out his own book *The Art of Drawing on Stone*. This was required reading for everybody interested in the subject: it is crisp and concise, and gives the reader clear instructions on what equipment is needed, how to use it and how to avoid pitfalls. He goes further and says that the image created by lithography is not a reproduction,

> but the original drawing itself. This is a feature peculiar to Lithography, and shows the immense benefit conferred on mankind by this admirable invention, by procuring to persons whose means are limited the power of possessing that which could formerly only be held by individuals of immense property . . . That which cannot be done in engraving, from the immense expense of getting up a highly finished plate, and the necessity of covering these expenses by an

extensive sale, may yet be done with considerable profit in Lithography.

Hullmandel set great store by science and scientists in his search for the ultimate in lithography, and sought the geologist William Buckland's advice about where the best form of calcareous limestone for the lithographic stones could be found. Buckland confirmed that there was no British stone suitable, and that the bed of limestone in the Danube valley in Bavaria was the best, uniting 'qualities of purity, whiteness, and hardness, in a greater degree than any which have been discovered'. Search for perfection in the production of a drawn line was a further goal of Hullmandel's. Lithography is an art 'entirely founded on Chemistry', he claimed, adding, 'it is impossible to say to what degree of perfection Lithography can be carried: its process being entirely chemical, is open to innumerable improvements'. Faraday who already knew Hullmandel both professionally and socially, had no doubt about the utility of Hullmandel's lithographic method. 'I have no hesitation in stating,' he wrote,

> that having been acquainted with, and having witnessed your method, and other methods of preparing Lithographic Drawings, I know yours to be strikingly peculiar and different from the others, and from a consideration of the chemical principles of the art, should expect your process to possess that superiority which the testimony of Artists, competent to judge, assure me that it has.

Among the many artists 'competent to judge' the efficacy of Hullmandel's process, the one closest to Faraday was his young brother-in-law George Barnard, with whom he made a small group of lithographs in 1825. These, one of which – *Cottage among Mountains*, dated 25 April 1825 – is signed by both Faraday and Barnard, were undoubtedly made and printed on stones in Hullmandel's workshop.

Charles Hullmandel was a man of many talents. Having been brought up in a French-speaking musical household in London, it is not surprising that he should become a talented amateur musician, organising musical parties at home and on the river, concerts and theatrical events, and composing his own music. One of his productions was the amateur theatrical event *Le Chanoine de Reims*, in

February 1825, which Faraday attended, keeping the lithographed poster in his scrapbook: the part of Le Chanoine was played 'by Mr Hullmandel, in his 3rd appearance as that character'. Confirming Hullmandel's musical abilities, James Duffield Harding noted in his diary: 'Went with Hullmandel to Covent Garden Theatre to hear him perform his Langham Waltz before Chas Mathews and Madame Vestris.'

The watercolour painter James Duffield Harding was one of Hullmandel's most loyal and talented artist collaborators. Together they brought lithography further into the public eye in 1822, when the *Gentleman's Magazine* published a lithograph of Harding's drawing of Netley Abbey, Hampshire. The text with the illustration described how 'some thousands, all equally good' had been taken from the single chalk drawing 'by a new process invented by Mr C. Hullmandel of Great Marlborough-street . . . establishing the important desideratum in lithography, of multiplying copies to an almost indefinite extent, and at the same time ensuring the impressions being uniformly good'. There are countless entries in Harding's incomplete sequence of diaries from 1828 into the 1850s that read 'called at Hullmandel's', or 'Hullmandel called'. They show Harding's relentless application to the task in hand: he is forever going to Hullmandel's to retouch prints, to the country to draw trees, to the British Museum to draw from sculpture or prints, and to conversazioni, often in Hullmandel's company. Harding, who was in his early twenties when he first worked with lithography, had been one of John Pye's apprentices, and had also worked as a draughtsman in Peter Frederick Robinson's architectural practice, when Robinson was designing the Egyptian Hall for William Bullock. He became an active and diligent teacher of watercolour painting, numbering Princess Sophia, the fifth daughter of George III, among his many pupils. Harding's other interests included the theatre and attending lectures, among which he notes that he went to Faraday's lecture at the Royal Institution on Electrical Induction in January 1838.

It is true to say that without Harding as his artist Hullmandel might never have progressed as far as he did in showing the finesse and subtlety, quite apart from high print-runs, that lithography could bring to image-making. In 1831 the *Literary Gazette* would say: 'Lithography appears now to be capable of anything.' Hullmandel made a scrapbook of 'Specimens of Early Lithography by Hullmandel and by J. D. Harding with his [Hullmandel's] MS notes', in which he stuck the 'first drawing on stone by me in 1818' – a view of Tivoli – and the 'first drawing on stone by J. D. Harding in 1820', *Château of the Counts of St Martin, Valley of Aost*. Further pages show examples of variations on the chalk-drawing manner of lithography, and include 'the brush style' (1831), 'the stump style' (1835), 'the steel brush or inverted style', and 'the tinted style' (1835). All these manners, which move lithography away from the chalk-drawing style of Géricault's lithographs, show that the medium was capable of matching the effects of watercolour, aquatint and even wood engraving. As Hullmandel himself put it, 'the art of lithography admits of many different styles; such as ink drawings either by lines or dots, etchings or engravings, chalk and imitation of wood-cuts, and of acqua-tinta'.

The flourishing of engravers and gradually lithographers in London meant that images were now available far and wide. The meanest broadsheet had always had its woodcut image – a satire against the government or the king, a portrait of a notable worthy, a gruesome hanging – and print shops displayed engravings in their windows for all to see. While line engraving on metal still occupied the upper end of the market by carrying the finest and most expensive imagery available, lithography was reaching new, wider markets entranced by its ability to integrate colour into the process. A cheaper alternative for the mass market and for advertisements, however, was woodcutting. Engraving on copper, or latterly steel, involved the artist in creating the image by gouging out the lines with a metal burin, sometimes with the aid of a ruler or compass for straight lines or regular curves. The ink settled into the engraved lines, from where it transferred under pressure to the paper. The artist of the woodcut sliced the image with a knife out of a plank or block of wood, and inked the uncut wood: the ink stayed out of the engraved lines. Thus woodcuts had a generally darker cast than line engravings. The particular advantage, however, was that woodcuts were quicker to make, from cheaper materials, and images could be printed in large quantities within a page of type. This is something that could not be done with copper and steel engraving, nor yet with lithography.

Advertisements with woodcut illustrations were cheap to make and were posted with announcements, bye-laws and other print on every available surface in the London streets. An energetic bill-sticker could put up between four hundred and four hundred and fifty bills in a day, for which he would earn one guinea. The displays of bills were known as:

> the open air Exhibitions of London . . . [having] all the boldness, if not much of the imagination and artistical skill of Salvator Rosa, and may compete the palm in roughness, at least, with the Elgin Marbles in their present weather-worn condition . . . The assiduity with which the 'Hanging Committee' of the great metropolis adorn the brick or wooden structure with a fresh supply of artistical gems every morning is amazing . . . There are rainbow-hued placards, vying in gorgeous extravagance of colour with Turner's last new picture. There are tables of contents of all the weekly newspapers, often more piquant and alluring than the actual newspapers themselves . . . Then there are pictures of pens, gigantic as the plumes in the casque of the Castle of Otranto . . . spectacles of enormous size, fit to grace the eyes of an ogre; Irishmen dancing under the influence of Guinness's Dublin Stout or Beamish's Cork Particular.

The Newcastle artist Thomas Bewick developed a sophisticated form of woodcutting, by adapting the practice of line engravers and engraving the image on the end of a block of hard wood such as box. His delicate and characterful pictures of animals and birds in his *General History of Quadrupeds* (1790) and other books took precision of imagery and mass-production to a hitherto impossible level. Bewick's wood engravings reached such extreme precision that they could be indistinguishable from line engraving. The engraver Pierre-François Godard ruefully admitted that the English were now rattling the French:

> [The English] are taking this art so far that one can scarcely distinguish the burin that they use from that of copper engraving. Innumerable pupils are acquiring this skill in England . . . Already English fictions, where the reputation has been established, and

works of natural history are embellished with wood engravings, which all arouse curiosity, and save the expense of engravings printed from copper. It is clear that if the English example is not quickly [followed], they will take over the printing from all countries of current publications in which illustrations play an essential role. We have very few engravers on wood here, and there is hardly anyone . . . who can rival the talent of the Englishman Bewick.

Bewick had come to London in October 1776, where he found work with line engravers and was encouraged to engrave for the Mint. He hated London, however, finding it to be 'a world of itself, where everything in the extreme might at once be seen: extreme riches, extreme poverty, extreme grandeur, and extreme wretchedness – all of which were such as I had not contemplated before . . . I tired of it, and determined to return home.' Nevertheless, Bewick's effect on London, and indeed on the entire European illustrated book trade, grew rapidly. Though working in Newcastle, he influenced the capital from afar, both by his publications and by the gradual influx during the early nineteenth century of artists who had either been his pupils or had been influenced by him, such as Robert Branston, Luke Clennell, John Jackson, Charlton Nesbitt and Thomas Robinson. Even Bewick was surprised at the heights of expression that could be conjured from wood engraving, and noted that one of his apprentices, Henry White, developed the technique of imitating the sketchy pencil-and-ink cross-hatching of the drawings of George Cruikshank, one of Dickens's illustrators. The apogee of Bewick's influence was reached in the 1840s and 1850s when the *Illustrated London News* was published every week from 1842, each issue carrying at least thirty wood engravings.

John Thompson, who learned wood engraving in London from Robert Branston, was able to create a minuteness of detail previously achieved only in copper or steel engraving. This gave him a particular value when working with publishers because engraved woodblocks, like woodcuts, could be printed with letterpress so that image and text appeared together on the same page. John Britton and John Murray were among the many publishers who saw the commercial value of combining word and image, and who employed John Thompson as a wood engraver. As Maria Callcott reminded Murray when they were working together on *Little Arthur's History of England* in 1833, '[Thompson] is very obliging and this you know is not the first time he has been busy for *us*, as he cut the blocks for our Giotto &c – and is now at work on a little design of Mr Callcott's. We have great respect for him.' Wood engravers were as dynastically minded as engineers. While Bewick created generations of pupils, Thompson and his younger contemporary Thomas Robinson spawned their own extended wood-engraving tribes. Thompson's brother Charles moved to Paris where he set up as a wood engraver, creating yet more competition for indigenous French book illustrators. His sister Eliza and daughters Isabel and Augusta practised wood engraving, as did his son Charles Thurston Thompson, before the latter became captivated by an even more precise reproductive medium, photography.

Thomas Robinson began business as a wood engraver in Spa Fields, Islington, and he also came to create a dynasty of engravers and artists. His son Thomas became a wood engraver, and his grand-sons Thomas, Charles and William Heath Robinson became artists and illustrators. One of the older Thomas Robinson's clients was the radical William Cobbett who, for speed and immediacy, employed wood engravers rather than line engravers to create the imagery to illustrate his political tracts. Wood engravings and woodcuts, being urgent and declamatory, lent themselves per-fectly to the haste with which Cobbett wanted his *Rural Rides* out on to the streets. They also matched the strident style of this extended weekly examination of the social and political condition of the country. Sending a landscape sketch to Thomas Robinson, Cobbett urged:

> In the landscape, *leave out the houses, town &c entirely*. Leave the fig-ures as I saw them; leave the hop-ground, which you will extend over part occupied by the farm-house; and enclose all with high trees, so that there shall be no distant view. Keep the branches of the trees in the foreground, as you have them now, and keep the *gate* and hedge which will remain; and also a gate at the further side of the ground may improve the picture. You will be so good as to lose no time.

Engravers, whether on metal or wood, worked in cramped, unhealthy conditions. Wood engravers, who unlike steel engravers or lithographers produced images rapidly for news journals, were thus faced with the additional pressures of night work. In the workshop of the wood engraver William Linton, as described in the 1860s, there was:

> a row of engravers at work at a fixed bench covered with green baize running the length of the room under the windows with eyeglass stands and rows of engravers. And for night work a round table with a glass lamp in the centre, surrounded with a circle of large clear glass globes filled with water to magnify the light and concentrate it on the blocks . . . the experienced hands in the best light, the 'prentice hands between.

The 1820s and 1830s saw a gradual and irreversible flowering of refined forms of image-making in which scientific discovery was put to the direct service of art. The ancient craft of copper engraving was given a new backbone and a new commercial lease of life by the introduction of steel plates; lithography, the art 'entirely founded on Chemistry', reached a peak of perfection through the mastery and business acumen of Charles Hullmandel and James Duffield Harding; and in 1839 the multiple processes of photography began to be publicly revealed. Central in this renaissance in image-multiplication were both Michael Faraday and J. M. W. Turner, the former through his commanding position in science in London and his direct friendships with artists and his encouragement of their work, the latter through the ubiquity of his art and his insistence on the highest quality being achieved in the reproduction of it.

Across his career Turner befriended and co-operated with dozens of engravers who used both copper and steel plates, in line engraving, mezzotint and aquatint, although he had only one published experience with lithography. While always encouraging the pursuit of perfection in traditional reproductive methods, both Turner and Faraday characteristically looked further. Their vision, and their faith in the power of both science and art when each took cognisance of the other, led them to find a common delight in the romance and variety, potential and fertility, of photography. This new medium, in which a piece of paper or glass chemically prepared, and acted upon by the light of day, can produce thousands of identical printed impressions, was discovered, or rather announced, in 1839. Rapidly photography came to challenge engraving and lithography as a reproductive medium, and to revolutionise the way humanity would see the world around it. It would become a medium 'astonishing to the philosopher and the simple child'.

All London at a Grasp

~

F ROM THEIR SEATS in John Tatum's Theatre of Science in Dorset Street, members of the City Philosophical Society could see, painted on the ceiling, bulging clouds, a large eagle, and two figures negotiating a balloon across the skies. A long poem, written by one of the Society's members, and transcribed by Michael Faraday into his Common Place Book, describes the Society in session, and, incidentally, the scene on the ceiling:

> Two globes, three chairs and two green folding doors
> A clouded ceiling where an angel soars
> A small balloon that seems to pierce the skies
> And two strange forms the whole to supervise . . .
> While o'er the pit a gallery placed on high
> When the rude hand may grasp the mimic sky
> Seize the bold eagle that with claws extending
> To pounce on gentle philos seems intending
> Or snatch the car where venal Sadler rides
> And coarse Miss Thompson mounts with manly strides.

Beneath the balloon, the eagle and the striding legs a gathering of perhaps twenty or thirty students met on Wednesday evenings to watch Tatum's scientific demonstrations and discussions, and to talk and argue among themselves. 'Venal Sadler' in the poem is James Sadler, a chemist and entrepreneur who had many commercial interests in London, Portsmouth and Liverpool, and who was clearly well known to the students at the Theatre of Science. With his sons John and William Windham Sadler he dominated the intrepid world of 'aerostation', as ballooning was called, in the 1810s. All three were chemists specialising in gases – James Sadler, who held the official military position of Chemist to the Ordnance, built steam engines in Oxford, Bristol, Coalbrookdale and Portsmouth, experimented with steam locomotion and pioneered coal-gas lighting. He made the first hydrogen-balloon flight in England, from Merton Fields, Oxford in 1784, rising to 3,600 feet and travelling six miles in the half-hour flight. By 1815 he had made forty-seven ascents, mainly from London, where he exploited a sideline in gas production in also running a fizzy-water factory. He used his balloon as a trade mark on the bottles. James's elder son John assisted Humphry Davy at the Royal Institution, and, after a few years spent in Newcastle and Hexham smelting lead, returned to London where from 1810 he ran Captain Beaufoy's Chemical Works in Lambeth, and gave lectures on aerostation at the Surrey Institution and probably elsewhere. He took part in balloon flights with his father.

William Windham Sadler entered the world of gas at an early age, being apprenticed to his father, and becoming manager of his father's Liverpool Gas Light Company in 1817, aged twenty. William's solo flying days, however, began earlier, when he ascended from Cheltenham in September 1813, without his father, who was too heavy and had to get out of the basket. The following year, James and William Sadler launched their balloon three times at least in London, twice in July – on the 15th and 29th from Burlington House – and on 1 August with 'Mr Sadler junior' (that is, W. W. Sadler) alone in the basket, from St James's Park to celebrate victory over France.

This was a summer of general celebration in Britain, the year Napoleon had been defeated, captured and exiled to Elba, and when the Treaty of Paris was laying the foundations of a new Europe. Nobody believed that Napoleon could break out of Elba, re-establish his army and set another challenge to the Allies; but, of course, on 1 March 1815 he did just that. Nevertheless, between June and early August 1814 that was all in the future, and London was thronged with foreigners and vibrant with celebration. The party went on and on. In June the Czar of Russia, the King of Prussia and other European royalty stayed for a fortnight with their entourages and witnessed, *inter alia*, fireworks at Carlton House and three days of illuminations. Then in early August London celebrated the peace again, as well as the anniversary of the Battle of the Nile and the centenary of the royal House of Hanover of King George III. As William Jerdan remembered,

> Sight after sight, fête after fête, and extraordinary novelty after novelty, kept the imagination on the stretch, and seemed to plunge everybody into an activity for pleasure hunting, as if the British empire had been turned into one Greenwich fair. From morning to night there was nothing but whirl and delirium: there was no life but the present; all the past was forgotten, and what the future might bring forth was uncared for.

In Green Park a Temple of Concord was constructed, with a revolving central dome driven by machinery devised by Maudslay's of Lambeth, a mock medieval tower was built in Hyde Park, and a Chinese pagoda and bridge over the Serpentine. A sea-battle took place on the Serpentine between the British and American fleets (model sized), which the British resoundingly won, and culminated in another firework display. This ended when the pagoda and bridge were destroyed after the gas lamps lighting them over-heated and set the whole confection on fire. London's ebullient mood sparked the desire for celebratory balloon flights, and, given the short time available, only two clear days between the Sadlers' flights of 29 July and 1 August, it is extraordinary how rapidly the balloon could be launched, flown, landed, collected, returned and prepared for launch again. Early balloon launches were events designed to gather paying crowds and to mark special occasions.

There were three routes to creating a gas that would give a balloon lift. The first was hot air, perhaps the easiest to make in theory but providing flights of relatively short duration. This was the method used by eighteenth-century balloon pioneers, primarily Montgolfier, the hot air being captured from a blazing fire at the mouth of the tethered balloon until, inflated, the craft could float off its moorings. Away it went until the air cooled; and down the balloon came. This method, the cheapest of all, lasted in public practice into the nineteenth century. The second route was through the highly dangerous, labour-intensive and very smelly chemical process of reacting sulphuric acid, then known as vitriolic acid or oil of vitriol, with iron or, less usefully, zinc. This gave off hydrogen, known then as 'inflammable air', in copious quantities. The third method was coal gas, the same substance that was by the 1820s flowing through networks of lead pipes to light the streets and houses of London.

The Italian-born natural philosopher Tiberius Cavallo FRS wrote an influential early treatise on ballooning, *The History and Practice of Aerostation* (1785), and there published recipes for inflammable air, and methods of design and manufacture of balloons. To make enough hydrogen to inflate a moderately sized balloon, 12,000 cubic feet, three-quarters full, the aeronaut (as balloonists called themselves until the mid-nineteenth century) required about 1.5 tons of iron, the same weight of sulphuric acid, and about four or five times this weight in water. The strength of the acid would vary, depending on which shop you got it from, as Cavallo put it. In Cavallo's experience 4¼ ounces of iron and the same of acid will produce one cubic foot of hydrogen, so to collect the required 12,000 cubic feet this multiplies up to 3,380 pounds (one and a half tons) each of iron and acid, along with hundreds of gallons of water. Thus it needed intensive physical effort, with many helpers, carts and horses, a secure water supply, and large wooden vats, pipes and bladders to get a balloon off the ground. The kind of iron that Cavallo recommended for these quantities was not iron filings, which he found would coagulate in lumps in the bottom of the wooden casks, but shavings from iron cannon, as these allowed the acid and water to mix around them. The hydrogen was collected from this bubbling, sulphurous poison through water, and fed in pipes into the waiting balloon. A balloon filled with 12,000 cubic feet of hydrogen would raise 9,000 ounces, or 562½ pounds (a quarter of a ton). The third method was coal gas, derived from burning coal to red heat. Coal gas (hydrogen, methane and carbon monoxide) was not as easy to collect nor as effective in giving lift as the purer hydrogen made from acid and iron, but was safer and less prone to explosion. Coal gas did not become a practical option for aeronauts until commercial coal-gas plants were operating successfully in London in the early 1820s.

The balloon itself was best made of silk varnished with a special coating made from the residue of boiled holly or viburnum bark. This was otherwise known as bird lime, a sticky substance coated on to the branches of trees to trap birds. Cavallo gave the recipe: boil a vat of bird lime 'for an hour . . . until it ceases to crackle. Then pour on it a pound of spirits of turpentine. Boil for six minutes. Then pour all onto 3 lb boiling nut oil, stir well, and boil for 15 minutes. Leave for 24 hours to settle, decant the liquid, and brush this warm on the silk with a flat brush. One coat on each side of the silk.' The boat, or 'car', to be suspended from a net slung over the whole body of the balloon, should be made from wickerwork, Cavallo advised, covered with leather, well painted or varnished over. 'Thus it would be light and would float very well upon water . . . or striking against anything hard would not break.' For ballast, Cavallo recommended sand, to be thrown out of the car to gain height. The oars and rudders that some aeronauts fitted might look dramatic but were useless. Wear thick clothes, Cavallo advised, and a varnished coat of silk 'for passing through fogs, clouds and mists', carry ropes and a hook to prevent the basket from bouncing when it hit the ground, and take a speaking trumpet for hailing people on the ground, a memorandum book and pencil for taking notes, a watch that shows seconds, a barometer (one used for measuring the height of mountains that might get in the way), two thermometers, a hygrometer, a magnetic compass, telescope, sextant and an electrometer. Also something to eat and drink; but as Cavallo said, 'there is no need to mention [refreshments], since hardly any aeronaut will forget them'.

To prepare for their flights in July and August 1814, presumably with all three Sadlers working together as a team, the aeronauts assembled a couple of tons of cannon shavings, the acid in straw-bound glass carboys, water, carts, cranes, ladders, horses and men. The water at the St James's launch would have been pumped out of the canal in the Park, but for the Burlington House events it would most probably have had to come out of the mains, thus depleting the supply for everybody else in the neighbourhood. Cannon would have come from wherever redundant cannon were piled in these first few months of peace, and the acid transported on a series of rattling carts perhaps across Westminster Bridge from Beaufoy's Chemical Works in Lambeth, where John Sadler worked, and where James Sadler had built a gas-making plant. The ingredients were mixed in ten-foot-high wooden vats, which 'unremittingly pour[ed] out a stream of vapour in a state which required the constant effusion of cold water to keep the conductors from violent heating'. From the 'conductors', brass valves and connectors, the precious gas travelled through silk tubes and bladders into the balloon itself. The chemical assistants – led by John Sadler shall we guess – wearing heavy leather protective clothing, hats, boots and masks, carefully and steadily poured the acid on to the iron submerged in the water, and tried to avoid being overcome by the gases and heat. The organisers had to manage the growing crowds, and take the entrance fee – it cost 3s 6d to get into the enclosure at Burlington House. If it was a society launch, with royalty or the aristocracy involved, there would be lines of soldiers on parade, and a military band to entertain the onlookers. Ballooning was not just a matter of getting into the basket and taking off.

As the Sadlers' balloon swelled with its gas, its full beauty became apparent. It was painted with figures of the cardinal virtues, Faith, Hope and Charity, within columns, and with orange stripes above and clouds below. The car, decorated with the royal coat of arms, had Union Jacks projecting on poles at each end. There was an unexpected excitement in the courtyard of Burlington House as the 15 July flight was being prepared. A scaffolding collapsed, and precipitated twenty to thirty paying customers to the ground; however, 'this catastrophe produced nothing beyond a general laugh at the sufferers who were thus suddenly thrown from the best to the worst situation of the assemblage'. The 15 July flight, which rose slowly in still air, carried James and William Sadler. At the 29 July event, however, they had a further passenger, Miss Thompson, the 'coarse Miss Thompson' of the City Philosophical Society poem, described in the press as an actress 'renowned in the dramatic corps', and an 'inmate [sic] of the Sadler family'. The Times, which could not name her, described the woman as having 'a slight and delicate figure, in a common summer dress, a light silk hat, a muslin gown, a blue silk mantle and altogether in a costume which seemed to contemplate none of the vicissitudes to which an aerial voyage is liable'. This launch, which took place in gusty winds, was dangerous and dramatic: 'the balloon rushed upwards with a rapidity almost fearful, and shot off to the North West . . . No account of the aeronauts had reached Burlington House at 12 o'clock last night.'

When by six o'clock on 1 August the Sadlers' balloon was recovered, returned and fully inflated with hydrogen and ready to rise up from St James's Park, there was an unexpected delay. Queen Charlotte and her daughters, evidently not fully appreciating that timing in ballooning was critical, had not yet arrived. The large crowd grew restive. William Sadler's paying passenger on this voyage, Mrs Henry Johnstone, a 'new aspirant to celestial excursions', was already in the basket, but waiting for the royal party delayed the launch by twenty minutes. In this time the rope securing the netting to the valve at the top of the balloon came away, making the launch potentially dangerous. The Duke of Wellington stepped up to try to dissuade Mrs Johnstone from taking part, and to urge Sadler to abort the launch. But as *The Times* put it, 'this enterprising young aeronaut . . . feeling for the disappointment of the public, and for his own honour, was determined to go up, and he ascended about twenty four minutes past six', on his own. As well as his honour, Sadler considered the expense and effort already incurred in producing perhaps 12,000 cubic feet of hydrogen, and the disastrous effect on the crowd if this gas had to be rapidly released. So up he went:

> Whilst the balloon was still hovering over the Park, he threw from it a number of small paper parachutes with jubilee favours attached to them, bearing various inscriptions. When above the London-docks the balloon appeared for a short time nearly stationary, and it was not until a quantity of ballast was thrown out that a quicker motion could be given to it. On passing over Deptford, at a considerable height, Mr Sadler went through a cloud which left behind it on the railing of the car, and on various parts of the balloon, a thick moisture which soon became frozen; and Mr Sadler for a short time felt the cold as intense as in winter.

At perhaps 3,000 or 4,000 feet Sadler then had to wrestle with the rope that had caused the trouble at the launch, and release the now frozen valve. The balloon bucked and billowed, and seemed liable to fall into the river, so Sadler cut a gash in the fabric, and made a controlled crash-landing in Mucking Marshes on the Essex coast. With the help of a fisherman and a cart, he took the balloon and basket to

Gravesend, where he caught a post-chaise, and arrived for a planned royal reception at Buckingham House, tired, wet, but triumphant, at 3.30 next morning.

These were just three of dozens of balloon launches that are reported in the London newspapers in the 1810s. Craft rose from the royal parks and the courtyards of grand houses, from behind inns, from the greens at Islington, Pentonville and Hackney, and from the pleasure gardens of Ranelagh and Vauxhall. The Sadlers shared the glamour of ballooning with many others including S. D. Dean, the husband and wife team Mr and Mrs George Graham, Thomas Harris, Mr Hampton and Charles Green. They took their craft around the British Isles – Manchester, Liverpool, Sheffield and Dublin saw their and others' flights. These were spectacles which the public paid handsomely to watch, the money going into the aeronauts' and innkeepers' pockets. When Charles Green launched from the Mermaid Tavern, Hackney in June 1823 he gathered a large crowd on a sunny day. 'Whatever effect', *The Times* reported, '[the weather] might have had on filling the balloon, had certainly great effect of filling the pocket of the aeronaut.' Aerostation had its share of theorists, principally the Yorkshire baronet Sir George Cayley who put forward proposals to build balloons wafted through the air by paddles, sails or fans powered by on-board steam engines. Cayley went on to build, and to test, an early aeroplane.

There were accidents at balloon launches and landings, there were delays and riots, night ascents with fireworks, successful parachute descents, and disastrous ones, as in 1837 when Robert Cocking was killed when attempting to descend from 5,000 feet with a parachute of his own devising. William Sadler died while trying to land his balloon near Blackburn in 1824; his father never recovered from the shock. When the Grahams, accompanied by the Sadlers, attempted to launch a new balloon made of cotton rather than silk (and thus heavier) from Islington in August 1823, a delay of more than three hours prompted shouts, speeches and rioting from the crowd of some seven hundred people who had each paid 3s 6d to watch the event. Bricks and tiles torn from building sites were thrown, palings were broken down and people were trampled. *The Times* reporter was particularly incensed that among all this blood and broken bones a 'ruffian' injured two children when he threw them out of a swing 'that was in full course'. Accidents and injury on landing were usually restricted to the participants, or to those unfortunate enough to be in the wrong place at the wrong time when the balloon hit the ground. When a 'Montgolfier' hot-air balloon was being prepared for launch from a straw and wood furnace to mark the opening of the Croydon Railway in 1839, it broke away and took with it five people kicking and screaming as they clung to the ropes. Some dropped off; some flew away. After about a mile the balloon cooled and came down, but one man was caught by his foot, and hung upside down from the rigging. He bumped along the ground on his head for a while, and his leg came off, 'being attached by the tendons only. It has since been amputated, but he lies in a dangerous state.' The press relished the accidents.

Charles Green, the most intrepid and long-lived of all the aeronauts, was described by the playwright and author John Poole, who flew with him in September 1838, as 'the Great Captain of the Air', in 'complete control over the "Here we go up, up, up, and there we go down, down, down"'. Green was an affable, good-tempered man on the ground, more like a farmer than a flyer, but when he got into the air, he was the first ship's captain of the skies, direct, demanding and in charge. He died in his bed aged eighty-five, after more than five hundred ascents and descents. Green was the first aeronaut to show that the dangerous and laborious process of generating hydrogen with acid and iron could be done away with when he made his first ascent, from Vauxhall Gardens, on 19 July 1821, the day of the coronation of George IV, in his 16,000 cubic feet capacity balloon. He managed this by the simple expedient of filling up with household gas for lighting from the Piccadilly gas main. The balloon rose to 11,000 feet, and landed in Barnet.

With gas on tap, balloonists no longer had to be chemists, with supplies of iron and acid at their fingertips, but daring professionals who could concentrate on weather-patterns rather than the mixing of acids. A balloon floating through the air over London became a common sight, and led to a rapid change in perceptions. For those on the ground, there above was a heavier-than-air machine carrying men and women, dreams and imagination, up into the sky. For those in the balloon there were new perspectives and hitherto unseen views of the capital, and gradually people were able to grasp the scale and complexity of the metropolis by rising above it. Views of London from a height had traditionally been drawn or painted from Highgate Hill (looking south) and Greenwich (looking north). Constable's views from Highgate and Turner's from Greenwich put London into a perspective that all could experience by going to London's high points and seeing for themselves. All could identify with Dick Whittington, looking back at a London he was leaving behind, and turning again, or with Benjamin Robert Haydon and Henry Fuseli looking down at, and admiring together, London's permanent blanket of smoke. As the nineteenth century began, the bird's-eye views recounted in words and pictures by balloon-travellers were beginning to create a new understanding of the city, and to show how inexorably and mightily it was growing. The same view-point gave a new perspective on the human being.

Robert Havell, watercolourist, printmaker and colourman of 77 Oxford Street, created his panorama of London around 1806 from drawings which he can only have begun in a balloon. Around that date the many balloonists active in London who could have given Havell a ride included the Frenchman André Garnerin, who launched from Lord's cricket ground and the Vauxhall Gardens, and Francis Barrett, who launched from Greenwich and Vauxhall. Havell's response to his flight was the nine-feet-long Rhinebeck Panorama which showed London from the Tower to Chelsea, and way beyond following the serpentine windings of the Thames to a romantic, distant, misty Windsor Castle. The work is full of deli-cately handled detail and incident in which the artist relates human narratives as well as trying to express distance, urban topography and scale. Attempting to pack as much information into the image as possible, Havell omitted all idea of atmosphere and the reality of smoggy London. He drew his panorama before there had been any measurable development in writing about the view from a flying machine, as opposed to the view from high ground. About five years later, when James Sadler flew from the Mermaid Gardens, Hackney on 12 August 1811 with Captain Paget of the Royal Navy, Sadler recorded his passenger's response to the view from the basket.

Paget's speechlessness speaks eloquently for an ordinary man's inability to express the new-found perspective:

> The prospect . . . was beyond the power of description: the capital was at that time pronounced by Captain Paget to be a small village; nor could he be persuaded to the contrary, till the four bridges, namely, London, Blackfriars, Westminster and Battersea, which from their intercepting the river were rendered more conspicuous than other objects, were pointed out to him by Mr Sadler.

Early flyers seemed happier using abstractions to describe the insubstantial than definitive words to evoke the solid. They were more at home with the cloudscape than with the landscape below. Captain Beaufoy, of Beaufoy's Chemical Works, flew with George Graham in June 1824, and reported:

> On ascending above the clouds they appeared like a sea of frozen snow, with dark fissures between, and in some places the clouds opened, and gave us a distinct view of the metropolis and its environs. The sky above was beautifully blue, and the sun shone brilliantly, tinging with a silvery hue the tops of the wide expanse of clouds, and particularly those that rose like mountains above the others. There were still a few white clouds at a great distance above us . . . Whenever we caught glimpses of the earth through the clouds, the view was beautiful and interesting, but the sight of the silvery sea of clouds to the very verge of the horizon was truly magnificent.

There can be no earlier description of London from the air than the report of the first flight over the metropolis by Vincenzo Lunardi in September 1784, but even Lunardi admitted that he could 'find no simile to convey an idea of it. I could distinguish Saint Paul's and other churches, from the houses. I saw the streets as lines, all animated with beings, whom I knew to be men and women, but which I should otherwise have difficulty in describing. It was an enormous bee-hive.' These men admitted that they were groping for words. What they were experiencing in their cold, unnerving balloon-baskets was something shockingly radical. Captain Paget simply could not accept that what he was seeing was actually London below him, until he caught sight of the bridges. No human being had ever witnessed such a sight before, from so unsettling a perspective. James

Sadler, more experienced as a flyer than most, and matter-of-fact in his language, got to grips with what he saw below in one of the earliest clear descriptions of London from the air as he took off in his balloon from Burlington House on 15 July 1814:

> It was not we who seemed to rise, but everything beneath us to retire. In a few minutes we were more perpendicular with Leicester Square, and our prospect was grand; the whole of London, and its magnificent buildings, lay below us, with its surrounding fields, canals and parks; the beautiful serpentine form of the river, with its rich shipping, docks and bridges. We enjoyed this scenery for about fifteen minutes, and at a quarter before four o'clock entered a dense cloud which completely shut us out from all sight of the earth.

But then, in the clouds, even Sadler relapsed into near-meaningless poetics: he saw 'variegated colours reflected from the multitudinous congregation of vapours around us, and the effulgence of different lights'.

In an account written as a letter to a friend after his 1838 flight with Charles Green, John Poole described both looking up and looking down, with a dramatic use of metaphor. Looking up, he said 'you sit in a thing like a sauce boat and look up to a world floating above your head'. And looking down:

> Sights! There was all London at a grasp, made of baby-houses, and pepper-casters, and extinguishers, and chessmen, with here and there a dishcover – things which you call domes, and spires, and steeples. Oh the vanity of man! Then there were its squares and pleasant places, bedecked with gooseberry bushes, intersected by yellow strips, half a yard wide in curves and zig zags . . . [After dark] conceive yourself looking down on an enormous map of London, with its suburbs to the east, north and south, as far as the eye could reach, DRAWN IN LINES OF FIRE! For anything beyond this I must leave you to your own powers of conceiving; for, to speak frankly, my powers of describing are here at a dead halt.

Fourteen years later, one of Green's last passengers, the social reformer Henry Mayhew, flew with him over London. For Mayhew, who had spent many years interviewing men and women in London and writing his reports published as *London Labour and the London*

Poor (1851), the view of London was neither Sadler's 'grand prospect' nor Beaufoy's glimpses through clouds 'like a sea of frozen snow'. Nor was it Poole's 'pepper-casters, and extinguishers, and chessmen'. Instead it was more animal, sinister, having its own internal motion:

> The roadways striping the land were like narrow brown ribbons, and the river, which we could see winding far away, resembled a long, grey, metallic-looking snake, creeping through the fields . . . In the opposite direction to which the wind was insensibly wafting the balloon, lay the leviathan Metropolis, with a dense canopy of smoke hanging over it, and reminding one of the fog of vapour that is so often seen steaming up from the fields at early morning. It was impossible to tell where the monster city began or ended, for the buildings stretched not only to the horizon on either side, but far away into the distance, where, owing to the coming shades of evening and the dense fumes from the million chimneys, the town seemed to blend into the sky, so that there was no distinguishing earth from heaven. The multitude of roofs that extended back from the foreground was positively like a dingy red sea, heaving in bricken billows, and the seeming waves rising up one after the other till the eye grew wearied with following them. Here and there we could distinguish little bare green patches of parks, and occasionally make out the tiny circular enclosures of the principal squares, though, from the height, these appeared scarcely bigger than wafers. Further, the fog of smoke that over-shadowed the giant town was pierced with a thousand steeples and pin-like factory chimneys.

The balloon in which Charles Green flew both John Poole and Henry Mayhew was the largest flying machine of its time, eighty feet high from the basket to the zenith when inflated, 150 feet at its broadest circumference, and containing 85,000 cubic feet of gas: it was as tall as six double-decker buses piled one on top of another, and had the cubic capacity of thirty-five of them. It could raise two tons, that is its own weight plus one and a half tons of cargo. This, the *Royal Vauxhall* balloon, which Green built in 1836 for the proprietors of the Vauxhall Gardens, became a permanent attraction at the gardens. It first flew on 9 September that year, just as the social season had drawn to an end, and Vauxhall Gardens was preparing for the winter.

But shortly after lunch on 7 November Vauxhall Gardens came alive again, and the *Royal Vauxhall* balloon carrying Green, his financial backer the lawyer Robert Hollond and an Irish theatre producer Thomas Monck Mason rose up once again from its launch site. Three and a half hours later it was crossing high above the beach at Dover, heading out over the jelly-green sea towards Calais, the white cliffs 'melting into obscurity . . . sparkling with the scattered lights, which every moment augmented'. Over the Channel they saw 'the interminable ocean spread its complicated tissue of waves without interruption or curtailment', and found that 'an awful stillness seem[ed] to reign over its motions'. In northern France they passed over burning limekilns, lit up like ships in the darkness, and moved silently across forests and icefields as the sun rose again. When they landed at about half-past seven the following morning they found they had travelled nearly five hundred miles, and were near Weilberg, in the Duchy of Nassau. There they were greeted warmly, were entertained for days by princes, burghers and the people, and allowed their balloon to be given the honour of a new name: the *Great Nassau Balloon*. This stuck; and so for seventy years did the distance record they had set.

With the balloon on a carriage behind them, and the wicker basket given wheels and converted into a triumphal car, Green, Hollond and Monck Mason came home to a heroes' welcome in London. There they recounted their trip endlessly. Monck Mason wrote a rapid account, which was reprinted with a group of atmospheric drawings published as lithographs. His language evokes the height that the balloon reached, and in what is the earliest account of the experience of aerial travel to exotic distant regions, brings landscape description into the realms of astronomy:

> The whole plane of the earth's surface, for many and many a league around, as far and farther than the eye distinctly could embrace, seemed absolutely teeming with the scattered fires of a watchful population, and exhibited a starry spectacle below that almost rivalled in brilliancy the remoter lustre of the concave firmament above . . . The sky, at all times darker when viewed from an elevation than it appears to those inhabiting the lower regions of the earth, seemed almost black with the intensity of night; while by contrast no doubt,

and the remotion of the intervening vapours, the stars, redoubled in their lustre, shone like sparks of the whitest silver scattered upon the jetty dome above us.

Robert Hollond discussed the trip with Turner, and spoke to him with such a rich expression that the artist later wrote to Hollond to say that 'your Excursion so occupied my mind that I dreamt of it, and I do hope you will hold to your intention of making the drawing, with all the forms and colours of your recollection'.

The skyscapes that Green and his companions encountered, and which Hollond evidently described to Turner, created a refreshingly extended language of the imagination for art and science. Turner's paintings, which had in the first decades of the nineteenth century been firmly rooted at ground- or sea-level, were beginning to exhibit a higher, aerial perspective before the Nassau flight and Turner's ballooning dream. In *Juliet and her Nurse*, exhibited at the Royal Academy in April and May 1836, the viewer floats gently off the foreground parapet, and in the later 1830s and into the 1840s this rising aerial spirit develops not only in Turner but in the paintings of John Martin, David Roberts and others. Canvases such as Turner's *Modern Italy — the Pifferari* (1838, Glasgow Museums), David Roberts's *View of Rome* (1856, National Gallery of Scotland) and John Martin's *Plains of Heaven* (1853, Tate Britain) have modest elevations which show the wide landscape extent and distant horizons that could not all be seen from ground level. They do not fully separate the viewer from secure ground, but they do unsettle, and subtly suggest a gradual and guarded entry into a floating world.

Amid the serious responses to ballooning, the clowns had their play. Richard Barham, in *The Ingoldsby Legends*, quickly rushed off his long comic poem 'The "Monstre" Balloon' when the *Great Nassau* returned from Germany.

> Oh the balloon, the great balloon
> It left Vauxhall one Monday at noon,
> And everyone said we should hear of it soon
> With news of Aleppo or Scanderoon.
>
> . . .

Then they talked about Green – 'Oh! where's Mister Green?
And where's Mister Hollond who hired the machine?
And where is Monck Mason, the man that has been
Up so often before – twelve times or thirteen –
And who writes such nice letters describing the scene?'

When the aeronauts return home there will be entertainment and lectures:

And there, on a beautiful transparent screen,
In the middle you'll see a large picture of Green,
Mr Hollond on one side, who hired the machine,
Mr Mason on t'other, describing the scene;
And Fame on one leg, in the air, like a queen

. . .

Then they'll play up a tune in the Royal Saloon,
And the people will dance by the light of the moon,
And keep up the ball till the next day at noon;
And the peer and the peasant, the lord and the loon,
The haughty grandee, and the low picaroon,
The six-foot life-guardsman, and little gossoon,
Will all join in three cheers for the 'Monstre' Balloon.

When the cheering stopped, Charles Green got back to ballooning for entertainment, and Robert Hollond was elected to parliament, where in the fifteen years that he sat as MP for Hastings he made one speech only, on balloon-launched projectiles. Charles Green cut a lonely figure, going up and down in his balloon, sometimes on voyages with a scientific purpose, such as carrying Robert Cocking on his ill-advised and ill-fated flight to test his parachute. Thomas Carlyle, walking home to Chelsea one evening, saw Green suspended in the sky after a launch from Vauxhall,

throwing out all manner of fireworks, red, green and indigo-coloured stars, and transitory milky-ways, the best he could do poor devil. He was hanging a goodish way up in the air; quite invisible except a fluster of confused fireworks which looked very small in the great waste deep of things, and he did not last above half a minute in all. No paltrier phenomenon was ever contrived for the solacement of human souls. I figured the wretched mortal sailing thro' the chill clear moon-shiney night, destitute of *any* object now, and with peril of his life for the sake of keeping his life in; and had real pity for him.

It must have been Charles Green whom Michael Faraday observed in 1850 rising in a balloon one summer evening above Vauxhall. As Faraday watched the phenomenon of a heavier-than-air contraption being carried effortlessly up into the sky, Green emptied two or three bags of sandy ballast. The slanting sunlight turned the sand into a golden cloud which fell in a stream towards the earth. Then the stream appeared to stop and hang in the air, it and the balloon parting from each other very slowly. Faraday described all this in his diary, and added a characteristic scientific explanation of this extraordinary visual experience: 'It shews the wonderful manner in which [each] particle of this dusty cloud must have made its impression on the eye by the light reflected from it, and is a fine illustration of the combination of many effects, each utterly insensible alone, into one sum of fine effect.'

Faraday gave expression to one of the particular beauties of London that Mary Anne Flaxman, the sculptor's sister, had described as 'an atmosphere composed of gold dust', seen as she walked near Regent's Park on an earlier summer's evening. Earlier still, in 1802, Wordsworth had described London in his sonnet 'Composed upon Westminster Bridge' as 'all bright and glittering in the smokeless air'. Air, light and floating particles, from the water vapour hanging in fog to dust thrown up by traffic and the ballast thrown down by Green, created a combination of visual effects unique to London. While those left on the ground could look up at them through the smog, the balloonists saw the metropolis from a new, higher perspective.

12

1831: A Disturbance of the Needle

~

WILLIAM JERDAN, EDITOR of the *Literary Gazette*, opened the
year 1831 with the announcement that it was fifteen years since
he had taken on the editorship of the magazine. He saw no reason to
be modest. 'The Gazette enjoys, by many thousands, the greatest
circulation of any purely literary Journal ever published in England; and
it has risen to this eminence under the *absolute* control and direction
of its Editor, who is also the proprietor of *the largest* proportion of the
entire emoluments derived from this widely extended sale.'

To his admission that he was making pots of money out of the
Gazette, Jerdan might have added that he had an office in a central
part of London, at 362 Strand, nearly opposite Somerset House, with
a snuff manufactory on the left, and a steam-packet company on
the right. Jerdan's office door is prominent in Caleb Robert Stanley's
painting *The Strand looking Eastwards from Exeter 'Change*, in the
Museum of London. Eighteen-thirty-one was going to be a special
year for society, culture and science in Britain. The fat but friendly
spendthrift King, George IV, had died in 1830, and 1831 would, per-
force, be the year in which his successor William IV was crowned.
London therefore could expect a heavy dose of pageantry. The
Reform Bill, introduced in March 1831 by Lord John Russell, would
begin its difficult passage through both Houses of Parliament, changing shape and emphasis as it went, and so the capital would have to
brace itself for civil disturbance. A site would finally be chosen in
1831 for the National Gallery so that the nation's growing collection
of pictures could be housed in spacious and appropriate accom-
modation. Thus London could look forward to old master paintings
coming more clearly into public focus and understanding than they
could ever have been in 100 Pall Mall. As the New Year began, the

replacement for London Bridge was nearly complete, and its opening in 1831 would be part of the natural course of ceremonial events. So London could expect lavish celebrations on the river, an easier flow of traffic between Westminster and Surrey, and an easier flow for the Thames. But most significantly, in his crepuscular basement laboratory in the Royal Institution, Michael Faraday followed a train of thought, and discovered how to induce and generate electricity. This was a giant leap not for London, but for humanity.

Reform in the monarchy, reform in parliament, reform in the way old master paintings were presented to the public, reform on the river, and a spark of electricity that prompted a flash of scientific insight: these were the first among many changes and harbingers of change which were channelled into one year, 1831. But the year that began with the insistent beat of political and urban reform ended, for many tragically, with the arrival of an unprecedented cholera epidemic in which thousands died in London, and hundreds of thousands in the rest of Britain and in Europe.

The success of Jerdan's *Literary Gazette* rested heavily on the editor and proprietor keeping an eye out not only for events and activities to praise, but also for some to castigate. Jerdan kept his finger on the pulse of London through fifteen years of reporting on art, science and belles-lettres. Where he detected cultural ill-health, he issued instructions for treatment. In January 1831 he turned his attention to the management of the British Museum. Montagu House was now being nibbled away by demolition, and encroached upon from right and left by Smirke's two new wings. As the new rooms were completed, so the collections were moved out of dark and infested basements and into the light of day. This revealed damage and distress to the objects, and while knowing that tens of thousands of pounds were being spent on building rooms for their public display, Jerdan pounced on the fact that some of the stuffed birds were falling to bits: 'A large and elegant apartment has been opened to the public during the last week, containing a collection of foreign birds, the greater part of which are in a very bad state of preservation.'

Jerdan went on to say that the collection housed above the King's Library in the new east wing had been created from gifts of sailors and travellers, and that the condition of the objects was a shame and an embarrassment: 'for who will collect, or make presentations, if these, as has hitherto been the case, lie for years neglected in obscure cellars?' Warming to his theme Jerdan castigated the British Museum authorities yet further: 'The collection of fossil univalves is excellent. Where are the bivalves? And, before we quit this subject, let us be allowed to express a hope that the public will not long be debarred access to the mineralogical collections.' Nothing much seems to have changed in the management of the Museum's stores since, in the 1800s, Richard Reinagle found the head, beak and legs of a dodo in a pile of bird and animal carcases awaiting sorting in a basement, and then lost them again; or when a crate of lithographic stones was sent to the museum, and just vanished: 'If they are here Hawkins thinks that they must be in some one of the boxes which Wilkinson nailed up . . . Without more definite directions . . . I know not where to lay my hands on them.'

One difficulty that the British Museum was failing to overcome was drastically falling visitor numbers. A question asked in a House of Commons committee drew attention to the fact that the Museum was closed on Tuesdays, Thursdays, Saturdays and Sundays, and that visitor numbers had fallen from a peak of 132,000 in the late 1820s to 68,000 in 1830. The radical MP Joseph Hume acknowledged that the British Museum was useful, but added, 'the only question is whether it might be rendered more useful'. It appeared that visitors' interests were misdirected; the King's Library, so the Museum's Standing Committee was told, attracted 'a great press of visitors' in 1831, giving 'great inconvenience to readers'. As a result non-readers were marshalled at one end to see the Library; but of course they wanted to look at the new marvel of architecture, with its unprecedented width made possible only by Smirke's use of iron beams. When Johann Passavant visited the British Museum in the late spring of 1831, he was as depressed by what he saw as were Jerdan and Hume:

> On the tiptoe of expectation we entered the doors of the British Museum, and how deeply we were disappointed by the first *coup d'oeil* of the interior . . . Those who remember the apartments which were first allotted to the collection of sculpture, will sufficiently understand and sympathise with my indignation at seeing those

222

magnificent specimens of the purest antique, which had adorned the Parthenon, and glistened beneath the sunny skies of Greece, here crowded in a dirty, dark apartment, and loaded with the defiling accumulations of London soot and dust. Preparation, however, was making for a more suitable dwelling place, which will be hailed with pleasure by all those who honour art in her purest and noblest form.

With more enterprise and flexibility than was possible at that time in the British Museum, Robert Burford opened a new panorama in his show rooms in Leicester Square in January. Burford was one of the new generation of entrepreneur showmen. Rather younger than William Bullock, he was just as energetic, though more single-minded in his approach to crowd-pulling. Burford owned and managed two panorama showplaces, in the Strand and in Leicester Square, and to collect the store of views from which panoramas could be painted by his hired artists, he crossed Europe drawing cities from vantage points such as steeples and hill-tops, and crossed the Atlantic to draw New York. His January offering in Leicester Square was, as the *Gentleman's Magazine* reported, Quebec from the Heights of Abraham, 'a magnificent view of the bold and romantic land which surrounds [the town], intersected by the gigantic river St Lawrence, and the sinuous St Charles . . . For pictorial effect no panorama we remember exceeds this of Quebec, and the manner of its execution is highly creditable to the artist.'

Burford had an army of artists working for him, as well as soldiers and administrators resident across the globe, who sent landscape drawings home for wholesale enlargement. In 1831 alone he presented panoramas of Hobart (March), of Bombay (June) and in December of Florence. These were mysterious, distant and, to most people, inaccessible places, many of which were reported upon in the newspapers; so what did they look like? Burford and others attempted to provide answers to that question. Passavant was impressed by the plethora of panoramas available, a number added to in 1831 by the completion of Decimus Burton's Colosseum in Regent's Park built to display a grand view of London at sunrise from the cupola of St Paul's. This had been drawn, as were many other panorama studies, using Cornelius Varley's Patent Graphic Telescope. Thus, on the largest possible scale, with panoramas coming and going, and, on the small scale, a host of foreign birds displayed in a new gallery at the British Museum, no Londoner could fail to see his or her city in the early 1830s as anything but the centre of a world of natural splendour.

The decision to build the National Gallery of Painting and Sculpture on the site of the grand range of royal stables near Charing Cross was taken in 1831. The *Gentleman's Magazine* was among the first to break the story with a long account in its March edition of the proposals to renew the area bounded on the north by the King's Mews and on the east by Charing Cross and the Strand. The trustees of what was briefly called the Royal National Gallery of Painting made it clear to the Treasury in 1828 that 100 Pall Mall, the former home of Sir John Julius Angerstein beside Carlton House, had become unsuited to its purpose. 'The House . . . is totally inadequate . . . The smallness of the space it embraces not admitting of the Pictures already possessed by the Public being advantageously arranged and still less furnishing the means of placing any future additions that may be made to it.'

It was not just the modest size of the house that was a problem, but the fact that the sheer weight of pictures and their frames on the domestic walls had contributed to the deterioration of the building to the point where it was considered unsafe. It was also a severe, and acknowledged, fire risk. The national collections had now grown in the four years since the nucleus of thirty-eight pictures were purchased by parliamentary grant from Angerstein's estate in 1824: works by Claude, Rubens, Rembrandt, Cuyp and Sebastiano del Piombo among them. The following year the pocket-sized *Madonna of the Basket* by Correggio was purchased, and in 1826 Titian's six-feet-long *Bacchus and Ariadne*. These were, then as now, considered to be masterpieces of world class, their importance never questioned. Between 1824 and 1828 twelve other works were added by gift and purchase, and when the Marquis of Stafford presented Rubens's gigantic canvas *Peace and War* in 1828 the house was already full to bursting point. In that same year the bequest of sixteen paintings from Sir George Beaumont entered the collection, and other benefactors, such as the Rev. Holwell Carr, were queuing up to die and leave their pictures to the nation. These were indeed the *nation's* paintings, quite separate and distinct from the royal collection scattered around palaces at St James's, Hampton Court, Windsor and the recreated Buckingham Palace at the further end of the Mall. While the trustees had briefly referred to their charge as the 'Royal National Gallery', by 1830 the word 'Royal' had been dropped for ever.

The trustees had already done some scouting of their own for new premises for the National Gallery, and their eyes had fallen on the buildings to the north of Charing Cross. They told the Treasury in 1828 that 'the Upper Gallery and contiguous rooms of the King's Mews, Charing Cross, might be made suitable for the purpose of displaying the National Collection to great advantage and at no considerable expense'. The building was still in use as stables, but even the prospect of some of the King's horses on the ground floor did not deter them. The event that changed the situation was the demand by the Office of Woods and Forests, the body that controlled urban development outside the City of London, to drive a new street between Pall Mall and the Carlton House site. The trustees of the National Gallery must have seen this coming: it was the climax of Nash's grand plan for a new north–south thoroughfare which had been creeping towards them from the undergrowth in Regent's Park for more than ten years. The creation of this street, Waterloo Place, meant that 100 Pall Mall would have to be demolished, although in reality there was a race between that event and the house collapsing under the weight of paintings and their frames.

Among other locations considered for the National Gallery was one further along Pall Mall, next to St James's Palace, and the vacant Carlton House site. Joseph Hume reminded the House of Commons that 'there was an empty palace [Carlton House], which had cost £600,000, and that would afford these pictures a very comfortable resting place'. Hume was evidently out of touch, because Carlton House had been demolished four years earlier; nevertheless it was good fodder for the parliamentary reform lobby. Inexorably, opinion was favouring the King's Mews, with or without the horses, and William Wilkins and Sydney Smirke, the younger brother of Robert

Smirke, presented plans to show how this might be turned into a picture gallery. Sydney Smirke proposed to take the roof off, insert skylights and divide the ground-floor space into a series of recesses, 'similar to the side chapels of a Catholic Church, with the exception that the light, instead of coming from behind the altar and opposite the eyes . . . will *here* be *before* the picture, and screened from the eyes'. This would create ample space to take the paintings, and allow the upper floor in the centre of the building to be used for the temporary storage of the records from the law courts, which were themselves being demolished and rebuilt. Subsequently, the upper rooms would be converted into galleries for 'hanging cartoons, sketches and other subordinate works of art'. Nevertheless, this suggestion was rejected and, instead of the proposed side-chapel method of hanging pictures, the gallery came to have the rectangular rooms of Wilkins's scheme.

The King's horses vacated the Mews in 1829, and until Wilkins's plans were adopted in 1831 the building at the top of the sloping ground newly named Trafalgar Square became home not only to the law records, but also to a pride of tired old lions which had been caged there since their eviction from Exeter 'Change menagerie in the Strand. Initially, the new building was intended to house both the nation's paintings and its sculpture currently displayed and stored in the British Museum. This proposal would have obliged the Elgin Marbles to be trundled once more through the streets of London. The Royal Academy was to be moved from Somerset House to a replica of the Parthenon in the centre of Trafalgar Square, facing the National Gallery. The Parthenon proposal, and the moving of the sculpture, was soon dropped, but the Mews site was retained for the National Gallery, to be shared, after a subsequent decision, with the Royal Academy. Being approximately equidistant from the fashionable west and the poor east of London, the National Gallery would in theory be equally accessible to all. Until demolition work on the Mews began, the lions could still be heard across the square, roaring into the night. As a direct result of collateral changes that accompanied John Nash's redevelopment of the central swath of London, from Regent's Park to St James's Park, the creatures came briefly to Trafalgar Square. In their former home, a large dilapidated building which stuck out and obstructed the traffic flow at the west end of the Strand, they had been causing a nuisance by frightening passing horses and pedestrians. Mary Lamb had often heard them roar at midnight as she travelled home along the Strand.

Exeter 'Change was a grubby and dispiriting old zoo that made William Bullock's Egyptian Hall seem positively elegant. This building and those around it were demolished to make way for a crisp new stucco residential development, shops, a gallery for watercolour painters, a school, an arcade and, in due course, another 'national gallery', the privately run National Gallery of Science. The replacement for Exeter 'Change, Exeter Hall, a building designed by John Peter Gandy, was constructed for multiple use – religious worship, temperance meetings and concerts – and was big enough to accommodate a choir of seven hundred. Speaking at its opening in March 1831, John Hoppus, the 'dull and inaudible' Professor of Philosophy at the University of London, outlined the three causes, religion, charity and science, that Exeter Hall was to promote: 'Religion was the parent, charity the daughter and science the handmaid . . . Inquiry was alive and the mind of man could not be repressed, and in proportion, as a union was formed between religion, charity and science, would the happiness of man be increased.' The philosophy that the nation's paintings should be available to all the nation's people, and thus be housed and displayed at the interface between rich and poor London, was in tune with the mood which surrounded the difficult passage of the Reform Bill through parliament in the course of 1831 and 1832. The siting of the religious, temperance and musical foundation of Exeter Hall at this same interface was a further manifestation of the mood.

On 22 April 1831, following the bitterly fought first defeat of the Reform Bill, parliament was dissolved, and the Prime Minister, Lord Grey, called a general election. This sent campaigners for reform into immediate action, which five days later took the ostensibly benign form of 'illuminations', by permission of the Lord Mayor of London. Householders were expected at the very least to put a lighted candle in their windows to mark their support of the floundering bill, and to avoid being attacked by the mob: 'All persons [were] compelled either to illuminate, or to see their property destroyed . . . The Bishop of Winchester and Mr W. W. Wynn, seeing the mob approach, placed candles in their windows, which thus escaped.'

The mob moved noisily and aggressively from Temple Bar, past Somerset House where Royal Academicians were completing the hang of their annual exhibition, down the Strand and into Pall Mall. There the satisfying crash of broken glass and howls of anguished householders filled the air. Then on they went to St James's Street, shouting, chanting and throwing stones, the embryonic and inadequate force of metropolitan police being powerless to stop them. They reached the gentlemen's clubs, where they broke the windows of Crockford's, Jordan's, the Guards and other club houses, and moved along Piccadilly to Hyde Park Corner. There they shattered windows in the Duke of Wellington's Apsley House. The Duchess of Wellington happened just to have died, and her body lay still in the house. When a policeman announced this to the mob and appealed to their better nature they changed direction and, buzzing and swarming, moved up Park Lane. There the hundreds of men and women resumed their shouting and jeering and hurling of stones, and 'broke some windows in the Duke of Gloucester's house. They then demolished the whole of the windows in the Marquis of Londonderry's mansion, and, having done similar damage to the premises of other gentlemen . . . broke Sir Robert Peel's windows'.

Following the crowd in the trail of stones, broken glass and fury was the bemused but observant middle-aged German painter Johann Passavant. He had arrived in London in April 1831 to tour England, where he came upon this swath of destruction. He was a painter who believed he had failed at his profession, not being, he thought, a match for his beloved Raphael. So he took to travelling, with a determination to see as many Raphaels in Italy, France and England as he could, to gather material for a comprehensive book on the master. To this end he procured invitations to the richest houses in the land, starting with London. That he did not take one look and turn for home when he saw Apsley House and other buildings attacked suggests that he considered the movements of the mob to be one of the excitements of London in 1831, an experience of civil disorder to set against the sinuous beauties of Raphael: 'It was my fate to see [Apsley House] the day after the general illumination for reform, upon which occasion the London populace had found no better way of expressing their patriotism in the cause, and their detestation of its enemies, than by smashing the windows of the principal Tory residences.'

At a crowded meeting in the Crown Tavern in Museum Street, Bloomsbury a month later, the National Reform Association was founded out of the failure of the Reform Bill. Among the leaders of the association were Francis Place, friend of Alexander Galloway, and Joseph Hume. The furious destructive power that had driven the mob through London on 27 April was now condensed into the affirmative action expressed in the Association's Declaration and Resolutions:

> The evils inseparable from mis-government, having at length pressed upon the people with a severity too great to be any longer quies-cently endured, their first efforts have been directed to put an end to a system, the workings of which have entailed upon them such accu-mulated ills . . . The enemy is strong, and must be met with proportionate firmness.

Revolution was feared, indeed in some quarters, which included the drawing room of Apsley House, it was considered a certainty. Harriet Arbuthnot, a friend and confidante of the Duke of Wellington, wrote in her journal: 'The Duke has lost heart entirely. He thinks revolution is begun and that nothing can save us . . . He foresees nothing but civil war and convulsions.'

Despite the public expression of fury, and Wellington's misgivings, cultural life in London carried on, as it had to. The first exhibition of the Society of Painters in Watercolour was held in March and April at the Society's new gallery in Suffolk Street to the north-west of Trafalgar Square, within sound of the mob and of the lions. 'Rocked, as it were, in the storm of political agitation, our artists continue to produce their bright creations with as much persever-ance as if all around partook of the tranquillity which belongs to their own pursuits and character.' The Royal Academy opened its exhibition on time, two days after the mob had flooded past its win-dows. At the annual dinner on 30 April, as the damage in the streets was being cleared away, Academicians held their annual dinner to which they invited a small army of members of the government and establishment, including five dukes, a marquis, eleven earls, two archbishops and the ministers of nine foreign nations spanning the globe from Brazil and America to Russia. The Royal Academy became each year a focus of attention through its annual exhibition, and the platform for a rousing speech of encouragement to culture. This year the speech was given by the Lord Chancellor, Henry Brougham, one of the leading government advocates of reform. He told the assembled guests, among them Sir James Willoughby Gordon, Sir Anthony Carlisle, John Nash and Samuel Rogers, of the unifying effects of the arts, and the power and principle of patronage: 'It becomes all of us, then, most diligently to foster them. It is the duty of government, it is the interest of the country. No station is so exalted, no fortune so splendid, as not to derive lustre from bestowing such patronage; no lot so obscure as not to participate in the benefits they diffuse.'

One of the most startling paintings in the exhibition was Constable's *Salisbury Cathedral from the Meadows*, the ninth work in the artist's celebrated series of 'six-footers' – indeed, at just over seven feet long, an extended six-footer. The senior and long-serving Academician Sir William Beechey saw the work on Constable's easel at an advanced stage, and remarked: 'Why *damn* it Constable, what a *damned* fine picture you are making, but you look *damned* ill – and you have got a *damned* bad cold.' Coughing and sneezing as he evidently was during the last stages of making the painting, the artist created a dramatic rainbow arching over the silvery-grey form of the cathedral. A cart, shining after the rain like a wet pageant-gilded wagon, is being drawn across the river where swallows dip in the late afternoon light. Constable has here conjured up the kind of apocalyptic weather more usually found in John Martin's or Turner's paintings, with bright pools of light interspersed with deep foreground and distant shadow. But the storm is passing. Constable's loose, flickering paint upset the *Times* correspondent, who, describing the painting as 'a very vigorous and masterly landscape', immediately suspected vandalism: 'Somebody has spoiled [it] since it was painted, by putting in such clouds as no human being ever saw, and by spotting the foreground all over with whitewash. It is quite impossible that this offence can have been committed with the consent of the artist.'

Turner showed seven paintings at the Academy in 1831, a year in which Constable was one of the handful of Academicians who laid the exhibition out, the hanging committee. *The Times* was as perplexed about Turner's paintings as it had been about Constable's *Salisbury Cathedral*: 'Turner is one of the most provoking of painters.' It praised his *Caligula's Palace and Bridge* as 'one of the most beautiful and magnificent landscapes that ever mind conceived or pencil drew', but went on to add that in some other pictures he had disgraced 'the high powers that dwell in him by caprices more wild and ridiculous than any other man out of Bedlam would venture to indulge in'. Being praised and vilified in equal measure at the same time was not an unusual state of affairs for Turner. Both he and Constable had reached the stage in their careers (both were well-known Academicians, both in their mid-fifties) when they were allowed some indulgence by the press: they could pull off a bizarre performance and get away with it, but they were nonetheless held on a tight rein. The *Morning Chronicle* called Turner 'The Yellow Admiral', while the *British Press* had said a few years earlier: 'we find the same intolerable yellow hue pervading everything . . . yellow, yellow, nothing but yellow, violently contrasted with blue'.

A painting of particular topicality among Turner's exhibits of 1831 was *Life-Boat and Manby Apparatus going off to a Stranded Vessel making Signal (Blue Lights) of Distress*. This was prompted by the sudden intervention into London scientific and marine society of the irascible Norfolk barrack-master and seaman Captain George Manby, who had instituted around the British coast a series of emplacements of small cannon which would fire a rope into the rigging of a ship in difficulties offshore. Many lives were lost each year in shipwrecks close to the shore, and Manby's invention allowed a physical link to be established between ship and shore, enabling crew and passengers to be brought to safety. Manby was practised at irritating officialdom with his inventions and ideas, among them the production of a self-righting lifeboat, the pressurised fire-extinguisher, and the use of the Arctic as a self-contained penal colony. Having given lectures for Michael Faraday at the Royal Institution in 1830, he managed the following year to get himself elected a Fellow of the Royal Society.

In a masterpiece of public relations which may have influenced the course of Manby's election, Turner's painting was hanging in the exhibition rooms of Somerset House when the vote on Manby's fellowship was taken in the Royal Society's rooms on the floor below. Manby and Turner had a number of friends in common who were Fellows of the Royal Society, including Faraday, the banker Dawson Turner and the portrait painter Thomas Phillips, as well as Manby's proposer for the fellowship, the surgeon Thomas Pettigrew, who gave such good parties in Savile Row. Although any one of them might have brought Manby to Turner's notice, Manby's campaign was famous from at least as early as 1812 when he performed a public demonstration of his apparatus across the Serpentine. The subject of the painting – rough sea, blustery shore, shipwreck – was vintage Turner, and the entire episode a prime example of the successful integration of scientific, artistic and practical ideas, action and perhaps friendly co-operation between the Royal Society and the Royal Academy within the walls of Somerset House.

There was no friendly co-operation in 1831 between Turner and Constable, however. Admiring though they were of each other's art, they had a difficult personal relationship which particularly aggravated Constable. He described Turner as 'watchful and savage', and in landscape painting, with some bitterness, as 'Lord over all'. Their antipathy came to a head at a party at the home of the elderly General Edmund Phipps in Mount Street, Mayfair. Phipps, who had followed a successful military career with a second career as the Tory MP for Scarborough, was a collector who regularly entertained artists and other collectors. He had, as Farington noticed, a loud laugh. This could be heard happily entertaining groups of artists, including David Wilkie, Benjamin Robert Haydon and John Jackson RA, who referred to themselves as 'the clique'. At one of Phipps's parties, in late April or early May 1831, Constable and Turner were among the guests, as was their fellow painter David Roberts, who left a vivid account of a quarrel:

> Constable, a conceited egotistical person . . . was loud in describing
> to all the severe duties he had undergone in the hanging of the [1831

Academy] exhibition. According to his own account nothing could exceed his disinterestedness or his anxiety to discharge that Sacred Duty. Most unfortunately for him a picture of Turner's had been displaced after the arrangement of the room in which it was placed . . . Turner opened upon him like a ferret; it was evident to all present Turner detested him; all present were puzzled what to do or say to stop this. Constable wriggled, twisted and made it appear or wished to make it appear that in his removal of the picture [*Caligula's Palace and Bridge*] he was only studying the best light or the best arrangement for Turner. The latter coming back invariably to the charge, yes, but why put your own there [*Salisbury Cathedral from the Meadows*]? I must say that Constable looked to me and I believe to every one else, like a detected criminal, and I must add Turner slew him without remorse. But as he had brought it upon himself few if any pitied him. My own opinion of Constable may be mistaken, but he was not only an egotist in his own laudation, but what was far worse he was abusive and not sparing of any one else, a rare thing in a man of talent.

As the year progressed, and the noise of private quarrels intermingled with the sound of the mob passing through the darkening streets of London, a murderous strain of *cholera morbus* was being transmitted across the globe from the Pacific islands, through China, India, Russia, into Germany and Holland, and across the sea by trade vessels to Britain. It made landfall first in Sunderland, on the north-east coast of England, where in November 1831 dozens of cases of individuals vomiting, purging, turning blue and dying from cholera were reported. The *Literary Gazette* was one among many publications that plotted the course of the disease towards Europe, by publishing lurid stories of the misery abroad, a journalistic technique that racked up public anxiety at home. 'Accounts from Russia state that . . . the artificial heat produced at Moscow . . . by the use of furs, and by the large stoves in the houses, have prolonged [cholera's] existence, and that great apprehensions are entertained that, on the approach of spring, its violence and rapidity of communication will be entirely restored.'

All this upset even the most sanguine of people. The usually levelheaded Thomas Carlyle told his wife in August, 'Mrs B[uller] dying of terror for the *cholera* . . . John [Jefferies] is terrified about cholera.'

Others thought they had actually caught it months before it arrived. In August, Elizabeth Barrett Browning wrote that her father 'has had a violent attack of cholera. He is weak and low in consequence of it, – and is going out of London for two days, to regain his strength by changing the air.' Whatever disease he had, it was not cholera. The *Literary Gazette* published a map of the progress of the disease, and in November quoted a highly regarded physician: 'The pestilential cholera travels not with the erratic course of a contagious distemper, but with a march steadily progressive, in a particular direction.'

The late King, George IV, who had been crowned with such inspired, expensive and luxuriant ceremony in 1821, was spared by his death the sight of his sumptuous coronation robes being sold off at public auction. Under the hammer on 9 June 1831 went the mantle, the ruff, the shoes and the 'fine kid trousers, of ample dimensions, and lined with satin': all of these he is pictured wearing in Thomas Lawrence's coronation portrait. The enormous trousers were knocked down in Phillips's auction rooms for only twelve shillings, while 'the sumptuous crimson-velvet coronation mantle, with silver star, embroidered with gold', which had cost more than £500 to make, was sold for 47 guineas. Less than a week later, on Tuesday 14 June, eight weeks before his coronation, the new King, William IV, opened the 1831 session of parliament on a glorious summer day, following the Whig victory in the general election. Thomas Babington Macaulay witnessed the scene from the balcony of the Athenaeum, a club spared by the marauding mob because its members, being artists, scientists and men of letters, were generally perceived to be in favour of parliamentary reform. Writing to his sister Hannah, Macaulay told how he saw:

> the King returned through St James's Park in the midst of an innu-
> merable multitude. The view was not very distinct, but was, I think,
> finer on that very account. A cloud of dust was raised by the tramp-
> ing; and the trees in some degree obscured the procession. The whole
> had something of that hazy gorgeousness which characterises Turner's
> pictures. The long succession of state carriages, white horses, red liv-
> eries, heralds in coats of Cloth of Gold, life-guards with helmets and
> cuirasses, passed through a roaring ocean of heads and waving hats
> with a kind of dim magnificence which was quite delightful.

This was one of the few fine and warm summer days in London in 1831. Rain fell heavily and often this year, particularly in August when thunderstorms brought floods and lightning damage to the City, and knocked a pinnacle from the west end of Westminster Abbey. On 8 September, during the coronation of King William and Queen Adelaide, the wind was 'rattling and tearing amongst the canvas canopies of the stands'. In the summer of 1831 a tempest of another kind became a counterpoint to the tempestuous weather, to the uncertain politics and to the approach of disease. Music and its performance in London was shaken to its roots in June when the Italian violinist Nicolò Paganini gave a series of performances at the King's Theatre, for which he initially demanded £4,000 a show. The capital was the last stop on his tour of European cities, including Prague, Vienna and Paris, where Goethe had seen him in action: 'I lack a base for this column of sunbeams and clouds,' Goethe wrote. 'I heard something simply meteoric and was unable to understand it.' A report from Prague gave warning of Paganini's personal magic that London was so soon to witness:

> Paganini is a meteor, even in these days of scientific refinement, whose splendour we are not likely to gaze upon again. I admit that his exterior is rather forbidding than inviting, and yet there is something very remarkable about it. He is thin; his clothes hang loose about his limbs; and when he stoops to make his bow his body wriggles after so extraordinary a fashion that the spectator every instant expects the upper part of his figure to sever itself from the lower, and both of them to tumble to pieces into a heap of bones.

Paganini's extraordinary technique came from a medical condition that allowed extreme and unnatural flexibility in his limbs and fingers, enabling him to draw sequences of notes from the violin that no healthy hand or finger could manage. Because of this sinister dexterity Paganini was said to be in league with the devil, and to encourage this demonic notion he wore a black cloak and arrived at performances in a black carriage drawn by a black horse. Describing Paganini's appearance, the *Times* critic wrote that 'you may not believe half of what I am telling you, and I am not telling you half of what there is to be told'.

Here in London, the home of romantic artists and scientists, was a romantic performer, *par excellence*. Charles Babbage took David Brewster to a concert, and Jerdan spotted the peculiar quality of this 'god of the bow': 'It is not simply such command of an instrument as never was witnessed before – it is the production of music which may literally be said to ravish the sense . . . Like a magician he appears to persuade or compel [his violin] to do what to others would be impossible.' But Jerdan also saw through the transparent musical genius and discovered the venal man. Paganini, who was reported to have earned £10,000 for eighteen performances, kept on declaring 'last nights', thus encouraging the public to a yet greater frenzy of ticket-buying: 'No one ought to begrudge to unequalled powers even lavish reward; but it is disagreeable to see trick and char-latanry added to the fair claim of merit and genius.'

When Paganini the romantic and revolutionary violinist had at last packed up his fiddle and sailed for home, William Cobbett, the revo-lutionary Englishman, stood trial at the Guildhall in July 1831 charged with libel, 'with intent to raise discontent in the minds of the labourers in husbandry, and to incite them to acts of violence and to destroy corn, machinery, and other property'. Cobbett spoke with characteristic eloquence and subtlety in his defence, and summed up by declaring that 'a flash of lightning which set fire to a barn or rick might do much good. This trial might do a great deal of good; it had done a great deal already, as it had enabled him, in the presence and hearing of this great audience, to cast off those vile slanders which had been circulated against him.' At the end of the trial, the jury failed to decide a verdict, and Cobbett was acquitted.

Having opened parliament in June, the new King had another opening to perform before he was crowned. With much pageantry, on 1 August he and Queen Adelaide walked across the new London Bridge from the London to the Surrey side. A canvas pavilion, flanked by soldiers in fake medieval armour, had been erected at the London end, with an awning four hundred feet long running prac-tically the whole length of the bridge. This tended to spoil the effect of the elegant lines of the structure on opening day, but nevertheless the King and Queen emerged at last waving and smiling and show-ing themselves to the cheering populace. The opening of Rennie's bridge, six years in the building, was the first triumphant civic event of the new reign. The King, the personification of the temporal power of the nation, gave due credit and homage to the City of London, the seat of the nation's financial and mercantile power. Calling at the top of his voice as the tent flapped and fluttered, he paid tribute to 'the great work which has been accomplished by the citizens of London ... We are commanding a most extraordinary instance of their skill and talent.' The King proposed a timely and diplomatic toast to 'the trade and commerce of the city of London'. George Jones's painting of the scene (London, Sir John Soane's Museum) shows a large and enthusiastic crowd greeting the King and Queen, the crowd including a number of Jones's artist and architect friends, among them Turner, Chantrey and Soane.

Walking slowly across the bridge to the Surrey side of the river, the King and Queen threw medals, specially struck for the occasion, to their subjects gathered around and below them, on boats, on the parapets and on the Surrey approaches. Just as the couple reached the end of the bridge, up from the bank of the river rose a gas balloon carrying the intrepid aeronauts Charles Green and Richard Crawshay, rising up and up into the sky until they were carried out of sight. William Jerdan noticed the rapidity with which images of the opening ceremony were published. He cited lithographs after Clarkson Stanfield and Thomas Allom appearing within days of the opening, evoking 'a true and lively idea of the gay scene which presented itself on the new bridge when the royal party promenaded it'. Of the lithograph of the subject after Thomas S. Cooper he declared: 'There is no end to London Bridge! This a gay coloured affair, of which the *coup d'oeil* is flashy enough.'

Despite the fact that his portrait appears in George Jones's painting of the opening of London Bridge on 1 August, Turner was actually three hundred miles away at the time, bumping along the toll roads near Carlisle. He had left town at the end of July for Scotland, but it was not so much the weather that preoccupied him as the extent of the journey ahead. He travelled by coach to Edinburgh, via Carlisle and Abbotsford in the Scottish Borders where he would meet Sir Walter Scott, and then go on to the Western Isles, which he planned to visit by steamboat. Benjamin

Robert Haydon made a steam-boat journey from London to Margate in a strong gale on or around 24 or 25 August. Far from being dismayed, the experience empowered him, and inspired him with an idea for a picture:

> the subject will be a Margate Steamer *after a gale!* What characters! – I have engaged all the musicians to come & sit, and the Captain is so delighted, that he says it will be the making of his vessel, and I shall have every accommodation to make drawings . . . It shall be at least as good as the Mock Election – I think if it make a hit the Steam Company ought to give me a ticket for Life.

Haydon does not appear to have started the painting, but the opportunity briefly raised his spirits, and stimulated his sense of adventure. Less than a week later, in the same series of rainstorms, Michael Faraday left London with his wife for Hastings. After they had ridden through the rain on the roof of the carriage wrapped up in rubber capes, he observed: 'I do not think any body ever fares so well on a coach as we do. Others on the outside were wet & cold those within dry but so stewed up that I envied not their lot.'

Beside Faraday in his bag was an iron ring wound with two separate coils of wire. With this, a battery and a small magnetic compass, he had on 29 August discovered at his work bench in the Royal Institution that when one of the coils was connected to the battery, electricity momentarily flowed in the other coil: 'Immediately, a sensible effect on the needle. It oscillated and settled at last in original position,' he wrote in his laboratory diary. When the wire was disconnected, he noticed 'again a disturbance of the needle'. Faraday knew he was on to something, and wrote to tell Sir Richard Phillips, the editor of the scientific journal *Annals of Philosophy*: 'I am busy just now again on Electro-Magnetism and think I have got hold of a good thing but can't say; it may be a weed instead of a fish that after all my labour I may at last pull up.' What Faraday had discovered was the phenomenon of electro-magnetic induction, the electrical principle behind what became to be known as the transformer.

Turner came home from his 1831 journey carrying with him sketches and watercolours to illustrate the poems of Walter Scott, and the idea for one of his greatest steam-boat paintings, *Staffa, Fingal's*

Cave (New Haven, Paul Mellon Center). Haydon's journey to Margate ended in the evaporation of his idea of a steam-boat subject, but when Faraday returned from Hastings on 21 September with some newly wound coils, he began a series of solitary experiments which culminated on 17 October with his discovery of how to generate alternating-current electricity, the discovery which showed that the days of the Steam Age were beginning to be numbered. In the four weeks between Faraday's return from Hastings and his generation of alternating-current electricity, the hopes of political reformers were raised to the heights as the Second Reform Bill was passed by the House of Commons with a Whig majority of 109. But after five days of further debate in the Tory-dominated House of Lords it was thrown out, and it appeared that the nation was back to square one. This sparked a series of marches and meetings around Britain in protest, the alternating currents of politics flowing powerfully throughout London at precisely the same time as Faraday was creating and identifying an alternating current of electricity in his Royal Institution coils.

The first meetings in London to protest about the failure of the Reform Bill took place the Saturday after the House of Lords vote on 8 October. The largest filled the Horse Bazaar, Marylebone to overflowing. An estimated thirty thousand men and women were unable to get into the square, so they walked patiently to Hyde Park, where fifty thousand now regrouped on the north bank of the Serpentine. There they were told that as they were outside the parish of St Marylebone the meeting was illegal, but that if they moved to Regent's Park they would be free to assemble. Once again they slowly went north, their numbers now swollen to eighty thousand, tramping the streets to show their support of parliamentary reform:

> If any thing could have cooled the ardour of the people, who however proved themselves as ardent as patriotic, it was this demand upon their patience after waiting above an hour at the Bazaar, and dragging through the Park for an hour more; but nothing daunted they proceeded in good humour, to the Regent's Park and arrived there between one and two o'clock. Several wagons were placed at the lower part of the grounds and the assembled multitude, which before the chair was taken must have amounted to 80,000 persons,

formed themselves on the rising ground into a sort of semi-circle and the wind being in their faces, the majority could hear the proceedings.

They were addressed by Joseph Hume, who told them that:

> it was no ordinary occasion which had called them together, and in the great and important measures they were about to discuss, every man from the King to the Peasant had a deep interest . . . They would tell the petty pitiful majority of the House of Lords that they had rights as Englishmen as sacred as their own and that an oligarchy which had usurped their rights should be compelled to relinquish their tyrannical power which they had so long exercised against the people.

The overall tenor of the October meetings and marches was peaceable and festive, with good humour and celebration as the processions ebbed and amalgamated and flowed through the capital. Perhaps twenty thousand people joined another huge crowd in and around the widest and most exclusive street in London, Portland Place. The people spilled out across the New Road and into Regent's Park as they gathered to march.

> There may perhaps have been other parishes in the procession . . . The numbers of the procession were variously estimated by the newspapers at from 70,000 to 300,000 – I think about 70,000 is near the truth, but taking into consideration the crowds which met and accompanied us on the line of march there might have been nearer 500,000. All the windows of the streets through which we passed were crowded with spectators the greater part of whom were elegantly dressed ladies, and Ribbons – Flowers – and Cockades were frequently showered upon us as we passed, accompanied with loud cheers waving of handkerchiefs and expressions of sympathy. At many points of the road we were saluted with bands of music, some playing the dead march, others God save the King – and Rule Britannia. Church bells tolled out as we passed. Flags and other items were hung out and with the exception of the mere City most of the Shop windows were closed, and business was suspended even in the private streets.

But even as the marchers carried their message to warn parliament of the demand for political reform, cholera was approaching. Giving as much information as they could, the Privy Council had approved

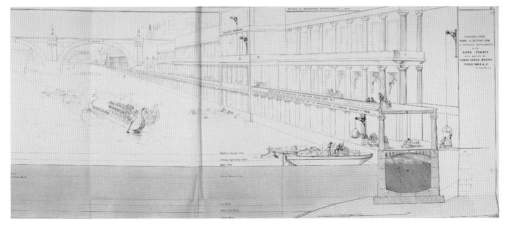

John Martin's proposal for the London Bridge terminus of his scheme to reshape London's sewage system. This lithograph accompanied Martin's submission to a parliamentary inquiry on Metropolitan improvements in 1838. It was not adopted

Regent Street Quadrant, attributed to Charles Wild. The elegant curve of the Piccadilly Circus end of Regent Street shown just before it was completed, c.1820. Now demolished

Interior of Sir John Soane's Museum, with the Sarcophagus of Seti I by John Michael Gandy. Created by Soane in the 1820s and 1830s, the Museum is virtually unchanged, and is open to the public

A View of Cheapside in the City of London by W. Duryer and T. M. Baynes. Looking west, with the tower of St Mary-le-Bow, and St Paul's Cathedral in the distance. The artists of this lithograph are as interested in the details of the roofscape as they are in the pattern of the traffic below

Above: The Strand from Exeter 'Change by C. R. Stanley. On the left is the office of William Jerdan's *Literary Gazette*, and in the background on the right is the corner of Somerset House, beside St Mary-le-Strand church

AUTHOR OF THE POLITICAL REGISTER.

Left: William Cobbett (1763–1835) by Daniel Maclise; politician, traveller, reformer. The eloquent and passionate journalist–politician was charged in 1831 'with intent to raise discontent in the minds of the labourers'. He defended himself, and won

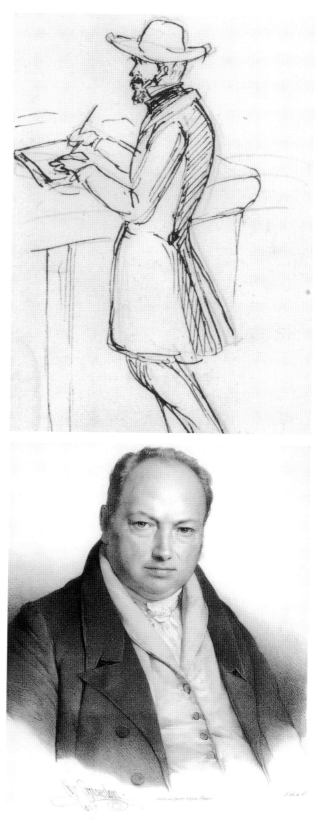

Thomas Carlyle (1795–1881) by Edward Matthew Ward; writer. Carlyle is standing at a desk in the British Museum Reading Room filling out a request slip for a book

Henry Maudslay (1771–1831) by Charles Etienne Pierre Motte; engineer, inventor. 'First, *get a clear notion* of what you desire to accomplish, and then in all probability you will succeed in doing it'

Mary Somerville (1780–1872) by Sir Francis Chantrey; mathematician and writer. Preparatory drawings for Chantrey's marble bust of Mary Somerville, commissioned for the Royal Society

Sir John Soane (1753–1837) by Sir Francis Chantrey; architect. A learned and determined architect and collector, whose ill-temper and vanity was balanced by his talent for throwing impressive parties

Sir Robert Smirke (1781–1867) by Edward Hodges Baily; architect. The 'ingenious young man' who rose with determination and skill to become architect of the British Museum, King's College, the Custom House, the General Post Office and the Royal Mint

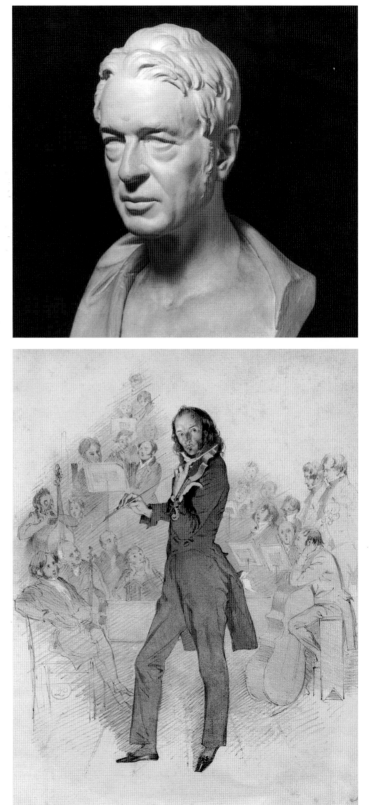

Nicolò Paganini (1782–1840) by Daniel Maclise; violinist. His extraordinary violin technique came from a medical condition that allowed an unnatural flexibility in his limbs and fingers

The Great Exhibition: Transept of the Crystal Palace, looking north, photograph by Henry Fox Talbot, 1851. Another photographer's camera, removed during exposure, is just discernible to the right of the fountain

The Great Exhibition: South Transept of the Crystal Palace, photograph by Henry Fox Talbot, 1851 the precautions against the disease recommended by the Board of Health. These were widely circulated throughout the country in pamphlets such as *Directions to Plain People as a Guide for the Conduct in the Cholera*. But if 'plain people' felt reassured by the official recommendations, there were many thousands of much plainer people who would have been completely unable to manage. Among the precautions recommended were:

> hot lime wash the walls of your houses from the cellar to the garret; this must be done by all, and often;
>
> open all windows, and thoroughly air every room several times a day;
>
> sprinkle all floors occasionally with chloride of lime [bleaching powder];
>
> lock away every article of furniture, dress, carpets, blankets, clothes etc not actually wanted in some retired room;
>
> let the room in your house intended for the reception of the sick be large and airy;
>
> let every house that can afford it be provided with a tin slipper bath, ready to be filled with water at the shortest notice;
>
> every village ought to be entirely cleared of beggars;
>
> have no more in your family than you can avoid. The fewer persons the better.

Then as a final exhortation, 'use wine in moderation; no spirituous liquors. Keep yourselves calm and composed; it will be much in your favour.'

God was rapidly called upon in a manner approved by hurried and anxious officialdom. Only days after the disease had been reported in Sunderland, HM Printing Office distributed by coach parcels of prayers on 5 November, a date usually reserved to celebrate escape from calamity rather than to mark its approach. The Vice-Chancellor of the University of Oxford received this covering note in his parcel of prayers:

> Sir – We have this day forwarded by coach from the Bolt-in-Tun, Fleet Street, a parcel addressed to the Vice-Chancellor of Oxford containing 100 copies of a Form of Prayer to be used during the continuance of our Danger from the Pestilence now spreading over a great part of Europe, which we trust will come safely to your hands.

Out in the depths of the country there were people who thought the cholera was all a Tory plot to stifle dissent. William Cobbett reported a conversation he had had with a Hampshire farm labourer:

'And this cholera morbus, Sir, don't you think it's a sort of shoy hoy to frighten us out of the reform?'

'Not exactly that,' said I, 'but when one of your children has got the hickups—'

'Ay,' said he, interrupting me, 'then my dame tells it some frightful lie and away goes the hickups.'

'Just so,' said I.

'Ay,' said he, 'but they won't frighten us by their cholera morbus, and make us content with potatoes and water.'

Francis Place was more ruminative about the ill-luck of the disease appearing when it did, and the possible consequences. Writing to Joseph Hume in December he predicted:

The cholera will spread all over the country, and by the time the [Reform] Bill shall have reached the Third Reading, and the country shall have become tired, if not wearied out and disgusted, we shall have quarantine regulations against our shipping in all parts of the world. The consequences may be a great impediment to navigation, diminution of trade and commerce, embarrassment, stagnation, panic, multitudes of people discharged in all our great manufactories.

The official remedy for those unfortunate enough to have caught the disease was a concoction of white wine, whey, spices, hot brandy and water or sal volatile. A teaspoon of this mixture was to be given to the patient frequently. Alternatively, five to twenty drops of peppermint, cloves and cajeput (tea tree oil) should be administered in a wineglass of water, or in very severe cases from twenty to forty drops of laudanum in any of the above mixtures. Sir Anthony Carlisle confirmed this to be the best treatment when he lectured to the Mechanics Institute on the cholera. He recommended it should be continued 'if repeated by the stomach, until retained, to be followed by bed, blankets and warm drinks such as wheys mixed with laudanum'. Another recipe, recommended by a surgeon on HM Hospital Ship *Canada*, was one drachm of nitrous acid, one ounce of peppermint water and forty drops of tincture of opium taken every three to four hours. The real problem was that nobody knew for certain how to cure the disease. John Hogg, a physician younger and more informed than Carlisle, described the course of cholera in cool, unequivocal language:

> The disease generally began by relaxation of the bowels without pain, the evacuations being colourless, no other symptom was observable; the second stage was indicated by spasmodic pains of the bowels, and incessant evacuations, cramps of the stomach, vomiting of colourless fluid, cramps in many of the muscles, particularly in the calves of the leg, and at the pit of the stomach, excessive torture and prostration of strength, sinking of the pulse, and shrinking of the body generally, particularly of the features; a clammy sweat broke out, no urine was passed. In the third stage the body was altogether collapsed and cold, the vomiting, purging and cramps subsided, the pulse was no longer felt, the breathing was slow and heavy, the voice shrill and weak, the tongue was often cold, and even the breath was chilling; the vital powers were completely prostrate, and the body became of a deep livid or blue colour, insatiable thirst came on, an occasional evacuation of a chocolate-like fluid took place, and death closed the scene; the intellects remaining calm and collected to the last. The disease was uncertain in its duration, it seldom lasted beyond thirty-six hours, and not infrequently cut the patient off in six, or even less.

With reform agitation and disappointment in the air, and the approach of a murderous disease, the nation was in the autumn of 1831 uneasy with itself. In early October, during another heavy rainstorm, the new King's College was opened beside Somerset House in buildings designed by the busy Robert Smirke. King's College was founded on the royal and religious principles of the Church of England, in retaliation to University College in Gower Street, which had driven God out of its constitution when founded in 1827. As the *Evening Standard* put it, 'with such a seminary in a prosperous position, there will be neither motive nor excuse for any parent to inflict upon his offspring the disgrace of education in the infidel and godless college in Gower Street'. The Bishop of London gave a homily at the ceremony on the duty of combining religious instruction with intellectual culture, and the College Principal, the

Rev. William Otter, gave another weighty lecture, the whole event lasting four hours. It was, as the *Literary Gazette* admitted, 'An inauspicious day for this interesting ceremony. The political agitation of the moment, and the badness of the weather, conspired to deprive it of much of that *éclat* which would doubtless otherwise have attended its start into being.' King's College had engaged a formidable group of professors, including Charles Lyell, who held the chair of Mineralogy and Geology, and Charles Wheatstone, the Professor of Experimental Philosophy, or, as we might put it today, of Scientific Research. It would not be long before cracks began to appear in the establishment when Lyell resigned in 1833 in protest at the college council's refusal to allow women to attend his lectures in case they might be led into dangerous areas of irreligious thought by his advanced views on the age and formation of the earth.

Of the many books on scientific subjects published or resonating to full effect in the course of 1831, three had a profound influence. Charles Lyell's *Principles of Geology* (1830) looked down into the earth, and argued that the planet was formed over a length of time unimaginable to the human mind, and that fossils and rock formations marked the gradual shaping of the global landscape. This process Lyell called Uniformitarianism. Mary Somerville's *The Mechanism of the Heavens* (1831) looked up to the stars, and was a translation and interpretation for English readers of *Mécanique Céleste* by the French mathematician and astronomer Pierre Simon Laplace. Neither the original French edition nor Somerville's translation were books for the general reader, crammed as they were with passages of abstruse mathematics, but Somerville graced her work on a difficult text with language rich in imagery which revealed the universe to be an organism with regular and predictable functions.

Mary Somerville was popular with her fellow scientists and mathematicians, not only because she was extremely clever and wrote well, but also because she had beauty and elegance, and a winning smile. She and her husband, the modest military physician William Somerville, gave splendid parties in Hanover Square, and her unique combination of grace, brains, generous hospitality and friendship made the stiffest scientist go weak at the knees. The astronomer Sir James South remarked, with about as much tact as he could muster, that Mary Somerville had modesty, 'that rare thing in a woman'. In the world of science, William and Mary Somerville were a royal couple.

Mary Somerville's style in *The Mechanism of the Heavens* is 'easy, clear and vigorous', as the naval captain and author Basil Hall told her: 'You never fail in a sentence or a paragraph. Each point is made out . . . Nothing is exhausted or squeezed to the uttermost & yet everything is satisfactory . . . So that the whole hangs together in a good harmonious maze, if I may so call it, like the heavenly bodies themselves.' Now that Humphry Davy was dead, and given that Michael Faraday did not write books, Mary Somerville was the only scientific writer who could engage the uninformed reader and carry him or her along in a comprehensible flow of ideas. Maria Edgeworth saw the point, and quoted some Somerville back to her:

> The great simplicity of your manner of writing . . . suits the scientific sublime – which would be destroyed by what is commonly called fine writing . . . Page 58 a beautiful passage on the propagation of sound. It is a *beautiful sentence* – as well as a sublime idea:
>
>> 'So that at a very small height above the surface of the earth the noise of the tempest ceases and the thunder is heard no more in those boundless regions where the heavenly bodies accomplish their periods in eternal and sublime silence.'
>
> Excuse me, in my trade as a sentence-monger.

Even a painter persevered with it, though the algebra defeated him. Thomas Phillips, both a Fellow of the Royal Society and a Royal Academician, told Mary Somerville: 'I thank you for the book but there is much I am sorry to say in it which partakes so little of the line of Beauty, viz: [here a line of mock algebra] that it might as well be in the old Chaldaick for me.'

Mary Somerville brought fresh poetic expression to the appreciation and understanding of science. Though fully in tune with the art and literature of her day – she knew Turner, and held long conversations with him – she had no use for the kind of proto-aestheticism that drove Keats's youthful disdain and fear of scientific discovery. Keats had written in his long poem *Lamia*, published in 1819, about a serpent which turned into a beautiful woman with tragic consequences: 'all charms fly', Keats wrote, 'at the mere touch of cold philosophy'. Philosophy, by which here Keats meant ordered scientific study, would not only 'clip an angel's wing', but also 'unweave a rainbow', thus sucking the poetry from nature and life. Somerville would have none of this, and through her writing, first in *The Mechanism of the Heavens* and latterly in *On the Connexions of the Physical Sciences* (1834), she asserted a moral authority for poetic metaphor and language to be the clearest medium by which established facts of science could be transmitted to a wide lay audience, male and female, now prepared and eager for understanding and involvement.

How could the scientific establishment in London acknowledge Mary Somerville's towering qualities? This was a question her friends and colleagues chewed over in their clubs and smoking rooms. Patronage was not enough. They could not elect her a Fellow of the Royal Society, as she patently deserved, because she was a woman. For the same reason she could not be quietly recommended for a knighthood. So they decided in 1831 to do the next best thing: the President and Fellows commissioned Francis Chantrey to carve her bust, at a cost of 200 guineas, to stand in the meeting room of the Royal Society. By February 1832 they had collected sixty-four subscribers. Mary Kater, the wife of Henry Kater FRS, wrote a womanly aside to Mary Somerville when she passed on the news: 'They only do themselves honour by conferring on you the only one they had it in their power to bestow.' Nevertheless, subscriptions petered out in 1835, when only £156 had been pledged, and it is not clear if the final sum was ever raised. While Chantrey completed the bust before he died in 1841, it was not delivered to the Royal Society until 1842.

The timing of this accolade to Mary Somerville of a Chantrey bust came at a pivotal moment in the Royal Society's history. Not only was 1831 the year of the arrival of cholera, of Paganini, of electromagnetic induction, of William IV, of London Bridge, and of the final struggle before the Reform Bill became law, it was also the year in which the Royal Society was forced to look at its own administration and answer brutal and determined criticism heaped upon it by Charles Babbage, one of its most formidable Fellows. It had always had its share of rivalries and incompetence, as Stephen Rigaud heard from a former Royal Society Secretary and Librarian, the mathematician Stephen Lee:

> Since I left Somerset House I have had innumerable queries respecting matters which the most careless Clerk might have furnished them with . . . But little else can be expected whilst such men as Davies Gilbert & Mr Pond are suffered to have any thing to do with the affairs of the Society or the Observatory.
>
> Are you aware that the coefficients C & D in the supplement to the Nautical Almanac for the present year are almost all wrong, thanks to that accomplished Mathematician & Astronomer John Pond Esq under whose superintendence they were completed.

Babbage's attack came in his polemic *Reflections on the Decline of Science in England and on Some of its Causes* (1830) which, while reflecting on the neglect of science as a subject in universities, castigated the Royal Society *inter alia* for the sloppy way it elected its Fellows, for falsifying minutes, for cronyism in appointments to official scientific advisory posts in government, for twisting the criteria by which Royal Society medals were awarded, for inefficiency, and for much else. For years Fellows had been elected more because they were good fellows or influential members of the established order than because as scientists they would make good Fellows. The circumstances of the election of Samuel Rogers, the banker–poet, to a fellowship in 1796 had, more than thirty years later, hardly changed. Babbage exposed the system by wry humour, saying that, to be elected, a gentleman had to get three Fellows to sign his certificate:

> At the end of ten weeks, if A.B. has the good fortune to be perfectly unknown by any literary or scientific achievement, however small, he is quite sure of being elected as a matter of course. If, on the other hand, he has unfortunately written on any subject connected with science, or is supposed to be acquainted with any branch of it, the members begin to inquire what he has done to deserve the honour; and unless he has powerful friends, he has a fair chance of being black-balled.

Babbage exaggerated for effect of course, but if he could only name one example to illustrate his case he could have chosen the instance of the election of Michael Faraday to a Royal Society fellowship. This took place in January 1824, but only after a seven-month campaign by Faraday's supporters against fierce opposition orchestrated by Sir Humphry Davy. The ease with which John Jebb, Bishop of Limerick and author of religious works; Horatio Walpole, 3rd Earl of Orford, and Major-General Sir John Malcolm, soldier and historian of India and Persia, were elected Fellows of the Royal Society in the same year as Michael Faraday's difficult passage is eloquent by comparison. Admitting a distinguished woman scientist and writer into their fellowship, even if only in the cold and partial form of a marble bust, was a small but significant step in the Royal Society's journey towards reform.

The event in the Royal Society's calendar equivalent to the Royal Academy's annual dinner in April was held towards the end of each year. On 30 November 1831, the President of the Royal Society, the scientifically inclined uncle of William IV, Prince Augustus Frederick, Duke of Sussex, appeared in full court dress to chair the anniversary meeting. In his speech to Fellows the Duke stressed the importance of 'cultivating intercourse with similar institutions abroad', and pledged himself to 'promote science and harmony amongst the Fellows of the Society'. He also announced that if Fellows failed to pay their annual subscriptions they would be struck off and would forfeit the honoured initials FRS. This was only mildly coded language which took due note of criticisms of the Society that had grown out of Babbage's attacks, the issue behind the subscriptions being that it was clear that too small a proportion of Fellows were practising scientists – as little as 30 per cent in the early 1830s.

The Thames Tunnel, which had inched its way beneath the Thames from Rotherhithe to a point in the middle of the river, was silent in 1831 except for the echoing chatter of sightseers. 'The Tunnel is lighted by gas, is dry and warm, and the descent is by safe and easy staircase. Admission 1/-,' the press advertisements read. But nothing else stirred, no engineers, navvies or bricklayers had been working there since January 1828, when the tunnel flooded disastrously. It may now have looked as if London was not going to have what was to be the first link in a chain of tunnels that became the basis of its nineteenth- and twentieth-century underground transport system. Brunel father and son were not short of suggestions for what to do with the truncated tunnel. Turn it into a wine cellar, said the poet Thomas Hood in his 'Ode to M. Brunel': 'build a bin or two . . . stick up a sign, the sign of the Bore's Head'. Another, the amateur poet Thomas Gent, wrote forty-seven lines in the *Athenaeum* journal 'On the Rupture of the Thames Tunnel':

> Every poor Quidnunc [gossip] now condemns
> The Tunnel underneath Old Thames
> And swears, his science all forgetting,
> Friend Brunel's judgment wanted *whetting*;
> 'Tis thus great characters are dish'd
> When they get *wetter* than they wished.

Marc Brunel took his mind off the tunnel by busying himself in surveys for improvements to the Oxford Canal and navigation on the Medway. His son and associate Isambard Kingdom Brunel, with prodigious energy, shuttled around the nation devising and implementing drainage schemes in Essex, and a new dock at Monkwearmouth, Sunderland. In London Isambard designed and built a thirty-feet-diameter observatory at Kensington for James South, with a revolving dome and machinery constructed by Maudslays of Lambeth. This was completed in May 1831. He submitted his entry for a competition to build a suspension bridge across the Avon Gorge at Clifton, Bristol, and in June 1831 his Egyptian-inspired proposal was accepted by the Clifton Bridge Committee. Isambard Brunel's ambitions were not limited to London, nor yet to Bristol or the British Isles. Before the Clifton Bridge, 'the ornament of Bristol and the wonder of the age', was begun, and before his Great Western Railway had fully negotiated its course between London and Bristol, Brunel was devising a steam ship, the SS *Great Britain*, to ply the Atlantic. But for a few inches of dockside masonry, Brunel's dream would have become a reality in his lifetime: a traveller would buy a ticket in London, take a train from Paddington Station to Bristol Temple Meads, put up at Brunel's hotel at Temple Meads, and, from nearby Bristol Docks board the *Great Britain* which would embark on a Wednesday to make landfall across the Atlantic in New

York harbour two Wednesdays later. Unfortunately, the dock at Bristol was just too narrow to accommodate the *Great Britain* regularly, so she made her Atlantic sailings to and from Liverpool instead.

After four years of campaigning, and attempted money-raising and lobbying, Brunel father and son accepted what they thought was reality. 'Tunnel is now, I think, *dead*,' Isambard wrote in his diary on 6 December 1831. 'The Commissioners have refused on the ground of want of [financial] security. This is the first time I have felt able to cry at least for these ten years.' Nevertheless, Brunel was not a man to languish for more than a moment, for he continued with an attitude that grew more positive as each word flowed on to the page: 'Some further attempts may be made – but – it will never be finished now in my father's lifetime I fear. However, nil desperandum has always been my motto – we may succeed yet. *Perseverantia*.' Around the entry he drew a thick black ink frame.

Twenty-one days later, as the old year began to turn into the new, and as Isambard Kingdom Brunel turned his attention to other, more viable projects, a journey began which would put the problems and purpose of the Thames Tunnel into a sharp perspective. Early on the crystal-clear afternoon of 27 December 1831, a three-masted naval brig, HMS *Beagle*, sailed out of Plymouth harbour on a five-year voyage of exploration which would take it around Cape Horn to the Galapagos Islands off the coast of Chile. On board was the young naturalist Charles Darwin.

13

'Now You Young Architects, There's a Fine Chance for You!'

∼

THE ARCHITECT JOHN Nash was a high-living, politically astute spendthrift, who turned bankruptcy and litigation into a fine art, and who was well over retirement age when in 1812 he began to transform London. He was born in 1752 the son of a Glamorganshire millwright, but died a sophisticated and cosmopolitan party-giver of renown, and an entrepreneur, loved and reviled in equal measure, who trailed lawsuits and quarrels even beyond the grave. For the Prince Regent, later George IV, he built, or severely improved, three palaces, and planned a fourth; for patrons in England, Wales and Ireland he built dozens of houses from *cottages ornées* to country castles; and for himself and his curious family he designed a pocket-castle in the Isle of Wight, and two London mansions in succession. In his house in Lower Regent Street, his second grand house in London, Nash lived 'like a prince', according to Karl Friedrich Schinkel who visited him on his English tour in 1826. Schinkel, coming from outside the hothouse professional and social world that Nash inhabited, observed the *mise-en-scène* with a detached but nevertheless flabbergasted eye:

> Stairway upwards, the walls covered in beautiful imitation green porphyry, model of the Parthenon on the landing, excellent imitation wood in the doors. Magnificent drawing room, white and gold . . . The hall – Raphael's Loggie pilasters and pediments finely painted, faithful, purple background of the side niches, where casts have been mounted of the best statues and busts of antiquity. Below, books bound in morocco, slabs of red marble. Plaster architectural models on the tables, lighting by means of round openings in the ceiling and small lamps at the side. In the other rooms, copies of the best paintings, Titian's Naples Danae.

Nash had married well: his second marriage, in 1798, was to Mary Anne Bradley, seventeen years his junior, who came to him with a fortune and a family to spend it on. His parties became the talk of the town, and from even as far away as Italy expatriate Englishmen seemed to speak of little else. The architect James Pennethorne, a promising and attentive young pupil of Nash, who also happened to be one of Nash's wife's sons, wrote from Milan to Robert Finch in Rome in August 1825:

> We had the pleasure to meet here 2 English friends, who gave us all the news from the Isle of Wight – being themselves from there & who told us of a Grand Fete Mr Nash is giving at his Castle having visiting him the Dukes of York, Clarence & Cambridge – & it is not impossible but uncertain that His Majesty will join them there.

That is how the architect lived. As a boy he had been 'a wild, irregular youth', a trait that he managed to control in his architecture, even if he failed wholly to do so in his private life. The control he achieved in his architecture reached no greater effect than his series of revolutionary amendments to the townscape of London. This was not a grand plan, nor was it the realisation of a lifelong dream: it evolved as it did under Nash's direction following a series of lucky events which came with a sequence and timing that not even the most optimistic of gamblers would dream of banking on. Very London.

Nash was already a wealthy and successful architect by 1806 when, aged fifty-four, he was appointed architect to the Office of Woods and Forests. Underpinning his success in the years before and during the Regency was his surprising friendship with the Prince of Wales, who became Prince Regent in 1811. The former was well practised in political and business manoeuvre, a genius at pleasing clients and at handling and reinterpreting frothy architectural style on a palatial scale. The latter was an extravagant royal playboy given little responsibility but having palatial ambitions and large trousers. Physically, they were both unremarkable; neither of them had a natural bodily beauty. The short, stout Prince shone in the fine clothes he wore, and within the sycophantic retinue and malleable system that surrounded him; the architect, a 'thick, squat, dwarf figure, with round head, snub nose and little eyes', as Nash described himself, talked and laughed, made jokes and flattered, was courteous and gentlemanly, but, above all, delivered. He was a subtle courtier, which led to rumours that his second wife, who had a number of children around her skirts when they married, had been a productive mistress of the Prince of Wales. This gave fuel to the gossips, and brought forth in the press scurrilous cartoons. It may, if proved, help to explain the Prince's gratitude and his patronage of Nash, or it may not; but what Nash certainly had in full measure was the successful architect's essential ability to engage with and assist his client.

So Nash had the Prince of Wales behind him. Then, by fortunate timing, in 1811 King George III was declared insane and the Prince became Prince Regent; and that same year the lease on the 510-acre Marylebone Park with its cluster of farms reverted to the Crown. This of course had long been expected, though the Prince's ambition to build a new, grand palace there had not. Nash rapidly produced a splendid set of plans, published in 1812, which went much further than a palace in the Park, and cast a thoroughfare one and a half miles south to the Prince's present palace of Carlton House. In 1813 Sir James Wyatt, who had been running the Office of Works very badly for seventeen years, conveniently broke his neck, and his job, the management and development of royal and government build-ings, was divided between John Nash, John Soane and Robert Smirke: Nash got the royal palaces, Soane the Law Courts, Smirke the British Museum. So by the end of 1813 Nash had the Office of Woods and Forests under his control, and had also taken over that part of the Office of Works that suited him just perfectly.

His initial plan for what rapidly became known as Regent's Park incorporated dozens of villas arranged among trees and water in an informal setting to create visual surprises at every turn. This closely followed eighteenth-century rules for Picturesque landscape arrange-ment. In engaging the Picturesque, Nash was nearly a century behind the times in terms of taste, but his plan gave the Park an instant sense of history that had taken the best part of a hundred years to develop in such landscaped gardens as Stowe in Buckinghamshire. Never had there been so rich an opportunity for landscape and resi-dential development in London on this scale. These houses would be leased to London's new money: bankers, successful tradesmen, lawyers, politicians. There were to be terraces of houses, a double circus for elegant parade, wooded lawns and acres, a lake and glimpses of the Regent's Canal, a pantheon commemorating the great and the good of Britain's past, and the royal palace. Then, in a southerly direction there was to be another circus on the New Road (now Marylebone Road) leading to Portland Place, whose line had been set in the 1770s. Land ownership in London being too complex and expensive to tamper with, Nash saw that the realistic option was to work with the existing street plan. James Wyatt had made his own attempt to solve the problem, which proposed a new road crashing violently through Soho in a series of jerky movements down to Piccadilly. Nash, however, offered a neat left curving turn at the bottom of Portland Place, a continuing southward line assimilating Edward Street and Bolsover Street, a crossing point at Oxford Street with a new circus, and a continuation slightly to the east of south which devoured the existing Swallow Street, roughly equidistant between Burlington House to the west and Golden Square to the east. He had the political and financial sense to spare such settlements and gathering places as Carnaby Market, near Golden Square, which Cornelius Varley had drawn with his Patent Graphic Telescope in 1801 (Museum of London). The route then made a graceful curve eastwards – the Quadrant, lined on each side with arcades and balconies – to keep to the edge of Soho, and at Piccadilly another circus re-established the north–south line and permitted a right-angled turn to allow traffic to proceed gently downhill to Waterloo Place as far as Carlton House.

Nash widened the existing street line as he went. He did not offer a straight triumphal avenue, as might have been expected in Paris or Berlin, but taking account of existing conditions allowed his route to find its own way naturally like a root through the foundations of London. This gave him the opportunity to insert 'eye-catchers' at the end of vistas, such as All Soul's Church in Langham Place, and the colonnaded curve of the Quadrant. At other points there were visual surprises to the right and left, for example the façade of the Haymarket Theatre which Nash rebuilt at the end of a side street off Lower Regent Street. This radical amendment to the town plan rescued the capital from an inertia brought on by the collision of rich estates in the west and the City in the east, which had squeezed to overcrowding the poorer housing in between. The east and the west, rather than the centre, was where London's money was held; the centre – the markets at Covent Garden, Hungerford and the Haymarket, the workshops of Long Acre, the inns, eating houses, theatres, and the countless small service businesses in this tightly packed area – was where money was spent, made and lost, and where tens of thousands of people lived. This was London's hub and heart.

Nash described his proposed route as 'a boundary and a complete separation between the Streets and the Squares occupied by the Nobility and the Gentry . . . and the narrow Streets and meaner Houses occupied by mechanics and the trading part of the community'. But this was a street not a wall, as in late-twentieth-century Berlin, and a boundary of separation of this kind is also a place where communities come together. London's population grew by about 10 per cent annually in the first decades of the nineteenth century, a rate which had increased to nearly 20 per cent by mid-century. This put extreme pressure on the finger of land which had developed on the medieval street patterns bounded by the west–east lines of Oxford Street and Holborn in the north, and the Strand and the Mall to the south. Lawyers, parliamentarians and bankers who worked in Westminster and the City began during the eighteenth century to live in the new estates in the west. To travel between home and work they had to squeeze themselves and their carriages along the existing sclerotic east–west arteries. It gradually became impossible. As a result the west and the east of London became different planets. John Richardson remarked: 'The inhabitants of the extreme east of London knew nothing of the western localities but from hearsay and report, and, *vice versa*, those of the west were in equal ignorance of the orientals.' Before Nash, London was a city on an east–west axis; after Nash the opportunities for easier north–south travel through the metropolis were open. By encouraging a new vertical flow through London towards the Thames the improvements also offered benefits to development south of the river.

The first part of John Nash's improvements to London, which

began with the building of Park Crescent in 1812, took over fifteen years to complete. Among Nash's great skills was his ability to orchestrate clients, financiers, landowners, traders and the Prince Regent into a great enterprise. Money poured in; money evaporated. Speculators, who included Nash himself, made money and lost it. Charges of corruption laid against Nash were investigated by a House of Commons committee, and thrown out. There were financial casualties, but the juggernaut rolled on in a generally northerly direction from Waterloo Place, with outcrops of building appearing up and down the central spine as opportunities arose. By the time Regent's Park, Regent's Canal and Regent Street were completed, the title that they honoured had disappeared from national life as the Prince Regent became King George IV in 1820. Now king, he tired of Carlton House, and the proposal for a palace in Regent's Park was abandoned. The number of villas in the Park was drastically reduced to fewer than ten. The King turned his attention to renovating and extending Buckingham House, at the far end of the Mall, into Buckingham Palace, another job he gave to Nash. Carlton House, 'this unhonoured pile', which was originally to be the climax of the southerly end of Regent Street, fell to the demolishers in 1827. Some of its parts were distributed: its chimney-pieces went to Windsor Castle, its Ionic columns to Buckingham Palace, and eight of its Corinthian columns to create the two porticoes on either side of the main entrance of the National Gallery.

With Carlton House reduced to rubble, the site temporarily became a rubbish heap, 'a mound as arid and unsightly as the sand hills which fence the coasts of Holland and Egypt'. Nash's scheme reached journey's end with a flourish a few dozen yards further south at Carlton House Terrace, a highly misleading name for a range of buildings that are infinitely grander than a terrace, and were conceived and built after Carlton House had vanished. The relentless southerly snip-snip of John Nash's street-cutting led to astounded comment in the press and correspondence which mixed delight and anxiety. Regent Street, in particular, had reorganised London at a stroke. Everything about it was new and bright and unfamiliar. The only comparable thoroughfare was Piccadilly, but Piccadilly is more or less straight and flat, and offered few surprises. One cannot really see down Piccadilly, but one can see up Regent Street, with its slow uphill rise, and its curve, a line of beauty that reminded those equipped to appreciate it of the curve of the High Street in Oxford. As each pedestrian or traveller passed along Regent Street, so its vista and its pleasures evolved before the eye. A visitor from Salisbury wrote in 1829: 'Rose before six. Walked down Regent Street, before the smoke curled from a single chimney; so that we could enjoy a view of this magnificent street as it was free from all vapour and mist.' Regent Street was home to fashionable shops, a fashionable church – Hanover Chapel – and at least two fashionably amusing museums, the Cosmorama and the Microcosm, the latter being described as a 'world within a world, a minute nature' around whose fourteen microscopes for the 'amusement of the curious' the proprietor, Mr Carpenter, guided his visitors.

Despite appearances, John Nash did not have all the best jobs. London in the 1820s and 1830s offered rich pickings for architects and speculators. In this golden age of London construction Sir John Soane designed the Bank of England, the Law Courts and the Offices of the Board of Trade; Sir Robert Smirke – when not working on the British Museum – designed King's College, the Carlton Club, the Royal College of Physicians (now Canada House) and the General Post Office, and came to the rescue of the crumbling Custom House; Charles Barry designed the Reform and Travellers Clubs; C. R. Cockerell the Hanover Chapel in Regent Street; Decimus Burton the Athenaeum and the Regent's Park Colosseum; William Wilkins the National Gallery; Benjamin and Philip Wyatt (sons of Sir James) remodelled and refaced Apsley House for the Duke of Wellington; and so it went on. John Richardson looked back from the early 1850s on how:

> Knightsbridge and Hyde Park Corner have, like other places, been improved. The handsome shops and houses which now form the southern side of the road have succeeded the small, dirty row of shops and sheds that stood there once. The turnpike has been removed; a weighing stone for wagons, that partly blocked up the road has disappeared; the wall which blocked out all view from the road into the park has been superseded by iron rails; triumphal arches have been erected; and Apsley House, originally a dingy brick

building, and very appropriately called by Sheridan the 'Dusthole' of London, has been transformed into an edifice of stone, with some pretensions to architectural beauty.

Robert Finch, 1,500 miles away in Rome, became the butt of the frustrations of young architects who could not seem to break the stranglehold of the established architectural system. Ambrose Poynter, who did eventually make a living as an architect working in the Gothic, Norman and Tudor styles, fulminated to Finch about the injustice of architectural competitions. He had entered the competition to design the new Post Office, but, as he told Finch in 1824:

> The *job* is now given – tell it not in Gath – to Smirke!!! – Lord Lonsdale patronized Smirke & as Ld Lonsdale is a Ld of the Treasury, & has nine rotten boroughs to boot, of course Smirke must be the choicest of architects. The outcry is universal – had Soane got it, no one need have grumbled his talents are a premium. Had Cockrill [*sic*] got it no one need have grumbled – it would have shewn a disposition to encourage a rising man – but that a man of . . . despicable taste should be thrust in for no earthly reason except the most bare faced corruption, is more than flesh & blood can patiently sit under . . . I am sick of the very idea of competitions, when the only reward even of success is to be robbed of one's design and thrust aside. However, I have set a term to this hopeless & losing pursuit – & if that time passes without some improvement in my prospects, I quit architecture for ever.

Another of Finch's young architect correspondents, John Davies, had come home from Italy in 1822 to find London 'in some places . . . very much changed':

> Not the City, Cheapside, the Strand &c are the same scene of bustle and confusion as ever, but the *West End* is a new world to me. Canals have been cut. Where used to be green fields I now see the masts of vessels. New roads new streets new crescents, terraces, squares, churches &c &c the change is wonderful. London is rendered more vast more magnificent but still there is rather more of bricklaying than of Architecture.

Davies there put his finger on the essence of the scheme: the Nash transformation of London was a series of interconnected private-development initiatives which stopped and started within their own errant timetables, but have subsequently become dressed up as if they were one *grand projet*. We can use the French term to describe it, but French it was not; it was English and irregular. Further, given the number of speculative builders, developers and financiers involved, the quality of the bricklaying, and anything else connected with the construction, was often suspect. Money, too, was volatile, as the fragile state of banking illustrated. One moment, May 1825, enthusiasm and wild expenditure: 'there appears to be an immense quantity of capital everywhere . . . and people are speculating mad. Shares are to be had in any thing you may fancy from Gas to Oysters. What think you to a Steam Company for washing linen and brushing coats.' The next, September 1825, banks crashed all over England taking speculators with them. Turner expressed a sanguine, countryman's view a few months later: 'Look at the crash in the mercantile world and the check that must follow, but the trouts will be found in the pool and the gudgeon in the shallow . . . while everything jogs on as usual, every one for himself, but at a more rapid trot notwithstanding steam boat liability, banks and stoppages.'

John Nash, by now seventy-three, did not stop when he reached St James's Park. Yet another young architect recently returned from Europe, Thomas Leverton Donaldson, reported to Finch in 1825 that 'among the projects now afloat that of street cutting is the most popular'. He went on to say that Nash had his eye on another improvement, a new system of streets linking Charing Cross, via Seven Dials, with the British Museum. This came as a result of the parliamentary vote in 1824 of £40,000 to expand the British Museum, beginning with the King's Library. Development of the Museum did not lead to universal public delight, but instead to loud complaints from those in the west of London that it was not adequately accessible from their direction. Donaldson continued to Finch: 'The nobs in the West End, enraged that so many good things should be so far Eastward, made a great noise in Parliament. The Government anxious to justify their proposition in Parliament desired Mr Nash to form an ample & noble access thereto as the West enders complained that they could not get at the Museum at all.' Nevertheless, no 'ample & noble access' to the British Museum was ever built.

Thomas Donaldson, who had attended Turner's Perspective lectures as a student at the Royal Academy, became a Silver Medallist in architecture in 1817. He travelled widely in Italy, Greece and Asia Minor, meeting Turner in Rome on the way. The two men had become close enough friends to travel together to Naples in 1819, where they saw Vesuvius in eruption. Donaldson, appointed the first Secretary of the Institute of British Architects on its foundation in 1834, had been a youthful admirer of John Nash, whom he later described as the architect 'to whom this Metropolis owes so much of its present improved arrangements and superior style of embellishment'. One of the duties that the Institute took upon itself was public education about architecture of all periods, a role which drew it to publish in 1835 a booklet setting out the basic questions to which people who had buildings of any kind in their care should know the answers. Though his name is not given on the title page, Donaldson was the author of this thoroughly modern document. Although initially of limited reach – the first edition ran to only 1,000 copies – it was translated into French and German, and went to a second edition in 1841. The booklet, with its extraordinary but illuminating title *Questions upon Various Subjects Connected with Architecture, Suggested for the Direction of Correspondents and Travellers, and for the Purpose of Eliciting Uniformity of Observation and Intelligence in their Communications to the Institute*, pioneered the clear official English to which twentieth- and twenty-first-century official government information leaflets aspire. It gave, and encouraged further search for, information on different building types and periods, from ice house to attic. Its emphases reflected the architectural interests and anxieties of the early nineteenth century, of which one of the most important factors in successful urban development in the 1830s and 1840s was the safe and correct construction of sewers:

> There is hardly any subject more important to the practical man than the mode of sewerage adopted for the relief either of a building or a city . . . The sewer constructed by Mr Nash in Regent Street was egg-shaped, and consisted of three half-brick rings, as Fig. C; where

the width was six feet in the clear, the height from the bottom to the top was only six feet six inches.

Though assiduous and hard-working, Donaldson realised that there was a great price to pay for the accumulation of architectural knowledge, and he sounded off to Finch about it. He complained that 'most of the [architectural] opportunities are engrossed by men of extensive interest but little talent':

> Is it not lamentable to think that those who have spent a fortune in the study of their art, who have suffered every privation amongst the savages who possess the remains of Antiquity in search of pure examples, who have exiled themselves from their families & friends for years, yet when they return must starve if they truckle not to the follies of their employers . . . To this state of things now verges the profession from the dastardly grovelling unmanly conduct of some of our most eminent Professors who seem to be using every artifice to trick each other out of their occupation.

One major disaster, emblematic of the pressures and temptations on architects and builders, was the collapse of the Custom House on the bank of the river at London Bridge as a result of shoddy workmanship. This could not be explained away in an exchange of letters. London's Custom House had been built to David Laing's designs in 1817. Through poor supervision, and fraudulent use of inadequate materials, the building had insufficient foundations: where oak had been specified for piles, beech had been used; where brick was required as infilling for arched ceilings, the builders had poured rubble. Part of its façade fell down in December 1824, and the floor of its main hall collapsed a month later. Donaldson described the situation: 'The failure of the construction of the Custom House here has caused a very great sensation . . . The walls they say threaten ruin & it is supposed that the damage may be from 60 to 150,000£. The profession are in a sad consternation at the disaster which is not only a terrible loss to the country but a sad disgrace to the Architect.' Robert Smirke, whose office was already busy designing the new British Museum buildings, was brought in to sort out the shambles. Laing was ruined, and left London. His fate became 'a beacon of warning to the young architect in particular, not to trust *to others* in matters of serious moment . . . still . . . if one architect failed in this work, the *quid pro quo* can be adduced in favour of another who succeeded, and *Smirked at the job!*'

Almost exactly ten years after the Custom House fell down, London suffered another disaster. The complex of medieval and later buildings at Westminster that comprised the Houses of Lords and Commons was severely damaged by fire on the night of 16 October 1834. The fire was an accident, caused by human over-exertion, too hot a furnace and unmaintained flues. In the basement of the House of Lords servants were burning piles of wooden tally sticks, which had for decades recorded expenditure. The situation ran out of control, and the building caught fire, rapidly becoming a magnificent spectacle. John Constable, with his two sons, watched the blaze from a hackney cab on Westminster Bridge. From the north-east the staff of the College of Arms near St Paul's Churchyard saw the glow over the rooftops from their windows: 'Our minds are wholly engrossed by the dreadful calamity at Westminster!' the Lancaster Herald at the college wrote the next day. 'Now gentlemen!' said the porter in the Royal Academy Library, 'now you young architects, there's a fine chance for you; the Parliament House is all afire.' Mary Somerville saw it all from Chelsea, where she and her husband 'had a fine view of the conflagration which was fearfully grand, but less damage has been done than was expected and happily Westminster Hall is saved'. From the west the former soldier Sir Richard Jackson saw it first from Piccadilly, overlooking Green Park:

> The flames arose above the dark masses of Westminster Hall & the Abbey, through the windows of which they were also seen & gave the appearance of all being enveloped by them. On approaching the Abbey, which was safe, from the direction of the wind, the anxiety of the spectators, and efforts of the [fire?]men were directed towards the preservation of the Hall, which was for many hours in the greatest danger, as the adjoining buildings form'd an extent of floating fire, which I never saw equalled except when $\frac{1}{3}^{\mathrm{d}}$ of Copenhagen was burning.

Jackson hurried over to Westminster where he saw firemen and troops working together to try to control the blaze. He noticed a fellow military man in the mêlée, Lord Hill, one of Wellington's generals, who stayed at the scene until three o'clock in the morning directing troops. Jackson gave these men 'great credit for their ready effectiveness & steady behaviour', and found the attitude of 'the mob', as he predictably described them, 'very satisfactory. The aweful scene really seemed to be, what it ought, one of universal interest.'

The crowds watching the fire came from all sections of society in London: the children of those who had danced when the Albion Mills burned down in 1791 were there, so too were those who had wept when Nelson's body was drawn on its catafalque up Ludgate Hill in 1805, and those who had broken windows in Pall Mall in April 1831 and gathered in quiet protest in Portland Place the following October. The history of London is marked by the gatherings of its crowds. Turner was one of the crowd when the fire was at its height, and it was he who came to transform the fire's 'universal interest' that Richard Jackson evoked into a reality. Hurrying from his house in Queen Anne Street down Bond Street or Regent Street, Turner will have first seen the blaze from about the spot where Jackson saw it, where the flames 'arose above the dark masses of Westminster Hall & the Abbey'. He crossed the Mall and St James's Park, and reaching Palace Yard made spirited pencil studies of the crowds in his sketchbook. One Academy student, John Green Waller, recorded in his diary that Turner, Clarkson Stanfield and some students went out on to the river to watch, and either by boat or by crossing Westminster Bridge Turner reached the opposite bank, and stayed there until first light.

In his studio, probably within the next few days, Turner made a series of watercolour studies, and then left the idea to simmer in his mind. The fire in the Houses of Parliament destroyed not only the medieval debating rooms of the Commons, but also drew a line under the old order, already undermined by the Reform Act. It prompted a fresh start, even if on the face of it this was only architectural. Turner responded to the fire slowly, but with a gathering and characteristic bravura. The following January, when the official report on the fire was being prepared for publication, he arranged for a standard three-feet-by-four canvas to be delivered in its frame to the British Institution in Pall Mall. There was, on delivery, very little paint on the canvas, 'a mere dab of several colours, and "without form and void", like chaos before the creation'. These words were written by the painter Edward Rippingille, a fellow exhibitor at the 1835 British Institution exhibition. Turner had exhibited at the British Institution before, but not since 1814 when he had had a row with the management, a committee of peers and gentlemen of overwhelmingly Tory inclination, and had not subsequently darkened its doors. One of them was Lord Lowther who, as Ambrose Poynter complained, had 'nine rotten boroughs to boot'. Very early in the morning, 'at the earliest hour allowed', Rippingille remembered, Turner began to paint his picture. This was a 'Varnishing Day' at the Institution, one of the few days before an exhibition's opening when senior exhibitors were allowed to put finishing touches to their paintings, or to varnish them. It was very much against the spirit of this concession to attempt to paint a picture from scratch.

But that, nevertheless, was what Turner did. He had evidently prepared the ground for what was a piece of private theatre, with he himself as the star. 'The managers knew that a picture would be sent there, and would not have hesitated, knowing to whom it belonged, to have received and hung up a bare canvas, than which this was little better. Such a magician, performing his incantations in public, was an object of interest and attraction.' With fellow artists including Etty and Rippingille at his side, Turner worked steadily. An audience gathered as he plied his brushes, palette knife and paints until, after more than three hours, he gathered his tools together, put them into his painting box, snapped it shut, and without saying a word to anybody, or even looking at his picture, slipped away from the gallery, down the stairs and away into the street. What Turner had created in those few hours on the gallery wall was a great conflagration to which he gave a very specific and pointed title – event, place and time: *The Burning of the House of Lords and Commons, 16th October, 1834* (Philadelphia Museum of Art). On the left in the distance are the Houses of Parliament ablaze; on the right Westminster Bridge in sharp perspective lit by gas globes and crowded with spectators; in the foreground more crowds of men and women packed together on the river bank, and on small boats on the water. The painting is a terrifying unity of sky and fire and stone and water, and in its time and place of first showing it carried a powerful political charge.

Choosing to paint this subject directly on the walls of the Tory establishment, Turner was sending a message. Performance, public appearance and the appearance of magic were activities which he both shied away from and embraced. 'He is a sort of Paganini,' the *Morning Chronicle* had averred in 1832, 'and performs wonders on a single string – is as astonishing with his chrome as Paganini is with his chromatics.' In the Houses of Parliament on fire, Turner had found a subject that combined a man-made cataclysm with contemporary history. In his past career the cataclysms that Turner had painted had either been natural – storms, avalanches, natural destruction – or biblical – the Deluge, a plague of Egypt. Only some of the storms had he actually witnessed. Here, however, was an event which galvanised London, destroyed the building that nurtured its democracy, and had symbolically cleared away a corrupt system. And, as well as all that, Turner had actually seen it all happen.

After the British Institution exhibition, Turner painted the subject again for his own beloved democratic institution of artists, the Royal Academy. He had done it once for the Lords, he did it once again for the Commons. The second version takes the spectator a step back from the fire, further down the river towards Waterloo Bridge (Cleveland Museum of Art). The sky is slightly lighter, and dawn is beginning to sweep the stars away. The same vast crowd is present as the giant column of flame and smoke is reflected in the river. As a pair these two paintings have the same relationship to each other as do the opening and the closing movements of a great romantic symphony, a tumultuous beginning with the statement of powerful themes, and a final heaven-storming grandeur, reprise and farewell. London would not be the same after the destruction of the Houses of Parliament, just as the art of painting would never be the same after the career of J. M. W. Turner.

The site of the old Houses of Parliament was cleared after the fire. More was demolished than was ever consumed by the flames, and within five years a new design had been adopted. The foundation stone was laid in 1840, and construction began. Rising now beside the river was a Gothic palace of unprecedented dimensions, designed by Charles Barry and Augustus Pugin, members of a new generation of architects who together created a building in which it was intended that British liberty should be preserved and democracy nurtured.

By April 1839 plans had advanced so far as to draw Sir Goldsworthy Gurney back from his Cornish retreat to propose a new system of oxygen lighting for the building. Just as much as roads, the river and water pipes were the threads connecting London, so were people and their aspirations, opinions, actions, and their reinventions of themselves. Gurney, having given up on his ambitions for steam road transport, had developed his new, bright oxygen-powered 'Bude' light and wanted to see it installed in the rebuilt House of Commons. He applied to Joseph Hume, who had now risen to become an influential and respected Whig MP, a man of the establishment, and *inter alia* Chairman of the Select Committee on the Lighting of the House of Commons. Faraday had spoken a few weeks earlier at the Royal Institution on Gurney's 'Oxy-oil Lamp', and now Hume approached Faraday to ask for his help in sorting out an argument over the new lighting which had arisen in parliament. The Tory Sir Frederick Trench MP complained of the danger of explosion from the light, and asked for a scientific assessment of the safety of this innovation, whose name had now expanded to the 'Philosophical Oleo-Oxygen Bude Light'. 'There never was a more dangerous, a more injudicious, or a more impractical experiment than that which is about to be made,' Trench claimed. Faraday was the man with a rock-solid reputation for speaking intelligibly on practical scientific matters, and he was the obvious recourse for a Select Committee chairman: 'I would not trouble you on this occasion if I was not anxious to remove all grounds of alarm and give Mr Gurney a fair opportunity of making his experiment.' Faraday's advice prevailed and as a result the new system of lighting was installed experimentally in the old House of Lords, where the Commons had been sitting since the fire.

The twenty-six years that it took to build the new Houses of Parliament were just those years during which London transformed itself from European capital to the premier imperial city of the world. William IV died in 1837, to be succeeded by his eighteen-year-old niece Victoria, whose youth, fragility and gender set a challenge. George IV and William IV had been brothers who had produced no legitimate heirs. Victoria, however, emerged from a fresh stem of the root of George III, her father being the late King's fourth son Edward, Duke of Kent. While London's physical growth and mercantile development carried on unchecked by radical change in the monarchy, Victoria's assumption marked a new beginning. The Georgian era had closed; now Londoners could begin a fresh, new optimistic state as Victorians. Thomas Donaldson expressed the extent of London's metamorphosis in his inaugural lecture as Professor of Architecture at University College, London, in 1842:

> Only thirty years ago [London's] streets were obscure and narrow, the public monuments rare, her river spanned only by a limited number of bridges. Now, however, the magnificent line of Regent Street, the recent improvements of the Strand and London Bridge, the removal of mean edifices from Charing Cross . . . the appropriation of Regent's Park and the erection of lines of palaces in Pimlico and north of the New Road at once impress the foreigner with exalted notions of our rapid progress in the arts of civilized life, and of our riches and resources.'

Impressing the foreigner was a central motive in the architectural development of London. But, at more or less the same time as Donaldson was praising the success of the embellishment of London, Cornelius Varley, artist, inventor and teacher, lectured the Royal Institution of British Architects on the squalor that remained. Up to the late 1840s, water continued to be pumped out of the filthy Fleet river in the summer and into carts for spreading over the roads of Camden and St Pancras to keep the dust down. 'This whilst drying and long after, spread a feeling of most filthy closeness over the whole neighbourhood . . . Each watering rewetted the preceding filth and so kept increasing the evil.'

Unlike other European capitals, London in the 1830s and 1840s was not centred on the court. Friedrich von Raumer observed at a rout at a ducal house that 'among us [Berliners], uniforms, crosses, stars, orders etc would have swarmed in such a company; here nothing of the sort was to be seen: every man decorated or encumbered with such things was a foreigner'. Thus already differentiated socially and in manners from its European neighbours, London took further leaps, raising its horizons and ambitions far beyond Paris, Berlin or St

Petersburg. The London docks were not being built in the 1820s and 1830s for trade with France, Germany and Russia only, but to take in the cloths of the Orient, the porcelain of China, the sugar and rum of the West Indies, the cotton of America, the spices and exotic woods of Africa. Rotherhithe, Wapping and the Isle of Dogs were now the portals to the world through which imports and exports passed.

Despite the fact that in 1831 he had briefly – for all of five minutes – thought that the Thames Tunnel was dead, Isambard Kingdom Brunel continued to proselytise and campaign for his father's great creation. Less than a month after the flood which closed down the workings for seven years, Michael Faraday blew life into the tunnel by making it the subject of the final meeting of the 1827 season of Friday Evening Discourses. The *Literary Gazette* was deeply impressed by Faraday's disquisition: 'a more clear and luminous explanation of the ingenious and scientific means devised by Mr Brunel for the accomplishment of his object, it is impossible to imagine'. The main difficulty that the Brunels and their workmen faced was what the workmen called 'live earth', the beds of gravel and semi-fluid mud that 'sometimes rushed upon the men like water'. The ordinary earth and clay were, to the workmen, 'mere holiday business', as Faraday expressed it. Isambard Kingdom Brunel was himself part of an audience at the Society of Arts listening to another lecture on the engineering difficulties of constructing arches in brickwork. Sitting still and listening to somebody else speak about a subject that he himself knew intimately was too much for Isambard, and he threw in a few observations from his seat. But then, 'carried away by his ardour', he proceeded to dominate the evening from his position in the audience. He did not realise, however, that William Jerdan was sitting directly behind him, straining to hear. The ubiquitous editor of the *Literary Gazette* was nevertheless frustrated: 'only a few unconnected sentences could be gathered; and this is all the apology we have for no report of an address delivered with great enthusiasm and vivacity'. Parts of the nation, in particular investors whose money had poured into the big hole at Rotherhithe, had already had enough of the Brunels and their tunnel, as doggerel in the *Comic Annual* of 1839 pointed out. Bundling Marc and Isambard together, the poet exclaimed:

> Burn all bores and boring topics;
> Burn Brunel - aye, in his hole!

London was the focus of intricate circles of concurrent building and money-making activity in the 1830s and 1840s. Put more baldly it was the fastest-growing city in the world, and the largest city the world had ever seen. While the docks handled the flow of goods in and out, London's factories tested ingenuity, manufactured goods, employed people and secured profits. Despite bank scares and crashes, invested profits brought a wealth which went to expand docks, to improve shipping, to construct commodity exchanges, to create more profits. The building of squares and terraces continued on the western side of London and south of the river, attracting more moneyed people to spend and invest. London grew for decades, spreading into the country around it like a stain. As early as the 1780s a child in Clapham remarked, 'If they go on building at such a rate, London will soon be next door to us.' He did not have long to wait, as the medieval boundaries of villages and hamlets burst under pressure from developers, and new terraces seeped out along the highroads. So rapid was the growth that Benjamin Disraeli despaired of the chaos of building. He urged greater control and reflection, suggesting that since the navy was more successful after an admiral had been shot – a reference to the execution of Admiral John Byng in Portsmouth in 1757 – it might be a good thing to hang an architect. Of the rows and rows of streets in London Disraeli wrote:

> Pancras is like Marylebone, Marylebone is like Paddington . . . All those flat, dull, spiritless streets, [resemble] each other like a large family of plain children, with Portland Place and Portman Square for their respectable parents . . . The Inns of Court, and the quarters in the vicinity of the port, Thames Street, Tower Hill, Billingsgate, Wapping, Rotherhithe, are the best parts of London; they are full of character; the buildings bear a nearer relation to what the people are doing than in the more polished quarters.

'The present is a speculating age!' cried the poet Allen Davenport in 1827. 'London! When will thy encroachments end?' he asked.

> Build up the space; let Bath and London join!
> Extend her to Newcastle on the Tyne!

Let all our cities be together thrown,
And make old England one imperial town.

The ready catalyst that made a productive reaction possible between art, science and technology was ample cash flow, but there was also the determination to succeed, and bloodymindedness, that despite volatile funds drove engineers to the very limits of their capacities to attain their goals. Two Indian visitors to London in 1840, Jehangeer Nowrojee and Hirjeebhoy Merwanjee, were deeply impressed by the Thames Tunnel: 'To any persons except Englishmen,' they wrote, 'the work would have presented insurmountable difficulties, and would never have been attempted.' They might more realistically have said 'to any persons except Brunels'; and the Brunels were of French extraction.

The Thames Tunnel reached the Wapping side of the river in the spring of 1841. The first person to make the complete crossing beneath the river was Marc's three-year-old grandson, Isambard's son, another Isambard Kingdom Brunel, who was passed hand to hand through the first small gap in the mud at the Wapping end. Two years later, on 25 March 1843, swept out, paved, gas-lit and dry, the tunnel opened to fanfares and celebration. William Jerdan reported in the *Literary Gazette* a remark that Brunel had got his 'great *toe-nail* (tunnel)' under the Thames. Marc Isambard Brunel confounded his son's fears and lived to see the tunnel opened, to receive a baronetcy and to take part in the celebrations. This 'eminent, modest and persevering mechanic', as Sir Richard Phillips had described him, did not, however, receive on completion the £5,000 payment that he had been promised years before.

The tunnel proved that, while the Thames and its winding curves was London's wall of defence from abroad, it need no longer be a barrier for Londoners travelling in and around their city. In theory the tunnel meant that the east end of London had its own route into Kent, without the need for travellers to use the City and west-end bridges, and allowed easier access between the commercial dockyards on the northern bank and Greenwich Naval Hospital and Woolwich Military Academy to the south. Further, the tunnel would cut journey times from London docks to the naval dockyards at Chatham, suggesting that its building was a strategic decision as well as a commercial and engineering one. But in the end the proposed carriage ramps at each entrance were never built on account of cost, and until it was taken over by the railway at the end of the century, the Thames Tunnel was a pedestrian route only, a mere curiosity, the place for fairs, markets and novelty banquets: beautiful and extraordinary, but useless.

This was not the first time that a Brunel engineering endeavour had triumphed over commercial sense, nor would it be the last. The Clifton suspension bridge went from Bristol to nowhere in particular, and the steamship the *Great Eastern*, conceived in 1852, had ceased to be commercially viable by the time she was launched six years later. The opening of the Thames Tunnel was Marc's triumph; Isambard had long been drawn into other projects. While Marc, suffering from the after-effects of repeated strokes, passed his final years in a bathchair looking out across St James's Park towards the termination of Nash's scheme, Isambard's Great Western Railway pressed westwards out of London from Paddington, by way of one Brunel engineering triumph after another: the viaduct at Wharncliffe, the bridge at Maidenhead, the tunnel at Box. These all led towards Bristol, the SS *Great Britain*, the Atlantic Ocean and the United States of America.

14

John Martin and the Watering of London

~

THE NASH MASTER plan largely succeeded, and its effects are with us today. The curve of Regent Street and its dramatic climax at All Soul's Church remains, even after the demolition and total rebuilding of the street when the ninety-year leases first came to an end in the 1910s and 1920s. But, of master plans that failed, the most spectacular was proposed neither by an architect nor by an engineer, but by John Martin, painter and engraver of scenes of urban and biblical apocalypse. Developing an ambition to create a renewed and healthy city watered from the redirected River Colne in Buckinghamshire, Martin, who had grown up in the bracing air of the Northumberland moors, advocated a cleaned-up River Thames which would revitalise London. An embryonic version of this idea had been put in place in the seventeenth century, when the New River was created by diverting a Hertfordshire spring into London as far as Sadler's Wells. But by the 1820s the metropolis was sprawling beyond its boundaries, and beginning to suffocate in its own ordure. This is what Shirley David Beare, the co-proprietor of Hatchett's Hotel, 67 Piccadilly, had to say on the subject:

> A slender portion of common sense . . . authorizes me to affirm, that a stream which receives daily the evacuation of a million human beings, of many thousand animals, with all the filth and refuse of the various offensive manufactories, which of necessity must be carried on in one of the most populous cities of Europe, cannot require to be analysed except by a lunatic, to determine whether it ought to be pumped up as a beverage for the inhabitants of the metropolis of the British empire; the question which you will decide is not whether a few grains of this abominable filth can by chemical process be extracted from a bottle of water taken here and there, and subjected

to the process of tea-kettle elaboratory, but whether, without any process at all, this stream, palpably known to contain all this mass of filth, should continue to be supplied.

Beare had to serve this water to his guests, among them the 'first families' of the nation. His was the hotel favoured by visitors and newcomers: Cyrus Redding had stayed there when he first came to London in 1806. A more circumspect witness, speaking on Martin's behalf, was William Somerville, Physician to the Royal Hospital, Chelsea. He found the water at Chelsea, being higher up river, tolerable and bearing no comparison to that 'which was supplied for years to my house in Hanover Square, which was not only frequently but generally extremely impure, foetid and offensive, it deposited enough to render its colour blackish'.

Clean water supply was an issue that dominated public discussion. Despite severe frost and heavy snow in London in January 1829, five hundred people attended William Brande's lecture on water supply to London at the Royal Institution. Martin's plans were timely, and were designed to end once and for all the supply of filthy water through domestic taps. They bore early fruit with his paper *Mr John Martin's Plan for Supplying with Pure Water the Cities of London and Westminster, and of Materially Beautifying the Western Parts of the Metropolis*, 1828. This proposed to take water from the Colne at Denham in Buckinghamshire, and carry it by aqueduct and tunnel via Northolt to a reservoir and a 7,500 square feet swimming pool at Paddington. There 'one thousand persons could enjoy the comfort and salubrity of bathing'. This was eighty feet above the Thames at high water, and so from Paddington water could be distributed to houses through a network of pipes running into central London. The supply would in theory be ample, and the surplus water would flow in a waterfall to an ornamental pond in Bayswater, under Bayswater Road to Kensington Gardens, then down by another series of waterfalls to the Serpentine, into Hyde Park, beneath Knightsbridge, down into the grounds of Buckingham Palace, and on through a series of lakes to Green Park, St James's Park and out into the Thames at Whitehall. This would be public waterworks on a scale, ambition and beauty to rival any in Europe, and make a cool, clean, liquid swath through London.

Martin amended and changed the focus of his plans in the light of objections from Buckinghamshire and Middlesex landowners, and of changes in the infrastructure of London, for example the replacement of the old London Bridge in 1831. He also turned his attention to London's sewer system, not only to preserve the quality of the river, but also to save the sewage for reuse:

> If the largest proportion of the richest manure is thrown away, where is the supply for keeping up the produce of the land to come from? . . . Is it not probable that a too ignorant waste of manure has caused the richest and most fertile countries such as Egypt, Assyria, the Holy Land, the South of Italy etc., to become as barren as they now are?

There was money and use in sewage, Martin insisted, and he was determined that it should not be wasted. He was passionate about his scheme, lobbying support wherever he could find it. The musician William Ayrton, a regular guest at Martin's soirées, and a Fellow of both the Royal Society and the Society of Antiquaries, was one target: 'The object is of so much importance, not only to the health of London, but to the agriculture of the country at large, and the means of effecting it are considered by the engineers so efficient and practicable, that I hope that the interest you formerly took in my entire plan may be continued to this separated portion.'

Among the greatest champions of the scheme was Thomas Donaldson who, at Michael Faraday's invitation, gave a public lecture on the subject at the Royal Institution in March 1833, and once again the *Literary Gazette* spread these new ideas. There would be a grand sewer built of iron, brick and stone running from Westminster parallel to the river, at the same inclination of seven inches per mile, and receiving all the drainage in its course. Above the sewer would be a colonnaded promenade, lit by sewer gas, for pedestrians and carriages. At the Tower, where there would be a barrage to create a placid harbour in the Pool of London, the sewer would turn away from the river, 'using the moat if permitted . . . to Regent's Canal where the grand receptacle should be made from which the soil could be transported by barge and canal to various parts of the country'.

Having a sewage pond near the plush new houses in Regent's

Park may have been a flaw in Martin's scheme: it would certainly create a stink. A similar system was proposed for the south bank of the river. Donaldson estimated the cost of the works to be £60,000 per mile, for seven-and-a-half miles, 'less cost than one of our bridges'. The sewer would be open at each end, with a fire at one end to draw the bad air from the drains, 'to become so purified as not to injure the external atmosphere'.

Later embellishments of Martin's scheme included mounting a railway line on top of the aqueduct bringing water from Buckinghamshire: this would now be part of the Chiltern Line, had it been realised. But it was all becoming too complex and grandiose, with further ideas being bolted on as if on a whim. South of the river, Martin suggested that water from high up the Thames at Teddington should be pumped into a reservoir in Richmond Park, from there in pipes cross the river on cast-iron pillars at Barnes to supply the villas of Fulham, Chelsea and Kensington, and further as far as Regent's Park. So, with a great filthy river running through it, London would also be watered from two directions by pumped and piped pure water. Donaldson advocated the scheme to the Institute of British Architects on 29 February 1836, and three days later it was accepted by a committee of MPs, Fellows of the Royal Society and Royal Academicians, chaired by the Duke of Grafton, formerly the Whig MP Lord Euston.

John Martin leaped the gap between painting and science, engineering and its application, theory and practice, art and society. His plans, so vocally supported by parliamentarians, by scientists including Faraday and Charles Wheatstone, and by Academicians including Turner, Etty and Eastlake, ran into the sands of the parliamentary select committees. To the 1838 Select Committee on Metropolis Improvements Martin submitted six elaborate plans, elevations and sections of his proposals culminating in a perspective view of the London Bridge end of construction, looking not unlike Nash's Carlton House Terrace. Here was London dressed up as Babylon, colonnades, walks, a barrage and elegant lighting. A dedication was carved on to an entablature: 'Dedicated to Alderman Sir Matthew Wood Bt. MP and the Hon. Members of the Committee for the Improvement of London Aug 1st 1838.'

Consideration of Martin's plans was only one of the tasks of Alderman Wood and his committee. Their main duty was to look at channels for east–west communication which 'are not more numerous, and only in a very few instances more spacious, than they were at the beginning of the seventeenth century'. One gentleman with time on his hands carried out his own traffic survey in Ludgate Street (that is, Ludgate Hill), the main road linking Fleet Street with St Paul's Cathedral, on 'an ordinary day of business', 13 September 1842. He sat in his parlour window with a pencil and paper, and across the twelve hours between 9 a.m. and 9 p.m. counted 2,014 omnibuses, 6,552 cabs and carriages, and 72,096 pedestrians. With over 80,000 individual journeys up or down Ludgate Hill, this was not London at its busiest, but nevertheless there was still an average of twelve carriages or omnibuses and about one hundred passers-by every minute. London's traffic just got thicker: eight years later the City of London Police reported one thousand vehicles and five thousand pedestrians an hour between 9 a.m. and 6 p.m. on a Friday in late November 1850 in Holborn.

Seven or eight architects and engineers put forward ideas to Wood's committee for consideration, including some which eventually came to fruition, such as opening the routes from Oxford Street along Theobald's Road to Hackney, and along High Holborn towards Aldgate. When Martin was examined by the committee, his opening exchange with the chairman was: 'I believe you are well known as a painter?' 'I believe I am tolerably well known.' Martin might have gathered from this and from what rapidly followed that he was wasting his time dedicating his scheme to the committee. The chairman's report showed that the days of Martin's ideas were numbered:

> It is obvious that the improvement of a great city in these essential particulars must generally carry with it a very considerable degree of embellishment also; but the Committee, though by no means insensible to the public gratification which mere embellishment . . . is calculated to afford, have in the prosecution of these inquiries regarded it as a matter of insubordinate importance.

But they didn't say yes, and they didn't say no; so Martin persevered. Five years later, in 1843, he was called to the Royal

Commission on Improving the Metropolis, where he faced competition from some new quarters. Among them was the staunch Tory MP, and former army officer, Colonel Sir Frederick Trench, a virulent opponent of the Reform Bill, who had described it as 'rash, improvident and revolutionary'. Trench was everything that Martin was not: militaristic (he rose by automatic promotion to general in 1854), Tory (a 'disinterested and devoted supporter' of Sir Robert Peel) and grandiose: his proposals made Martin's seem restrained. Objecting to Nash's plans for Regent Street in 1825, Trench urged the King to build a palace in Hyde Park, with an approaching avenue two hundred feet wide running from the new palace to St Paul's. For the north bank of the Thames, Trench proposed a colonnaded embankment comparable to terraces at Genoa and Nice. Unlike these, however, Trench would run a railway on top of columns fourteen feet high, which having wooden rails and wheels, and being propelled by rope pulley, would be silent and smoke free. The railway, Trench argued, would be a source of great profit.

Trench's proposals were given no more than the polite attention that Martin's received. The most effective opposition to Martin came from James Walker, the President of the Institution of Civil Engineers, who had submitted his own scheme, and who supported an alternative sewerage proposal from the builder and developer Thomas Cubitt. Walker objected to Martin's scheme because in his view it would interfere with the incessant traffic of colliers and their access to the wharfs, and Martin criticised Cubitt's sewerage proposals because the manure would be wasted by not being made available to farmers for fertilising the fields. They were fighting like cats in a bag, with Martin being forced on to the defensive, to suggest that his ideas had been stolen by his opponents. His arguments had not greatly developed over the past decade, and some of the evidence and phraseology that he used to the 1843 committee he had also offered in earlier encounters. Martin concluded that 'nothing would be easier than to re-model with little labour what may have cost the original projector years of serious study and reflection; and the credit ought surely to belong to him'. The 1843 commission rejected Martin's proposals outright, saying that his claims 'were not considered equal to those of other Plans prepared for the same object . . .

and we felt . . . that we should not be justified in making it the subject of further enquiry'. John Martin the amateur had been squeezed
out by Walker, Cubitt and the professionals. His was an outdated
romantic approach to solving London's water and sewage problems
cloaked in the architectural embellishments of Egypt or Babylon.
Even the recycling of the sewage was a kind of romantic expression,
the harvest of nature returned to nature to flower again at harvest.

Nevertheless Martin continued to press and lobby the government. As a director and shareholder of the Metropolitan Sewage
Manure Company, he wrote in 1846 to urge Sir Robert Peel to support the company's bill in the House of Commons which repeated
the call for a great sewer to be constructed along the Thames. The
bill successfully became an act, 'notwithstanding . . . a very violent
opposition from various quarters', as Martin confided to William
Ayrton. He continued to paint and to exhibit – in 1846, while lobbying Peel about sewage, showing at the Academy landscapes with
titles that reflected the calm that he could now only find through his
art: *Cornfield – Sitting on the Stile, Evening: Coming Storm* and *The Brook*.
Martin gave much of his fortune, his reputation as an artist and his
mental health to his engineering schemes. Other improvements that
he proposed included a circular railway running around the central
areas of London, uniting the city – the forerunner of the Circle Line,
completed in 1884. That Martin failed ultimately as an urban reformer,
and that the transformation of London took a further fifty years, is
due not to his inadequacy but to the inability of the governing elite
to understand that an artist's vision could come off the canvas and
into the street. It cannot have helped his cause that two of his elder
brothers were known to be insane: William, a crackpot inventor and
pamphleteer in Newcastle, who threatened his enemies with damna-
tion and prophesied the destruction of the nation, and Jonathan who
set fire to York Minster in 1829 and was sent to Bedlam for his pains.
Near the end of his life, Martin said to his son Leopold: 'Oh my
boy, if only I had been an engineer! Hundreds with me would have
been thousands. Instead of benefiting myself and a few only, I
should have added to the comfort, prosperity and health of mankind
in general.'

Martin finally gave up his practical attempts to revitalise London in 1852, and returned to painting on the enormous scale that had occupied him in the 1820s. His final statement as an artist were three vast canvases, *The Last Judgement*, *The Plains of Heaven* and *The Great Day of His Wrath* (London, Tate Britain), painted from the last years of the 1840s until his death in 1854. When Arthur Cleveland Coxe, the Bishop of Western New York, visited him in 1851 he was hard at work on *The Last Judgement*. This was 'full of his mannerism, and sadly blemished by offences against doctrinal truth', the Bishop wrote, 'but not devoid of merit or of interest'.

Frederick Trench, who had vehemently opposed Nash's improvements to London, and who contributed to the demise of Martin's grand plan, was nevertheless a pioneer of sorts. He was one of the movers of the proposal to erect a colossal statue to the Duke of Wellington on top of the triumphal arch designed by Decimus Burton opposite Apsley House. He sought brass cannon to melt down for the work, to be made by Matthew Cotes Wyatt, another son of Sir James Wyatt. He searched London for redundant ordnance, and received four and a half tons of cannon from Sir Francis Chantrey. Through fellow army officers, and with the help of his friend the Duke of Rutland, and of William Jerdan and the *Literary Gazette*, he commandeered or otherwise appropriated nearly forty tons of cannon to create the work. This was the largest bronze sculpture yet made in Britain: thirty-five feet high, twenty feet in diameter around the belly of the horse, the Duke's body alone weighing two and a half tons. When the forequarters of the horse came to be cast in September 1845, William Jerdan was present, and wrote in the *Literary Gazette*:

> The flow of so large a quantity of molten metal from the furnace to the receptacle whence it descends to fill the mould is a very grand and remarkable phenomenon . . . The dazzling red stream throws up clouds of vapour of every prismatic hue, the green tinges prevailing; but blues, yellows, and various graduations of red, rolling along both in these clouds and in flames emitted from, accompanying and hovering over the lava torrent.

London, in the middle years of the 1840s, was at one of its recurring heights of confidence and wealth. Napoleon was long gone; so was cholera. Steamers paddled up and down the Thames; a tunnel burrowed beneath it; balloons floated above it; the new Houses of Parliament were rising beside it; railways courteously avoided coming anywhere near it. This was a modern, thriving world city. The crash in railway investment and the collapse of banks (1847) was in the future, as were the Chartist demonstrations (1848), the return of cholera (1848), and the war in the Crimea (1853–6). The creation of an enormous equestrian figure of the Duke of Wellington was a luxury that London believed it could afford. It was of course much lampooned. *Punch* had pleasure in making a joke of it; old soldiers shook their heads at it – one, the retired army captain turned painter George Jones, described it as 'that monster on the arch'.

Turner is thought to have been, with Jerdan, among the 'considerable party of scientific and literary men and artists' present at the casting ceremony. Whether he was there or not, he nevertheless thought deeply about the significance of the production of so clearly symbolic and celebratory an object. Two years after the casting had taken place, and a year after the bronze horse and rider had been winched to the top of the arch, Turner exhibited at the Royal Academy his painting *Hero of a Hundred Fights*, showing Wyatt's statue emerging in one piece (a poetic necessity, though a technical impossibility) from the flames of the furnace. Like London.

15

'Astonishing to the Philosopher and the Simple Child'

~

THE SULPHUROUS ATMOSPHERE obscured, coloured and dis-
coloured London. 'Fog everywhere,' as Dickens put it in the
opening paragraphs of *Bleak House* (1853). 'Fog up the river . . . Fog
on the Essex marshes . . . fog drooping on the gunwales of barges
and small boats.' We might add fog in the Strand, fog in the National
Gallery, fog seeping through the skylights of the British Museum and
flowing about the battered bodies of the Elgin Marbles. In the year
of the publication of *Bleak House* Michael Faraday gave formal advice
to select committees on the cleaning of the multifarious deposits of
fog from old master paintings, and four years later on the damage
done by smoke, dust and fog to the surfaces of the Elgin Marbles. In
the 1830s, however, he had had some more homely and easy-going
advice for his artist friends on how to avoid the penetrations of fog.

Faraday recommended to many of these friends that they rigor-
ously test the durability of pigments before risking permanent
damage to their pictures from the atmosphere. He suggested to
Charles Hullmandel, Turner and his own brother-in-law George
Barnard that they put sample paint trials out in the sun, part covered
up and part exposed, so as to measure the differences in fading and
colour change. William Henry Fox Talbot, artist, traveller, amateur
scientist and persistent explorer in the fields of image reproduction,
noted in early February 1839 that 'copper plates for engraving, if
kept in London, become tarnished by sulphurous vapours'. This was
well known, but, particular as he was, he jotted this observation
down at the beginning of a pair of notebooks in which he recorded
his thoughts and practices during experiments to create 'photogenic
drawings', permanent images of objects and buildings captured on

chemically coated paper. He had since 1834 been making 'photo-genic experiments' both in London and at his country house Lacock Abbey in Wiltshire, where he made a particularly curious discovery. Having left a partially covered sheet of paper coated in silver nitrate out in the sun, he brought it indoors and left it in the dark. The paper had not apparently been affected by the sunlight, but coming across it a few hours later Talbot found that the side of the paper he had exposed to the sun had darkened. He wrote about this in an art-icle in the *Philosophical Magazine* of July 1835, as part of a general essay 'On the Nature of Light', and followed the discovery up with further experiments.

This curious phenomenon was not really new. For centuries the black box with the pin hole, the *camera obscura* – literally, 'dark room' – had been known and had been played with, and the inverted image created by it had been studied, described and drawn. In 1802, Humphry Davy, Thomas Wedgwood and Sir Anthony Carlisle found that they could briefly hold a faint image, having discovered a method of coating paper or leather with a silver-nitrate solution and passing a bright light on to it through a picture painted on glass. They could not keep the image for more than a few minutes before it gradually faded away. Carlisle claimed to have taken the experi-ment somewhat further than simply passing light through coloured glass, and had worked with reflected light from objects. 'About forty years ago I made several attempts,' he wrote, 'with my lamented friend Mr Thomas Wedgwood to obtain and fix the shadows [that is, the images] of objects by exposing the figures painted on glass, to fall upon a flat surface of shamoy [chamois] leather wetted with nitrate of silver.'

Among the subjects they attempted to capture with 'imperfect [though] absolutely startling' results were 'plaster of Paris casts, and from *life*'. Carlisle made his reminiscence in February 1839, only a few months before he died, at a time of sudden general hubbub about the new science, or art, of photogenic drawing. The labora-tory trial by Davy and his friends was one harbinger of a change in human affairs that began slowly at first, but then, from January 1839, came with a gathering rush. This, the beginnings of a public under-standing of the principles of photography, had a long shadow falling before it. It might have started earlier, in June 1831, when Brewster, Fox Talbot and Herschel breakfasted together at Babbage's house, and Herschel told the company that he had caused light to precipitate a calcium salt on paper. But he had astronomy on his mind, and did no further work on the discovery before 1834 when he left for four years in the Cape of Good Hope, where he seems to have forgotten all about it.

Henry Fox Talbot had corresponded with Faraday on scientific matters throughout the 1830s, and together on 25 January 1839 the pair gave a brief account of the principles of what they called 'photogenic drawing' at the end of a Friday Discourse at the Royal Institution on the polarisation of light. It was a pre-planned footnote to an hour or more of discussion and demonstration on the properties of light. Faraday and Fox Talbot displayed a group of examples, including images of lace, and of the reticulations on an insect's wing seen through a microscope. 'I do not profess to having perfected an Art,' Fox Talbot wrote, 'but to have *commenced* one.' Experiments over the previous ten or fifteen years in France by Joseph Niepce and Louis-Jacques Daguerre had led to the creation of highly detailed images on glass and subsequently metal, a process that became known as the daguerreotype. The process – but not all the chemical details – had been first introduced to the French public at the Academy of Sciences in Paris on 7 January, and this prompted Fox Talbot to reveal the full details of his process lest it be thought that he had used Daguerre's work to further his own.

The date that is generally recorded for the first announcement of photography in Britain is, however, six days after the Royal Institution meeting, 31 January 1839, when Fox Talbot read his paper on the subject to Fellows of the Royal Society. His choice of title was highly significant and gave a direction to the initial ambition of the discovery: 'Some account of the art of photogenic drawing, or, the process by which natural objects may be made to delineate themselves without the aid of the artists' pencil'. There is a rightness about the timing of these two meetings which allowed photography, the art which brought fine image-making within the reach of all, to be announced first at the Royal Institution, and only subsequently at a gathering of scientists at the Royal Society. A week or so later, Fox

Talbot published his account of 'The Art of Photogenic Drawing' in the *Athenaeum*, and in the February issue of the *Philosophical Magazine*. There he explained the process, and suggested some uses: for silhouette portraits, for copying glass paintings, for copying engravings, for delineating sculpture and for taking images of architecture, landscape and external nature. It could become a new art form, and Fox Talbot made it all as clear as he could, unlike in France where the details of Daguerre's process remained a state secret. Present at the Royal Society meeting, and at a subsequent one there on 21 February, was the Secretary, John Children, who took something of what he had heard from Fox Talbot home with him, and discussed it with his married daughter, Anna Atkins.

Six weeks after Fox Talbot presented his paper, Sir John Herschel spoke at the Royal Society on 14 March 1839 under the title 'Note on the Art of Photography, or the application of the Chemical Rays of Light to the Purposes of Pictorial Representation'. At the meeting Herschel, who subsequently withdrew his paper after having doubts about its conclusions, displayed twenty-three of his photographs, including 'a sketch of his telescope at Slough, fixed from its image in a lens'. Public discussion of what was rapidly accepted as 'photography' blossomed immediately. A fortnight before Herschel's lecture, the chemist John Thomas Cooper exhibited photographs of ferns at the Botanical Society, and rapidly advertised for sale in the *Athenaeum* 'photogenic-drawing paper', prepared by his own technique. By May 1839 Cooper was giving a lecture-demonstration on photography to the Society of British Artists. Concurrently, Talbot considered exhibiting his photographs at the Colosseum in Regent's Park or the Cosmorama in Regent Street. Photography had become a sudden public sensation, like the velocipede, Bloomers or the iPod.

Public educational activity in photography grew rapidly, and still, 170 years later, amateur photography remains a staple of evening classes everywhere. It is clear from the vocabulary in the titles of papers by Talbot and Herschel, where words like 'art', 'delineate' and 'drawing' abound, that the first priority of pioneers of photography was to enlarge its usefulness as a reproductive artistic medium – indeed, the purpose of Davy, Carlisle and Wedgwood's 1802 experiments was to copy paintings and sculpture. Michael Faraday picked up the thread again at the end of March 1839, and spoke informally to another large audience of lay people at the Royal Institution about further applications of the discovery, as devised and amended by the painter William Havell who had found a quick way of copying engravings by photographic action.

William Havell, a first cousin of the intrepid Robert Havell who had flown in a balloon with his pencil over London in 1806, was a talented but pedestrian landscape painter. He developed a process that he called 'photogeny' by which he made a photographic copy of his own sketch of Rembrandt's etching *Faust Raising a Spirit*. Havell sent a proof, aided by 'the perfection of Mr Cooper's sensitive paper', to Faraday to display in the Royal Institution, asserting that 'there can be no doubt of its becoming a most interesting Art, for multiplying designs by a most simple process'. As Havell described it, the process was not that simple, but a complicated method of covering the etching with a glass plate, stopping out the lighter areas with opaque white lead, the middle tints with semi-opaque white, and scratching the lines out of the painted areas with a knife or etching needle. The etching was then removed, a sheet of sensitised paper substituted, and the whole thing exposed to the sun. This was not, of course, a photograph of the engraving, but a redrawing of a tracing of it by light on paper, a *cliché verre*. Havell had been present when Fox Talbot and Faraday introduced the new discovery on 25 January, and from his letter to Faraday had clearly learned enough to go home and try it himself. Fox Talbot's own practice of making negative images dissatisfied Havell, and prompted him to experiment further with the medium, using a series of portrait heads after the Italian baroque painter Guercino as his subject matter. The particular interest for Havell, as for Faraday, was that 'it is quite clear that artists may by considering the above methods multiply original sketches or designs, ad infinitum, they never wear out, may be altered, improved, retouched at pleasure, requiring no printing presses, any number may be exposed to the light at the same instant'.

The motive force behind photography came as much from art and artists as from science – of the early pioneers Daguerre was a painter and a stage designer, Fox Talbot an amateur artist, William Havell and William Lake Price watercolour painters, and J. T. Willmore an engraver. Photography followed lithography in being an early cross-ing point in the history of culture where a perfectible scientific technique brought into being, to revolutionary effect, a new artistic medium. J. T. Willmore and William Brockedon between them pushed the boundaries of knowledge in photography. Brockedon sent a 'photogenic drawing' to the ageing Manchester scientist John Dalton, and the portrait painter Thomas Phillips expressed an anx-iety for the old reproductive methods: 'I am very much obliged to you for the sight of Mr. Willmore's etchings (Photogenic). Alas for the Printers! Though the Engravers may yet flourish at least with the etching needle. The Art is however exceedingly curious and may yet produce some extraordinary effects.'

In raising the subject of photography at the Royal Institution right at the beginning of its genesis, Faraday was flagging up inter-ests which, for him, had much wider implications. He had a developing interest in the chemistry of photography and of photo-graphic varnishes, which he discussed and tested with Herschel in 1839 and 1840. He welcomed anybody who could contribute to photographic advances, for example Alfred Swaine Taylor FRS, a chemist and forensic scientist who specialised in cases of poisoning. Taylor had found ways of improving on Fox Talbot's technique, and through exhibiting Taylor's 'photogenic drawings' in the same few weeks that he showed Fox Talbot, Herschel and Havell's results, Faraday enriched, widened and freed the debate. Together Faraday and Taylor produced at least one 'photogenic drawing', an image of *The Wooden Bridge* by Augustus Wall Callcott. A decade later, Faraday and Fox Talbot experimented together with flash photography, by spinning a printed disc in front of the camera, discharging a battery and capturing the printed letters 'as sharp as if the disk had been motionless', as Fox Talbot told Faraday the following day: 'If a truly instantaneous photographic impression of an object has never been obtained before (as I imagine that it has not) I am glad it should have been first accomplished at the Royal Instn.'

While photography in London was already the stuff of advertise-ments, evening classes and a multiplicity of methods, an announcement backed by the French government on 19 August 1839 at the Academy of Science in Paris put Daguerre's method of fixing an image on glass into public ownership. The French government had done a deal with Daguerre in which they would give him a large sum of money, and he would reveal the whole process to the world. The broad difference between the English and the French methods was that images created by the former were printed on paper, in negative, and were reproducible; while the latter produced jewel-like images, with intense detail, on glass or metal, but could not be multiplied. The American inventor Samuel Morse realised the potency of the daguerreotype immediately on first seeing one: 'You cannot imagine how exquisite is the fine detail portrayed. No painting or engraving could ever hope to touch it.'

When the French announcement came, London scientists were in Birmingham, at the biennial meeting of the British Association for the Advancement of Science in the Philosophical Institute, Cannon Street. They had been treated to an exhibition of fifty-six photogenic drawings by Fox Talbot in what must have been the first real exhibition of photographs ever mounted. Talbot was immediately called upon to explain Daguerre's process to the gathering, which he did by conjuring up a complex and potentially dangerous process involving clouds of iodine gas, fragile glass plates and precisely measured angles. Already the possibilities of the use of colour in the new art were being considered, leading Talbot to observe that 'these facts serve to illustrate the fertility of the subject, and show the great extent of yet unoccupied ground in this new branch of science'. One gets the impression that Talbot here used the word 'science' because his audience in Birmingham was composed of scientists. Had he been called to explain Daguerre's process at, let's say, the Society of British Artists, he would surely have described it as 'this new branch of art'. One shortcoming of Daguerre's process was immediately spotted: this was the fragility of the surface of the image – one touch and that part of the image was brushed away. Thus a new kind of varnish was eagerly sought to protect the surface, something that came to exercise the ingenuity of Faraday and Herschel.

News travelled. A scientist in America, the Liverpool-born chemist John Draper, Professor of Chemistry at the University of New York, had by March 1840 succeeded in producing portraits by Daguerre's method which had 'all the beauty and softness of the most finished mezzotint engraving'. He at first dusted the sitter's face with white powder, but soon found that this was not necessary, and that with exposure times of between twenty and ninety seconds in even dim sunshine the Daguerre process could render 'each button, button-hole and every fold'. From her exile in Italy, Mary Somerville wanted to help Herschel with photographic experiments. 'It is impossible to obtain any continued account of the progress of the Daguerreotype from the beginning up to the present time,' she wrote to Herschel in 1843. Having the rich Italian light around her, she offered her expertise: 'Can I not be of any use to you . . . by trying or repeating experiments on the beams of an Italian sun and even a phase of the moon which are so beautiful and so bright.'

The most significant implication of Faraday's excitement about photography is his grasp of its potential in image reproduction. This chimes clearly with his interest in the other commercial reproductive methods, lithography and steel engraving, and he will have been well aware of the meeting held at the London Electrical Society in August 1841 when William Grove lectured 'On a voltaic process for etching Daguerreotype plates'. Displaying examples of his electrically etched plates, Grove concluded: 'Instead of a plate being inscribed as "drawn by Landseer, and engraved by Cousins", it would be "drawn by Light, and engraved by Electricity".' Having had the opportunity to look closely at some of Grove's 'Photographic Etchings', Faraday told him: 'They are very good & surely must lead to something excellent.'

Photography also touched Faraday's sense of vanity. In the 1840s to 1860s he became one of the most photographed figures in public life, in images that seem to be largely self-directed: there are pictures of Faraday seated, standing, holding a magnet, posing with his wife, and posing with another scientist, J. F. Daniell. In photographs taken by the three leading commercial pioneers, Antoine Claudet, Richard Beard and John Mayall, Faraday is shown looking at the camera, taking no notice of it, as full length or as vignette. Every kind of pose is there, and we may draw the conclusion that the image of Faraday that Faraday wanted posterity to grasp was one made by the technique in which science and art held hands: the photograph.

It is revealing that William Brockedon showed such immediate interest in the development and potential of the photograph. In

1839 he was heavily committed to the production of his 'Prominent People', his own exceptional collection of over one hundred portrait drawings of his wide circle of friends and acquaintances. It was the practice among men and women of intellect and fashion in the nineteenth century to make collections of portraits, often by gift or exchange, of their circles of friends. Faraday was very proud of his collection of portrait engravings of fellow scientists, and showed them to friends and visitors. Photography rapidly took over this practice, and by the mid-1840s the clear implication in the words 'family album' had come widely to mean that the medium involved was photography.

Turner was another artist who, in the course of the 1840s, became intrigued by photography and its possibilities. Of the older generation, his fascination with the subject was shared not only by William Brockedon and William Havell, but by others including the miniature painter Sir William Newton and the Brighton traveller turned photographer William Constable who had in 1806 travelled from New York to New Orleans by boat, mule and on foot. Some time in the late 1830s Turner's friend Samuel Rogers had brought daguerreotypes to London from Paris. John Ruskin recounted that Rogers showed the daguerreotypes to a group of artists, including Turner, when they came to dinner. Turner was late to arrive, and talking among themselves the other artists considered that the discovery would injure Turner particularly. When Turner did arrive, they uttered the negative reaction which echoed the warning of Samuel Morse, 'our profession is gone'. Turner, however, had a good look at the daguerreotypes, and said, 'We shall only go about the country with a box like a tinker, instead of a portfolio under our arm.' Which is to say: 'We can learn how to use it, and can take the paraphernalia with us on our travels.'

His near-contemporary Sir William Newton could not be further in intention from Turner as an artist. As miniature painter-in-ordinary to Queen Victoria, and before her to William IV, he was a royal favourite (which Turner was not), and, in 1837, was knighted, which Turner was not. His miniature portraits, precise and homely, neat and pernickety, attracted the kind of client who had difficulty with Turner's chromatic later works. But, like Turner, who as well as enjoying Rogers's daguerreotypes spent many hours watching John Mayall at work in his Strand studio and having his picture taken, Newton became intrigued by photography. He attended meetings of Brockedon's Graphic Society addressed by Fox Talbot, and went on to experiment with Fox Talbot's calotype process. In 1852 Newton exhibited his photographs at the Society of Arts in the first public exhibition of photographs to be held in England. The Graphic Society, founded in 1833 by William Brockedon, met regularly at the Thatched House Tavern in St James's. Their meeting of 13 March 1839 was a watershed, because there fifty or more members, including the engravers J. T. Willmore and John Pye and the lithographer John Duffield Harding, assembled to discuss the implications of photography on their work. Picking up on the ability of photography to reproduce paintings, they were both expressing their anxiety and identifying opportunities for the future. Willmore subsequently wrote an impassioned letter to the *Literary Gazette* claiming priority in the invention of photography over Fox Talbot, and describing his and other artists' unsuccessful efforts to patent their discovery earlier in the 1830s, in the fear that otherwise photography might threaten their livelihood.

A year after the publication of the facts of photography, Charles Eastlake's translation of Goethe's *Farbenlehre*, or *Theory of Colours*, was published. Turner carefully read and, paragraph by paragraph, annotated his copy with comments that reveal how well he was versed in the technical language of optics. He uses in his marginalia the terms 'dioptrics' and 'catoptrics', words which refer to the process of refraction and reflection, and against the paragraph where Goethe discusses an experiment of placing light-sensitive paper under yellow-red and blue-red glass and looking at the difference on exposure, Turner has written the word 'Deguerreotype [*sic*]'. These words and terms are among many which were becoming common coin among interested and intelligent members of the public, such as those who attended Friday Evening Discourses in Albemarle Street, and witnessed scientific advance interacting with artistic understanding.

Entrepreneurship followed closely on the heels of scientific advance. Within ten years of Fox Talbot's announcement, Richard

Beard, Antoine Claudet and John Mayall were in full commercial production of photography in London. Beard forced the pace through his clever snatch at the ownership of the patent rights for the production of daguerreotypes in England; in rivalry with Beard, Claudet set up one of the two earliest daguerreotype studios in London in 1841, and improved the practice radically; and Mayall, who came on to the scene in 1847, rapidly dominated it through technical brilliance, innovative skill, staying power and business sense.

Richard Beard was the Devon-born entrepreneur who made a fortune as a partner and later owner of a London coal merchant company at Purfleet Wharf, Blackfriars, and Regent's Park Basin. As we saw in Chapter 8, he was a prodigious correspondent to *The Times*, writing a dozen or more letters to the Editor in 1834 and 1835 on the subject of the supply, quality and weighing of coals. The trade in coal did not satisfy him, however, and another of his particular talents was that he had a nose for a successful patent. He took one out for colour printing on fabrics in 1839, and in that same year began negotiations with Daguerre's agent in London to buy English patent rights for the new photographic process. In 1840 he went on to buy the English rights on the American Wolcott camera, which operated with a concave mirror to intensify the available light. This could only take very small daguerreotype images, no more than one and a half inches by two, but by focusing the light into an intense beam it shortened the sitting time to four or five minutes. He and the inventor Alexander Wolcott made public experiments with the new camera in the Medical Hall, Holborn, in August 1840, and when in March the following year Beard had opened his daguerreotype studio in London, he had acquired the full rights to operate the process in England.

Beard had an eye for the main chance. His interest in photography was not of the same kind as that of Daguerre, Fox Talbot, Herschel, Faraday or Claudet, who were keen to investigate its science and development; rather he saw it as a money-making opportunity. When he corresponded with Fox Talbot, as he did in 1842, it largely concerned the complex courtesies of legal and commercial rights. Beard must take the credit, as a scientific and photographic layman, for seeing the business opportunity of Daguerre's discovery, and acting on it rapidly. He made a great deal of money out of selling licences to operators in towns and cities throughout England and Wales, and in his studios charged one guinea for a head-and-shoulders, and two guineas for a full-length image. At the height of his supremacy he made, reputedly, £125 a day. But Beard went a step too far, and in 1850 was declared bankrupt after a series of prolonged court cases over patent infringements. He was ruthless in asserting his rights to the process, by taking legal action to protect his interests. His opponents included Claudet and Mayall.

As Beard's *Times* correspondence reveals, he desired a public platform, and as a coal merchant had created one that made him into a strident voice for his industry. Evidently this was not high enough for him, and in 1841 he created a new platform in the shape of a photographic studio on the roof of the Polytechnic Institution in Regent Street. This he opened on 23 March, and three days later his assistant, the chemist and teacher John Goddard, gave a demonstration lecture on the daguerreotype at the Royal Institution. On the roof of the Polytechnic Institution, as *The Times* put it, Beard – or rather John Goddard – carried on his 'magical process'.

> From the roof, which is constructed of blue glass of about a quarter of an inch thick, a very powerful light is obtained, and it is so ingeniously contrived as to revolve with the sun. In a portion of the room, nearly in the centre, an elevated seat is placed, on which the party whose likeness is to be taken sits with his head reclining backwards. In this position the sitter is told to look into a glass box, in an opposite direction, about five feet from him, in which is placed the metallic plate to be impressed with the portrait. Having done so for a few seconds, he descends, and a few minutes afterwards a faithful likeness is presented to him. The likenesses we saw were admirable, and closely true to nature, beauties and deformities being alike exhibited.

By April 1842 Beard was operating also from 31 Parliament Street, Westminster, and had studios in King William Street, City Road and New Millman Street. Among his earliest clients was the elderly Maria Edgeworth who wrote home to her sister Fanny Wilson a sparkling account of being photographed in Beard's studio, revealing clearly how labour-intensive, even industrial, the daguerreotype process was:

You are taken from one room into another up stairs and down and you see various people whispering and hear them in neighbouring passages and rooms unseen and the whole apparatus and stool on a high platform under a glass dome casting a *snapdragon blue* light making all look like spectres and the men in black gliding about.

Beard's Polytechnic studio was seen as one of the special attractions of the Institution, as a *Times* advertisement revealed: 'The colossal electrical machine worked by steam power . . . the appearance of the aurora borealis . . . the Orrery – Diving Bell and Diver . . . Photographic portraits taken daily by Mr Beard.'

Beard's main rival in the early years of the 1840s was the Frenchman Antoine Claudet who had run a glassworks near Paris, until, in 1829, he moved to London and opened a glass shop and warehouse at 89 High Holborn. Claudet was the purist to Beard's opportunist; he did the work and made the innovations himself, rather than paying others to do it for him. When the daguerreotype process was revealed in 1839, Claudet returned to Paris to take instruction from Daguerre himself, and in advance of Beard purchased a licence to practise the technique in London. He opened a studio in June 1841 on another hospitable roof, that of the National Gallery of Science in Adelaide Street, off the Strand. So, by the early summer of 1841, the roofs of two institutions of scientific education, no more than a fifteen-minute walk apart in London, housed elaborate glazed gazebos bristling with brand-new photographic equipment in glowing walnut and gleaming brass, and turntables, plush curtains, tripods and mirrors. Both Beard and Claudet were seeking clearer air and light free from the urban shadows of central London. Tramping up long flights of steps with camera, glass plates and chemicals became a regular practice for Claudet, as for Beard and his clients, for one of Claudet's earliest assignments was to take a series of plates to create a panoramic view of London from the top of the Duke of York's Column in Waterloo Place. This was engraved on wood for the *Illustrated London News* in 1843 in a piquant clash of invention: the quickest and newest means of taking an image, combined with the slowest (and possibly oldest) means of reproduction. Claudet's main income came from making portraits. One sitter, the photographer and writer Thomas Sutton, reported that he was instructed 'to sit there, still as death': 'I was seated . . . in the full blazing sunshine and after about an exposure of a minute the plate was developed . . . My eyes were made to stare until the tears streamed from them and the portrait was of course a caricature . . . I paid a guinea for it. It has since faded.'

All this innovation and entrepreneurship was soon to be put at risk by intemperate fighting in the law courts. Claudet's purchase of personal operating rights from Daguerre brought him into immediate conflict with Beard, the latter believing that he owned complete rights. As a wealthy, and as he perhaps thought invulnerable, businessman (he sold his coal-merchant business in 1843), Beard took out an injunction to close Claudet down. He failed, and after expensive hearings in the Vice-Chancellor's Court and the Court of Chancery (1841–4), Claudet was able to continue unthwarted. His business expanded fast, *The Times* reporting in July 1842 that he was 'succeeding rapidly now the merits of his process have become generally known. The Queen Dowager [Queen Adelaide, widow of William IV] has honoured him with a visit, and has had her likeness taken.' Queen Adelaide did not have to sit in the full sun, as had Thomas Sutton. There were a number of grades of lighting available, depending on what the sitter desired, or could bear. The hardy could sit out in full sunlight with their eyes unblinking for the few minutes the process took. Those like, Maria Edgeworth, of a more delicate nature could sit inside the blue-glazed gazebo that both Claudet and Beard had constructed. *The Times* tried to explain why the glass had to be blue:

> Blue and white are the only lights that are capable of making any impression on the prepared silver plate, and therefore when a likeness is taken it must either be in the pure light, or in light admitted through a blue medium. The laboratory, therefore, is illuminated by red and yellow glass, as the plate goes here after the likeness is taken, merely for the purpose of being washed, &c., and it is essential that no light should be admitted which would affect it.

Behind the sitter Claudet had the clever idea of introducing a painted canvas backdrop, like a theatre flat, that could transport the subject to a ballroom, to a continental marine promenade, to Paris, Vienna, St Petersburg, or anywhere.

Victory over Beard allowed Claudet's practice to go from strength to strength. He cared about improving photographic technique, and in 1841 presented papers to both the Royal Society and the French Academy of Sciences on using chlorine and bromine to speed up the process. The innovation of using red light in the dark-room was his, and he patented it. He opened a studio at the Colosseum in the clearer air of Regent's Park, and in 1851 opened what he called his Temple of Photography at 107 Regent Street. There he had a gallery of photographs of his own and other photographers, and, with Beard tottering beneath the weight of self-imposed lawsuits, Claudet became the grand old man of commercial photography in London, 'the Van Dyck of photography' as the *Athenaeum* came to call him. Nevertheless, he had his detractors. David Brewster, himself no spring chicken, called him 'the oldest photographer, and, therefore, probably the most prejudiced', and accused him of creating 'grim anamorphoses of humanity . . . which, though a terror to the domestic circle, have the merit of showing us how we shall look in a winding sheet or under the more ghastly phase of a *post-mortem* examination'. Claudet retorted: 'If this be true, Sir David has taken a great and lively interest in ascertaining how he shall look under the painful circumstances described, as I have had the honour of taking his portrait many times, and on the last occasion about six weeks ago.'

The daguerreotype portrait process gradually became obsolete. When Claudet retired and handed his practice over to his son Henry in the early 1860s it had been long superseded by the paper negative process pioneered by Henry Fox Talbot. Shortly after he died in December 1867 Claudet's Temple of Photography burned to the ground, and all his records, equipment and daguerreotypes were reduced to ashes. Beard had long since got out of photography, although despite previous bankruptcy he continued in business with his son Richard until the late 1850s. He exhibited at the Great Exhibition in 1851, and in 1852 wrote to *The Times* claiming priority on the method of enamelling daguerreotypes that he was using in his King William Street studio. Beard ended his career as a 'medical galvanist', selling zinc- and copper-wire belts to cure rheumatism, sciatica and toothache.

John Jabez Edwin Mayall was a much travelled Yorkshireman who in 1847 set up a commercial studio offering daguerreotype portraits. His father had been a manufacturing chemist near Huddersfield, and, after some years working with his father, John Mayall spent the early 1840s in the United States where he lived in New York and Philadelphia. There he and an English partner Samuel van Loan started a daguerreotype business, Mayall himself also travelling the eastern United States, where he made images of the Niagara Falls and other landscape subjects. He and van Loan were rapidly and distinctly successful, winning a silver medal in 1844 for their daguerreotypes from Philadelphia's Franklin Institute. After becoming sole proprietor of the Philadelphia business, trading under the name 'Professor Highschool', Mayall sold up in 1846 and came back to England where he worked briefly for Antoine Claudet, and by April the following year had set up the American Daguerreotype Institution at 433 West Strand, four doors east of Nash's Lowther Arcade.

Mayall began by opening an exhibition in his new rooms to display what it was he did, and could do. He showed 140 of his own daguerreotypes, astounding in their quantity, quality and intensity of image. There were a dozen or more portraits, numerous views in the United States, tableaux, stories in pictures, landscapes and a photograph of the Rosetta Stone. From the evidence of their titles, at least forty-five can only have been made in England – Mayall worked fast, there were views in the Strand, at Windsor and Stratford-on-Avon, and portraits of Faraday, Grove, Lyell, Herschel, Rennie and Brewster. Exhibits added later included photographic tableaux illustrating 'before and after' the 1847 slump in value of railway shares on the stock market. An early advertisement in *The Times* stressed Mayall's American background, which Mayall himself did little to dispel. He described himself there as 'Professor Highschool, late of Philadelphia, US', who had made 'New discoveries in Daguerreotype . . . which take Daguerreotype portraits by an entirely new process, of a degree of delicacy, depth of tone, and lifelike reality, never previously attained by himself or any other photographic artists'.

As his American success revealed, Mayall was a very good businessman, technically adept and innovative in his craft, highly ambitious and accomplished at flattering his clients. He had an uncanny knack of knowing where to 'place' his pictures. He took a daguerreotype portrait of the American scientist Joseph Henry, when, as the first Secretary to the Smithsonian Institution, Henry came to London in 1851 to see what was going on. Mayall perspicaciously gave the portrait to Michael Faraday, who told Henry, 'We look at your face painted in light by Mr Mayall & I dare say it is like. He and nature together have made you look very comfortable.' Henry responded that 'the presentation of the daguerrotypes was a proposition of Mayall himself which I did not know he had carried into execution'. Mayall rose to become a court photographer, creating many important images of Queen Victoria, Prince Albert and other members of the royal family. When he came to take her portrait in 1855, Queen Victoria referred to him as 'the oddest man I ever saw'. He had clearly convinced the Queen that he came from the west. She wrote: 'He is an American and a tremendous enthusiast in his work.'

An early client of Mayall's busy studio, where artists and scientists came and went, was an inquisitive elderly gentleman and his lady who seemed to be unusually interested in what went on in the studio. The client did not give his name, and led Mayall to believe that he was a senior lawyer. According to an account Mayall later wrote about the incident, he took the client's photograph many times, across many return visits. The photographs were posed in various ways: in one the old man was seen reading; in another he wore robes and a large floppy hat; others were quite straightforwardly posed. The gentleman watched Mayall grind lenses, and on one visit stayed for 'some three hours, talking about light and its curious effects on films of prepared silver'. They discussed the spectrum, and the visitor was particularly taken with Mayall's photographs of the Niagara Falls, in which he had caught the fleeting impression of the rainbow. Whenever he came to the shop this visitor always seemed to have 'some new notion about light' to discuss. Mayall showed him a new six-inch lens from Paris, and he looked at it and through it with surprise and admiration.

Mayall eventually got the old gentleman's name out of him. 'Mr Turner', he was told, and after this his visits became so frequent that he became known to the staff in the shop as 'our Mr Turner', and they put out a special chair for him. One wonders why Mayall, having met the old man over so long a period, having talked very intelligently with him about light and colour and having known his name to be Turner, was so bone-headed as to continue to think that his visitor was a lawyer. But the charade continued for nearly two years, and through many visits. 'Mr Turner' sent Mayall customers, and comforted him when the younger man fretted about the legal battle he was involved in over patent rights with Richard Beard. Turner, himself a clever businessman, reassured him: 'No, no; you are sure to succeed; only wait. You are a young man yet. I began life with little, and you see I am now very comfortable . . . You'll come out alright, never fear.'

The visitor was, of course, J. M. W. Turner. Like the best fiction, the story ends in a revelation, and a disappearance. Turner had been coming to Mayall's shop for two years, when, on 21 April 1849, he attended a soirée given by the new President of the Royal Society, the Earl of Rosse, in Somerset House. The House was bright with London Lights: Roderick Murchison was there, as was Thomas Donaldson, George Jones, Richard Westmacott, William Jerdan, Antoine Claudet, John Rennie, John Farey, John Martin, Sir William Newton and William Grove. They examined models of Rosse's gigantic telescopes, of Marc Brunel's block-cutting machine which, after forty years' service, was still in active use in naval dockyards, and they looked at a display of photographs by Claudet and Mayall. John Mayall was there too, and he and Turner talked as they had so often done in the past. Then up came a man who knew them both, and tried to introduce them to each other, saying to Mayall, 'Do you know that he is *the* Turner?'

When after this revelation he had pulled himself together, Mayall offered to carry out any experiments in light and the spectrum that Turner might require, and help him work out his ideas about the treatment of light and shade. They parted on the understanding that Turner would call once again at Mayall's shop. But he never did; and they never met again. Turner's friendship with Mayall is an extraordinary instance of the depth of the old painter's engagement with one or another aspect of science and technical progress. Progress in photography in the early 1840s was as much about technical improvements in chemistry and optics as it was about image-making, and it is significant that Turner showed as profound an interest in Mayall's lens-making activities as he did in his practice of photography.

John Mayall was an exceptional individual whose business skill and technical prowess caused him to do very well out of the embryonic photographic industry. Among his innovations were the carte-de-visite, in which wallet-sized photographs mounted on card were produced in great numbers; and at the other end of the scale he offered photographic enlargements. One of these, a full-size standing figure of the Baltimore philanthropist George Peabody, was the largest photographic image yet made. Mayall also introduced the vignetted photograph, created by spinning a card with an excised star in front of the camera lens. This resulted in a photographic image with a stylishly blurred edge, comparable to small-scale engravings whose lines fade away into the paper. These he called 'crayon portraits'. By the time of his death in 1901 Mayall's influence had spread over the globe, not only through the travels of his minuscule cartes-de-visite but by way of the ten studios in London, four in Brighton, one in Kingston-on-Thames and three in Melbourne, Australia. These he and his many children managed together.

While Beard, Claudet and Mayall were energetically carving out careers and attempting to make fortunes in commercial photography, others, like Herschel, Fox Talbot and John Children's daughter Anna Atkins developed the scientific potential of photography. *The Times* looked back at recent progress when it reviewed the exhibition of photographs at the Society of Arts in December 1852 – a total of 784 exhibits:

> By its [photography's] operation the fine arts acquire a special machinery long wanted, and still imperfectly appreciated. As the manufacturer calls to his aid the loom and the steam-engine, the artist, with a sublimer effort of intellectual power, can henceforth use the sun and the camera to multiply and extend his labours. The man of science, too, finds in it a new help in gaining that degree of permanence which is

required for delicate and minute observation. Photography already aspires to mark the wanderings of the stars, and opens up new marvels to microscopic research. What printing was to the literature of the world, this promises to be to art and philosophy.

Anna Atkins, a member of the small circle of scientific friends which included her father, Herschel, Faraday, Fox Talbot and the Somervilles, was an accomplished artist who in 1823 drew more that two hundred lithographs of shells to illustrate her father's translation of Jean-Baptiste Lamarck's *Genera of Shells*. She was also a botanist, and an active member of the Botanical Society. Immediately the practice became known she became intrigued by photography, and in 1841 her father wrote to Fox Talbot to tell him so: 'When we return to Kent my daughter and I shall set to work in good earnest till we completely succeed in practising your invaluable process . . . I have also ordered a camera for Mrs Atkins from Ross.' Anna Atkins's contribution to the history of photography is her pioneering set of three volumes, *Photographs of British Algae: Cyanotype Impressions*, which she and family friends and servants produced in a kitchen industry between 1843 and 1853. As a botanical and scientific illustrator, Atkins knew the difficulties of accurately depicting a plant or a shell with a pencil. Photography, and in her case the cyanide-based process 'cyanotype' developed by John Herschel, cleared that problem away. As a result, the most humble of plants were the first to be captured by the currently most advanced of scientific processes. The results, in the rich blue that suffuses the paper, present a level of visual information that transcends the ethereal beauty of the images. All the folds, creases and veins in the plants are laid out, every frond, hair and pollen speck are there before us more than 150 years after those plants were picked. Anna Atkins did not exhibit her work in her lifetime, but, continuing his account of the 1852 Society of Arts exhibition of photography, the *Times* reviewer observed a wonder that Atkins would have shared:

> To think that a piece of paper or glass physically prepared, placed in a camera, and acted upon by the common light of day, will retain an exact image of the most fleeting objects, from which thousands of impressions may be printed, is one of those marvellous results actually astonishing to the philosopher and the simple child.

John Herschel returned from four years' astronomical experiment at the Cape of Good Hope in June 1838. He was received in London like the hero he was, the man who had identified and numbered more than four thousand double stars and nebulae in the southern skies. He returned home with perfect timing, for although he was well aware of his friend and correspondent Henry Fox Talbot's experiments with photography, it was not until January 1839 that he heard about Daguerre's discoveries. Rapidly he set about making improvements to Daguerre's technique, by creating a negative image that could be printed and multiplied. Herschel was, like Faraday, not a man to obfuscate, or keep new scientific ideas within a limited priestly coterie. He wrote about the importance of clarity of language in scientific endeavour, and urged fellow scientists to avoid terms that tend to 'clothe [science] in a strange and repulsive garb, and . . . [assume] an unnecessary guise of profundity and obscurity . . . Not to do this is to deliberately reject the light which the natural and unencumbered good sense of mankind is capable of throwing on every subject.' It was Herschel who coined the word 'photography', which stuck.

16

The Crystal Palace

~

A S ANNA ATKINS CREATED her delicate blueprints of fragile plant structures, the growth of a sequence of fragile plant-like forms in Hyde Park was astonishing Londoners with its rapidity and scale. The Crystal Palace, designed by Joseph Paxton, 'not a regular architect', as *The Times* described him, was being constructed in the Park to house the Great Exhibition of the Works of Industry of All Nations, to open on May Day, 1851. The Great Exhibition, an event with unprecedented ambitions to bring the whole world, and its tide of natural and man-made products, flowing though London like another river, was launched by Henry Cole at a public meeting in October 1849. To make the announcement Cole chose the Egyptian Hall in Piccadilly, home of so many strange and wonderful ideas. Cole was then a middle-ranking but ambitious and effective government official who had been an assistant keeper of the Record Office and a reformer of the postal system. The Great Exhibition and its organisation transported Cole from a back office to the most influential position in the teaching and promotion of standards of art and design. Out of the foundations of the Great Exhibition evolved the Victoria and Albert Museum, and Cole was its first director. 'Spices from the east,' Cole promised his Egyptian Hall audience in 1849, 'the hops of Kent and Sussex, the raisins of Malaga, and the olives of the Pyrenees . . . the steam-engine in all its endless applications . . . the looms of the Dacca muslin weavers, and the last new power-loom made by Messrs. Roberts.'

The presiding genius behind the Great Exhibition was not Cole, however, but the Queen's husband, Prince Albert. As the Queen's consort, and father of their (by 1850) seven children, this was an adventure of sufficient scale to absorb Albert's intellectual and physical energies. He was not yet thirty when he first pursued, with the Society of Arts, the idea that a comprehensive exhibition of manufactures be held in London. Throwing his unique social and political influence, his drive and charisma, into the project, he whipped committees together, raised money and wrote rousing advocacies for the exhibition. He secured the Hyde Park site, dealt with criticism and appointed Henry Cole. The event was intended to be a great exhibition not only of the works of all nations, but of the works of all Britons. A published statement, almost certainly written by Prince Albert himself, made it clear that while it was expected that princes would be exhibitors, as well as 'the most scientific agriculturalist' and 'skilful manufacturers' and 'artists of the greatest genius', it would also be open to 'the cottager who cultivates any seed of remarkable excellence, the cottager's son who invents any implement of increased usefulness . . . the cottager's daughter who works more elegant pillow-lace than the common or plaits straw in a new and more beautiful way'.

In the months leading up to the Exhibition, when the construction work was an event of intense public interest, a publican, John Smith, celebrated the extra money that would be circulating in London just as a result of the increase in visitors and their spending power. He calculated that another river, an extra £7 million, would flow through London's tills: 'if London was full to overflowing in 1814, to celebrate the beginning of peace, with representatives of a few nations as guests, how much more full will it be in '51 with the whole world as guests?'

Like Anna Atkins, Joseph Paxton was a gardener, one who not only nurtured plants, but created bulbous and reticulated plant-like forms to house them. His hothouse for the Duke of Devonshire at Chatsworth (1840) created the ideal living space for the giant lily *Victoria Regia*, among hundreds of other species. He built another smaller hothouse near by, at Darley Dale in Derbyshire. Atkins's native plant specimens, Herschel's star systems and Fox Talbot's lace were subjects whose intricate beauties could only be fully revealed by photography. So too Paxton's Crystal Palace. Unlike the plants, the star systems and the lace, however, the Crystal Palace was a structure of a kind that did not exist before the invention of photography, so subject and medium could gradually reveal their intricacies and potential together, and their technological, scientific and artistic development could proceed hand in hand.

With his Crystal Palace, Paxton stretched the aesthetic language and structural technology of the greenhouse to its absolute limits. Long before the first sheet of the 900,000 square feet of glass had been fitted, the building was named the Crystal Palace by the *Illustrated London News*. Its panes, each forty-nine inches long, were made by a process perfected by James Chance and Co. of Birmingham, and were the largest pieces of sheet glass made commercially anywhere in the world. The ironwork was cast in Smethwick, and all travelled to the site by rail. Thus the height and the sparkle in the roof were both the gift to the Crystal Palace from Birmingham. The name Crystal Palace, which stuck to it all through its construction, its presentation and its rebuilding in Sydenham in 1854, reflected something of the affection that Londoners felt in its creation. The name also justified Paxton's guiding principle when he proposed a building in cast iron and glass, describing it as 'the least objectionable structure to occupy a public park . . . whilst, at the same time, a building of this description would be in every point of view best adapted for the purposes of the Exhibition'. There was to be not a vestige of stone, brick, mortar or plaster in the building, indeed no material that needed water as a medium, to avoid condensation against the glass. It would be 1,851 feet long – a size to mark the year of festivity – with a central transept of just over four hundred feet. The central nave would be high enough, at 108 feet, to accommodate an existing line of elm trees in the park. The language used to describe the parts of the Crystal Palace – 'transept', 'nave', 'aisle', 'crossing' – were those usually associated with cathedrals, the only buildings on a comparable scale known to all.

One clever technique adopted by Paxton was to make a virtue of the gentle slope in the ground, upwards from west to east. This allowed people at the west entrance to see the entire spectacle ranging up ahead of them, a similar effect to that experienced in Regent Street. Overhead, the aisles and transepts were shaded by canvas awnings so that sunlight did not overwhelm or overheat the interior; only the nave was left uncovered, with the result that, as prints of the interior suggest, the sun shafted down into the central space and lit it brilliantly and dramatically. The ironwork on its interior facings was painted to a scheme created by Owen Jones – blue, white and yellow for the verticals; blue, white and red for the curving girders; and red, white and yellow for the roof bars. 'My object', Jones told a meeting of the RIBA in 1850, 'is now to show that [the Crystal Palace's] grandeur may be still further enhanced by a system of colouring which, by marking *distinctly* every line in the building will tend to increase the apparent height, as well as its length and its bulk.'

After the exhibition, Paxton proposed that the building should be converted into a permanent winter garden, with walkways and carriage drives running through it. He himself predicted that the Crystal Palace would become the ancestor of all domestic conservatories, which in the early-twenty-first century have become the blessing and the curse of the suburbs. He told his audience at the Society of Arts in November 1850 that 'I have no doubt but many structures similar to that at Darley will be attached to dwelling houses, where they may serve as sitting-rooms, conservatories, waiting-rooms or omnibus-rooms.'

Work began in Hyde Park in late September 1850, and within a month the site had sprouted with columns and their footings. Steam from engines driving saws curled among the elm trees, which were already dropping their leaves as the building went up around them. A dozen engines carried out a dozen specialist tasks: one machine stirred putty, another drew lengths of guttering through a paint trough and on through an aperture lined with brushes. Men and boys scuttled about with an urgent despatch to ensure that this building was ready in time, while officials continued to doubt they would do it: 'The builders had been pushed out by the painters; the painters, in their turn, had been elbowed out by the carpenters, who began to put up many of the fittings before the painting was finished . . . each succeeding act pressed hard upon its precursor.'

Turner, by now an old man helped along by his companion Sophia Booth, visited the site in January 1851, and reported on the speed of its construction: 'The Crystal Palace has assumed its wonted shape and size . . . it looks very well in front because the transept takes a centre like a dome, but sideways ribs of Glass frame work only Towering over the Galleries like a Giant.' At just the same time that Turner was taken to see the Crystal Palace, Thomas Carlyle described it to his brother John as a 'monster of a giant birdcage', having 'the effect of Solomon's Temple as the old sixpenny pictures gave it us':

> Once its use is over [Paxton] can build it again into two streets of dwelling houses, into a village of iron cottages, or a world of garden greenhouses, without losing a pound of the substance employed (putty excepted). That I call clever; the rest is like to be all fudge and boisterous ostentation: I already have my own *thots* about flying far away from London till it is all over!

Carlyle admired the panache with which Paxton handled the construction, and the speed with which, by January 1851, he was driving it to completion: 'Never in the world's annals, I believe, was there a *building* of such extent finished in ten times the *time* by hand of men; – and here Paxton (whose ingenuity is the soul of it, and *enables* him to employ tens of thousands on it at once) has got it all but ready as per contract.' Nevertheless the Crystal Palace had its snags. During the March storms of 1851 it began to leak, 'taking in floods of rain, – drip, drip in all corners, – and thousands of sparrows also fluttering about, getting ejected by *poison*.'

The younger generation of photographers had reached the height of their powers when the Crystal Palace was under construction. Nevertheless, it is curious that there appear to be no surviving photographs of the Crystal Palace in course of erection; for a record of this transitory period we have to look to the long-exercised practice of wood engraving in the *Illustrated London News* and elsewhere, or to written description. The reason for this is not hard to find. During the day the site swarmed with more than two thousand workmen, in urgent and deliberate activity to complete the monster building in the allotted six months. Carts rattled, cranes creaked, steam engines coughed and rallied as thousands of girders were swung into place, and the 900,000 panes of Birmingham glass were delicately bedded down. There was no time for a photographer to say 'Hold still for five minutes please!' and at night there was no light to take photographs. So, for example, as a record of the extraordinary moment when the workmen greeted Prince Albert on his visit to the construction site on 5 December 1850, we must rely on *The Times*:

> As the Prince was leaving the Exhibition . . . a large bell at the entrance was sounded, and in an instant, from every part of the huge pile, the 2000 men employed came scrambling onward to give him a parting cheer. It was a remarkable spectacle to see so large a body of people approaching in so many different ways, some slipping down columns, others skipping along joists, and balancing themselves dexterously along girders. At last they all formed themselves in a semicircle round the spot where the Royal carriage was drawn up. As they awaited in respectful silence the Prince's appearance, a brewer's dray entered the gates with 250 gallons of beer, and, as if by instinct, they recognised that the grateful supply was for them. Of course they welcomed the dray with cheers. His Royal Highness, on taking his departure, was saluted with enthusiastic hurrahs.

Once opened, by the Queen Empress accompanied by Prince Albert on 1 May 1851, the Great Exhibition was truly the world's platform for the 'Works of Industry of All Nations'. The smallest screw from Birmingham and the most complex 'pen-knife' from Sheffield could be found on display; the most intricately carved sideboard from France; the largest vase from Germany; James Nasmyth's steam hammer, Maudslay's steam engines, Hullmandel's lithographs, Martin's engravings, and John Varley's patent graphic telescope were all there. The enormous construction – 'building' does not seem to be quite the name for it – was crammed with objects displayed clearly and systematically in a manner that set new standards for museums. The public signage was of a new, modern order, the national displays being clearly indicated, and routes around the building being marked in a manner derived from railway stations. Journalists, however, were still confined by long practice to use painting as their metaphor. The opening impression was conjured in tumbling sentences by the *Illustrated London News*:

> The first *coup d'oeil* of the Building on entering the nave was grand and gorgeous in the extreme. The vast dimensions of the Building,

the breadth of light, partially subdued and agreeably mellowed in the
nave by the calico coverings placed over the roof, whilst the arched
transept soared boldly into the clear arch of heaven, courting, admitting and distributing the full effulgence of the noonday sun the bright
and striking colours and forms of the several articles in rich
manufactured goods, works in sculpture and other objects displayed
by the exhibitors . . . were blent into an harmonious . . . picture of
immense grandeur.

For the same reason of too much uncontrollable movement, there
are few surviving photographs of the Great Exhibition in full swing,
one of them being a daguerreotype by Mayall. Henry Fox Talbot,
however, embarked bravely with his assistant Nicholas Henneman on
a commission to photograph the building and a selection of the
exhibits during the opening months, and together they took more
than 150 different subjects. One of these, a view inside the Crystal
Palace transept looking north, reveals something of the complication
of photography in the early 1850s: a shadowy figure, who must have
moved into or out of shot during exposure is seated left, while an
after-image of a camera and tripod suggests that another busy photographer also got in the way of Fox Talbot's lens. Fox Talbot was
expected to produce enough prints from his photographs to illustrate
140 sets of the four-volume *Reports of the Juries of the 1851 Exhibition*.
A total of 21,700 photographic prints would be required, a practically
impossible industrial-scale operation for the time. If many of the
volumes, bound in red morocco leather, failed to receive illustrations, enough were illustrated to reveal the scale and complexity
of the Great Exhibition undertaking: wood engravings could not
do it justice. There are photographs of the interior looking in all
directions which do not show individual displays, but do reveal the
curious conglomerations of objects in the nave and transepts – an
immense Greek amphora, a steam engine, a grand marble statue, a large
rubber boat. Of the exhibits that had to be taken outside into the Park
to be photographed there is a gleaming steam winnowing machine
and its associated parts with, in the background, Baron Marochetti's
noble bronze equestrian figure of Richard Coeur de Lion controlling
his spirited charger and waving his sword aloft. Technology met art;
scientific advance met sculptural historicism at the Great Exhibition.

But it is one particular photograph of the Crystal Palace that tells: this is of the South Transept from just beyond the original gate posts into Hyde Park. To the left there is a small classical gate lodge, and fixed to the gate posts can be seen a poster, headed EXHIBITION, and another inscribed NOTICE. So far, so very ordinary. But behind, towering upwards and menacingly forwards, is the baleful white iron-creased whale of a building, topped by a semi-circular toothed fan of decorated ironwork the size of the Sadlers' hydrogen balloon, and looking like half a cogwheel of more gigantic an engine than even Henry Maudslay could imagine. The windows are covered by linen blinds, but one of them on the first floor has, accidentally or through its failure, fallen down, evoking a moment of human error in this extraordinary venture.

The royal opening was 'captured' by the court painter Henry Courtney Selous in an expansive group of stiff-as-a-shaving-brush figures lined up under a palm tree in the centre of the Crystal Palace: the Queen is there, Prince Albert, a line of princes and princelings, and ambassadors from every corner of the earth. The Archbishop of Canterbury is intoning a prayer, with thousands of invited guests looking on from the banks of balconies. The colours in the painting are primary and gorgeous; 'hazy and indistinct' it is not. Though completed in 1852, this group portrait (London, V&A) is of exactly the same kind as George Jones's account of the opening of London Bridge by William IV in 1831 (London, Sir John Soane's Museum), or, painted in quite different circumstances, to the *Trial of Queen Caroline, 1820* by Sir George Hayter (London, National Portrait Gallery). The genre goes yet further back to seventeenth-century Dutch group portraits; but the point to be made here is that in recording this great expectation of twentieth-century modernism, Prince Albert and his advisers chose the tried, tested and tremendously impressive over the new and contentious medium of photography. Technically, although with difficulty, a photograph could have been taken to mark the opening of the Crystal Palace; but it was not.

Within the aisles, transepts, nave and walkways, thronged with crowds of visitors from All Nations, could be found a display of 145 (according to the catalogue, but actually very many more) photographs by photographers from all those nations whose savants and scientists had struggled with the photographic principles of daguerreotype and calotype – overwhelmingly from Great Britain, the United States and France. In the exhibition catalogue Photography came not in the Fine Arts section, but as part of the Philosophical Instruments category of the Machinery section, between Spectacles and Magnets: thus, within the philosophy of the exhibition, Photography was considered to be a science rather than an art. On display were examples of one of the largest daguerreotypes yet made, *Bacchus and Ariadne* (twenty-four inches by fifteen) by Mayall, and of Mayall's 'crayon portraits'; there were images of the sun by Claudet, enamelled daguerreotypes by Beard, and an image of smallpox vaccine taken from a cow by the pioneering William Constable. The man who brought all these photographs and photographic equipment together was Charles Thurston Thompson, the son of the wood engraver John Thompson, with whom he trained, and the husband of Henry Cole's sister-in-law.

The leitmotif that linked every space in the Crystal Palace was its display of sculpture from all over the world – although chiefly from Britain, the United States, France, Germany and Italy. There were startled nymphs, there was a dying gladiator, and under this light, organic, modern structure a marble Andromeda still found herself chained to a rock in the well-tried antique manner. The 'artists of the greatest genius', as the prospectus for the Great Exhibition promised, were still those who found themselves chained to the rocks of antiquity, rather than being freed, like the engineers who created the Crystal Palace, into the creation of free-flowing organic forms.

The six months of display had its share of unexpected excitements. In September it was the target of a demonstration of Bloomerism by a group of men and women dressed in light, billowing short-cut trousers, Bloomers. They were hooted at by the exhibition visitors while handing out leaflets advertising a lecture on Bloomerism in Finsbury, and then disappeared. Yet more exciting was the near-collision into the Crystal Palace of an escaped balloon, piloted by Mr and Mrs Graham. This caught on a post as it was lifting off from Batty's Hippodrome at the entrance to Hyde Park, and a hole was torn in it. The balloon rose up, descended, rose again, all the while leaking gas and heading erratically towards the Great Exhibition with its grappling irons flying at the ends of their ropes. There were about 35,000 people inside, as the Grahams careered overhead, knocking down a line of flagpoles one by one, throwing all their sand ballast on to the Palace and shattering some glass in a desperate attempt to rise upwards. They missed the Palace by a whisker, and were seen disappearing eastwards over the Park where they ended up demolishing the parapets and chimneys of a line of houses on the other side of Piccadilly. The Grahams survived.

When the doors closed for the last time on the Great Exhibition on 15 October, the exhibits were rapidly removed, leaving the colossal shimmering structure empty and naked and, for the first time in its existence, as vulnerable as the dried wings of a butterfly. Benjamin Brecknell Turner photographed the vast interior in images which leap the decades and take us directly to 1930s and 1940s photographs of industrial buildings on, by comparison, a modest scale. It is curious that two of the pioneering figures in nineteenth-century photography, as in painting, are named Constable and Turner. The photographer whose work captured the inspiring scale and construction of the Crystal Palace most succinctly, however, was Philip Delamotte, who, like Thompson, was the son of an artist – the watercolour painter William Delamotte. Philip was commissioned to record the process of reconstruction of the Crystal Palace when, a year after the Great Exhibition closed, it was bought and moved in its entirety to a new site overlooking London at Sydenham. Delamotte's photographs ranged from the preparation of the site and the re-erection of the nave to the grand opening ceremony on 10 June 1854 when the Queen returned once again to the Crystal Palace. In front of swathes of her waiting subjects, filling tiers of balconies behind her, Queen Victoria and her consort Prince Albert look like a pair of woollen-draped dolls, surrounded by a platform party of woollen dolls. Evidently, what Henry Selous could accomplish in oil paint on a large canvas was simply impossible yet in a photograph. Delamotte, like Brecknell

Turner before him, could evoke scale and plant-like fragility, and wide extended spaces and the pouring in of light. But, on the scale required for the opening of the Crystal Palace, neither he nor photography could yet do grandeur.

A World of Wonders in Itself

ONE BY ONE during the course of the half-century, London Lights began to fade and die. Joseph Farington fell down stairs from the gallery of Didsbury parish church, near Manchester, where he was visiting his brother's family in the final days of 1821. He had been attending Evensong, it had been raining, and he slipped, tumbled and cracked his head on the stone floor. He had started his diary for that day, 30 December: 'Rose 10 after 8. A dull moist morning. Therm^r at noon 44½. Wind West.' Marianne Farington concluded the entry with a sense of detail of which her uncle would have been proud:

> his hands encumbered with Hat, Umbrella and prayer book – his feet equally so with Golloshes he was unable to recover from a slip of his feet and went down the flight of stairs with great rapidity and force – such as to project himself beyond the stairs – so that his head came with heavy fall on the pavement of the Church floor. The vital spark was gone. He neither looked, spoke, moved – or breathed again.

Emerging horizontally and at speed from the staircase, Farington departed with the same despatch with which he wrote his daily diary. His place as the independent, highly personalised and private chronicler of the world of art and society in London was taken by Benjamin Robert Haydon, a man of whose attitudes and behaviour Farington disapproved.

For his part, Haydon ended a furious life of antagonism and frustrated genius by shooting himself in the head on 22 June 1846, and when that did not work having the presence of mind to slit his own throat with a razor. On his gravestone in the old Paddington churchyard, beside his five dead children, and in the shadow of the grave of

Mrs Siddons who had pronounced him such a success twenty-six years earlier, were words he chose for himself: 'He devoted forty-two years to the improvement of the taste of the English people in high art and died broken-hearted from pecuniary distress.'

Humphry Davy, much to his wife's anxiety, got the wanderlust and in March 1828 left England on a long continental tour. He had become increasingly demanding and querulous, restless and disappointed, and sought a role. Though remaining the President of the Royal Society, he was no longer in the forefront of science, and found himself, scientifically speaking, extra to requirements. For John Murray he wrote two books of poetic and wistful reflection, *Salmonia: or Days of Fly Fishing*, first published anonymously in 1828, and *Consolations in Travel, or the Last Days of a Philosopher*, which he wrote as his own consolation on his final travels. Murray published this posthumously in 1830. A letter from Lady Davy to John Murray, written probably in the middle or late 1820s, reveals something of Davy's inner difficulties in his latter years: 'I am sure you will receive him in a room alone, as he is unequal to seeing strangers, and consequently he makes rather an effort to go to you.' Jane cared for Humphry from a distance. Although in Ljubljana her husband found Papina, an innkeeper's daughter prepared to travel with him as a 'kind and affectionate nurse', Jane naturally fretted, telling John Murray to hurry news of the production of *Salmonia* to Sir Humphry, by then in Rome. 'I think him both as a liberal citizen whose inventions have benefited his country, and as to Universal Fame, and *present* suffering, one entitled to your chiefest consideration, and I do pray you to prove this by any immediate attention to his wishes.' Jane rushed from London to Humphry's bedside in Rome when she heard of a deterioration in his health. Although she arrived in time to begin to bring him home, he died en route in their 'wretched Inn' in Geneva on 28 May 1829. He was buried outside the city walls in the Cemetery of Plainpalais.

Thomas Hope died among the sparkling lamps and the marble and gilt splendour of his house in Duchess Street in February 1831, and was whisked away to be buried at the Hope family house, Deepdene in Surrey. Charles Lamb died after a fall at home in Edmonton, Middlesex, in December 1834, having passed his last years in a fever of depression and drunkenness. His mad and beloved sister Mary survived him by thirteen years. Both John Nash and John Soane died in the houses that they had created for themselves, the one a frothy and extravagant island castle, the other an austere town house, and both were buried in tombs of their own designs. Nash was in severe financial straits at his death at East Cowes in May 1835, having only his one castle left; John Soane, catching a chill caught descending his staircase at night in January 1837, died a wealthy man and a knight of the realm, and left his house to the British nation which cherishes it still. Sir Francis Chantrey died in his armchair, by his fire, 'of a spasm of the heart' in 1841; Charles Hullmandel of a brain haemorrhage in 1850; Sir James Willoughby Gordon and John Farey both in 1851, the one of bronchitis, the other of heart failure. Turner, lying in bed looking out over the Thames at Chelsea, succumbed to heart disease in the dying days of December 1851. 'Had you not better take a glass of sherry?' he asked his doctor on being told that his days were numbered.

Fifty years after Richard Porson's death, his favourite drinking den, the Cider Cellar in Maiden Lane, remained a place of informal education and enlightenment. William Makepeace Thackeray gathered his friends there for pre-publication readings from his novel *The Newcomes* (1853–5) in which the cellar appears as 'The Cave of Harmony', a place where 'welsh-rabbits [toasted cheese] and good old glee singing' could be had. It was always a haunt of the literati and of literary aspirants and desperadoes, and was named in Thackeray's *Sketches and Travels in London* as the final stop in the fall of the dissolute MP Arthur Rowdy, 'who was known to go to Vauxhall, and had even been seen, with a comforter over his nose, listening to "Sam Hall" [a miserable song about a man on his way to be hanged at Tyburn] at the Cider Cellar'. By the late 1850s it provided a platform for comic public discussions with music, and mock parliamentary debates on current issues, which drew such crowds that it had to be extended to accommodate them. These events, organised by the impresario and publican Renton Nicholson, the self-proclaimed 'Lord Chief Baron', continued the Cider Cellar's role as a place of informal education with alcohol, until the building was demolished in the 1860s.

William Jerdan, Cyrus Redding and Charles Babbage had enough time on their hands towards the ends of their lives to compose their minds and their memoirs. Written sometimes long after chains of events had taken place and looking back on them, memoirs are reflections of a different kind to diaries, which, like Farington's and Haydon's, are written hot, on the spur of the moment. Generally speaking, memoirs justify, and can fudge chronology; diaries report in real time. Humphry Davy under the guise of writing treatises on fishing and travel followed a third path of personal historical record, leaving a rich autobiographical trace amid his allusive descriptions of grayling and of the Colosseum by moonlight.

At the beginning of his *Passages from the Life of a Philosopher* (1864) Babbage observes why it is that others might want to write their memoirs: some did it to stave off boredom, he said; some in case another person might do them down in their memoirs; yet others 'for fear that the vampires of literature might make [their life] their prey'. Babbage claimed no such negative purpose for himself, but instead intended to write an account of the genesis of his calculating machines, 'rendered less unpalatable by relating some of my experience amongst various classes of society . . . in which I have occasionally mixed': thus a technical history with social interludes. Jerdan, more prolix yet than Babbage, took seven pages to outline his reasons for embarking on an account of 'that perplexing subject, MYSELF', believing that 'without presumption, I can truly assert that my stores are very considerable both in variety and value'. Jerdan thought he would be dead before anybody read his memoirs, though he was wrong in this, and lived on until 1869. 'What egotism is autobiography?' asked Cyrus Redding, after precisely describing the view from his desk, and carrying on anyway: 'These desultory memoirs are commenced on the west side of Hampstead Hill. Palatial Windsor is seen rising proudly in the distance. The spire of Harrow, like a burial obelisk ascending in another direction.'

These autobiographers all looked back on their lives and made various justifications for their actions. Another, however, the Rev. John Richardson, whose *Recollections of the Last Half-Century* were published in 1855, took a different, more prescient view. In his *Enquiry into the Condition of those Industrial Classes who have really represented England at the Great Exhibition* (1851) he revealed in his opening remarks inklings of what we now know as global warming. Reflecting on how, in 1851, the 'deep snows and severe frosts of the protracted winters' were forgotten, and how the Thames 'is no longer conscious of the strange burden of the roasting ox', he found a cause in the agricultural improvements of the previous decades: 'The felling of forests, the draining of marshes, the more uniform and skilful cultivation . . . are assigned as causes adequate to account for the climatorial and atmospheric change.'

Melancholy reflections of this kind carry rich echoes into our own time: it is the sorry lot of the prophet to address the deaf. John Martin's proposed improvements in the water supply of London in the 1830s would not have come in time to prevent the 1831–2 cholera outbreak, but they might have prevented or mitigated those of 1848–9 and 1853–4. It was not until the mid-1850s that polluted water was proved to be the cause of cholera, and not until 1859 that work began on London's present sewerage system. Mary Somerville voiced the horrors of the 1853–4 outbreak. She was writing from Florence, and from hearsay: 'The Board of Health are blamed for it because they did nothing to improve the state of London since the last time it raged, and when they saw it coming now they opened the sewers which is the cause of the present violence – such men deserve the severest punishment.'

The railways came late to London, compared to Birmingham and the industrial north-west and the north-east of England. They also kept away from the centre, the first termini being positioned in an irregular ring of perhaps a mile radius from Trafalgar Square. Like the forts or gatehouses of a medieval city, they looked outwards into the country beyond. Both Euston Station, for Robert Stephenson's London and Birmingham Railway, and a temporary Paddington Station, for Brunel's embryonic Great Western Railway, were opened in 1838, but the other termini came later, King's Cross and Liverpool Street in the 1850s, Victoria and St Pancras in the 1860s, Marylebone in the 1890s. The iron roofs of the London stations, and latterly of such exhibition halls as the Royal Agricultural Hall, Islington (1861), remain as living reflections of the Crystal Palace projected into the twenty-first century. These are now lit, permanently, by electricity;

in the 1840s, however, Euston and Paddington went to sleep at night, their gas lamps turned down to a minimum, until a night train drew up in the distance awaiting a signal to enter. Then, magic: 'That instant every gaslight on and above a curve of 900 feet burst into full power. The carriages, cabs &c appear, comparatively speaking, in broad daylight, and the beautiful iron reticulation which sustains the glazed roof appears like fairy work.'

William MacRitchie, a church minister from Clunie, Perthshire, visited London in 1795. He came and left by horse-drawn carriage, lit not by gas or electricity but, if lit at all, by candle or oil light. MacRitchie wrote this in his diary:

Monday 10th August 1795: Leave London. Look back with indescribable mixture of feelings on this vast metropolis well termed 'a world of wonders in itself'. Think on all I have seen, and suffered, and enjoyed, in the City and its environs. Ruminate on its magnificence; its extent; its populousness; its riches; its poverty; its dissipation; its luxuries; its vanities; its vices; its virtues.

Some things never change.

Dramatis Personae

The men and women whose lives interact within the pages of this book

Ackermann, Rudolph (1764–1834)	Designer, entrepreneur, salesman
Allom, Thomas (1804–72)	Architect, artist
Angerstein, John Julius (1735–1823)	Banker, collector
Arbuthnot, Harriet (1793–1834)	Diarist
Atkins, Anna (1799–1871)	Botanist, pioneer photographer
Aubert, Alexander (1730–1805)	Astronomer
Austen, Jane (1775–1817)	Author
Ayrton, William (1777–158)	Musician, writer on music
Babbage, Charles (1792–1871)	Mathematician, mechanician
Banks, Sir Joseph (1743–1820)	Botanist, President of the Royal Society
Barry, Sir Charles (1795–1860)	Architect
Barry, James, RA (1741–1806)	Artist
Beard, Richard (1801–85)	Coal merchant, entrepreneur of photography
Beare, Shirley David	Hotelier
Beaumont, Sir George, Bt (1753–1827)	Collector, patron, benefactor
Belzoni, Giovanni Battista (1778–1823)	Strongman, Egyptologist
Beuth, Peter Christian William	German official, visitor to London in 1826
Bewick, Thomas (1753–1828)	Artist, wood engraver, author
Blake, William (1757–1827)	Artist, poet
Boulton, Matthew (1728–1809)	Engineer, entrepreneur
Bowerbank, James (1797–1877)	Geologist, botanist
Boydell, Josiah (1752–1817)	Artist, art dealer, local politician

Braithwaite, John (1797–1870)	Engineer
Bramah, Joseph (1748–1814)	Engineer, inventor
Brewster, David (1781–1868)	Scientist
Britton, John (1771–1857)	Artist, art dealer, publisher
Brockedon, William (1787–1854)	Artist, traveller, inventor
Brunel, Isambard Kingdom (1806–59)	Engineer
Brunel, Sir Marc Isambard (1769–1849)	Engineer, inventor
Bullock, George (1782/3–1818)	Furniture designer, salesman
Bullock, William (early 1780s–after 1843)	Showman, collector, entrepreneur
Burford, Robert (1791–1861)	Panorama owner, entrepreneur
Burton, Decimus (1800–81)	Architect
Callcott, Sir Augustus Wall, RA (1779–1844)	Artist, administrator
Callcott, Maria (1785–1842)	Traveller, author
Canova, Antonio (1757–1822)	Sculptor, visitor to London in 1815
Carlisle, Anthony (1768–1840)	Physician, teacher
Carlisle, Nicholas (1771–1847)	Antiquary
Carlyle, Thomas (1795–1881)	Author
Cavallo, Tiberius, FRS (1749–1809)	Balloonist
Cayley, Sir George (1773–1857)	Inventor, aeronaut
Chantrey, Sir Francis Leggatt, RA (1781–1841)	Sculptor
Children, John (1777–1852)	Scientist
Claudet, Antoine (1797–1867)	Photographer
Clement, Joseph (1779–1844)	Machinist, inventor
Cobbett, William (1762–1835)	Politician, traveller, author
Cochrane, Thomas, Lord (1775–1860)	Naval officer, politician
Cockerell, Charles Robert, RA (1783–1863)	Architect
Cocking, Robert (1775/6–1837)	Balloonist, inventor
Cole, Henry (1808–82)	Administrator
Coleridge, Samuel Taylor (1772–1834)	Poet
Conrath, Thomas	Museum attendant
Constable, John (1776–1837)	Artist

Constable, William (1763–1861)	Traveller, photographer
Cooper, John Thomas	Photographer
Coxe, Arthur Cleveland	US Churchman, visitor to London in 1851
Cracherode, Clayton Mordaunt (1730–99)	Collector
Craig, William Marshall (d. 1827)	Artist
Crowe, Rev. William (1745–1829)	Churchman, poet, teacher
Cubitt, Thomas (1788–1855)	Property developer
Davenport, Allen (1775–1846)	Shoemaker, radical and poet
Davies, John (1796–1865)	Architect
Davy, Jane (1780–1855)	Hostess, wife to Sir Humphry Davy
Davy, Sir Humphry (1778–1829)	Scientist, author, traveller
De Quincey, Thomas (1785–1859)	Author
Delamotte, Philip (1821–89)	Photographer
Deyerlein, George (d. 1829)	Lathemaker
Dighton, Robert (1751–1814)	Engraver, singer and thief
Donaldson, Thomas L. (1795–1885)	Architect
Donkin, Bryan (1768–1855)	Engineer
Edgeworth, Maria (1767–1849)	Author
Egan, Pierce (1772–1849)	Author, journalist
Englefield, Sir Henry, Bt (1752–1822)	Antiquary, scientist
Ericsson, John	Engineer
Etty, William, RA (1787–1849)	Artist
Faraday, Michael (1791–1867)	Scientist, teacher, churchman
Farey, John (1791–1851)	Engineer, author
Farey, John, the elder (1766–1826)	Geologist, surveyor
Farington, Joseph, RA (1747–1821)	Artist, diarist
Fawkes, Walter (1769–1825)	Landowner, radical
Finch, Robert (1783–1830)	Traveller, diarist,
Fly, Rev. Dr Henry, FRS (1744–1833)	Churchman
Fuseli, Henry (1741–1825)	Artist

Galloway, Alexander (1776–1847)	Engineer, local politician
Garnerin, André (1769–1823)	Balloonist
Garnett, Thomas (1766–1802)	Physician, writer, natural philosopher
Géricault, Théodore (1791–1824)	Artist, visitor to London 1820–1
Goldham, John	Billingsgate fishmonger
Gordon, Lieutenant-Colonel James Willoughby (mid-1770s–1851)	Soldier
Gordon, Julia Willoughby	Artist
Gough, Richard (1735–1809)	Antiquary
Gray, Edward Whitaker (1748–1806)	Museum curator
Green, Charles (1785–1870)	Balloonist
Gurney, Sir Goldsworthy (1793–1875)	Inventor
Hall, Basil (1788–1844)	Naval officer, traveller, writer
Hallam, Henry (1777–1859)	Historian
Hamilton, William Richard (1777–1859)	Administrator
Hancock, Walter (1799–1852)	Engineer, inventor
Harding, James Duffield (1797–1863)	Artist, lithographer
Havell, Robert (1769–1832)	Artist, artists' colourman
Havell, William (1782–1857)	Artist, pioneer of photography
Hawkins, Edward (1790–1867)	Numismatist, museum curator
Hawthorne, Nathaniel (1804–64)	US writer, visitor to London in 1855
Haydon, Benjamin Robert (1786–1846)	Artist, diarist
Henry, Joseph (1797–1878)	US scientist, visitor to London in 1837
Herschel, Sir John (1792–1871)	Astronomer, pioneer of photography
Herschel, Sir William (1738–1822)	Astronomer
Herzen, Alexander (1812–70)	Russian émigré in London, writer
Hogg, John	Physician, author
Holland, Henry (1788–1873)	Physician
Hollond, Robert (1808–77)	Balloonist, politician
Holtzapffel, John Jacob (1768–1835)	Lathemaker

Hope, Thomas (1769–1831)	Designer, collector, author, host
Hoppus, John (1789–1875)	Theologian, philosopher, teacher
Hullmandel, Charles (1789–1850)	Pioneer of lithography
Hullmandel, Nicholas-Joseph (1756–1823)	Musician, French émigré
Hume, Joseph, MP (1777–1855)	Radical politician
Jackson, John, RA (1778–1831)	Artist
Jackson, Sir Richard	Soldier
Jameson, Anna (1794–1860)	Pioneer art historian
Jenner, Edward (1749–1823)	Physician, discoverer of vaccination
Jerdan, William (1782–1869)	Journalist
Jones, Captain George, RA (1786–1869)	Soldier, artist
Jones, Owen (1809–74)	Designer
Kater, Henry (1777–1835)	Scientist
Keats, John (1795–1821)	Poet
Kingston, John	Government official
Knight, Thomas Andrew (1759–1838)	Botanist
Laing, David (1774–1856)	Architect
Lamb, Charles (1775–1834)	Author
Lamb, Mary (1764–1847)	Author
Landseer, Charles (1799–1879)	Painter
Landseer, John (1769–1852)	Engraver
Lawrence, Sir Thomas (1769–1830)	Artist, President of the Royal Academy
Leslie, Charles Robert, RA (1794–1859)	Artist, author
Lever, Ashton (1729–88)	Collector, museum curator
Lloyd, Mary (née Potter) (b. c.1825)	A child across the span of this book
Lovelace, Ada, née Byron (1815–52)	Mathematician
Lunardi, Vincenzo (1759–1806)	Balloonist
Lupton, Thomas (1791–1873)	Artist, engraver
Lyell, Charles (1797–1875)	Geologist
Lysons, Samuel (1763–1819)	Antiquary

Macaulay, Thomas Babington (1800–59)	Historian, politician
MacRitchie, Rev. William	Churchman, diarist
Manby, Captain George (1765–1854)	Inventor, entrepreneur
Marcet, Alexander (1770–1822)	Physician
Marcet, Jane (née Haldimand) (1769–1858)	Scientific writer
Martin, John (1789–1854)	Artist
Maudslay, Henry (1771–1831)	Engineer, entrepreneur
Mayall, John (1813–1901)	Pioneer of photography
Monck Mason, Thomas	Balloonist, theatrical producer
Monkhouse, Thomas	City merchant
Muir, William (1805–88)	Machine-tool maker, inventor
Murchison, Roderick (1792–1871)	Geologist
Murray, John (1778–1843)	Publisher
Nares, Edward (1762–1841)	Churchman, historian
Nash, John (1752–1835)	Architect
Nasmyth, Alexander (1758–1840)	Artist
Nasmyth, James (1808–90)	Engineer, artist
Newton, Sir William (1785–1869)	Artist, pioneer of photography
Nicholson, Renton (1809–61)	Publican
Otter, Rev. William (1768–1840)	Churchman, teacher
Paganini, Nicolò (1782–1840)	Violinist, visitor to London in 1831
Parkinson, James (1730–1813)	Collector, museum curator
Passavant, Johann (1787–1861)	Painter, traveller, author
Paxton, Sir Joseph (1801–65)	Gardener, structural engineer
Peale, Charles Willson (1741–1827)	American naturalist, visitor to London
Perkins, Jacob (1766–1849)	Engineer, inventor
Pettigrew, Thomas (1791–1865)	Surgeon, antiquary
Phillips, Sir Richard (1767–1840)	Author, publisher, journalist
Phillips, Thomas (1770–1845)	Portrait painter
Phipps, General Edmund (1760–1837)	Soldier, politician, host
Place, Francis (1771–1854)	Leather worker, tailor, radical politician

Pond, John (1767–1836) — Astronomer
Poole, John (1785/6–1872) — Dramatist
Porden, Elizabeth (1795–1825) — Poet
Porden, William (bapt. 1755–1822) — Architect
Porson, Richard (1759–1808) — Classicist, teacher
Poynter, Ambrose (1796–1886) — Architect
Pugin, Augustus (1812–52) — Architect
Pye, John (1782–1874) — Artist, engraver

Raumer, Friedrich von (1781–1873) — German historian, visitor to London 1830s
Redding, Cyrus (1785–1870) — Journalist
Reinagle, Richard (1775–1862) — Artist, teacher
Rice, Charles — Museum attendant, tavern singer
Richardson, Rev. John — Churchman, author
Rigaud, Stephen Peter (1774–1839) — Mathematician
Rippingille, Edward (1798–1859) — Artist, critic
Ritchie, Joseph (?1788–1819) — Surgeon, explorer in Africa
Roberts, David (1796–1864) — Artist
Robinson, Thomas (1806–85) — Artist, wood engraver
Rogers, Samuel (1763–1855) — Banker, collector
Rossi, Charles (1762–1839) — Sculptor
Rudge, Edward (1763–1846) — Antiquary, botanist
Rumford, Benjamin Thompson, Count (1753–1814) — Scientist, inventor, administrator

Sadler, James (1753–1828) — Balloonist, gas engineer
Sadler, John (1779–1838) — Balloonist
Sadler, William Windham (1796–1824) — Balloonist
Sala, George Augustus (1828–96) — Journalist, playwright
Sass, Henry (1787–1844) — Artist, teacher, host
Saunders, George (1762–1839) — Architect
Say, William (1768–1834) — Artist, engraver
Scharf, George (1788–1860) — Artist, lithographer
Schinkel, Karl Friedrich (1781–1841) — Architect, visitor to London in 1826
Schopenhauer, Johanna — Visitor to London in 1800
Seaward, Samuel (1800–42) — Engineer, inventor
Selous, Henry Courtney (1803–90) — Artist

Shee, Sir Martin Archer (1769–1850) Artist, President of the Royal
Academy

Shuckburgh-Evelyn, Sir George, Scientist
Bt (1751–1804)

Siddons, Mrs Sarah (1755–1831) Actress

Simond, Louis American visitor to London
in 1810–11

Singer, George (1786–1817) Electrician

Smirke, Robert (1780–1867) Architect

Smirke, Sydney (1798–1877) Architect

Soane, Sir John, RA (1753–1837) Architect

Somerville, Mary (1780–1872) Mathematician, scientific author

Somerville, William (1771–1860) Traveller, physician

Southey, Robert (1774–1843) Poet

Sowerby, James (1757–1822) Naturalist, artist

Stanfield, Clarkson, RA Artist
(1793–1867)

Stodart, James (1760–1823) Cutler, entrepreneur

Talbot, William Henry Fox Artist, photographer
(1800–77)

Tatum, John (?c.1776– ?) Scientist, teacher

Taylor, John (1757–1832) Journalist

Taylor, Michael Angelo, MP Politician
(1756/7–1834)

Thackeray, William Makepeace Author
(1811–63)

Thompson, Charles Thurston Photographer
(1816–68)

Thompson, John (1785–1860) Artist, wood engraver

Thomson, Henry, RA (1773–1843) Artist

Ticknor, George (1791–1871) US historian, visitor to London
in 1835

Townley, Charles (1737–1805) Collector, host, benefactor

Trench, Colonel Sir Frederick Soldier, engineer, politician
(c.1777–1859)

Turner, Benjamin Brecknell Pioneer of photography
(1815–94)

Turner, Dawson (1775–1858) Banker, botanist

Turner, Joseph Mallord William, RA (1775–1851)	Artist, teacher
Turrell, Edmund (d. 1838)	Engraver
Varley, Cornelius (1781–1873)	Artist, inventor
Walker, James (1781–1862)	Engineer
Walker, Thomas (1734–1836)	Lawyer, author
Ward, James, RA (1769–1859)	Artist
Watt, James (1736–1819)	Engineer, inventor
Wedgwood, Thomas (1771–1805)	Pioneer of photography
Westmacott, Sir Richard, RA (1775–1856)	Sculptor
Wheatstone, Sir Charles (1802–75)	Scientist, teacher
Whitworth, Joseph (1803–87)	Engineer, inventor
Wilkie, Sir David, RA (1785–1841)	Artist
Willmore, J. T. (1800–63)	Artist, engraver, pioneer of photography
Wordsworth, William (1770–1850)	Poet
Wyatt, James (1746–1813)	Architect
Wyatt, Matthew Cotes (1777–1862)	Sculptor

Notes

ABBREVIATIONS

Ants	Society of Antiquaries of London
Babbage	Charles Babbage, *Passages from the Life of a Philosopher*, 1864
Balston	Thomas Balston, *John Martin 1789–1854: His Life and Work*, 1947
Baron	Xavier Baron (ed.), *London 1066–1914: Literary Sources and Documents*, vol. 2: *Regency and Early Victorian 1800–1870*, 1977
BL	British Library
BM	British Museum
Bodleian	Bodleian Library, University of Oxford
Carlyle, *Letters*	C. R. Saunders *et al.* (eds), *The Collected Letters of Thomas and Jane Welsh Carlyle*, 30 vols
Coleridge, *Notebooks*	Kathleen Coburn (ed.), *The Notebooks of Samuel Taylor Coleridge*, 1957–2002, 5 vols
Constable, *Correspondence*	R. B. Beckett (ed.), *John Constable's Correspondence*, 1962–75, 8 vols
Davy, *Works*	John Davy (ed.), *The Collected Works of Sir Humphry Davy Bart*, 1839, 9 vols
Evans	Joan Evans, *A History of the Society of Antiquaries*, 1956
FD	Kenneth Garlick, Angus MacIntyre and Kathleen Cave (eds), *The Diary of Joseph Farington*, 1978–98, 17 vols
FJ	Frank A. J. L. James (ed.), *The Correspondence of Michael Faraday*, 1991–, 6 vols

Gage	John Gage (ed.), *Collected Correspondence of J. M. W. Turner*, 1980
Gent's Mag.	*The Gentleman's Magazine*
Hamilton, *Faraday*	James Hamilton, *Faraday – The Life*, 2002
Hamilton, *Turner*	James Hamilton, *Turner – A Life*, 1997
Hansard	*Hansard's Official Parliamentary Report*
Haydon, *A&J*	Benjamin Robert Haydon, *Autobiography and Journal*, ed. Tom Taylor, 2nd edn, 1853, 3 vols
Haydon, *Diary*	W. B. Pope (ed.), *The Diary of Benjamin Robert Haydon*, 1960–3, 5 vols
Hist. Phot.	*History of Photography*
IET	Institution of Engineering and Technology, London
ILN	*Illustrated London News*
Jerdan	*The Autobiography of William Jerdan*, 1852–3, 4 vols
Jones	George Jones, *Sir Francis Chantrey RA: Recollections of his Life, Practice and Opinions*, 1849
Lit. Gaz.	*Literary Gazette*
NLS	National Library of Scotland, Edinburgh
ODNB	*Oxford Dictionary of National Biography*, 2004
Phil. Mag.	*Philosophical Magazine*
Phil. Trans.	*Philosophical Transactions of the Royal Society*
RA	Royal Academy of Arts, London
Redding	Cyrus Redding, *Fifty Years' Recollections, Literary and Personal*, 1858, 3 vols
RI	Royal Institution, London
RIBA	Royal Institute of British Architects, London
Richardson, *Recollections*	Rev. John Richardson, *Recollections of the Last Half-Century*, 1855, 2 vols
RI, *MM*	Frank Greenaway, Maurice Berman, Sophie Forgan and Donovan Chilton (eds), *Archives of the Royal Institution, Minutes of the Managers' Meetings, 1799–1903*, 15 vols, bound into 7 vols, 1971–6
RS	Royal Society, London
RSA	Royal Society of Arts, London

Schinkel	David Bindman and Gottfried Riemann (eds), *Karl Friedrich Schinkel, 'The English Journey', Journal of a Visit to France and Britain in 1826*, 1993
Simond	Christopher Hibbert (ed.), *An American in Regency England* [Louis Simond] – *The Journal of a Tour in 1810–11*, 1968
Thornbury	Walter Thornbury, *The Life and Correspondence of J. M. W. Turner RA*, 1862 (new edn 1897)
V&A, NAL	Victoria and Albert Museum, London, National Art Library
Walker	Thomas Walker, *Aristology, or the Art of Dining*, 1835; new edn ed. Felix Summerly [pseud. Henry Cole], 1881

PROLOGUE

1   'with a violence': Thomas Carlyle to Alexander Carlyle, 14 Dec 1824. Carlyle, *Letters*, vol. 3, p. 218.

2   'as a picturesque object': Nathaniel Hawthorne, *English Notebooks*, 1870, p. 319.

3   Humphry Davy's 'river of knowledge' metaphor: Davy, *Works*, vol. 8, p. 163.

4   'It is her largeness': Samuel Taylor Coleridge, 'The blossoming of the solitary date-tree', 1805.

5   John Goldham's evidence: *Report of Commissioners … on the Supply of Water to the Metropolis*, 1828, p. 71.

6   'nervous and romantic temperaments': *My Past and Thoughts. The Memoirs of Alexander Herzen*, trans. Constance Garnett, 1968, vol. 3, p. 1025.

6   'If one is not to be crushed': Herzen, *ibid.*, p. 1184.

CHAPTER 1: A DISPLAY OF SPLENDOUR

7   'My cellar's my camp': From a drinking song by George Alexander Stevens (1710?–84), actor and writer who was a habitué of the Cider

Cellar in 1780s. Quoted Henry C. Shelley, *Inns and Taverns of Old London*, 1909, p. 123.

8   Porson's calligraphy: his handwritten letter forms became the source for the modern printers' Greek font. See also William Jerdan, 'Richard Porson', *Men I Have Known*, 1866, p. 352.

8   'sluggish indolence of manner': FD, 18 Jan 1797, vol. III, pp. 752–3.

8   Farington reveals his height at FD, 5 Dec 1808, vol. IX, p. 3394.

8   In the latest complete edition Farington's diaries (Coll. HM the Queen, Royal Library, Windsor Castle) have been published in sixteen volumes (5761 pp.) and an index volume. Kenneth Garlick, Angus MacIntyre and Kathryn Cave (eds), *The Diary of Joseph Farington*, 1978–98.

9   'by speaking of his long previous fast': E. H. Barker, *Literary Anecdotes and Contemporary Reminiscences of Prof. Porson and Others* (1852), vol. 2, p. 11. William Maltby (1763–1854) succeeded Porson as Principal Librarian at the London Institution.

9   to drain the glasses left behind: Morchard Bishop (ed.), *Recollections of the Table-Talk of Samuel Rogers*, 1952, pp. 158ff.

9   Porson would drink ink: *Ibid.*, p. 163.

10   'pour forth a hundred lines of Homer': Barker, *op. cit.*, vol. 2, p. 62.

10   'every great Philosopher here': Anon, *Adventures Under-Ground: A Letter from a Gentleman Swallowed up in the Late Earthquake, to a Friend on his Travels*, 1750, p. 12.

10   'accidental and capricious': Jerdan, *op. cit*, p. 348.

11   'into which the mind of man could dive': *Ibid.*, p. 351. See also William Jerdan, *National Portrait Gallery of Illustrious and Eminent Personages of the Nineteenth Century*, 1831, vol. 2, unpaginated: 'It was a rich treat to listen to him in his best moods: though not eloquent, but, on the contrary, often perplexed and embarrassed, there was nothing pedantic, and his resources were astonishing – inexhaustible.'

11   'indecent sea bathing': 'Viator' [a.k.a. William Jerdan], *Observations on Indecent Sea-Bathing as Practised at Different Watering-Places on the Coast of this Kingdom*, 1805.

11   Jerdan's charm: Richardson, *Recollections*, vol. 2, pp. 196–7.

11   Murder of Spencer Perceval: Jerdan provides a plan of the House of Commons lobby, marking the positions of the people who were present when the shooting took place. Jerdan, vol. 1, p. 295.

12 Carlisle and the excrescence: FD, 5 Dec 1805, vol. VII, pp. 2655–6.

12 'men, like gamecocks,': *Ibid.*

12 George Butler's bequest: *Ibid.*, 3 Jan 1806, vol. VII, p. 2668.

12 Nelson's meal of macaroni: *Ibid.*, 19 Dec 1805, vol. VII, p. 2664.

13 'all in a blaze of light': Simond, pp. 30–1.

13 London in 1810: *Ibid.* p. 147.

14 'nine dukes to dine here': Bryant Lillywhite, *London Coffee Houses*, 1963, p. 548 (no. 1262).

14 Jonathan's Coffee House: Leopold Wagner, *London Inns and Tavens*, 1924, p. 68.

14 William Jerdan knew the inns: Jerdan, vol. 1, p. 90.

14 London carriage stops: *Post-Office Annual Directory*, 1806.

14 'the moment the *clock strikes*': William Gilly to Stephen P. Rigaud, 16 Apr 1830, Bodleian, MS Rigaud 61, vol. II, F-M, f. 55.

15 The sewers discharging into the river: Robert Southey, *Letters from England*, LXVI, 1808. Quoted Baron, pp. 49–50.

15 Turner's birthplace: Thornbury, p. 2.

16 Sandemanian chapel: *Manchester Guardian*, 27 Nov 1886.

16 'dark with light': Samuel Carter Hall, *Retrospect of a Long Life, from 1815 to 1883*, 1883, vol. 1, pp. 3–4.

16 'fat with human remains': John Hogg, *London as It Is*, 1837, p. 218.

16 William Wordsworth, 'Composed upon Westminster Bridge, September 3 1802'.

16 Pitt the elder's overturned coffin: Redding, vol. 1, p. 24.

16 Waterlogged army records: Letter J. Byron to Sir John Barrow, 3 Apr 1838, Bodleian, MS Rigaud, 60, f. 130.

17 John Bronowski, Introduction to *William Blake*, The Penguin Poets series, 1958, p. 9.

17 'the Furnaces of iron': William Blake, *Jerusalem. The Emanation of the Giant Albion*, 1804–c.1820, ch. 4, v. 89.

17 William Wordsworth, *The Prelude*, 1850, Book 7.

17 Jenner's handkerchief: FD, 17 Feb 1809, vol. IX, p. 3042.

17 'Teutha'; Jerdan, vol. 1, p. 118.

18 'antagonistically crowded precincts': *Ibid.*, vol. 2, p. 274.

18 The smell of London on a letter: Redding, vol. 2, p. 131.

18 Walking on the frozen river: *Ibid.*, vol. 1, p. 227.

18 One-way traffic in Albemarle Street: *ODNB*, entry on Humphry Davy, by David Knight.

18 'rattling engines': Charles Lamb, 'In Praise of Chimney-Sweepers', from *Essays of Elia*, 1823, Everyman edn, 1906, p. 128.

19 'carriages . . . inextricably massed': Thomas De Quincey, 'The Nation of London', *Autobiographic Sketches*, 1863, p. 184.

19 'the roar of Niagara': *Ibid.*, p. 182.

19 Angerstein on the growth of London: FD, 27 May 1814, vol. XIII, p. 4525.

19 'The great lengths of the streets': De Quincey, *op. cit.*, p. 184.

20 The Devonian sent out of his mind: Redding, vol. 1, p. 50.

20 Starlings: 27 Nov 1799. Coleridge, *Notebooks*, vol. 1 (1794–1804), p. 582.

21 'a pearl . . . through a burnt glass': John Constable to John Dunthorne Snr, n.d. [1801], Constable, *Correspondence*, vol. II, p. 26.

22 'occupants above and below': Friedrich von Raumer, *England in 1835*, 1836, vol. 1, p. 99.

22 'like a foolscap crown': Byron, *Don Juan*, canto X, v. 82.

22 'like the smoke of the Israelites': Haydon, *A&J*, vol. 1, p. 55.

23 'nearly a million of coal fires': Sir Richard Phillips, *A Morning's Walk from London to Kew*, 1817, pp. 130–1.

23 Smoke made London warmer: FD, 31 Dec 1796, vol. III, p. 734.

24 Edward Roberts's evidence: *Select Committee on Steam Engines and Furnaces*, 1819, p. 8.

24 Francis Chantrey on columns: Jones, Appendix, p. 298.

24 Smoke tunnel to Oxford: R. C. Kidd to Stephen P. Rigaud, 23 Oct 1829, Bodleian, MS Rigaud 61, vol. II, F-M, f. 213.

24 Robert Southey, *Letters from England*, Letter VII, 1808. Quoted Baron, p. 39.

24 'learned simplicity of the instruments': 24 Jan 1810, Simond, p. 28.

24 Lamb's 'natural hypochondria': Charles Lamb, 'The Londoner', 1802. Quoted Baron, p. 28.

25 'London itself is a pantomime': Charles Lamb to William Wordsworth, 30 Jan 1801. Quoted Baron, pp. 25–6.

25 'atmosphere composed of gold dust': Mary Anne Flaxman to Maria Denman, 12/14 July 1824, Flaxman Papers, vol. 3, BL Add. MS 39783, f. 28.

25 Farington in Norfolk: FD, 6 Nov 1805, vol. VII, p. 2645.

25 Jerdan in the navy: Jerdan, vol. 1, p. 76.

26 Turner's painting: *The Battle of Trafalgar, as seen from the Mizzen Starboard Shrouds of the Victory*, 1806, Turner Bequest, Tate Britain.

26 Early account of Faraday: William Goodhugh to William Jerdan, 14 Dec n.y. [c.1830s], Bodleian, Jerdan Papers, d. 113, ff. 223–4.

26 Fuseli's studio: Haydon, *A&J*, vol. 1, p. 28.

27 John Tatum: An advertisement in *The Times*, 28 Sept 1815, says that Tatum is opening his tenth annual series of lectures.

27 Redding leaves Reading: Redding, vol. 1, pp. 22–4.

27 Smirke and Lowther: FD, 15 and 16 Dec 1805, vol. VII, p. 2661.

27 Willoughby Gordon's marriage: Lord Moira to James Willoughby Gordon, 27 Oct 1805, Willoughby Gordon Papers, BL Add. MS 49500, ff. 116–17.

28 *Gent's Mag.*, vol. 76, pt 1 (Feb. 1806), pp. 65–72.

29 Nelson's motto: 'Let he who deserves it bear the palm.'

29 Farington's weather report: FD, 9 Jan 1806, vol. VII, p. 2670.

29 Josiah Boydell: FD, 4 and 7 Dec 1805, vol. VII, pp. 2654 and 2656.

29 'Arabian night's entertainments': FD, 18 Jan 1806, vol. VII, p. 2672.

29 Haydon's recollection of Nelson's funeral: Haydon, *A&J*, vol. 1, p. 41.

CHAPTER 2: CHAPEL, PARLIAMENT, THEATRE AND PANTHEON

31 Carlisle's appearance: J. F. Clarke, writing in the 1830s, when Carlisle was in his seventies. Quoted Brian Hill, 'The Crustacean Knight: Sir Anthony Carlisle FRCS, FRS 1768–1840', *The Practitioner*, vol. 206 (Dec 1968), pp. 950–5.

31 full court dress and a bag-wig: Constable, *Correspondence*, vol. VI, p. 186n.

31 Croonian lecture title: Journal Book, Part 1, 7 Nov 1805, part 2, 14 Nov 1805, RS Archives.

31 Terms of the bequest of William Croone: *The Record of the Royal Society*, 4th edn, 1940, p. 118.

32 Charles Lamb on Carlisle: Hill, *op. cit.*, n. 1.

32 Carlisle's experiments: *Phil. Mag.*, vol. 6 (1800), p. 372, and vol. 7 (1800), pp. 337–47; Thomas Wedgwood and Humphry Davy, 'An Account of a Method of Copying Paintings upon Glass and of Making Profiles by the Agency of Light upon Nitrate of Silver', *Journal of the Royal Institution*, vol. 1 (1802), p. 170.

32 Carlisle the fisherman: FD, 2 Aug 1809, vol. X, p. 3520.

32 'half starved Academicians': Haydon, *Diary*, 15 Oct 1808, vol. 1, p. 22.

32 Anthony Carlisle, 'Account of a monstrous lamb', *Phil. Trans.*, vol. 91 (1801), pp. 139–43.

32 Anthony Carlisle, 'Account of a Family Having Supernumerary Fingers and Toes', *Phil. Mag.*, vol. 44 (1814), pp. 17–21. See also Hamilton, *Faraday*, p. 132.

32 'He is considered *insane*': John Constable to Archdeacon Fisher, 17 Dec 1824, Constable, *Correspondence*, vol. VI, p. 186.

32 Anthony Carlisle, 'The Croonian Lecture on the Arrangement and Mechanical Action of the Muscles of Fishes', *Phil. Trans.*, vol. 96 (1806), pp. 1–12.

33 Interior of the Royal Society lecture room: 'Plans and descriptions of the rooms of the Royal Society and the Society of Antiquaries', RS Misc. MS XIII, 58/1–7.

34 The Society did not meet at Easter, Whitsun and Christmas.

34 Sybille Bedford, *A Legacy*, 1956; Penguin edn, 1964, p. 32.

34 'Elephant's tusk': Read on behalf of a non-member, Charles Combe, on 19 Feb 1801. *Phil. Trans.*, vol. 91 (1801), pp. 165–8.

34 William Herschel, 'On the power of penetrating into space by telescopes; with comparative determination of the extent of that power in natural vision, and in telescopes of various sizes and constructions', *Phil. Trans.*, vol. 90 (1800), pp. 49–85. Read 12 Dec 1799.

34 William Herschel, 'Observations of the changeable brightness of the satellites of Jupiter', *Phil. Trans.*, vol. 87 (1797), pp. 332–51. Read 1 Jun 1797.

34 Herschel's lecture on the nature of the sun: *Phil. Trans.*, vol. 91 (1801), pp. 265–318, 354–62. Read 16 Apr and 14 May 1801.

35 Charles Hatchett, 'Analysis of the earthy substance from New South Wales called Sydneia', *Phil. Trans.*, vol. 88 (1798), pp. 110–29. Read 8 and 15 Feb 1798.

35 George Shuckburgh-Evelyn, 'An account of some endeavours to ascertain a standard of weight and measure', *Phil. Trans.*, vol. 88 (1798), pp. 133–82. Read 1 Mar 1798.

35 Thomas Andrew Knight, 'On the ascent of the sap in trees', *Phil. Trans.*, vol. 91, pt 2 (1801), pp. 333–53. Read 14 May 1801.

35 Anthony Carlisle, 'On Muscular Motion', *Phil. Trans.*, vol. 95 (1805), pp. 1–30.

36 Samuel Rogers's nomination as FRS: EC/1796/13, RS Archive.

37 'the indefatigable Mr T. A. Knight': *Phil. Mag.*, vol. 39 (1812), p. 386.

37   The full list of 1805 Fellows is:

Warburg, Claus; no record

Rudge, Edward; Botanist and antiquary, FSA, traveller to Guiana

Morris, George Paulet MD; physician to Westminster Hospital

Blaquière, Hon. William; no record

Ferguson, Robert; Whig MP for Fife; amateur natural historian

Fermor, Hon. Thomas William, later Earl of Pomfret; soldier, became a general, FSA

Knight, Thomas Andrew; vegetable physiologist and horticulturalist

Holford, Robert; traveller

Smith, Sir William Cusac; barrister, Baron of the Court of Exchequer in Ireland

Cust, Hon. John, afterwards Earl Brownlow

Dysart, Frederick William, Earl of Bristol

Babington, William MD; physician and mineralogist

Rigaud, Stephen Peter; mathematician and astronomer

Murdoch, Thomas; late of Madeira

Barrow, John; Secretary to the Admiralty, explorer

Dysart, Wilbraham, Earl of

Loveden, Edward Loveden; of Buscot Park, Berkshire, MP, much married

Whidbey, Joseph; RN sailing master and engineer, sailed round the world with George Vancouver, worked with Rennie at Plymouth harbour

Dimsdale, Nathaniel, Baron of the Russian Empire, lately MP for Hertford

37   Founding of the Society of Antiquaries: BL Harley MS 7055, f. 1. Quoted Evans, p. 36. See also *Archaeologia*, vol. 1 (1770), Introduction, p. xxv; Ants MS 268. Quoted Evans, p. 58.

38   The Society of Antiquaries' ambitions: *Archaeologia*, vol. 1 (1770), Introduction, p. xxix; Ants MS 268. Quoted Evans, p. 58.

39   'over shaded this poor Society': John Vertue to William Stukeley, 8 Sept 1750, BL Add. MS 23091, f. 149. Quoted Evans, p. 103.

39   Proposed merger: David Boyd Haycock, '"The Cabals of a few designing members": The Presidency of Martin Folkes, PRS and the Society's First Charter', *Antiquaries Journal*, vol. 80 (2000), pp. 273–84.

39   'The arrangement and proper use of facts': *Archaeologia*, vol. 1 (1770), Introduction, p. ii.

40   Rev. John Watson, 'Druidical remains in or near the parish of Halifax in Yorkshire', *Archaeologia*, vol. 2 (1773), pp. 353–63 (read 21 Nov 1771); Sir Joseph Ayloffe Bt, 'An account of the body of King Edward the First . . . 1774', *Archaeologia*, vol. 3 (1775), pp. 376–413 (read 12 May 1774); Sir William Hamilton, 'Account of the discoveries at Pompeii', *Archaeologia*, vol. 4 (1777), pp. 160–75 (read 26 Jan, 2 and 9 Feb).

40   Sophie Forgan, 'Lecture Theatres, Laboratories and Repositories: Learned and Scientific Society Buildings', *RSA Journal*, vol. 135 (1987), pp. 702–4, 773–6.

40   Lack of space: Evans, pp. 174–5.

41   Gifts to British Museum: *British Museum Synopsis*, 1808, p. xxvi; A. E. Gunther, *The Founders of Science at the British Museum 1753–1900*, 1980, p. 24.

41   Bone of contention: Evans, pp. 174ff.

41   Support of George III: Raymond Needham and Alexander Webster, *Somerset House Past and Present*, 1905, p. 217.

41   G. A. Sala, *Twice Around the Clock*, 1859, p. 51.

41   *Archaeologia*'s irregular publication: vol. 15: 1806; vol. 16: 1812.

41   'temple of Morpheus': Bernard Nurse, 'George Cruikshank's *The Antiquarian Society*, 1812, and Sir Henry Charles Englefield', *Antiquaries Journal*, vol. 80 (2000), pp. 316–21.

42   'art of inactivity': Evans, p. 245.

42   Lysons's Yorkshire accent: FD, 16 Mar 1807, vol. VIII, p. 2989.

42   Anthony Carlisle, 'A description of five maces', *Archaeologia*, vol. 16 (1812), pp. 338–9. Read 7 Apr 1808.

42   Englefield's adultery: Mark Noble, *Memories of Fellows*, Society of Antiquaries (n.d.), MS 269, f. 87. Quoted Nurse, *op. cit.*, pp. 316–21.

42   Englefield smells of violets: Morchard Bishop (ed.), *Recollections of the Table-Talk of Samuel Rogers*, 1952, p. 109.

42   Robert Smirke, 'Account of some remains of Gothic architecture in Italy and Sicily', *Archaeologia*, vol. 15 (1806), pp. 363–6. Responses: *ibid.*, pp. 367–72 and 373–9.

42   'fat, contented, and rosy official': Jerdan, vol. 4, p. 32.

43   Royal Institution's founding intention: RI, *MM,* vol. 1, p. 1.

43   'as public as possible': Count Rumford to Messrs Cadell and Davies, Printers, 14 May 1800, Montagu Papers, d. 9, f. 341, Bodleian.

44   *The Times*, 12 Apr 1800.

44   Fees: Life membership was thirty guineas.

4   'so prim and respectable': RI, *MM*, 17 Feb 1800, vol. 1, p. 127.

45   Coleridge, *Notebooks*, vol. 1 (1794–1804), p. 1099.

46   William Marshall Craig: RI, *MM*, 10 Feb 1806, vol. 4, p. 144.

47   Discussion of Craig's lecture: FD, 27 Feb, 14 Mar 1806, vol. VII, pp. 2686, 2691. The quintet of conversationalists are, with Farington himself, Samuel Foart Simmonds FRS, FSA (1750–1813), a mad doctor and physician, and Proprietor of the Royal Institution; William Parsons FRS, an antiquary of Sackville Street; Samuel Lysons FRS, FSA (1763–1819), Director of the Society of Antiquaries, archaeologist; and Sir Henry Englefield FSA, FRS (1752–1822), Vice-President of the Society of Antiquaries, archaeologist and designer of scientific instruments. 'Ducros' is the Swiss topographical artist Louis Ducros (1748–1810) who worked extensively in Italy in the late eighteenth century.

48   Society of Arts 'premium' winners: Society of Arts minute book, Oct 1804–June 1805, pp. 253 ff, RSA Archive.

49   Over-full museum: Society of Arts minute book, 1808–9, pp. 50–1, 30 Nov 1808, RSA Archive.

50   James Barry RA, *Account of the Series of Pictures in the Great Room of the Society of Arts, Manufactures and Commerce at the Adelphi*, 1783.

51   Eric Shanes, 'Dissent in Somerset House: Opposition to the Political status-quo within the Royal Academy around 1800', *Turner Studies*, vol. 10, no. 2 (1990), pp. 40–6.

51   Subjects for Royal Academy 'premiums': RA Council Minutes, vol. 3, 29 Jan 1803.

52   Turner on the RA committee: *Ibid.*, vol. 3, 4 Mar, 26 Mar, 4 Apr 1803; FD, 24 Dec 1803, vol. VI, p. 2202; 11 May 1804, vol. VI, pp. 2319–20; RA Council Minutes, 24 Apr 1811.

CHAPTER 3: THE CIRCUITS THAT ILLUMINATED LONDON.

53   Knowledge as a river: Davy, *Works*, vol. 8, p. 163.

54   'The perception of truth': Anon [Humphry Davy], 'Parallels between Art and Science', *The Director: A Weekly Literary Journal*, no. 19, vol. 2 (30 May 1807), pp. 193–8.

54   'the fluency of an Italian improvisatore': John Ayrton Paris, *The Life of*

Sir Humphry Davy Bart, LLD, 1831, vol. 1, p. 6.

54 'everything seemed alive': Davy, *Works*, vol. 1, p. 119.

54 'a votary of fashion': *Ibid.*, p. 263.

54 'a smirk on his countenance': Paris, *op. cit.*, vol. 1, p. 120. Quoted in the book's review in *Lit. Gaz.*, 1 Oct 1831, p. 632.

54 'humming some angler's song': Davy, *Works*, vol. 1, p. 100.

54 'poring over crucibles': *Ibid.*, p. 136.

54 Laetitia Barbauld, *Eighteen Hundred and Eleven, a Poem*, 1812.

55 Davy's verse: Paris, *op. cit.*, p. 119.

55 Great Missenden: Hamilton, *Turner*, p. 119.

56 'Nature and her effects': J. M. W. Turner, Lecture V (1818), BL Add. MS 46151 H, ff. 25v-41v. Quoted in John Gage, *Colour in Turner*, 1969, p. 209.

56 'From what appeared to me to be': Humphry Davy, *Consolations in Travel, or the Last days of a Philosopher*, 1830, Dialogue the First.

56 'to renew my stock of metaphors': Quoted Paris, *op. cit.*, vol. 1, p. 92.

56 'highly pleasurable thrilling': Davy, *Works*, p. 272.

56 'Nothing exists but thoughts': *ibid.*, p. 290.

57 Thomas De Quincey, 'The Nation of London', *The Works of Thomas De Quincey* (ed. Daniel Sanjiv Roberts), 2003, vol. 19, pp. 109–31.

58 Jane Marcet, *Conversations on Chemistry*, 1806; 1817 edn, pp. v–vi.

58 Cyrus Redding, *Yesterday and Today*, 1863, vol. 2, p. 130.

59 *ODNB*, entry on Robert Finch, by Alan Bell.

59 Rev. Henry Fly, DD, FRS, FSA. Sub-Dean of St Paul's, Confessor to the Royal Household, Minister of the Trinity Church, Minories, London. *Gent's Mag.*, May 1833, pp. 281–2.

59 Robert Finch's diary, 6, 10, 16 Dec 1813; Bodleian, Finch Papers, e.6, ff. 49v and 56v. Dr Evans is Lewis Evans (1755–1827), astronomer and mathematical master at the Royal Military Academy, Woolwich.

59 Clarissa Wells: Hamilton, *Turner*, pp. 147–8.

60 Robert Finch's diary, 3, 9 Nov, 10 Dec 1813, 21 Jan 1814, Bodleian, Finch Papers, e.6, ff. 7v, 14v, 50v, 104v.

60 'You shall not quiz poor chemistry': Clarissa Wells to Robert Finch, n.d. [late Jan 1814]. Bodleian, Finch Papers, d. 17, ff. 33–4.

60 Advertisement in *The Times*, 28 Sept 1815.

60 'Explain why smoke ascends': Anon [possibly William Hone], 'Quarterly Night, Oct 2nd 1816', long poem transcribed within

Michael Faraday's Common Place Book, vol. 1, f. 137, IET Archive.

61   City Gas-Light Co. next door: Advertisement in *The Times*, 23 Jan 1817.

61   Michael Faraday's notes to John Tatum's lectures, 4 vols, RI Archive, F4B1–4.

61   Tatum's pupils: Frank A. L. James, 'Michael Faraday, The City Philosophical Society and The Society of Arts', *RSA Journal*, Feb 1992, pp. 192–9; Hamilton, *Faraday*, pp. 137–8.

62   Tatum references: *Phil. Mag.*, vol. 50 (1817), pp. 42–5 and 353–8; vol. 51 (1818), pp. 438–9.

62   Singer: *The Times*, 31 Oct 1808; Singer and Accum: *Phil. Mag.*, vol. 31 (Jun–Sept 1808), pp. 327–8; Sowerby: *Phil. Mag.*, vol. 32 (Oct 1808–Jan 1809), p. 373; Crowe: RI, *MM*, 11 Jul 1808, vol. 4, p. 372. For a full overview of science lecturing and exhibitions in this period see Iwan Rhys Morus, *Frankenstein's Children: Electricity, Exhibition and Experiment in Early-Nineteenth Century London*, 1998.

62   Abbott's letters are lost, but most of Faraday's survive because Abbott kept them meticulously. They ultimately found their way to the archive of the Institution of Electrical Engineers, subsequently the Institution of Engineering and Technology. FJ, vol. 1, passim.

62   'The best form for a lecture room': Michael Faraday to Benjamin Abbott, 1 Jun 1813, MS SC 123, IET Archive. FJ, no. 23.

63   George Saunders: Elected a subscriber to the RI for life in 1800, and, as did Soane and Holland, gave his services free. RI, *MM*, 14 Mar, 12 May 1800, vol. 2, pp. 16, 79.

63   'How have I wished the Lecture finished': Michael Faraday to Benjamin Abbott, 1 Jun 1813, MS SC 123, IET Archive. FJ, no. 23.

63   Sir George Porter and James Friday (eds), *Advice to Lecturers – An Anthology taken from the Writings of Michael Faraday and Lawrence Bragg*, 1974.

63   gentle and deliberate movements: Michael Faraday to Benjamin Abbott, 11 Jun 1813, IET MS SC 123. FJ, no. 25.

64   Wells's botanical illustrations have since disappeared.

64   Robert Finch's diary, 11 Nov 1813, f. 16; Bodleian, Finch Papers, e.6.

64   Change of lecture time at Antiquaries: Evans, p. 126.

65   'which sometimes bordered on 1000 persons': RI, *MM*, 27 Jan 1800, vol. 1, pp. 93–4.

CHAPTER 4: A PELICAN IN A CHICKEN RUN

66 'in all studious and curious persons': British Museum Act, 26 George II, c. 22, Section I, p. 333, and Section IX, p. 341. Quoted Marjorie L. Caygill, 'From Private Collection to Public Museum', *Enlightening the British: Knowledge, Discovery and the Museum in the Eighteenth Century*, 2003, pp. 18–28.

66 Neil Macgregor: *Guardian*, 22 Oct 2005.

66 'the largest, the completest and most the magnificent' house: Pierre Grosley, *A Tour to London; or new Observations on England and its Inhabitants*, trans. Thomas Nugent, 1772, vol. 2, p. 23; 'An Architect' [John Carter], 'Montague [*sic*] House (British Museum), *Gent's Mag.*, vol. 84, pt 1 (May 1814), pp. 458–9.

67 its drains backed up: BM, Committee Minutes, 2 Nov 1758, C476.

67 'The collections . . . are in the greatest confusion': Peter Ascanius to Carl Linnaeus, 1755, J. E. Smith, *Correspondence of Linnaeus*, 1821, vol. 2. BM Cuttings Books, vol. 1, C55.1, BM Archive.

67 Visitor numbers: 1803 – 11,904; 1806 – 11,824; Jan to Jun 1807 – 6,815. These figures were given by the British Museum and reported in *The Times*, 21 Sept 1807. David M. Wilson, *The British Museum – A History*, 2002, p. 81, gives the full year's figure for 1807 as 13,046. This rose to 29,000 in 1812. BM Cuttings Book, vol. 1, p. 29, BM Archive. By comparison, the annual spring and summer exhibition at the Royal Academy in Somerset House attracted men and women in much greater numbers: for example, about sixty thousand people attended the 1799 exhibition, over ten or twelve weeks. RA Council Minutes, vol. 3, 29 Jul 1799; *British Museum Statutes and Rules*, 1808, pp. 113–20.

67 *Visits to the Leverian Museum; containing an account of several of its principal curiosities, both of nature and art: intended for the instruction of young persons in the first principles of natural history*, 1805, pp. iii, 139–40.

68 Rev. William MacRitchie, *Diary of a Tour Throughout Great Britain in 1795*, 1897, p. 90.

68 Winning lottery ticket displayed: *Visits to the Leverian Museum*, 1805, p. 145.

68 C. Willson Peale, *Discourse Introductory to a Course of Lectures on the Science of Nature, 1800*, p. 20.

68 Banks's attitude to Lever: FD, 9 Jul 1806, vol. VIII, p. 2807.

69   William Jerdan, 'William Bullock', *Men I Have Known*, 1866, p. 70.

69   Green flock wallpaper: *Gent's Mag.*, vol. 84, pt 2 (Jun 1814), pp. 557–60.

70   Decorative frescoes: The artists were Charles de la Fosse (1636–1716), Jacques Rousseau (1631–91) and Jean-Baptiste Monnoyer (1634–99).

70   Crocodile: A. E. Gunther, *The Founders of Science at the British Museum 1753–1900*, 1980, p. 23.

71   In 1808 the three departments of the Museum evolved into four: Department of Printed Books, Department of Manuscripts, Department of Natural History and Modern Artificial Curiosities, and Department of Antiquities, Coins and Medals (incorporating Prints and Drawings).

71   Reading Room Register: BM Archive. Joseph Planta (1744–1827), Principal Librarian; Samuel Ayscough (1745–1804), Assistant Librarian.

71   Readers: Britton, 13 May 1809; Sass, 8 Jul 1809, 'recommended by Mr Soane'; Paytherus, 14 Jan 1809.

72   The Magna Carta displayed: *A Lady Travels, Journeys in England and Scotland from the Diaries of Johanna Schopenhauer*, ed. and trans. Ruth Michaelis-Jena and Willy Merson, 1988. Quoted Baron, pp. 173–4.

72   'We had no time allowed to examine anything': Simond, p. 44 (18 Apr 1810).

72   Hatchett's mineral collection: *British Museum Synopsis*, 1808, p. xvii.

72   'scattered and lost in the dust': Gunther, *op. cit.*, p. 32.

73   Sloane's mineral collection: *Ibid.*, p. 33.

73   Lost dodo parts: *Penny Magazine*, vol. 3 (4 Jan 1834), p. 4.

73   Robert Dighton, print thief: Antony Griffiths, 'The Reverend Clayton Mordaunt Cracherode (1730–99)', *Landmarks in Print Collecting*, ed. Antony Griffiths, 1996, pp. 43–64.

73   William Beloe sacked: FD, 9 Jul 1806, vol. VIII, p. 2809.

74   Arrangement of sculpture in Townley Wing: BM Committee Minutes, 13 May 1808, C2379, BM Archive.

74   New garden roller requested: *Ibid.*, 13 May and 11 Jun 1808, C2380 and 2390, BM Archive.

74   Royal opening: *The Times*, 4 Jun 1808. BM Committee Minutes, 11 Jun 1808, C2386–7, BM Archive.

74   George Saunders, *A Treatise on the Design of Theatres*, 1790; facsimile reprint, Benjamin Blom, New York, 1968.

75   'each stone as it fell': Robert Smirke, MS notes on Journal in Greece,

RIBA Library. Quoted St Clair, *op. cit.*, p. 139.

76 Turner's drawings of Lowther Castle reproduced in James Hamilton, *Turner's Britain*, 2003, figs 73–5.

76 'Robert Smirke so ingenious': FD, 16 Dec 1805, Vol. VII, p. 2661.

77 'When a foreigner first arrives at a town': Saunders, *op. cit.*, pp. vii–viii.

77 'about £700 per annum': FD, 2 Apr 1808, vol. IX, p. 3253.

77 Smirke's minimum fee: *ODNB*, entry on Sir Robert Smirke, by Richard Riddell.

78 'one of the worst public servants': Lord Liverpool to 9th Duke of Richmond, 8 Jan 1814, BL, Add. MS 38568, f. 224.

78 Gas lighting in courtyard: BM Committee Minutes, 14 Feb 1818, BM Archive.

78 The dog from Baffin's Bay: *The Times*, 21 Jan 1819.

79 Reading Room moves upstairs: BM Committee Minutes, 8 Jul 1809, C2424, BM Archive.

79 Request to draw from the Elgin Marbles: W. R. Hamilton to Thomas Daniell, 21 Jan 1812, Montagu Papers, d. 7, f. 366, Bodleian.

80 'The first thing I fixed my eyes on': Haydon, *A&J*, vol. 1, p. 92.

81 'stowed away in the damp rooms': *Select Committee on the Condition, Management and Affairs of the British Museum*, 1835, Q3381–3, p. 245.

81 Conrath's diary: Quoted Marjorie Caygill and Christopher Date, *Building the British Museum*, 1999, p. 21.

81 Felicity Owen, 'Sir George Beaumont and the National Gallery', *'Noble and Patriotic' – The Beaumont Gift, 1828*, National Gallery, 1988, p. 11.

81 Attendance figures: 1824 – 112,804; 1829 – 68,100; 1836 – 383,157. Quoted in John Pye, *Patronage of British Art*, 1845, p. 227, and in BM Cuttings Book, vol. 1, C55.1, BM Archive.

81 Faraday's Common Place Book, vol. 1, p. 444, IET. Actually, the Museum closed at 4 p.m. From 1837 it was also open in August and September.

82 Visitor numbers to the Reading Room; water closets installed: BM Standing Committee, 14 Jan 1832, BM Archive.

82 Fifty-five books: *Select Committee . . .* , 1835, Q1315–16, p. 99.

82 Treasury grant of £8,000: 26 Feb 1831.

82 Damage to Townley Venus: 4 Jan, 16 Feb and 10 Mar 1832.

83 'one of the finest rooms in the world': *Select Committee . . .*, 1835, Q3965, p. 285.

83 'its old crazy cupola': *Old Humphrey's Walks in London*, 1843.

83 Auction sale of material from Montagu House: Newspaper unknown, 1843, BM Cuttings Book, vol. 2, p. 80, C55.1, BM Archive.

83 'The building is in a very insecure state': *Select Committee . . .* , 1836, Q5425, p. 128.

83 'I must have expressed myself ill': T. B. Macaulay to Robert Smirke, 10 Oct 1830; Smirke Papers, BL Add. MS 60745, f. 145.

83 'no other colour than that of stone': Robert Smirke to Chairman of Trustees, BM Standing Committee, 10 Aug 1833, BM Archive.

84 'formerly the walls of the Egyptian Gallery': Sydney Smirke, 5 Mar 1859; BM Archive, Original Papers, vol. 62.

84 Seven painters killed: *The Times*, 5 Sept 1837.

84 The extent of public interest: *Select Committee . . .* , 1836, Q5477, p. 448.

84 Delay in building work: *Select Committee on the Plans and Estimates for the Completion of the Building of the British Museum*, 1838, p. 3.

85 Richard Westmacott: BM Standing Committee, 14 Feb 1818, 9 Dec 1820, 13 Jan 1821, BM Archive.

85 Gifts of casts of Elgin Marbles: *Select Committee on the Plans and Estimates for the Completion of the Building of the British Museum*, 1838, Q60–7, p. 14.

85 Charles Rice appointed as attendant: BM Standing Committee, 18 Nov 1837, BM Archive.

85 Laurence Senelick (ed.), *Tavern Singing in Early Victorian London:, The Diaries of Charles Rice for 1840 and 1850*, 1997, p. 12. The entry quoted is for 8 Jan 1840. '"Analysation" by W. Moncrieff. Sung by me Augt 1841 C.R.'; *ibid.*, pp. 246–8.

CHAPTER 5: THE TRAFFIC OF MIND

86 Canova in London: Katharine Eustace, '"Questa Scabrosa Missione" – Canova in Paris and London in 1815', in Katharine Eustace (ed.), *Canova Ideal Heads*, Ashmolean Museum, Oxford, 1997, pp. 9–38 and passim.

86 Wellington hissed at the theatre: Lord Combermere to James Willoughby Gordon, 9 Oct 1815, Willoughby Gordon Papers, BL Add. MS 49507, ff. 170–1.

87 'grand génie': Haydon, *Diary*, 28 Nov 1815, vol. 1, p. 484.

87 Canova at Woburn: Hugh Honor, 'Canova's Three Graces', in

H. Honor and A. Weston-Lewis (eds), *The Three Graces – Antonio Canova*, 1996, pp. 19–45.

87 'sculpture at such a height of perfection': FD, 21 Nov 1815, vol. XIII, p. 4738.

87 'alone worth the journey from Rome': Richard Cook to Dawson Turner, 22 Dec 1815, Dawson Turner Papers, 0.13.11/208, Trinity College Library, Cambridge.

87 'when he smiles': Haydon, *Diary*, 19 Nov 1815, vol. 1, p. 481.

88 'a most pleasing example of the harmony': 5 Dec 1815. Quoted Eustace, *op. cit.*, p. 25.

88 Canova at Carlton House: Timothy Clifford, 'Canova in Context', in Honor and Weston-Lewis (eds), *op. cit.*, 1996, p. 14.

88 'the happy year of 1815': From a letter, written in Italian, by W. R. Hamilton to Canova, 4 May 1816, quoted Eustace, *op. cit.*, p. 30. 'Il felice anno di 1815, che ha stabilito la pace di Europa, e restituito alla bella Italia i suoi capi d'opera.' The recipients were William Richard Hamilton, the Duke of Wellington, Charles Long and Viscount Castlereagh. The *Ideal Heads* that they were given are, respectively, in the Ashmolean Museum, Oxford; the Wellington Museum, Apsley House; the Kimbell Art Museum, Fort Worth, Texas; and a private collection.

88 'The people we hate most in the world': 'Thinks-I-to-Myself' [Edward Nares], *A Serio-Ludicro, Tragico-Comico Tale*, 1812 [many editions, this from 9th edn], p. 201.

89 'a country living, out of sight': *ODNB*, entry on Edward Nares, by Nigel Aston.

89 'In London, wherever you are *not*': 'Thinks-I-to-Myself', *op. cit.*, p. 201.

89 Soirée days: Redding, vol. 1, (1858), p. 247; 'our friendly Monday soirée'. John Martin to William Ayrton, 25 Feb 1831, Ayrton Papers, vol. 5, BL Add. MS 52338, f. 109; M. B. Hall, *All Scientists Now*, 1984, p. 23; Alexander Gilchrist, *The Life of William Etty*, 1855, vol. 2, p. 193; Balston, pp. 84–6; letter Michael Faraday to John Martin, 23 Dec 1828, FJ, no. 382; Ellen Jacobson to Dawson Turner, 23 Jun 1828, Trinity College, Cambridge, Dawson Turner Papers, 2.P1.3; Maria Graham to John Murray, 25 Feb and 6 Mar 1821, Murray Archive, NLS; Jerdan, vol. 3, p. 17.

90 Pot-Luck Club and Graphic Society: Jerdan, vol. 3, p. 17; William Brockedon to John Murray, 18 Jul 1833, Murray Archive, NLS. Graphic Society membership lists are in the RA Library.

91 'Gregson, the Pugilist': FD, 20 and 30 Jun, 29 Jul 1808, vol. IX, pp. 3300–1, 3306, 3320–1. Among those present, beside the host Lord Elgin himself, were painters and sculptors Benjamin West, Thomas Lawrence, Joseph Nollekens, Francis Bourgeois, Thomas Stothard, William Westall, Thomas Rossi, Henry Thomson, Matthew Wyatt and John Flaxman, the former Ambassador to Prussia Francis Jackson, the antiquary Joseph Windham, a minister (Woodforde) and a group of connoisseurs, Charles Greville, William Locke and Mr Wolff. For William Richard Hamilton see Eustace, *op. cit.*, pp. 101–5 and passim. Allan Cunningham, *The Life of Sir David Wilkie*, 1843, vol. 1, p. 222–3.

92 Colburn: *A Memoir of Zerah Colburn Written by Himself*, 1833, pp. 37–8; Hamilton, *Faraday*, p. 132; Anthony Carlisle, 'An account of a family having Hands and Feet with Supernumerary Fingers and Toes', *Phil. Trans,* vol. 104 (1814), pp. 94–101. Carlisle refers to the poly-dactylic giant in II Samuel 21: 20, and I Chronicles 20: 6. Anthony Carlisle, 'Account of a Family Having Supernumerary Fingers and Toes', *Phil. Mag.*, vol. 44 (1814), pp. 17–21. See also Anthony Carlisle, 'Some particulars respecting the arithmetical powers of Zerah Colburn, a child under eight [*sic*] years of age', *Phil. Mag.*, vol. 40 (1812), pp. 119–25. Haydon, *Diary*, May 1813, vol. 1, p. 309.

93 Dinner times and customs: Walker, pp. 2, 65 and passim; John Hogg, *London as It Is*, 1837, p. 339.

94 Farington, Jerdan and Taylor: FD, 15 and 17 Apr 1817, vol. XIV, pp. 5002 and 5004; Jerdan, vol. 2, p. 69–73. John Taylor, *Poems on Various Subjects*, 1827, vol. 2, pp. 73–4.

95 Sass: E. Phelps (ed.), *Recollections of an Academician by John Callcott Horsley, RA*, 1903, p. 24. Quoted *ODNB*, entry on Henry Sass, by Robin Hamlyn.

95 Charlotte Street: There were at least fourteen Charlotte Streets in London, one being distinguished from another by a nearby road or square being written into the address.

96 Hatchett's Hotel: Redding, vol. 1, p. 24.

96 Almack's: James Gant, *The Great Metropolis*, 1837, pp. 5–6, 43.

97 Tom and Jerry: Pierce Egan, *Real Life in London*, 1821; 1905 edn, vol. 1, pp. 10–19, 148, 229–31. Pierce Egan, *Life in London: A Play in Three Acts depicting Day and Night Scenes of Tom, Jerry, Logic & Co*, 1818, p. 12; W. T. Moncrieff, *Tom and Jerry; or, Life in London. An Operatic Extravaganza*, first performed Adelphi Theatre, Nov 1821.

98 Rudolph Ackermann's gas lighting: Americo Cabral de Mello, 'On Gas Light . . . and its Economical Application', *Phil. Mag.*, vol. 44 (1814), pp. 368–70.

98 Hope's rout: *The Times*, 10 May 1802.

99 Hope offers tickets to Academicians: FD, 7 Feb 1804, vol. VI, p. 2235.

99 Hope's guests: Maria Edgeworth to Sophy Ruxton, 16 May 1813, Christina Colvin (ed.), *Maria Edgeworth – Letters from England 1813–1844*, 1971, p. 56.

99 Hope's house: J. D. Passavant, *Tour of a German Artist in England*, 1836, vol. 1, p. 224.

99 Dinners: Walker, pp. 9, 14–15, 17, 29, 51–4; Simond, p. 147; W. M. Thackeray, 'A Word about Dinners', *Sketches and Travels in London*, 1848; World's Classics edn, 1904, p. 276.

101 Interior decoration: D. R. Hay, *The Laws of Harmonious Colouring adapted to House Painting*, 1828, p. 25.

102 'Above, there is a blaze of light': Morchard Bishop (ed.), *Recollections of the Table-Talk of Samuel Rogers*, 1952, p. 235.

102 Rogers's lighting: ML [Mary Lloyd], *Sunny Memories*, vol. 1, 1879, p. 8.

CHAPTER 6: A MUTTON CHOP AT 5 O'CLOCK

103 'the Immortal Dinner': Haydon, *A&J*, vol. 1, pp. 384–8; *Diary*, vol. 2, pp. 173–6; Penelope Hughes-Hallett, *The Immortal Dinner*, 2000, pp. 80–1.

105 'most money-making part of my business': V. Nolte, *Fifty Years in both Hemispheres, or Reminiscences of the Life of a Former Merchant*, 1854, pp. 405–6.

105 Haydon on Chantrey: Haydon, *A&J*, vol. 2, pp. 160–1.

105 'honest, dull-headed, perhaps stupid': Nolte, *op. cit.*, pp. 405–6.

106 Jerdan on Chantrey: William Jerdan, *Men I Have Known*, 1866, p. 114.

106 Chantrey encouraging sitters to move: Nolte, *op. cit.*, p. 406.

106 Somerville on Chantrey: Mary Somerville to Woronzow Grieg, 21 Jul 1834, Mary Somerville Papers, MSIF-1, Bodleian.

106 Chantrey as a host, and characteristics: Jones, pp. 23–4, 56, 98, 134, 170, 180, 215, 241. 'Stokes' is the stockbroker Charles Stokes, a regular guest and a mutual friend. See entry on Charles Stokes by James Hamilton in *Companion to J. M. W. Turner*, 2001, pp. 309–10.

107 'the spots in Carrara marble': Humphry Davy Notebooks, 14g, p. 45, RI Archive.

107 'I'm afraid I shall never like Mr Chantrey': Ada Byron to Mary Somerville, postmarked 8 Jul 1834. Somerville Papers, dep. c.367, Bodleian.

107 Chantrey's invitations: Francis Chantrey to Charles Babbage, 11 May 1826, BL Add. MS 37183, f. 283; 30 Nov 1829, BL Add. MS 37184, f. 442; 13 Apr 1832 ['1831' is written, but the postmark is 14 Apr 1832], BL Add. MS 37186, f. 331; 11 Dec 1839, BL Add. MS 37191, f. 273. *The Life of James Watt* by François Arago was published in 1839.

108 Chantrey's income from Watt and Boulton: A. Yarrington, I. D. Lieberman, A. Potts and M. Baker (eds), 'An Edition of the Ledger of Sir Francis Chantrey RA, at the Royal Academy, 1809–1841', *The Walpole Society*, vol. 56 (1991/2), Watt: nos 36, 124a, 136b, 192a, 193a, 194a, 195a, 270b, 301b; Boulton: no. 228a.

109 'the most attractive visitor': Samuel Smiles (ed.), *James Nasmyth, Engineer – An Autobiography*, 1883, p. 153. For the date of the installation of the furnaces, see Yarrington *et al.*, *op. cit.*, no. 214a. The size of the large furnace is given in David Brewster, *Letters on Natural Magic*, 1832, p. 311. Babbage's visit: Babbage, p. 158.

109 Chantrey's Munro equestrian figure: Yarrington *et al.*, *op. cit.*, no. 211a.

109 'The further *corner* of the room': Brewster, *op. cit.*, p. 311.

110 'I have seen much of [Brewster]': Charles Babbage to John Herschel, 20 [or 23?] Jun 1831, RS Archive, HS.2.262.

110 The Difference Engine: Babbage, p. 51; Anthony Hyman, *Charles Babbage, Pioneer of the Computer*, 1982, p. 124.

111 Dorset Street: This is a different Dorset Street to the one off Salisbury Square where John Tatum had his Theatre of Science.

111 'I propose that the Calculating Engine': Charles Babbage to J. Herschel, Dec 1832 and Apr 1833, RS Archive, HS.2.275, 279.

111 'Babbage's parties are the best': Charles Darwin to Caroline Darwin, 27 Feb 1837. Frederick Burkhardt and Sydney Smith (eds), *The Correspondence of Charles Darwin*, vol. 2: *1837–1843*, 1985, pp. 8–9.

111 'This figure moved her arms': ML [Mary Lloyd], *Sunny Memories*, vol. 1, 1879, pp. 51ff. (essay on Charles Babbage).

111 Mary Potter: *Ibid.*, pp. 17, 51. Rev. J. P. Potter became a subscriber to the RI on 7 Feb 1825, RI, *MM*.

113 'by [Babbage's] special invitation': *The Life, Letters and Journals of George Ticknor*, 1876, 12 Jul 1835.

113 'Mr Babbage would have been burned for a conjuror': Friedrich von Raumer, *England in 1835*, 1836, p. 46.

113 Wellington and the Empress Eugénie: Babbage, pp. 179–80.

113 Ada Byron and Babbage: Ada Byron to Mary Somerville, n.d. [before Jul 1835], Somerville Papers, dep. c.367, Bodleian. Ada Byron to Mary Somerville, postmark 19 Mar 1834, Frank Buckland, 'Souvenirs of the Life of Lady Murchison', *Land and Water*, 13 Feb 1869. Ada Byron to Mary Somerville, 8 Nov 1834, Somerville Papers, *loc. cit.*; Charles Babbage to Ada Byron, 10 Jun 1835, Lovelace-Byron Papers, dep. 168, Bodleian. Benjamin Woolley, *The Bride of Science: Romance, Reason and Byron's Daughter*, 1999; Hamilton, *Faraday*, pp. 311–21.

114 'I saw [Mrs Charles Lyell]': [Mrs] Murchison to Mary Somerville, 6 May 1833, Somerville Papers, *loc. cit.*

114 'I do fear the Machine will be the death of him': Mary Somerville to Ada, Lady King, 3 Jul n.y. [1836], Lovelace-Byron Papers, dep. 174, Bodleian.

114 so that the carriages could go in convoy: Ada Byron to Mary Somerville, postmarked 26 Nov 1834, Ada Byron to Mary Somerville, Thursday morning, postmarked 28 May 1835. Somerville Papers, *loc. cit.*

115 'the *harum-scarum* extraordinary things': Ada Lovelace to Woronzow Grieg, 31 Dec 1841, Somerville Papers, dep. c.367, Bodleian.

115 'I hope you still find pleasure': Mary Somerville to Ada Byron, 28 Feb 1835, Murray Archive, NLS.

115 Mary Somerville's paper read to the Royal Society by her husband: Hamilton, *Turner*, p. 223.

115 'naturally modest': Maria Edgeworth to her stepmother, 16 Jan 1822, C. Colvin (ed.), *Maria Edgeworth: Letters from England 1813–44*, 1971, pp. 321–2.

115 'little bootikins': Maria Edgeworth to Mary Somerville, 6 Nov 1823, Somerville Papers, dep. c.370, Bodleian.

116 'The style is easy, clear and vigorous': Basil Hall to Mary Somerville, 27 Dec 1831, Somerville Papers, *loc. cit.*

116 'Humble a man of art as I am': Martin Archer Shee to Mary Somerville, n.d. [1831], Somerville Papers, dep. c.372, Bodleian.

116 The Somervilles' financial troubles: Elizabeth C. Patterson, *Mary Somerville and the Cultivation of Science 1815–1840*, 1983, pp. 170ff.

116 Mary Somerville's copyright: Mortgage deed, 26 Oct 1838, Murray Archive, NLS.

116 'if [Saba] is not already your friend': Henry Holland to Mary Somerville, n.d. [1834], Somerville Papers, dep. c.370, Bodleian.

116 'I shall be happy to come on Wednesday': Charles Lyell to Mary Somerville, n.d., Somerville Papers, dep. c. 371, Bodleian.

117 'Having found no difficulty': William Wollaston to Francis Chantrey, Saturday morning, 29 May 1824, University of Durham Library. I am grateful to Professor David Knight for this reference.

117 'purity of the English language': Charter of Incorporation of the Royal Literary Society, 1824, *Transactions of the Royal Literary Society*, 1829, vol. 1, pp. 1–5.

117 Reached the ears of George IV: Edward W. Brabrook, *The Royal Society of Literature of the United Kingdom: A Brief Account of its Origin and Progress*, 1891, pp. 3–4.

117 'the Saint Sebastian of his days': Jerdan, vol. 2, pp. 37ff.

118 'Mr Soane used to receive parties': Redding, vol. 1, p. 247.

118 On Samuel Taylor Coleridge: *Ibid.*, vol. 3, p. 64; Thomas Carlyle's Journal, 26 May 1835, quoted in J. A. Froude, *Thomas Carlyle: A History of his Life in London 1834–1881*, 1890, vol. 1, p. 47.

118 On Walter Scott and Samuel Rogers: Redding, vol. 3, pp. 23, 269.

118 Morchard Bishop (ed.), *Recollections of the Table-Talk of Samuel Rogers*, 1952, intro, p. xix. See also Robert K. Wallace, 'The "sultry creator of Captain Ahab": Herman Melville and J. M. W. Turner', *Turner Studies*, vol. 5, no. 2 (1985), pp. 2–19.

118 On Madame de Staël: Redding, vol. 1, p. 244.

119 'when, in a moonlight morning': *Ibid.*, vol. 3, p. 315.

119 'The world looks often quite spectral': Jul 1835, Thomas Carlyle's Journal, quoted in Froude, *op. cit.*, vol. 1, pp. 56–7.

119 'the voice of London': Merton M. Sealts Jr (ed.), *The Journals and Miscellaneous Notebooks of Ralph Waldo Emerson*, vol. 10 (1847–8), p. 553.

120 'Babbage continues eminently unpleasant': Thomas Carlyle to John A. Carlyle, 24 Nov 1840, Carlyle, *Letters*, vol. 12, pp. 335–6.

120 'There were fat people': Thomas Carlyle to Margaret Carlyle, 8 Mar 1838, Carlyle, *Letters*, vol. 10, p. 38.

121 On Sir John Soane's house: J.D. Passavant, *Tour of a German Artist in England*, 1836, vol. 1, p. 261.

121 'Sir John will not live or die in peace': John Britton to William Jerdan, 25 Mar 1835, Jerdan Correspondence, vol. 1, ff. 64–5, MS English Letters d. 113, Bodleian.

121 'Ohone! Ochone!': 'Lament', in Rev. Richard H. Barham, *The Ingoldsby Legends*, 1840; 1903 edn, p. 596.

122 On Soane's soirée: B. R. Haydon to Mary Russell Mitford, quoted Eric George, *The Life and Death of Benjamin Robert Haydon*, 1948, p. 139. Mary Anne Turner to Dawson Turner, 1 Apr 1825, Dawson Turner Papers, Trinity College Library, Cambridge, 2.LL1.6.

CHAPTER 7: EVERY TOOL HAD A PURPOSE

124 'It was to oblige you': Bodleian, MS Rigaud 61, vol. II, f. 39, 21 Feb 1815.

124 About eighty men on his payroll: *First Report from the Select Committee on Artizans and Machinery*, House of Commons, 1824, vol. 5, 24 Feb 1824. See also *ODNB*, entry on Alexander Galloway, by Michael T. Davis.

124 Galloway's invoice: Bodleian, MS Rigaud 61, vol. II, f. 30, 19 and 25 Nov 1814.

125 'The flywheel of your engine': *Ibid.*, f. 39, 21 Feb 1815.

125 'one of the cleverest men': *ODNB*, entry on Alexander Galloway, and Mary Thale (ed.), *Autobiography of Francis Place 1771–1854*, 1972, p. 142.

125 'to assist the grand work': Alexander Galloway to Francis Place, 19 Aug 1829, Place Papers, BL Add. MS 37950, f. 39.

126 'a man entirely devoted to the cause of freedom': Count Alerino Palma, *Summary Account of the Steam Boats for Lord Cochrane's Expedition . . . for the Service of Greece*, 1826, p. 4.

126 'that is, in plain English', and 'There were specimens of excellence': *Report . . . Artizans and Machinery*, vol. 5, 24 Feb 1824.

128 'I had lords and ladies': Matthew Boulton to J. L. Baumgarten, Aug 1767. Quoted Jenny Uglow, *The Lunar Men*, 2002, p. 211.

128 Mint production: *London Magazine*, vol. 3 (Feb 1821), p. 221.

129 'contained all the improvements': John Bourne (ed.), *A Treatise on the Steam Engine in its Application to Mines, Mills, Steam Navigation, and Railways*, by the Artizan Club, 1846, p. 18.

129 'The Public are requested to observe': Quoted Uglow, *op. cit.*, p. 495.

130 'when we consider the steam-engine': John Farey, *A Treatise on the Steam Engine – Historical, Practical and Descriptive*, 1827, p. 3.

130 Efficiency of engines in Cornwall: *Phil. Mag.*, vol. 52 (1818), p. 313. These figures are reported approximately monthly, and, depending on the type of engine, average around the figure given here.

131 'The productiveness of labour': Farey, *op. cit.*, p. v.

131 John Farey, *ODNB* entry by A. P. Woolrich.

133 On Elizabeth Pugsley: *Ibid.*

133 'crowded together about *400* inhabitants': Alexander Galloway to Francis Place, 9 Aug 1829, Place Papers, BL Add. MS 37950, ff. 30ff.

134 'only a mouthing common-council man': Samuel Smiles, *Industrial Biography: Iron Workers and Tool Makers*, 1864, p. 241.

134 Henry Maudslay, *ODNB* entry by R. Angus Buchanan.

134 'nearly the entire change': Charles Holtzapffel, *Turning and Mechanical Manipulation*, vol. 2, 1843, p. 647.

135 Accident at Galloway's works: *The Times*, 4 and 6 Sept 1824.

135 Accident at Maudslay's works: *The Times*, 25 May 1826.

135 '[Maudslay] a stout, friendly man': 2 Jun 1826, Schinkel, p. 81.

136 On the Holtzapffels: W. Greene Ogden Jr, *Notes on the History and Provenance of Holtzapffel Lathes*, 1987.

137 Schinkel and Beuth's tour of London: Schinkel, passim.

138 On Nasmyth and Maudslay: Samuel Smiles (ed.), *James Nasmyth – Engineer: an Autobiography*, 1883, pp. 121–8, 130–1, 147. Note that these recollections were written in Nasmyth's old age and filtered through Samuel Smiles's editorship. *Henry Maudslay*, Science Museum, 1971.

140 'Yes, very intimately': *Report from the Select Committee on the Arts and their Connexion with Manufactures*, House of Commons, 1836, vol. 9, pt 2, p. 29.

140 'Mere geometrical drawing': Smiles (ed.), *op. cit.*, pp. 173–4.

141 'First, *get a clear notion*': *Ibid.*, p. 172.

CHAPTER 8: THE VERY PULSE
OF THE MACHINE

143 'The most economical disposition': *Report from the Select Committee on the Arts and their Connexion with Manufactures*, House of Commons, 1836, vol. 9, pt 2, p. 29.

143 Toplis listed Western Literary and Philosophical Institute, Leicester Square; Marylebone Literary and Science Institute; Mechanics Hall of Science, Finsbury; Mechanics' Institution, Spitalfields; City of London Literary and Science Institute. *Ibid.*, pt 1, pp. 122–3, Q1560, 1566. At evening class in the London Mechanics' Institute in 1836 a tradesman could study from the following subjects: English grammar, writing, arithmetic, mathematics, practical geometry, architectural, mechanical, perspective, landscape and ornamental drawing, drawing the human figure, modelling, French, Latin, short-hand, literary composition, chemistry, experimental philosophy, geography, natural history and phrenology. *Ibid.*, Appendix 3.

144 Evidence to the Select Committee: Nasmyth, *ibid.*, pt 2, p. 29, Q308; Sass, pt 2, p. 23, Q232; Martin, pt 1, pp. 70–1, Q922–3.

145 Martin's sons drawing in the British Museum: John Martin to J. T. Smith, 16 Nov 1832, John Martin Correspondence, Queen Mary College Archive, WFD/JM/3.

146 John Martin's Sketchbook, Douce Bequest (1834), Ashmolean Museum, Oxford, 1863.1475.

147 Brockedon: The large-scale religious and historical dramas which Brockedon exhibited include *The Judgement of Daniel* (wrongly inscribed on its frame 'Jesus at the Temple'; 1817; Exeter Combined Court), *The Agony in the Garden* (1817; altarpiece, Dartington Church), *The Vision of Zechariah* (1821), *The Last Supper* (1825; altarpiece, formerly Christ Church, Hunslet, Leeds), *The Deluge* (1827), *Moses on Mount Sinai* (1835; formerly Christ's Hospital), *Christ Raising the Widow's Son at Nain* (St Saviour's, Dartmouth), *A Scene from Ossian* (formerly Dartmouth Guildhall) and *The Crucifixion* (Cornworthy Church, near Totnes).

147 William Brockedon, *ODNB* entry by Nicholas Alfrey.

147 Brockedon's lecture subjects: Hamilton, *Faraday*, pp. 210–12. Brockedon proposed many members to the Society of Arts, including T. L. Donaldson, John Martin and Henry Sass. Society of Arts Membership lists, 1813–25, RSA Archives.

148 On travelling with John Murray: Sam Smiles, *Memoirs of John Murray*, 1891, vol. 2, p. 464.

148 'goodly company even for Mr Hallam': William Brockedon to John Murray, 18 Jul 1833, Murray Archive, NLS.

148 'London is intolerably dull': William Brockedon to John Murray, 15 Sept 1837, Murray Archive, NLS.

148 'a striking and animated resemblance': *Lit. Gaz.*, 30 May 1835, p. 345.

149 *Report from the Select Committee on the Proportions of Tolls which ought to be paid by Carriages Propelled by Steam or Gas, on the Present State and Future Prospects of Land-carriage so Propelled, and on the Probable Utility to the Public*, 1831.

150 Devon toll: *Ibid.*, p. 8. There were twenty shillings in one pound sterling.

150 On Carlisle: Gurney refers to 'my friend Sir Anthony Carlisle' in his evidence to the 1831 committee.

151 Gurney's journey: Lord Hill to Sir James Willoughby Gordon, 23 Aug 1829, Willoughby Gordon Papers, BL Add. MS 49508, ff. 89–90. Report dated 3 Aug 1829, Willoughby Gordon Papers, BL Add. MS 49508, ff. 83–8.

151 Gurney's evidence: *Report from the Select Committee on the Proportions of Tolls*, pp. 5–7, 20–5, 31.

153 'Patent Philosophical Hay-tosser': An Inside Passenger [William Jerdan], *Personal Narrative of a Journey over-land from the Bank to Barnes*, 1829.

154 'the grand prize of public opinion': *Mechanics Magazine*, 24 Oct 1829.

154 'The powerful introduction of a blast bellows': *Mechanics Magazine*, 10 Oct 1829.

155 'These smacks are now replaced': Gummed insert, n.d., in *Reid's Leith & London Smack Directory*, 1819, Bodleian, Vet. A6 e.2207.

155 Davy and Faraday crossing the Channel: Hamilton, *Faraday*, p. 55.

155 Turner sailing to Scotland: 'King's Visit to Scotland' sketchbook, 1822, Tate, Turner Bequest, CC, ff. 1–8.

156 'the rate at which men were to walk': Hansard, 3rd series, vol. 6, pp. 289–90, 19 Aug 1831.

156 *Report from the Select Committee on the Frequent Calamities by Steam Navigation*, 1831, evidence of Capt. K. B. Martin, p. 32, and Q2062. The *Albion* did eventually founder, in a storm in 1837, near Marloes, Pembrokeshire. The bay, where bits of her wreckage can still be seen, was subsequently called Albion Bay. The *Royal William* reportedly

rammed the *Magnet*, her rival on the London-to-Margate voyage, and crushed her lifeboat. Letter to the *The Times*, 23 Jul 1831.

157   Richard Beard, letters to the *The Times*, 28 Feb, 4, 20, 29 Mar 1834; John Herschel, *Discourse on the Study of Natural Philosophy*, 1830, pp. 59–60. One guinea was £1 1 shilling. Tax level as at 1860.

158   'the avenues of a forest': *Murray's Modern London – A Visitor's Guide*, 1860, reprinted 2003, p. xix.

158   'The cockney talked of a jaunt to Margate': Redding, vol. 1, p. 37.

158   Charles Lamb, 'The Old Margate Hoy', *The Last Essays of Elia*, 1833, Everyman edn, 1906, p. 208.

159   Jarvis's Landing Place: F. Coghlan, *The Steam Packet and Coast Companion*, 1832, p. 61.

159   'the *London Engineer*': *Engineer*, 15 Oct 1897, p. 368; H. P. Spratt, *The Birth of the Steamboat*, 1968, pp. 90, 103–4.

159   Brent shipyard: J. Brent Streit, *The Brent Family of Shipbuilders*, 2000.

159   On Lord Cochrane: Ian Grimble, *The Sea Wolf: The Life of Admiral Cochrane*, 2001; Brian Vale, *The Audacious Admiral – Cochrane: The True Life of a Naval Legend*, 2005. Letter Maj. W. E. Cochrane to the Editor of the *Courier*, 10 Dec 1826, in Richard H. Galloway, *Refutation of Calumnious Statements concerning the late Alexander Galloway Esq, C.E., contained in the Earl of Dundonald's book entitled 'Life of Lord Cochrane'*, 1871, pp. 62–3. H. P. Spratt, *Transatlantic Paddle Steamers*, 1967, pp. 19–21. C. A. Finsterbusch, 'The Advent of Steam to the West Coast of South America', *Sea Breezes*, vol. 18 (Apr 1934), pp. 69–72. Maria Graham, *Journal of a Residence in Chile*, 1824, 7 Jul 1822, pp. 172–3. Douglas Dakin, 'Lord Cochrane's Greek Steam Fleet', *Mariner's Mirror*, vol. 39, no. 3 (1953), pp. 211–19. Maria Graham to John Murray, 5 Aug 1823, Murray Archive, NLS.

161   Fiona MacCarthy, *Byron, Life and Legend*, 2003, p. 481.

161   On Galloway: Count Alerino Palma, *Summary Account of the Steam Boats for Ld Cochrane's Expedition . . . for the Service of Greece*, 1826, pp. 4, 17. J. and S. Ricardo to Lord Cochrane, quoted in Thomas Dundonald and H. R. Fox Bourne, *The Life of Thomas Lord Cochrane*, vol. 1, 1869, pp. 332–3, 353. Richard H. Galloway, *Refutation . . .*, pp. 43–52. Galloway's letter to the *The Times*: 28 Aug 1826. Galloway and Cochrane's patent: *Phil. Mag.*, vol. 51 (1818), p. 395. Dakin, *op. cit.*, pp. 216–18.

163   William Cobbett, 'Rural Rides', *Cobbett's Weekly Register*, vol. 59 (7 Oct 1826), p. 86.

163 Cobbett's second attack: William Cobbett, 'Greek Cause!', *Cobbett's Weekly Register*, vol. 59 (28 Oct 1826), pp. 296–7. Richard H. Galloway, *Refutation* . . . , p. 48. Alexander Galloway to Francis Place, 19 Aug 1829, Place Papers, BL Add. MS 37950, ff. 38–41. Galloway's emphasis.

163 John Galloway describes the ship's sea-trials in a letter in *The Times*, 28 Apr 1827.

CHAPTER 9: HAYDON, GÉRICAULT AND BULLOCK AT THE EGYPTIAN HALL

165 Alpha Road is now named Rossmore Road. Haydon writes at length about the genesis of his *Christ's Entry into Jerusalem*, and about himself. Particular references used here are *A&J*, vol. 1, pp. 289, 319–20, 398–400. Charles Lamb's praise: 'Tabulum egregii', published in Latin in *Champion*, 7 May 1820, and in Lamb's own English translation, *Champion*, 14 May 1820. Quoted Penelope Hughes-Hallett, *The Immortal Dinner*, 2000, p. 100.

166 Farington on RA hanging committee: FD, 14 Apr 1820, vol. XVI, pp. 5492, 5496.

166 'God forgive him, I can't': Haydon, *Diary*, vol. 5, p. 429.

166 'all the world were fools': Richardson, vol. 2, p. 194.

166 Farington on Haydon: FD, 24 May 1809, *Recollections*, vol. IX, p. 3467.

166 'I was opposed': Haydon, *A&J*, vol. 1, p. 235.

167 British Institution's rules: *An Account of the British Institution for Promoting the Fine Arts* . . . , 1805, p. 4.

167 'We can all remember the loiterers and loungers': Anna Jameson, quoted William T. Whitley, *Art in England 1800–1820*, 1928, p. 110.

168 '[We] remained jammed in on the landing-place': *Lit. Gaz.*, 22 May 1819, p. 333.

168 'Og of Bassan': Redding, vol. 3, pp. 91–2.

168 'the fatigue and expense of a long': *An Account of all the Pictures Exhibited in . . . the British Institution, from 1813 to 1823, belonging to the Nobility and Gentry of England*, 1824, pp. x and xii–xiv.

169 'This was nothing but that usual want': Haydon, *A&J*, vol. 1, p. 349–50.

169 Haydon's *Macbeth*: Ibid., pp. 190–3.

170 'my preference for Men & Women': Jane Austen to Cassandra Austen, 18–20 Apr 1811. Dierdre Le Faye (ed.), *Jane Austen's Letters*, 2003, p. 179.

170 Isis and Osiris: The curious poses of the figures, classically rather than Egyptian-inspired, are discussed by Alex Werner in 'Egypt in London – Public and Private Displays in the 19th Century Metropolis', *Imhotep Today: Egyptianizing Architecture*, 2003, pp. 75–104.

170 'the whole of the known Quadrupeds': William Bullock, *A Companion to Mr. Bullock's London Museum and Pantherion*, 12th edn, 1812, pp. 1–2.

171 'the town was absolutely astonished': William Jerdan, *Men I Have Known*, 1866, entry on William Bullock, pp. 67–82.

171 'Such a man does infinite good': Jerdan, vol. 2, p. 88.

171 'still intire with the flesh on': William Bullock to Lord Liverpool, 24 Apr 1813, Liverpool Papers, BL Add. MS 38252, f. 265.

171 'an old, rusty, fusty head': John Constable to John Dunthorne Snr, 4 Feb 1799, Constable, *Correspondence*, vol. II, 1964, p. 23. Cromwell's head is illustrated in three gruesome photographs in *Archaeological Journal*, vol. 68 (1911), facing pp. 236–7, plates iv–vi.

171 'on the propriety of exhibiting such an article': William Bullock to Lord Liverpool, 24 Apr 1813, *loc. cit.*

172 'a very fine work of art': FD, 30 Mar, 4 Apr 1816, vol. XIV, pp. 4805, 4811–12.

172 Wicar displayed: *Ibid.*, 3 and 9 Jan 1817, vol. XIV, pp. 4952, 4955.

172 'finding that throwing open the British Museum': William Bullock to Lord Liverpool, 2 and 5 Apr 1819. Liverpool Papers, BL Add. MS 38276, ff. 138, 161.

173 'it is absolutely the same thing': Ambrose Poynter to Robert Finch, 26 Apr 1822. Finch Papers, d. 13, ff. 435–6, Bodleian.

173 'Passed an acute and miserable morning': Haydon, *Diary*, 7 Nov 1815, vol. 1, p. 479.

173 'Thus reasoning, I borrowed': Haydon, *A&J*, vol. 1, p. 152. Haydon's italics.

173 'I have a large family': Benjamin Robert Haydon to John Murray, 26 Nov 1828, Murray Archive, NLS.

174 'that blessed refuge for the miserable': Haydon, *A&J*, 9 Sept 1836, vol. 3, p. 47.

174 '4 more large knives and forks': Benjamin Robert Haydon to William

Newton, 25 Apr 1831, Haydon Letters, Queen Mary College Archive, WC/HA/15.

174 'The Academicians now say': Haydon, *Diary*, 11 Sept 1816, vol. 2, p. 45.

175 Egyptian Hall exhibition: Haydon, *A&J*, vol. 1, pp. 399–404. Criticisms of Haydon's exhibition were published in: *Annals of Fine Arts*, vol. 5 (1820), pp. 128–47; *London Magazine*, vol. 1 (May 1820), p. 581; *Blackwood's Magazine*, vol. 8 (Nov 1820), p. 219; *Examiner*, 27 Mar–22 Oct 1820 (in ten issues).

176 *London Magazine*, vol. 1 (May 1820), pp. 581–7. See also *The Times*, 5 Apr 1820.

177 Lorenz Eitner, *Géricault's Raft of the Medusa*, 1972, pp. 7–11. Advertisement for *Raft of the Medusa*, *The Times,* 13 Jun 1820, p. 1, col. 1. Invitation card reproduced Eitner, *op. cit.*, fig. MM. Géricault's lithograph, Musée Bonnat, Bayonne, inv 700. Géricault in London: Lorenz Eitner, *Géricault: His Life and Work*, 1982, pp. 210–17.

178 'people had left town': Haydon, *A&J*, vol. 1, p. 410.

178 Haydon's takings: FD, 24 Jun 1820, vol. XVI, p. 5526; Haydon, *A&J*, vol. 1, pp. 410–11.

178 Subsequent history of *Christ's Entry*: Haydon, *Diary*, vol. 2, p. 266n.

179 *Raft of the Medusa* private view: *Globe*, 12 Jun 1820. Eitner, *Géricault: His Life and Work*, p. 211. 'In this tremendous picture': *Lit. Gaz.*, 1 Jul 1820, p. 427. 'a fine performance': FD, 26 Jul 1820, vol. XVI, p. 5542.

179 Géricault at RA: *Morning Herald*, 24 Jun 1820, p. 3.

180 'great admiration for his talent': C. R. Cockerell's Diary, 16 Dec 1821, quoted Lee Johnson, 'Géricault and Delacroix seen by Cockerell', *Burlington Magazine*, CXIII (Sept 1971), p. 548.

180 Martin at the Egyptian Hall and the RA: Balston, pp. 33–4, 66; *Select Committee on Arts and Principles of Design*, 1836, pt 2, p. 71, Q824. Martin's son, Leopold, called *Clytie* 'a grand ideal; a bright and lovely landscape, an effort to portray the beauty of Claude when at his best and happiest, combined with the warmth and charm of Turner . . . My father had every hope that the picture might demand attention.'

180 'he stabbed his mother': Thornbury, p. 265.

181 'acquired immense applause': Balston, p. 40.

181 'The spectators crowd around it': Quoted *ibid.*, p. 48. From the *Examiner*, 1819.

181 'An inquisition without a Pope': *Report of Select Committee on Arts and their Connexions with Manufactures*, 1836, pt 2, Q1063.

181 'unjust and illiberal laws': Balston, p. 52.

181 Academicians who voted against Martin: FD, 6 Nov 1820, vol. XVI, p. 5577.

181 'the day before': Balston, p. 55.

181 'their ill-usage': *Report of Select Committee on Arts and their Connexions with Manufactures*, 1836, pt 2, p. 71, Q818.

182 'so vivid': W. T. Whitley, *Art in England 1800–1820*, 1928, p. 107.

CHAPTER 10: AS THE ART ADVANCES

183 Martin's appearance and home: Balston, pp. 44, 77, 170, quoting William Bewick, a young artist pupil of both Haydon and Martin. In W. P. Frith, *My Autobiography*, 1887, vol. 3, p. 37, this same sentiment is rendered as 'a very handsome man'. Allsop's Buildings later became Allsop Terrace. The terrace, just to the west of Baker Street Station, is now replaced by a block of inter-war flats.

184 'wootz': Michael Faraday and James Stodart, 'Experiment on the Alloys of Steel, made with a View to its Improvement', *Quarterly Journal of Science*, vol. 9 (1820), pp. 319–30. Hamilton, *Faraday*, pp. 153–6.

184 Perkins's technique: Faraday's Common Place Book, vol. 1, ff. 392ff., IET Archive.

185 Martin's engravings and workshop: Balston, pp. 95ff. Faraday to John Martin, 9 Mar 1827, FJ, no. 319; and 23 Dec 1828, FJ, no. 382. John Martin's 'Autobiographical Letter', *ILN*, 17 Mar 1849.

186 Bernard Barton, 'The Battle of Gibeon, verses illustrative of Martin's Joshua', *A New Years Eve, and other Poems*, 1828, pp. 105–8. Verse IV.

187 'with many most cordial grunts': *Art Journal*, 1863, pp. 87ff. Quoted Gage, p. 299.

187 'I have had a long conversation with Turner': Francis Chantrey to John Murray Jr, 8 Dec 1832, Murray Archive, NLS. Charles Heath's finances were in a precarious state at this time.

187 John Britton: See Brian Lukacher, 'Britton's Conquest: Creating an Antiquarian Nation, 1790–1860', *Landscapes of Retrospection*, 1999.

187 'George Baker has recommended': W. H. Hyett to William Upcott, 10 Dec 1816, Montagu Papers d. 7, f. 570, Bodleian.

188 Andrew Wilton, 'The "Keepsake" Convention: Jessica and Some Related Pictures', *Turner Studies*, vol. 9, no. 2 (1989), pp. 14–33.

188 On John Pye: *Phil. Mag.*, vol. 49 (1817), p. 419. 'Declaration of engravers that they will not become candidates for election into the Royal Academy', 10 Jul 1826, Pye Correspondence, V&A, NAL, MSL/1930/1211, f. 35. Signatories are John and Henry Le Keux, George Cooke, Edward Goodall, John Henry Robinson, William Finden, John Pye, George T. Doo, John Burnet. John Pye, *Patronage of British Art*, 1845, pp. 175, 183–6.

189 'kept . . . everything': E. R. J. Radcliffe to Sir Frank Short, 18 Jul 1820, Pye Correspondence, V&A, NAL, MSL/1930/1211, f. 2.

190 'Sent to the Earl of Egremont': Notebooks of John Pye, vol. 2, BL Add. MS 36935, ff. 13–14.

190 'it meant starvation': Alaric A. Watts, *Alaric Watts, a Narrative of his Life*, 1884, vol. 1, p. 308. Quoted Basil Hunnisett, *Steel-Engraved Book Illustration in England*, 1980, p. 39. Turner was exasperated by the delay, writing to Pye, 'Year after year rolls on and no proof of Ehrnbtein appears – I do request you to proceed (pray state your own time) or let me have the picture.' 2 Jan 1842. John Gage, 'Further Correspondence of J. M. W. Turner', *Turner Studies*, vol. 6, no. 1 (1986), p. 6 (no. 248a).

190 On Linnell's drawings of Piombo and Poussin: John Linnell to John Pye, postmark 15 Jan 1829, and 19 Apr 1832, Pye Correspondence, V&A, NAL, MSL/1930/1211, ff. 25, 27.

191 A copy of *Engravings from the Pictures of the National Gallery* is in the British Library, 746.e.8. Pye's list of drawings and plates for the engraving project, 1827–39, is in Pye Correspondence, V&A, f. 72. The subject by Claude was wrongly identified by Pye as '*The Annunciation*'. It is in fact *Hagar and the Angel*.

191 'the Art of Engraving never flourished as it now does': Charles Heath to Dawson Turner, 19 Feb 1825, Dawson Turner Papers, Trinity College Library, Cambridge, o.13.29/35.

191 'As the art advances': *Report of Select Committee on Arts and their Connexions with Manufactures*, 1836, p. 81, paras 944–5.

191 'Eight or ten years ago': James Grant, *The Great Metropolis*, 1837, p. 139.

191 'I work a lot in my room': 12 Feb 1821. Quoted Lorenz Eitner, *Géricault's Raft of the Medusa*, 1972, pp. 64–5.

192 J. and P. André, *Specimens of Polyautography*, 1803; Henry Bankes, *Lithography, or the Art of Making Drawings on Stone, for the Purpose of Being Multiplied by Printing*, 1813, ed. Michael Twyman, 1976; 'The Process of Polyautographic Printing', *Gent's Mag.*, vol. 78, pt 1 (Mar 1808), pp. 193–6; T. Fisher, 'Curious Specimens of Polyautography, or Lithography', *Gent's Mag*, vol. 85, pt 2 (Oct 1815), p. 297. 'On the Origin and Practice of Lithography', *Phil. Mag.*, vol. 49 (1817), pp. 215–18, 391.

193 A thing about cheese: The Earl of Moira challenged Willoughby Gordon to agree that cheese made in his dairy in Ayrshire was better than 'any which Cheshire, Lancashire or Gloucestershire can produce'. Earl of Moira to James Willoughby Gordon, 8 Jan 1808, Willoughby Gordon Papers, BL Add. MS 49502, f. 6.

193 On the Willoughby Gordons: James Hamilton, *Turner – The Late Seascapes*, 2003, pp. 4–7. See also: Paul Oppé, 'Talented Amateurs: Julia Gordon and her Circle', *Country Life*, 8 Jul 1939, pp. 20–1; Selby Whittingham, 'What You Will; or, Some Notes Regarding the Influence of Watteau on Turner and Other British Artists', *Turner Studies*, vol. 5, no. 1 (1985), pp. 2–25, and no. 2 (1985), pp. 28–48; Ian Warrell, *Turner on the Loire*, 1997, pp. 181ff.

194 'now I am looked upon as a fool': Charles Hullmandel to Richard Owen, 27 Jan n.y. [1820s], Owen Correspondence, Natural History Museum archive, 15/458/9.

194 'this high and lofty one': James Ward to Sir John Leicester, 14 Apr 1824; Douglas Hall, 'The Tabley House Papers', *Walpole Society*, vol. 38 (1960–2), p. 97.

194 Charles Hullmandel, *The Art of Drawing on Stone*, 1824, pp. v–vii. A modern edition is ed. Joan M. Friedman, 1982.

195 'I have no hesitation in stating': Michael Faraday to Charles Hullmandel, 12 Apr 1827; FJ, no. 321. Faraday records a recipe for lithographic ink in his Common Place Book, vol. 1, p. 399, IET Archive: '2 oz soap, 3 oz shellac, ⅛ oz tallow. 2 spoonsful of Venice turpentine – mixed completely. Then a small portion burnt off.'

195 Faraday's lithographs: Faraday's Scrapbooks, vol. 1, p. 27, RI Archive.

196 Faraday attended a Hullmandel theatrical: Michael Faraday to William Macready, 6 Oct 1837, FJ, no. 1040. Faraday's Scrapbooks, vol.1, p. 32, RI Archive.

196 'Went with Hullmandel': Harding Diaries, 22 Oct 1839, J. D. Harding Papers, Courtauld Institute Archive.

196 'some thousands, all equally good': *Gent's Mag.*, vol. 92, pt 2 (Nov 1822), facing p. 398.

196 Harding attends Faraday lecture: Harding Diary, 18 Jan 1838, J. D. Harding Papers, Courtauld Institute Archive.

197 'Lithography appears now to be capable of anything': A review of *Ruins of Kenilworth Castle*, published by Ebers & Co., *Lit. Gaz.*, 29 Jan 1831, p. 75.

197 Hullmandel's scrapbook: St Bride's Printing Library, London, 15582.K/B8.

197 'the art of lithography admits of many different styles': *Phil. Mag.*, vol. 56 (1828), pp. 232–5.

198 Bill-stickers' wages: *Grant's London Journal*, pt 1, no. 3 (Jan 1840), p. 18.

198 'the open air Exhibitions of London': William Weir, 'Advertisements', in Charles Knight, *London*, vol. V, 1843, p. ciii. Quoted Baron, pp. 375–6.

198 '[The English] are taking this art so far': Godard Collection, 11469, Alençon Library, France. MS text written into Godard's copy of *Traité historique et practique de la gravure en bois*, by Jean Michel Papillon (1766). Quoted James Hamilton, *Wood Engraving and the Woodcut in Britain, c1890–1990*, 1994, p. 28. Author's translation.

199 'a world of itself': Thomas Bewick, *A Memoir*, ed. Montague Weekley, 1961, p. 85. See also Jenny Uglow, *Nature's Engraver – A Life of Thomas Bewick*, 2006.

200 '[Thompson] is very obliging': Maria Callcott to John Murray, May 1833, Murray Archive, NLS.

200 The Robinson family: James Hamilton, *William Heath Robinson*, 1992, ch. 1.

200 'In the landscape, *leave out the houses*': William Cobbett to Thomas Robinson, 63 Margaret St, Spa Fields, n.d. [1820s/30s?], Robinson Papers, University of Reading Library.

201 'a row of engravers at work': Walter Crane, *An Artist's Reminiscences*, 1907, pp. 46–50.

201 Turner's *View of Leeds* was produced as a lithograph in 1823 by Harding, printed by Hullmandel. In the decade after Turner's death about thirty lithographs and chromo-lithographs after his work were produced.

202 'astonishing to the philosopher and the simple child': *The Times*, 31 Dec 1852.

CHAPTER 11: ALL LONDON AT A GRASP

203 'Two globes, three chairs': Anon [William Hone?], 'Quarterly Night, Oct 2nd 1816', transcribed by Michael Faraday in his Common Place Book, vol. 1, pp. 137–58, IET Archive. For discussion on the authorship of the poem, see Hamilton, *Faraday*, pp. 128–9.

204 Chemist to the Ordnance: Mary Mills, *The Early East London Gas Industry and its Waste*, 1999, p. 9.

204 James Sadler, *ODNB* entry by H. S. Torrens.

204 John Sadler, lecture announcement, *Phil. Mag.*, vol. 48 (1816), p. 235.

204 Sadler's balloon launches: 15 Jul 1814 (reported *The Times*, 16 Jul 1814), and 29 Jul 1814 (advertisement *The Times*, 28 Jul 1814; flight reported *The Times* 3 Aug 1814).

205 'Sight after sight': Jerdan, vol. 1, pp. 204–5; vol. 2, p. 31n.

206 Tiberius Cavallo, *The History and Practice of Aerostation*, 1785, pp. 219, 267, 281, 308.

207 James Sadler's building of a gas-making plant is described as 'a persistent story' by Mary Mills, *op. cit.*, p. 9.

208 'unremittingly pour[ed] out a stream of vapour': *The Times*, 16 Jul 1814.

208 Launch events: Burlington House launch advertisement, *The Times*, 28 Jul 1814; 16 Jul 1814; 30 Jul 1814 (Miss Thompson is named in unsourced cuttings in the Royal Aeronautical Society library); 3 Aug 1814; 4 Jun 1823.

210 George Cayley, 'On Aerial Navigation', *Phil. Mag.*, vol. 50 (1817), pp. 27–35; see also vol. 47 (1816), pp. 81–6, 321–9 and 429–31. *ODNB*, entry on George Cayley, by John A. Bagley.

210 Hampton's successful parachute jump over Kensington Gardens, *The Times*, 13 Aug 1839.

211 'ruffian' injured two children: *The Times*, 19 Aug 1823.

211 Disastrous flight from Croydon: *The Times*, 2 May 1839

211 'Here we go up, up, up': John Poole, *Crochets in the Air; or, an (un)Scientific Account of a Balloon trip, in a Familiar Letter to a Friend*, 1838, p. 26.

213 'The prospect . . . was beyond the power of description': *Phil. Mag.*, vol. 38 (1811), pp. 231–3.

213 'On ascending above the clouds': *The Times*, 19 Jun 1824.

213 Vincent Lunardi, *An Account of the First Aerial Voyage in England*, 1784, p. 40.

214 'It was not we who seemed to rise': *Phil. Mag.*, vol. 44 (1814), pp. 75–6.

214 'you sit in a thing like a sauce boat': Poole, *op. cit.*, pp. 3, 35, 65.

215 'The roadways striping the land': Henry Mayhew, *ILN*, 18 Sept 1852.

216 'melting into obscurity': Thomas Monck Mason, *Aeronautica; or, Sketches Illustrative of the Theory and Practice of Aerostation: Comprising an Enlarged Account of the Late Aerial Expedition to Germany*, 1838, p. 42.

216 [Thomas Monck Mason], *Account of the late Aeronautical Expedition from London to Weilburg accomplished by Robert Hollond Esq., Monck Mason Esq. and Charles Green, Aeronaut*, 1836, pp. 26 and 30. Quoted Gage, pp. 163–4.

217 'your Excursion so occupied my mind': J. M. W. Turner to Robert Hollond, n.d. [c.Dec 1836]. Quoted Gage, p. 205.

217 'Oh the balloon, the great balloon': 'The "Monstre" Balloon', in R. H. Barham, *The Ingoldsby Legends*, 1840.

218 Death of Cocking: *The Times*, 29 Jul 1837; letter Michael Faraday to the Editor, *The Times*, 1 Aug 1837; FJ, no. 1019.

218 'throwing out all manner of fireworks': Thomas Carlyle to Jane Welsh Carlyle, 21 Aug 1845, Carlyle, *Letters*, vol. 19, pp. 161–2.

219 'It shews the wonderful manner': Jun 1850, Thomas Martin (ed.), *Faraday's Diary*, 1934–5, vol. 5, 24 Jun 1850, para 10875, p. 309.

219 'an atmosphere composed of gold dust': Mary Anne Flaxman to Maria Denham, 12/14 Jul 1824, Flaxman Papers, vol. 3, BL Add. MS 39783, f. 28.

CHAPTER 12: 1831: A DISTURBANCE OF THE NEEDLE

220 'The Gazette enjoys': *Lit. Gaz.*, 1 Jan 1831, p. 1.

221 'A large and elegant apartment': *Lit. Gaz.*, 22 Jan 1831, p. 57.

222 Lost dodo parts: *Penny Magazine*, vol. 3 (4 Jan 1834), p. 4.

222 'If they are here': J. Forshall to Thomas Pettigrew, n.d., Pettigrew Letters, BL Add. MS 56229, f. 191.

222 The British Museum was useful: Hansard, 3rd Series, vol. 3, p. 432, 14 Mar 1831.

222 'a great press of visitors': BM Standing Committee Minutes, 11 Jun 1831.

222 'On the tiptoe of expectation': J. D. Passavant, *Tour of a German Artist in England*, 1836, vol. 1, p. 15.

223 Robert Burford, *ODNB* entry by Ralph Hyde.

223 'a magnificent view': *Gent's Mag.*, vol. 101, pt 1 (Jan 1831), p. 69.

223 Panoramas on display: *Lit. Gaz.*, 19 Mar 1831, p. 188; *Gent's Mag.*, vol. 101, pt 1 (Jun 1831), p. 541; *Gent's Mag.*, vol. 101, pt 2, p. 542.

223 Colosseum in Regent's Park: Passavant, *op. cit.*, vol. 1, p. 275.

224 New site for the National Gallery: *Gent's Mag.*, vol. 101, pt 1 (Mar 1831), pp. 201–7.

224 The Royal National Gallery of Painting: So-called at first meetings only, Trustees' Minutes, 7 Feb, 8 and 15 Jul 1828, vol. 1, 1828–47, National Gallery Archive, NG1/1.

224 'The House . . . is totally inadequate': Trustees' Minutes, 7 Feb and 15 Jul 1828, vol. 1, 1828–47, National Gallery Archive, NG1/1.

224 Likely collapse of 100 Pall Mall: National Gallery Archive, NG5/13/1(ii).

225 Alternative sites for National Gallery: Trustees' Minutes, 16 Dec 1830, vol. 1, 1828–47, National Gallery Archive, NG1/1.

225 Carlton House suggested for National Gallery: Hansard, 3rd series, vol. 4, pp. 991ff., 8 Jul 1831.

226 'similar to the side chapels': Sydney Smirke, descriptive plan for the conversion of the King's Mews into a Gallery, 1830, National Gallery Archive, NG5/13/2.

226 Lions in Trafalgar Square: *Gent's Mag.*, vol. 101, pt 1 (Mar 1831), pp. 201–7.

227 Lions roaring at midnight: Mary Lamb to Barbara Betham, 2 Nov 1814, Mrs Gilchrist, *Mary Lamb*, 1883, p. 201.

227 Exeter Hall: Percy Howard, 'The Passing of Exeter Hall', *Civil Service Observer*, vol. 13, no. 5 (May 1907). John Hoppus, *ODNB* entry by W. A. J. Archbold, revised by C. A. Creffield. *Gent's Mag.*, vol. 101, pt 1 (Apr 1831), p. 362.

227 'All persons [were] compelled': *Annual Register*, 1831, Chronicle, 27 Apr, pp. 68–9.

228 'It was my fate to see': Passavant, *op. cit.*, vol. 1, p. 166.

229 'The evils inseparable from mis-government': BM Place Collection, set 63, vol. 2, f. 9. Printed.

229 'The Duke has lost heart entirely': Francis Bamford and the Duke of Wellington (eds), *The Journal of Mrs Arbuthnot 1820–1832*, 1950, vol. 2, p. 420 (16 May 1831).

229 'Rocked, as it were': *Lit. Gaz.*, 2 Apr 1831, p. 218.

230 'It becomes all of us': *The Times*, 2 May 1831.

230 'Why *damn* it Constable': John Constable to David Lucas, 23 Mar 1831, Constable, *Correspondence*, 1966, vol. IV, p. 346.

230 Criticism of Constable and Turner: *The Times*, 6 May 1831.

231 'The Yellow Admiral': *Morning Chronicle*, 16 May 1831; see also Martin Butlin and Evelyn Joll, *The Paintings of J. M. W. Turner*, revised edn, 1984, no. 338.

231 'we find the same intolerable yellow hue': 30 Apr 1826; see Gage, no. 115, and Hamilton, *Turner*, p. 328, n. 83.

231 On Manby: Kenneth Walthew, *From Rock and Tempest, The Life of Captain George William Manby*, 1971, passim.

231 Manby lectures at the RI: Hamilton, *Faraday*, pp. 239–41.

232 Manby's demonstration on the Serpentine: *The Times*, 4 May 1812.

232 Constable on Turner: John Constable to Archdeacon Fisher, 10 Jul 1823 and 23 Jan 1825 respectively, Constable, *Correspondence*, 1968, vol. VI, pp. 125 and 191.

232 Phipps's loud laugh: FD, 25 Jun 1809, vol. IX, p. 3496.

232 'the clique': *ODNB*, entry on William Seguier, by Alistair D. Laing.

232 'Constable, a conceited egotistical person': Helen Guiterman, 'The Great Painter: Roberts on Turner', *Turner Studies*, vol. 9, no. 1 (1989), pp. 2–9.

233 Cholera reported in Sunderland: *Lit. Gaz.*, 26 Nov 1831, p. 764.

233 'Accounts from Russia state': *Lit. Gaz.*, 26 Mar 1831, p. 205.

233 'Mrs B[uller] dying of terror': Thomas Carlyle to Jane Welsh Carlyle, 15 Aug 1831, Carlyle, *Letters*, vol. 5, pp. 329 and 331.

234 'has had a violent attack of cholera': Elizabeth Barrett Browning to Hugh Stuart Boyd, 23 Aug 1831. P. Kelley and R. Hudson (eds), *The Browning Correspondence*, 1984, vol. 2, p. 325.

234 'The pestilential cholera': G. H. Bell, 'Letter to Sir H. Halford on the . . . proposed regulations for Cholera, Edinburgh, 1831', *Lit. Gaz.*, 12 Nov 1831, pp. 731–2.

234 Auction of George IV coronation robes: *Annual Register*, 1831, Chronicle, pp. 81–2. Trousers, lot 17 in the sale, held by Phillips in New Bond Street. Coronation mantle, lot 52.

234 'the King returned': T. B. Macaulay to Hannah Macaulay, 22 Jun 1831, Thomas Pinney (ed.), *The Letters of Thomas Babington Macaulay*, 1974, vol. 2, pp. 49–50.

235 Bad weather in London: *The Times*, 1 and 19 Aug 1831.

235 'rattling and tearing': *The Times*, 9 Sept 1831.

235 Paganini in London: *The Times*, 23 May 1831; *Lit. Gaz.*, 25 Jul 1829; p. 491, 11 Jun 1831, p. 381; 18 Jun 1831, p. 397; 2 Jul 1831, p. 429; 27 Aug 1831, p. 555. David Brewster, *Letters on Natural Magic*, 1832, p. 311. See also Alan Kendall, *Paganini: A Biography*, 1982.

236 Cobbett's trial: *Annual Register*, 1831, Chronicle, pp. 95ff.

236 William IV opens London Bridge: *Ibid.*, pp. 116ff.

237 Lithographs of London Bridge rapidly published: *Lit. Gaz.*, 13 Aug 1831, p. 526; 20 Aug 1831, p. 540; 27 Aug 1831, p. 555.

237 Turner travelling to Scotland: J. M. W. Turner to Sir Walter Scott, 20 Apr 1831, Gage, p. 169.

238 'the subject will be a Margate Steamer': Benjamin Robert Haydon to W. Newton, 26 Aug 1831, Haydon Letters, Queen Mary College Archive, WC/HA/16.

238 'I do not think any body ever fares': Michael Faraday to Edward Magrath, 2 Sept 1831, FJ, no. 511.

238 'again a disturbance of the needle': Thomas Martin (ed.), *The Diary of Michael Faraday*, 1934, 29 Aug 1831, vol. 1, p. 367, para.2.

238 'I am busy just now again': Michael Faraday to Richard Phillips, 23 Sept 1831, FJ, no. 515.

240 'it was no ordinary occasion': Place Papers, BL Add. MS 27790, ff. 8, 9 and 11.

240 'There may perhaps have been': Mr Powell's account of the Procession of October 1831, written on 22 May 1834, and transcribed by Francis Place. Francis Place Papers, *loc. cit.*, ff. 39–47.

241 'hot lime wash the walls': *Directions to Plain People as a Guide for their Conduct in the Cholera*, 1831, pp. 6ff.

241 'Sir – We have this day forwarded': Papers relating to the Cholera, 1831–2, Oxford, Bodleian, 1562.c.1.

242 'And this cholera morbus': *The English Chronicle and Whitehall Evening*

Post, 15–16 Nov 1831. Papers relating to the Cholera, 1831–2, Oxford, Bodleian, 1562.c.1.

242 'The cholera will spread': Francis Place to Joseph Hume, Dec 1831, quoted Graham Wallas, *The Life of Francis Place*, 1925, p. 287.

242 Treatments for cholera: Papers relating to the Cholera, 1831–2, Oxford, Bodleian, 1562.c.1; *The English Chronicle and Whitehall Evening Post*, 15–16 Nov 1831. *The Times*, 28 May 1831.

243 'The disease generally began': John Hogg, *London as It Is*, 1837, pp. 107–9.

243 'with such a seminary in a prosperous position': *Evening Standard*, 19 Jun 1828.

243 Opening of King's College: Gordon Huellin, *King's College London 1828–1978*, 1978, p. 10.

243 'An inauspicious day': *Lit. Gaz.*, 15 Oct 1831, p. 666.

245 'that rare thing in a woman': James South quoted in Mary Kater to Mary Somerville, 12 Apr 1832, Somerville Papers, dep. c.371, Bodleian.

245 'You never fail in a sentence': Basil Hall to Mary Somerville, 27 Dec 1831; Somerville Papers, dep. c.370, Bodleian.

245 'The great simplicity of your manner of writing': Maria Edgeworth to Mary Somerville, 31 Mar 1832, Somerville Papers, dep. c.370, Bodleian.

245 'I thank you for the book': Thomas Phillips to Mary Somerville, 22 Jun [1832], Somerville Papers, dep. c.371, Bodleian.

245 Somerville and Turner: James Hamilton, *Turner and the Scientists*, 1998, p. 68.

246 Somerville bust: Alison Yarrington, Ilene D. Lieberman, Alex Potts and Malcolm Baker (eds), 'An Edition of the Ledger of Sir Francis Chantrey RA, at the Royal Academy, 1809–1841', *Walpole Society*, vol. 56 (1991/2), no. 261b. 'List of subscribers to Chantrey's bust of Mary Somerville commissioned on behalf of the Royal Society Feb 1832', Somerville Papers, Bodleian. The sixty-four subscribers included Charles Babbage, David Brewster, Rev. Charles Buckland, Charles Parr Burney, Michael Faraday, Sir John Herschel, Charles Lyell, John Murray, John Rennie, Stephen P. Rigaud and Sir Jeffrey Wyattville. Mary Kater to Mary Somerville, 12 Apr 1832; John Lubbock to William Somerville, 23 Mar 1835, Somerville Papers, dep. c.371, Bodleian.

247 'Since I left Somerset House': Stephen Lee to Stephen P. Rigaud, 14 Nov 1831, Bodleian, MS Rigaud, 61, f. 258.

247 'At the end of ten weeks': Charles Babbage, *Reflections on the Decline of Science in England, and on Some of its Causes*, 1830, pp. 50–1.

248 Royal Society anniversary meeting: *The Times*, 1 Dec 1831.

248 Royal Society membership: *Notes and Records of the Royal Society*, 1939, p. 108.

248 Thames Tunnel advertisement: *Courier*, 22 Oct 1831; also many in the *The Times*.

249 'Every poor Quidnunc': *Athenaeum*, no. 6 (5 Feb 1828), pp. 84–5.

249 'the ornament of Bristol': Sir Abraham Elton, at the ceremony to mark the start of work on the Clifton Bridge, 18 Jun 1831.

250 'The Commissioners have refused': Isambard Kingdom Brunel's Diary, 6 Dec 1831, Brunel Collection, University of Bristol Library.

CHAPTER 13: 'NOW YOU YOUNG ARCHITECTS, THERE'S A FINE CHANCE FOR YOU!'

251 Nash's architectural output: Forty-three public buildings, eighty-six domestic buildings, in addition to his Regent Street and Regent's Park developments and a skirmish with the townscape of Leamington Spa. More than 50 per cent of his buildings, including the whole of Regent Street, have been demolished. Howard Colvin, *A Biographical Dictionary of British Architects, 1600–1840*, 3rd edn, 1995, pp. 687–94.

251 'Stairway upwards': 4 Jun 1826, Schinkel, pp. 89–91.

252 'We had the pleasure to meet here': James Pennethorne to Robert Finch, 25 Aug 1825, Finch Papers, d. 13, ff. 149–50, Bodleian.

252 'a wild, irregular youth': William Porden diary, 3 Jul 1812, Derbyshire Record Office, 03311/4/5.

252 'thick, squat, dwarf figure': A. T. Bolton, *The Portrait of John Soane RA*, 1927, pp. 351–5.

253 Regent's Park and Regent Street: J. Mordaunt Crook, *London's Arcadia: John Nash and the Planning of Regent's Park*, Soane Lecture, 2000, pp. 6–13. Hermione Hobhouse, *A History of Regent Street*, 1975, p. 19.

255 'The inhabitants of the extreme east': Richardson, *Recollections*, 1855, vol. 1, p. 3.

256 Corruption charges against Nash: *The Times*, 15 Jun 1829. See also Terence Davis, *John Nash, the Prince Regent's Architect*, 1973; John Summerson, *The Life and Work of John Nash, Architect*, 1980.

256 Carlton House demolished: *The Times*, 30 Mar 1827.

256 Distribution of parts of Carlton House: J. Mordaunt Crook and Michael Port, *The History of the King's Works 1782–1851*, vol. VI, 1973, p. 321.

256 'a mound as arid': *The Times*, 18 May 1830.

257 'Rose before six': John Hoppus, *Memories of a Wife*, 1856, 20 Oct 1829, p. 60.

257 Regent Street attractions: *Athenaeum*, no. 19 (28 Mar 1828), p. 299. Abraham Booth, *The Strangers' Intellectual Guide to London, 1839–40*, 1839.

257 'Knightsbridge and Hyde Park Corner have': Richardson, *Recollections*, 1855, vol. I, p. 19.

258 Colvin, *op. cit.*, p. 1141.

258 'The *job* is now given': Ambrose Poynter to Robert Finch, 2 Jan 1824, Finch Papers, vol. 5, ff. 449–50, Bodleian.

258 'Not the City, Cheapside': John Davies to Robert Finch, 18 Nov 1822, Finch Papers, vol. 5, f. 66, Bodleian.

259 'there appears to be an immense quantity of capital': J. Bennett to Robert Finch, 24 May 1825, Finch Papers, vol. 2, ff. 110–11, Bodleian.

259 'Look at the crash in the mercantile world': J. M. W. Turner to James Holworthy, 7 Jan 1826, BL Add. MS 50118, ff. 72–3.

259 'among the projects now afloat': Thomas L. Donaldson to Robert Finch, 19 Aug 1825, Finch Papers, vol. 5, ff. 160–1, Bodleian.

259 'The nobs in the West End': Thomas L. Donaldson to Robert Finch, 19 Aug 1825. Finch Papers, vol. 5, ff. 160–1, Bodleian.

260 Turner and Donaldson in Rome: Hamilton, *Turner*, p. 200.

260 Donaldson on Nash: Thomas Donaldson to William Behnes, 14 Jun 1838, on accepting Behnes's bust of John Nash on behalf of the RIBA, RIBA Archive, LC/1.

260 Royal Institute of British Architects, *Questions upon Various Subjects connected with Architecture suggested for the direction of correspondents and travellers . . .* , 1835, 2nd edn, 1841. Observation on Nash's sewers in Regent Street, p. 12. Donaldson lists this as one of his publications in his Common Place Book, p. 68, RIBA Archive, DoT/1/1.

261 'Is it not lamentable': Thomas L. Donaldson to Robert Finch, 14 Aug 1824, Finch Papers, vol. 5, ff. 150–1, Bodleian.

261 Collapse of Custom House: Mordaunt Crook and Port, *op. cit.*, vol. VI, p. 430.

261 'The failure of the construction': Thomas L. Donaldson to Robert Finch in Rome, n.d. [inscribed by Finch 'Recd Feb 21 1825'], Finch Papers, vol. 5, ff. 154–5, Bodleian.

261 'a beacon of warning': J. Noble, *The Professional Practice of Architects*, 1836, p. 22.

262 Houses of Parliament fire: Katherine Solender, *'Dreadful Fire!' Burning of the Houses of Parliament*, exh. cat., Cleveland Museum of Art, 1984.

262 Constable's drawings of the fire: C. R. Leslie, *Memoirs of the Life of John Constable*, 1951 edn, p. 237.

262 'Our minds are wholly engrossed': G. J. Beltz, College of Arms, to Rev. Dr Bliss, 17 Oct 1834, Bodleian, MS Rigaud, 60 f. 152.

262 'now you young architects': Richard and Samuel Redgrave, *A Century of Painters of the English School*, 1866, 2nd edn, 1890, p. 420.

262 'had a fine view of the conflagration': Mary Somerville to Woronzow Grieg, 20 Oct 1834, Somerville Papers, MSIF–1, Bodleian.

262 'The flames arose above the dark': Sir Richard Jackson to Sir James Willoughby Gordon, n.d. [late Oct 1834], Willoughby Gordon Papers, BL Add. MS 49508, ff. 171–4.

263 Turner's sketches of the fire: 'Burning of the Houses of Parliament Sketchbook (2)', Finberg CCLXXXIV; Turner Bequest, Tate Britain. Diary of John Green Waller FSA, Carlton College MS 317, ff. 54ff, University of London Library. Quoted Solender, *op. cit.*, p. 42.

263 Official report: *Report of the Lords of the Council respecting the Destruction by Fire of the Houses of Parliament, with Minutes of Evidence*, 25 Feb 1835, 63 pp.

264 Turner at the British Institution Varnishing Day: E. V. Rippingille, in the *Art Journal*, 1860, p. 100.

265 'He is a sort of Paganini': *Morning Chronicle*, 7 May 1832.

266 Gurney's 'Oxy-oil lamp': *Lit. Gaz.*, 23 Feb 1839, pp. 121–2. See also Michael Faraday to H. Williamson, 12 Feb 1839, FJ, no. 1142.

266 'There never was a more dangerous': Hansard, 3rd series, vol. 47, pp. 496–7, 23 Apr 1839.

266 'I would not trouble you': Joseph Hume to Michael Faraday, 29 Apr 1839; FJ, no. 1167.

267 'Only thirty years ago': Inaugural lecture given 17 Oct 1842; reported

Lit. Gaz., 22 Oct 1842, cutting inserted at f. 69 of Donaldson's Common Place Book, RIBA Archive, DoT/1/1.

267 Varley's lecture to RIBA: Cornelius Varley, 'The Drainage of London Its Nauseous and Dangerous Effluvia and the Means by which that Evil may be Entirely Removed', paper read to RIBA, Apr 1847, RIBA Archive, MS/SP/5/23, pp. 5–6.

267 'among us [Berliners]': Friedrich von Raumer, *England in 1835*, 1836, vol. 1, pp. 13–14.

268 'a more clear and luminous explanation': *Lit. Gaz.*, 30 Jun 1827, p. 410.

268 'only a few unconnected sentences': *Lit. Gaz.*, 16 Jan 1836, p. 42.

269 'Burn all bores': *Comic Annual*, vol. 10 (1839), p. 35.

269 'If they go on building at such a rate': William Temple, *British Prose Writers*, 1821, p. 122.

269 'Pancras is like Marylebone': *Wit and Wisdom of Benjamin Disraeli*, 1881, p. 193.

269 'The present is a speculating age!': Allen Davenport, 'London', from *The Muses' Wreath*, 1827; Malcolm Chase (ed.), *The Life and Literary Papers of Allen Davenport*, 1994, p. 79.

270 'To any persons except Englishmen': Jehangeer Nowrojee and Hirjeebhoy Merwanjee, *Journal of a Residence of Two Years and a Half in Great Britain*, 1841, p. 220.

270 his 'great *toe-nail*': *Lit. Gaz.*, 1 Apr 1843, p. 210.

270 'eminent, modest and persevering mechanic': Richard Phillips, *A Morning's Walk from London to Kew*, 1817, p. 45.

CHAPTER 14: JOHN MARTIN
AND THE WATERING
OF LONDON

272 Martin's ambition: Balston, pp. 120–32.

272 'A slender portion of common sense': S. D. Beare giving evidence to the 1828 Royal Commission on the Supply of Water to the Metropolis, quoted by John Martin in the *Select Committee on Metropolis Improvements*, 1838, p. 154.

273 Hatchett's Hotel guests: *Mogg's New Picture of London and Visitors' Guide*, 1844.

273 William Somerville's evidence: *Royal Commission for the Supply of Water to the Metropolis*, 1838, p. 52.

273 William Brande's lecture on water supply: *Lit. Gaz.*, 31 Jan 1829, p. 72.

273 Martin's plan: An earlier edition of this paper, which has not survived, was *Plan for Supplying the Cities of London and Westminster with Pure Water from the River Colne*, 1827.

274 'If the largest proportion': Martin's evidence to *Select Committee on Metropolis Improvements*, 1838, p. 153.

274 Lobbying support: John Martin to William Ayrton, 25 Feb 1831 and 11 Jul 1844, Ayrton Papers, BL Add. MS 52338, ff. 109, 112.

274 'using the moat if permitted': *Lit. Gaz.*, 30 Mar 1833, p. 200.

275 Martin's revised plan: John Martin, *A Plan for Abundantly Supplying the Metropolis with Pure Water from the River Coln, Forming at the Same Time a Railway*, 1834. Balston, pp. 124–5.

276 The committee's task: *Select Committee on Metropolis Improvements*, 1838, pp. iii–v.

276 Traffic flow in London: Extract from *The Times*, 15 Sept 1842; Faraday's Common Place Book, vol. 1, p. 450, IET. City of London Police Report, 22 Nov 1850, Great Exhibition Prospectuses etc, V&A, NAL, Exh. 1851.108, f. 3.

277 Trench's characteristics: Hansard, 3rd series, vol. 4, pp. 743–6, quoted *ODNB*, entry on Frederick Trench, by M. H. Port. BL Add. MS 40597, f. 393, 30 Dec 1846.

277 Trench's proposals: *Royal Commission on Improving the Metropolis*, Jan 1844, pp. 45–6.

277 Cubitt's proposal: *Ibid.*, p. 154.

278 Martin lobbies Peel: John Martin to Robert Peel, 8 May 1846, Peel Papers, BL Add. MS 40591, f. 242.

278 'notwithstanding . . . a very violent opposition': John Martin to William Ayrton, 14 Sept 1846, Ayrton Papers, BL Add. MS 52338, f. 118.

278 'Oh my boy, if only': Balston, p. 129.

279 'full of his mannerism': Arthur Cleveland Coxe, *Impressions of England; or Sketches of English Scenery and Society*, 2nd edn, 1856, p. 38.

279 Gift of cannon: 'Weight of Cannon Received from Sir Francis Chantrey', Wyatt Family Papers, WYFam/1/9/13, RIBA Archive. Correspondence between Matthew Wyatt, the Duke of Rutland and William Jerdan, c.1843, Jerdan Correspondence, d. 114, ff. 78 and 338, Bodleian.

279 'The flow of so large a quantity': *Lit. Gaz.*, 13 Sept 1845, p. 612.

280 'that monster on the arch': George Jones to William Napier, 22 Nov 1852, Napier Papers, MS Eng. Lett. D.242, ff. 94–5, Bodleian. John McCoubrey, 'The Hero of a Hundred Fights –Turner, Wellington and Schiller', *Turner Studies*, vol. 10, no. 2 (1990), pp. 7–11; Nicholas Alfrey, 'Turner and the Cult of Heroes', *Turner Studies*, vol. 8, no. 2 (1988), pp. 33–44; James Hamilton, *Turner and the Scientists*, 1998, pp. 111–14.

CHAPTER 15: 'ASTONISHING TO THE PHILOSOPHER AND THE SIMPLE CHILD'

281 Faraday's advice: Hamilton, *Faraday*, pp. 375–6. H. Bence Jones, *Life and Letters of Faraday*, 1870, vol. 1, pp. 377–8.

281 Fox Talbot's experiments: 6 Feb 1839. Larry Schaaf, *Records of the Dawn of Photography: Talbot's Notebooks P and Q*, 1996, p. 3. H. F. Talbot, 'On the Nature of Light', *Phil. Mag.*, 3rd series, vol. 7 (1835), pp. 113–18.

282 Sir Anthony Carlisle, letter in the *Mechanics Magazine*, vol. 39, no. 809 (9 Feb 1839), p. 329. Quoted Geoffrey Batchen, 'Tom Wedgwood and Humphry Davy: "An Account of a Method"', *Hist. Phot.*, vol. 17, no. 2 (1993), pp. 172–83. Thomas Wedgwood and Humphry Davy, 'An Account of a Method of Copying Paintings upon Glass and of making Profiles by the Agency of Light upon Nitrate of Silver', *Journal of the Royal Institution*, vol. 1 (1802), p. 170.

282 'imperfect [though] absolutely startling' results: *Lit. Gaz.*, 9 Feb 1839, p. 90.

283 On Herschel: John Herschel to Charles Babbage, 26 Jun 1831, RS Archive. Quoted Larry Schaaf, 'Herschel, Talbot and Photography: Spring 1831 and Spring 1839', *Hist. Phot.*, vol. 4, no. 3 (1980), pp. 181–204.

283 Fox Talbot's correspondence with Faraday: FJ, nos 558, 559, 644, 650, 722, 820, 933, 1122.

283 'I do not profess to have perfected an Art': Letter to the Editor from Henry Fox Talbot, *Lit. Gaz.*, 2 Feb 1839, p. 74. Henry Fox Talbot to William Jerdan, *Lit. Gaz.*, 2 Feb 1839, p. 73.

284 'The Art of Photogenic Drawing': *Athenaeum*, no. 589 (9 Feb 1839).

H. F. Talbot, 'Some account of the Art of Photogenic Drawing', *Phil. Mag.*, vol. 14 (Feb 1839), pp. 196–211.

284 'a sketch of his telescope': *Proc. Roy. Soc.*, vol. 4 (1837–43), pp. 131–3. Larry Schaaf, 'Sir John Herschel's 1839 Royal Society Paper on Photography', *Hist. Phot.*, vol. 3, no. 1 (1979), pp. 47–60.

284 John Thomas Cooper: FJ, no. 1163, note; *Annals of Natural History*, 1839, vol. 4, p. 212. *Athenaeum*, no. 594 (16 Mar 1839). *Mirror*, vol. 33 (11 May 1839), p. 298. Schaaf, *Records of the Dawn of Photography: Talbot's Notebooks P and Q*, p. 41.

285 Havell and Faraday correspondence: 23 Mar, 19 Apr 1839, FJ, nos 1154, 1163.

285 Havell, Willmore and Brockedon: See *Lit. Gaz.*, 30 Mar 1839, pp. 202–3; 13 Apr 1839, pp. 236–7 for further information about Havell and Willmore's involvement with photography. John Dalton to William Brockedon, 20 May 1839, NPG Archive.

285 'I am very much obliged to you': Thomas Phillips to William Brockedon, 17 Apr [1839], NPG Archive.

286 Photographic varnishes: Michael Faraday to John Herschel, 18 Jan 1840, FJ, no. 1234.

286 Callcott's painting: Repr. Stephen White, 'Alfred Swaine Tayler – A Little known Photographic Pioneer', *Hist. Phot.*, vol. 11, no. 3 (1987), pp. 229–35, fig. 5. Also: Lawrence Alt, 'Alfred Swaine Taylor (1801–80) – Some Early Material', *Hist. Phot.*, vol. 16, no. 4 (1992), pp. 397–8.

286 'If a truly instantaneous': Henry Fox Talbot to Faraday, 15 Jun 1851; FJ, no. 2437.

287 'these facts serve to illustrate': *Notices and Abstracts of Communications to the British Association for the Advancement of Science*, Birmingham, August 1839, p. 3–5.

287 'all the beauty and softness': *Phil. Mag.*, vol. 16 (Jan-Jun 1840), p. 535. J. W. Draper, 'On the process of the Daguerreotype and its application to taking portraits from the life', *Phil. Mag.*, vol. 17 (Sept 1840), pp. 217ff.

288 'Can I not be of any use to you': Mary Somerville to John Herschel, 12 Nov 1843, RS Archive, HS.16.347.

288 William Grove's lecture: *The Times*, 20 Aug 1841.

289 Faraday's portrait collection: L.-A.-J. Quetelet to Michael Faraday, 9 Sept 1850, FJ, no. 2323. Gertrude M. Prescott, 'Faraday, Image of the

Man and the Collector', in David Gooding and Frank A. J. L. James (eds), *Faraday Rediscovered*, 1985, pp. 15–31. Faraday's portrait albums are in the RI Archive, MS F1, H and I.

289 William Constable, *ODNB* entry by Phillipe Garner.

289 'We shall only go about the country': 'Rogers' Interview with Ruskin about Turner', Ruskin Foundation, MS 54C, Ruskin Library, University of Lancaster.

290 The Graphic Society membership lists are in the Royal Academy Library. Among the members in 1839 were William Brockeden, Thomas L. Donaldson, Sir William Newton, Peter Robinson, Henry Sass, J. T. Willmore, John Pye and Lewis Vulliamy, the architect of the columned façade of the Royal Institution. Michael Faraday and Charles Wheatstone were the only scientist members in 1839. See letter from J. T. Willmore in *Lit. Gaz.*, 6 Apr 1839, p. 215.

290 Willmore's letter: *Lit. Gaz.*, 6 Apr 1839, p. 215.

290 Turner's annotations: John Gage, 'Turner's Annotated Books: Goethe's "Theory of Colours"', *Turner Studies*, vol. 4, no. 2 (1984), pp. 34–52.

291 On Beard: Bernard V. and Pauline F. Heathcote, 'Richard Beard: an Ingenious and Enterprising Patentee', *Hist. Phot.*, vol. 3, no. 4 (1979), pp. 313–29. Photograph of Richard Beard published in *Hist. Phot.*, vol. 5, no. 3 (1981), p. 268 (correspondence from B. V. and P. F. Heathcote). C. G. Scott, 'Richard Beard, Newton Abbott and the Growth of Photography', *Hist. Phot.*, vol. 15, no. 1 (1991), pp. 13–15. R. Derek Wood, 'The Daguerreotype in England: Some Primary Material Relating to Beard's Lawsuits', *Hist. Phot.*, vol. 3, no. 4 (1979), pp. 305–9.

291 Beard and Wolcott: *The Times*, 25 Aug 1840. A. T. Gill, 'Wolcott's Camera in England, and the Bromine-Iodine Process', *Hist. Phot.*, vol. 1, no. 3 (1977), pp. 215–20.

292 'From the roof': *The Times*, 24 Mar 1841.

292 Beard's studios: Michael Pritchard, *A Directory of London Photographers, 1841–1908*, 1986, p. 35.

293 'You are taken from one room': Maria Edgeworth to Fanny Wilson, 25 May 1841, Christina Colvin (ed.), *Maria Edgeworth: Letters from England 1813–44*, 1971, pp. 593–4.

293 Polytechnic advertisement: *The Times*, 25 Apr 1842.

294 'I was seated': Thomas Sutton, *Photographic Notes*, 1856.

294 Claudet photographs Queen Adelaide: *The Times*, 19 Jul 1842.

295 'the Van Dyck of photography': *Athenaeum*, 25 Apr 1857, p. 538.

295 Brewster and Claudet quarrel: *The Times*, 15 and 17 May 1852.

295 Beard's priority claim: *The Times*, 18 Nov 1852.

296 On Mayall: he was born Jabez Meal, in Oldham, Lancashire. It is suggested that he altered his surname to Mayall during the early 1840s when he worked and travelled in the United States. On his return to England c.1846 he was indelibly 'Mayall'. *ODNB*, entry on Mayall, by Larry Schaaf. Leonie L. Reynolds and Arthur T. Gill, 'The Mayall Story', *Hist. Phot.*, vol. 9, no. 2 (1985), pp. 89–107; and 'The Mayall Story – A Postscript', *Hist. Phot.*, vol. 11, no. 1 (1987), pp. 77–80.

296 Mayall's exhibition is recorded in Thornbury, p. 351.

296 'New discoveries in Daguerreotype: *The Times*, 18 May 1847.

297 'We look at your face painted in light': Michael Faraday to Joseph Henry, 28 Apr 1851, FJ, no. 2416. Joseph Henry to Michael Faraday, 4 Jun 1851, FJ, no. 2430.

297 'the oddest man I ever saw': Queen Victoria's Journal, quoted H. and A. Gernsheim, *Queen Victoria*, 1959, p. 261.

297 Mayall's mystery visitor: Thornbury, pp. 351ff.

298 Royal Society soirée: *The Times*, 23 Apr 1849. The following day Mayall wrote a letter to the Editor of *The Times* to correct an error in the report 'that the only photographs exhibited there were mine': 24 Apr 1849.

299 Largest photograph: Larry Schaaf, 'Mayall's Life Size Portrait of George Peabody', *Hist. Phot.*, vol. 9, no. 4 (1985), pp. 279–88.

299 'By its [photography's] operation': *The Times*, 31 Dec 1852.

300 'When we return to Kent': John Children to Henry Fox Talbot, 14 Sept 1841, Lacock Abbey Collection, LA41–057. See also Larry Schaaf, *Sun Gardens: Victorian Photograms by Anna Atkins*, 1985. 'Ross' is the photographic instrument maker Andrew Ross, of London.

300 'To think that a piece of paper': *The Times*, 31 Dec 1852.

301 'clothe [science] in a strange and repulsive garb': J. F. W. Herschel, *Discourse on the Study of Natural Philosophy*, 1830, new edn, ed. Andrew Pyle, 1996, pp. 70–2.

CHAPTER 16: THE CRYSTAL PALACE

302 'not a regular architect': *The Times*, 6 Dec 1850.

302 'Spices from the east': *The Times*, 18 Oct 1849. For Henry Cole, see

Elizabeth Boynton, *The Great Exhibitor – The Life and Work of Henry Cole*, 2003.

303 'the cottager who cultivates': *A short statement of the nature and objects of the proposed Great Exhibition . . . appointed to take place in London in 1851 and its interest to all classes of people*, Great Exhibition Prospectuses etc, V&A, NAL, Exh.1851.108, f. 6.

303 'if London was full to overflowing': John Smith, *Remarks on the particular advantages which the Great Exhibition of 1851 is likely to confer on the tradesmen of the Metropolis*. Great Exhibition Prospectuses etc, V&A, NAL, Exh.1851.108, f. 7a.

304 'Crystal Palace' named: *ILN*, 19 Oct 1850, pp. 322–3; the name was repeated in *Punch*, 2 Nov 1850. It had already caught on.

304 'the least objectionable structure': Joseph Paxton, 'The Crystal Palace', address to the Society of Arts, 13 Nov 1850. *The Times*, 14 Nov 1850.

305 'My object', Jones told a meeting: Owen Jones, 'On the Decorations Proposed for the Exhibition Building, Hyde Park', paper read to the RIBA, 16 Dec 1850, RIBA Archive, MS/SP/10/38, f. 5.

305 'I have no doubt but': Paxton, *op. cit.*

305 Construction begins: *The Times*, 25 Oct 1850. *The Great Exhibition of the World's Industry*, 1851, p. 21.

305 'The builders had been pushed out': *Descriptive key to Mr H. C. Selous' Picture of the Inauguration of the Great Exhibition of 1851*, V&A, NAL, Exh.1851.186, f. 6.

305 'The Crystal Palace has assumed': J. M. W. Turner to Francis Fawkes, 31 Jan 1851, Gage, p. 323.

306 Carlyle on the Crystal Palace: Thomas Carlyle to John A. Carlyle, 12 Jan, 20 Feb, 29 Mar 1851; Carlyle, *Letters*, vol. 26, pp. 13–14, 36, 51.

307 'As the Prince was leaving': *The Times*, 6 Dec 1850.

307 'The first *coup d'oeil*': *ILN*, 3 May 1851, p. 349.

308 Mayall's daguerreotype: Repr. Leonie L. Reynolds and Arthur T. Gill, 'The Mayall Story', *Hist. Phot.*, vol. 9, no. 2 (1988), fig. 3.

308 Photographic illustrations to exhibition report: Nancy B. Keeler, 'Illustrating the "Reports for the Juries of the Great Exhibition of 1851": Talbot, Henneman, and their Failed Commission', *Hist. Phot.*, vol. 6, no. 3 (1982), pp. 257–70. Three illustrated sets of the volumes are in the V&A, NAL, Exh.1851.80–3.

309 South Transept photograph: Exhibition of the Works of Industry of all Nations, *Reports of the Juries . . .* , 1852, vol. 2, facing p. 437.

310 Bloomerism: *The Times*, 27 Sept 1851.

310 Balloon emergency: *The Times*, 17 Jun 1851.

EPILOGUE:
A WORLD OF WONDERS IN ITSELF

313 Farington's death: FD, 30 Dec 1821, vol. XVI, p. 5761.

313 Farington's disapproval of Haydon: FD, 24 May 1809, vol. IX, p. 3467.

314 'I am sure you will receive him in a room alone': Lady Davy to John Murray, n.d. [mid- to late 1820s], Murray Archive, NLS

314 a 'kind and affectionate nurse': David Knight, *Humphry Davy: Science and Power*, 1992, p.170.

314 'I think him both as a liberal citizen': Lady Davy to John Murray, 18 Dec 1828, Murray Archive, NLS.

314 Davy's death: Lady Davy to John Murray, 5 Jun 1829, Murray Archive, NLS.

315 Soane's death: Susan Palmer, *The Soanes at Home*, 1997, p. 83. Soane's house, 12 Lincoln's Inn Fields, is owned and administered for the nation by the trustees of the Sir John Soane's Museum.

315 Chantrey's death: *The Times*, 27 Nov 1841.

315 Willoughby Gordon's death: *The Times*, 6 Jan 1851.

315 Farey's death: *ODNB*, entry on John Farey, by A. P. Woolrich.

315 Turner's death: Helen Guiterman, 'The Great Painter – Roberts on Turner', *Turner Studies*, vol. 9, no. 1 (1989), pp. 1–9; Hamilton, *Turner*, pp. 309–10.

315 The Cider Cellar: W. M. Thackeray, *The Newcomes*, ch. 1; 'On Love, Marriage, Men and Women II', *Sketches and Travels in London* (1904 edn), pp. 300–1; 'A Night's Pleasure, IV and VI', *ibid.*, pp. 409ff. and 418ff. Renton Nicholson, *Rogue's Progress. The Autobiography of 'Lord Chief Baron' Nicholson*, 1860[?], 1966 edn intro. by John L. Bradley, pp. 327–9. J. E. Ritchie, *The Night-Side of London*, 1858, pp. 108–14.

316 'for fear that the vampires of literature': Babbage, p. vii.

316 'that perplexing subject, MYSELF': Jerdan, vol. 1, pp. 1–7.

316 'These desultory memoirs': Redding, vol. 1, pp. 1–5.

317 'The felling of forests': Rev. John Richardson, *The Real Exhibitors Exhibited, or an Enquiry into the Condition of those Industrial Classes who have really represented England at the Great Exhibition*, 1851, p. 1.

317 Polluted water: Stephen Halliday, *The Great Stink of London*, 1999. Mary Somerville to Woronzow Greig, 19 Oct 1854, Somerville Papers, dep. b.206, Bodleian.

317 Royal Agricultural Hall: Now the Building Design Centre.

318 'That instant every gaslight': Sir Francis Head, *Stokers and Pokers*, 1849.

318 'Leave London': Rev. William MacRitchie, *Diary of a Tour Throughout Great Britain in 1795*, 1897, p. 99.

A Brief Bibliography
of books published from the 1980s

Ackroyd, Peter, *London: The Biography*, Vintage, 2001

Fox, Celina, *Londoners*, Thames & Hudson, 1987

Fox, Celina, (ed.) *London – World City 1800–1840*, Yale University Press, in association with the Museum of London, 1992

Halliday, Stephen, *The Great Stink of London*, Sutton, 2001

Hibbert, Christopher, *London: The Biography of a City*, Penguin, 1980

Hibbert, Christopher, and Weinreb, Ben, *The London Encyclopaedia*, Macmillan, 1993

Inwood, Stephen, *A History of London*, Macmillan, 1998

Kynaston, David, *The City of London*, 4 vols. Chatto, 1994–2001

Pevsner, Nikolaus, *London*, 6 vols, (new editions, edited by Simon Bradley, Bridget Cherry), *Buildings of England Series*, Yale University Press, 1997–2003

Porter, Roy, *London: A Social History*, Hamish Hamilton, 1994

Sheppard, Francis, *London: A History*, Oxford, 1998

Stamp, Gavin, *The Changing Metropolis*, Viking, 1984

White, Jerry, *London in the Nineteenth Century: A Human Awful Wonder of God*, Jonathan Cape, 2006

Wilson, A. N., *London – A Short History*, Weidenfeld & Nicolson, 2004

The Village London Atlas – The Changing Face of Greater London 1822–1903, Guild, 1986.

Index